COLONIALISM ON THE PRAIRIES

FIRST NATIONS and the colonial encounter

Series Editor: David Cahill, Professor, School of History and Philosophy, University of New South Wales

Series titles in order of publication

Missionaries, Indigenous Peoples and Cultural Exchange
Edited by Patricia Grimshaw and Andrew May

The Conquest All Over Again: Nahuas and Zapotecs Thinking, Writing, and Painting Spanish Colonialism
Edited by Susan Schroeder

First World, First Nations: Internal Colonialism and Indigenous Self-Determination in Northern Europe and Australia
Edited by Günter Minnerup and Pia Solberg

Colonialism on the Prairies: Blackfoot Settlement and Cultural Transformation, 1870–1920
Blanca Tovías

Aboriginal Dreaming Paths and Trading Ways: The Colonisation of the Australian Economic Landscape
Dale Kerwin

City Indians in Spain's American Empire: Urban Indigenous Society in Colonial Mesoamerica and Andean South America, 1600–1830
Edited by Dana Velasco Murillo, Mark Lentz, and Margarita R. Ochoa

COLONIALISM ON THE PRAIRIES
Blackfoot Settlement and Cultural Transformation, 1870–1920

BLANCA TOVÍAS

sussex
ACADEMIC
PRESS
Brighton • Portland • Toronto

Copyright © Blanca Tovías, 2011, 2012.

The right of Blanca Tovías to be identified as Author of this work has been asserted in accordance with the Copyright, Designs and Patents Act 1988.

2 4 6 8 10 9 7 5 3 1

First published in hardocver 2011, reprinted in paperback with corrections 2012, by
SUSSEX ACADEMIC PRESS
PO Box 139
Eastbourne BN24 9BP

and in the United States of America by
SUSSEX ACADEMIC PRESS
920 NE 58th Ave   Suite 300
Portland, Oregon 97213–3786

and in Canada by
SUSSEX ACADEMIC PRESS (CANADA)
8000 Bathurst Street, Unit 1, PO Box 30010, Vaughan, Ontario L4J 0C6

All rights reserved. Except for the quotation of short passages for the purposes of criticism and review, no part of this publication may be reproduced, stored in a retrieval system or transmitted in any form or by any means, electronic, mechanical, photocopying, recording or otherwise, without the prior permission of the publisher.

British Library Cataloguing in Publication Data
A CIP catalogue record for this book is available from the British Library.

Library of Congress Cataloging-in-Publication Data
Tovías, Blanca.
Colonialism on the prairies : Blackfoot settlement and cultural transformation, 1870–1920 / Blanca Tovías.
  p. cm. — (First nations and the colonial encounter)
Includes bibliographical references and index.
ISBN 978-1-84519-307-2 (h/b : alk. paper)
ISBN 978-1-84519-540-3 (pbk. : alk. paper)
  1. Siksika Indians—Colonization. 2. Siksika Indians—Cultural assimilation.
 3. Siksika Indians—Folklore. 4. Siksika Indians—Religion. 5. Siksika Indians—Clothing. I. Title.
E99.S54T68 2011
978.004′97352—dc22

2010052468

Typeset and designed by Sussex Academic Press, Brighton & Eastbourne.
Printed by TJ International, Padstow, Cornwall.
This book is printed on acid-free paper.

Contents

List of Illustrations	vi
Series Editor's Preface, by David Cahill	viii
Acknowledgements	ix
Introduction: The Threads of Continuity	1
Note on Nomenclature	8

Part I The Blackfoot Sun Dance: Resistance and Persistence, 1877–1920

1 The Sun Dance: Invoking the Sacred	15
2 Colonial Conceits and Indictable Offenses	24
3 Honouring Creator Sun and Praying for Good Crops	46

Part II The Grammar of Blackfoot Leadership Dress, 1830–1920

4 Dress, Sacred Stories, and Worldviews	63
5 Fur Trade, Success, and Dress	84
6 The Longevity of Buckskins	100

Part III Ethnographic Encounters: Cultural Transactions and Translations

7 Between Orality and Text: The Encounter with "Salvage" Ethnography	115
8 Blackfoot Genres into Written History and Literature	129

Part IV The Oral Tradition in Contemporary Native Literature

9 Hero Quests, Sun Dancing, and the Story of "Scarface"	159
10 The Blackfoot Hero in James Welch's *Fools Crow*	168
11 Ethics in Emma Lee Warrior's *Compatriots*	179
Conclusion	188
Appendices 1–4	194
Notes	200
Select Bibliography	246
Index	293

List of Illustrations

The colour plates are located between pages 144 and 145; CP indicates that the illustration is in the colour plate section.

1.1 *Piegan Sun Dance camp* [1889], Glenbow Archive, Calgary, Canada, NA-118-16.
2.1 *Piegan (USA) encampment, Montana* [c.1890s], Glenbow Archive, Calgary, Canada, NA-1463-1.
2.2 *The Blackfoot Treaty (Treaty 7), 1877, Crowfoot speaking*, Glenbow Archive, Calgary, Canada, NA-40-1.
3.1 *George Gooderham, Honourary chieftanship ceremony, Blackfoot reserve, Alberta* [1931], Glenbow Archive, Calgary, Canada, NB-1-2.
3.2 *Blackfoot house and tipi, Blackfoot (Siksika) reserve, southern Alberta* [c.1908], Glenbow Archive, Calgary, Canada, NA-3322-12.
4.1 Karl Bodmer, Swiss, 1809–1893, *Piegan Blackfeet Man*, 1833, watercolour and pencil on paper, sheet: 12 3/8 × 10 in.; 31.4325 × 25.4 cm, Joslyn Art Museum, Omaha, Nebraska: Gift of the Enron Art Foundation, 1986, JAM 1986.49.290. CP
4.2 George Catlin, *Stu-mick-o-súks, Buffalo Bull's Back Fat, Head Chief, Blood Tribe*. 1985.66.149, Smithsonian American Art Museum. Gift of Mrs. Joseph Harrison, Jr. CP
4.3 Johann Hürlimann, after Karl Bodmer, Swiss, 1809–1893, *Chief of the Blood-Indians, War-Chief of the Piekann Indians, and Koutani Indian*, 1839, engraving and hand coloured aquatint on paper, Joslyn Art Museum, Omaha, Nebraska: Gift of the Enron Art Foundation, 1986, JAM 1986.49.542.46. CP
4.4 George Catlin, *Eeh-nís-kim, Crystal Stone, Wife of the Chief*. 1985.66.150, Smithsonian American Art Museum. Gift of Mrs. Joseph Harrison, Jr. CP
5.1 Karl Bodmer, Swiss, 1809–1893, *Encampment of the Piekann Indians*, 1833, aquatint, engraving, and watercolor on paper, Joslyn Art Museum, Omaha, Nebraska, JAM 43.Tab. CP
5.2 *Natawista Iksana, Blood woman, Alberta* [n.d.], Glenbow Archive, Calgary, Canada, NA-5014-1.

List of Illustrations

6.1 *Red Crow, head Chief of the Bloods*, Glenbow Archive, Calgary, Canada, NA-668-53.
6.2 *Crowfoot, during tour of eastern Canada* [1886], Glenbow Archive, Calgary, Canada, NA-182-2.
6.3 *Yellow Horse, head chief of the Blackfoot and his wife* [ca. 1910], Glenbow Archive, Calgary, Canada, NA-350-1.
8.1 AF 4702, *Wolf Collar's Story Robe*, 1961, moose skin, pencil, paint, string, 123.5 cm × 118.0 cm, Collection of Glenbow Museum, Calgary, Canada. CP
8.2 *Many Guns and wife, Siksika (Blackfoot) reserve, Alberta* [1919], Glenbow Archive, Calgary, Canada, NC-71-12.

Series Editor's Preface

DAVID CAHILL

Recent decades have witnessed a rise in self-awareness and self-assertiveness of First Nations peoples. This has brought indigenous histories, cultures, identities and politics into the mainstream of public and intellectual life, often in controversial manner. First Nations are beginning to receive the attention their welfare, cultures, and histories merit. For many of them, this has come after five centuries of contact with European powers and nation states. First Nations have variegated histories that are partly the result of their autochthonous cultures, their particular colonial experiences, and increasing integration into the world economy. Notwithstanding this wide variation, however, many of the colonial processes they have undergone are similar in nature. Generic colonial processes such as land rights, labour systems, miscegenation, evangelization, and the undermining of traditional laws by introduced legal systems have produced a wide variety of cross-cultural outcomes. Similarly, First Nations have been severally but variably transformed by profit–based economic systems with different values, by new gender and social roles, and new forms of education to wean indigenous children away from traditional values. In effect, new lifeways, a loss of autonomy, new judicial and fiscal systems, and bewildering multiple levels of government, have all posed immense obstacles to the social reproduction of indigenous nations.

First Nations across the globe underwent conquest that involved both violence and negotiation. Their responses were many and varied. There was resistance, most manifest in all types of rebellion as well as passive resistance. Then there were processes of accommodation by which they sought to realign traditional belief, value, and authority systems with those imposed upon them, forcefully or persuasively, by the colonial powers. Finally, there was also considerable opportunism and initiative, by which indigenous communities sometimes turned colonialism back on itself by appropriating colonial institutions and legal processes so as to optimize their own colonial condition. It is evident that conquest and settlement brought many deleterious consequences in its train, but the 'fatal impact' approach to the consequences of colonialism upon indigenous groups has always been far too simplistic, skimming over, as it does,

Series Editor's Preface

the many positive and creative adaptations of indigenous peoples to new and daunting challenges.

Most regions of the world were inhabited by indigenous peoples at the beginning of European conquest and colonization, from the late fifteenth century onwards. The Americas, both north and south, included urban civilizations as well as non-sedentary groups, and even today indigenous subjects are not always fully incorporated into the modern world, e.g. Amazonian tribes, who nevertheless manage to make their voice heard, sometimes to great effect, as for example in the 2009 victory of indigenous communities from the tropical Peruvian eastern lowlands over governmental and private development interests. In Oceania, including Australasia, conquests were often seaborne and sometimes took longer to grip, such that the impact of colonialism varied greatly according to region or province. Processes of conquest, colonization, and colonial control have taken place across Asia with a range of responses that often included major revitalization movements, as for example in Burma, Indonesia and the Philippines. Indigenous Africans experienced, well into the twentieth century, different types of colonial oppression. Still other vicissitudes of colonial and nation state control have been experienced in the Central Asian republics and Mongolia, while even Europe has its own indigenous inhabitants, the Sami of Scandinavia.

Some indigenous peoples have largely disappeared either wholly, or at least as cohesive social groups, for example the Guanches of the Canary Islands, who were largely extinct by the late sixteenth century. However, many descendants of supposedly extinct First Nations vigorously oppose the very idea that their culture and identity were obliterated by colonial rule. The rise of DNA analysis has sometimes given them reason to do so. The widespread public perception that indigenous inhabitants of Tasmania became extinct in the nineteenth century has been proven wrong, though no serious scholar ever believed it. DNA has similarly disproved the theory of the disappearance of the native peoples of California, long believed by academics and non-academics to have become extinct. Rather, it has been shown that some among them escaped a state-backed genocide, based on bounty hunting, by adopting western dress and passing themselves off as Mexicans. Now their story can be told (and compensation claims can be lodged). For many erstwhile colonies with large indigenous populations, the attainment of post-colonial independence — from the eighteenth century to even the present day — merely resulted in a substitution of European colonialism by internal colonialism, i.e., the continued (and sometimes worsened) exploitation of individual First Nations, exploitation that often had, and has, the explicit or tacit support of nation states. For First Nations, colonialism didn't die away in post-colonial societies, it merely metamorphosed — same horse, different rider.

Scholars, politicians, journalists, and activists of all kinds have interpreted First Nations' cultures, histories, and present-day social conditions in many different ways, sometimes marked by contempt for indigenous peoples. This is highly contested ground, with indigenous claim-making posing challenges to conventional interpretations of indigenous histories, especially in the treatment of the early colonial encounter itself. Indigenous groups have made demands for formal apologies by the State for the abuses attendant upon colonial rule, sometimes accompanied by a recasting of the indigenous past as a kind of Golden Age in which humankind lived in harmony with the natural environment. Not infrequently, this has restored an indigenous storyline to national histories from which they had been largely excluded. Simultaneously, indigenous stakeholders have pressed their case for compensation for their colonial suffering, sometimes viewed as an unbroken continuum to the present. This recompense has been sought in the form of financial payments to groups and individuals, as social and educational programs designed especially for indigenous claimants, and — most controversially — the return of lands alienated during the twin processes of conquest and colonization. Claims for the return of sacred items and ancestors' remains also attend this process. Indigenous land claims have sporadically provoked fierce resistance among stakeholders, especially from those present-day, non-native owners of lands alleged to be "tribal" homelands, many of whom dispute indigenous titles or entitlements. Beyond the question of land tenure and right of access to ancestral hunting and even spiritual territories, opponents of such historical rights exhibit a wider resistance, explicitly denying that colonialism was detrimental for indigenous peoples, and alleging that deleterious post-colonial conditions were and are due to their own inability to take advantage of the so-called civilizing possibilities ushered in by colonial rule and later post-colonial, sovereign governments. Put another way, their problems are entirely of their own making.

This denialism is the bane of productive debate. It embraces a wide range of opinions, ranging from journalistic contrariness to, in its worst manifestations, a crude racism, but is not necessarily unsophisticated for all that. Of more moment are contested questions of national, collective and even individual identity. Such debates and conflicts also represent a battle over History, of who should control normative versions of national history, national memory, and essentialised national myths. For example, in Australia, those who deny indigenous sufferings accuse their opponents of creating a "black armband" version of history. The latter respond that their critics, and especially denialists of whatever ilk, seek to "whitewash" national history, editing out shameful episodes of harmful white policies and actions from national history and nationalistic myth. Whether explicitly or implicitly, each camp accuses the other of falsification of the national history. This standoff is reminiscent of an earlier debate over

Series Editor's Preface

Spanish conquest and colonization in the Americas, in which partisans of the "Black Legend" were pitched against those of a "White Legend". This historiographical debate, which commenced in the sixteenth century, only petered out in the 1960s. It was resolved after a fashion, but only after a plethora of monographic, empirical studies settled many of the issues involved, such that proponents of both "Legends" were forced to resile from their more extreme assertions. Quite clearly, resolution of heated debates over First Nations histories will depend, in the final analysis, on the harvesting of a significant weight of empirical studies and theoretical refinement, as well as public debates entered into in good faith. A further avenue of progress through these questions lies in a comparative, cross-cultural treatment of the histories of First Nations peoples. An awareness of the historiography on indigenous nations in other world areas is usually absent from national debates over indigenous claim-making. The context for understanding First Nations everywhere should be international and global, not just local and national.

However, there is an abundant and rich empirical historiography, ethnologically informed, on First Nations, above all those of Canada, the United States, and Latin America. In the Asia-Pacific region, there are many New Zealand studies of Maori-Pakeha colonial relations that are variable in quality, but among which are superb analyses of warfare, religion and land tenure. There are also numerous studies of the colonial encounter elsewhere in Polynesia and Melanesia. The historiography on indigenous Australians is even more variable in quality, ranging from ill-informed journalism, through poorly researched essays, to a small cluster of first-rate empirical studies. In order to respond to the lack of comparative studies, there is an urgent need for a general series that would embrace the indigenous histories across national boundaries. It is envisaged that each volume in this Sussex Academic Press series will be informed by rich, first order research on First Nations globally. The series will focus especially on native peoples of North America, Mesoamerica and the Andes, Oceania, and Asia.

The present study by Blanca Tovías on the Blackfoot Nations of Canada and the United States crosses several borders: the 49th Parallel that artificially divides the Blackfoot of Alberta from their counterparts in Montana; two imperialisms and two colonialisms; and the two state-building experiments directed from Ottawa and Washington respectively. The colonial experiences of the Blackfoot in Alberta and Montana have been, despite many commonalities, vastly different. For the Blackfoot, as for many First Nations of North America, imperialism did not end with the creation of national states, but sometimes began or intensified thereafter. This study also transcends disciplinary boundaries: a complex historical study that draws upon literature, especially Native American literature, the whole viewed through an ethnological lens, generally, and specifically via a re-examination of the salvage ethnology of the late nineteenth and early twentieth centuries. Those salvage ethnologists sought to "rescue" the remains of once-pristine indigenous cultures believed to be on the verge of extinction, by recording (sometimes literally, by film and sound) those cultures before they disappeared entirely. Like all pioneers, they sometimes misunderstood, and got things wrong, yet in doing so they produced both an ethnology and a deeply flawed history of the Blackfoot nations that, over time, became almost canonical. By re-examining the salvage ethnologists' activities and sources, Blanca Tovías has simultaneously recovered and reinterpreted Blackfoot history in "emic" terms, i.e., from an insider perspective.

The propensity of Blackfoot scholars and elders to transmit their traditional knowledge, often in the form of stories or myths as well as winter counts and story robes, provides a fundamental point of departure for any understanding of Blackfoot culture in all its many dimensions and inflections. Other sources of information, especially valuable for the early era, come from contemporaneous accounts of travellers, agents, fur traders, mounted police and soldiers, and sundry other wayfarers. The most abundant primary sources on the treaty years and transition to sedentary lifeways are to be found in the inexhaustible (large and small) archives and research libraries of north-western North America as well as other specialist collections in the East, not least the personal and official papers of several of the pioneering ethnologists. Blanca Tovías has been indefatigable in tracking down and consulting these abundant primary sources. This juxtaposition of sacred stories, diaries and memoirs, ethnological fieldwork, and governmental and bureaucratic records, has produced a richly textured interdisciplinary history that balances narrative with thematic approaches.

There is now a large corpus of historical, literary and anthropological works on the colonial encounter in the north-western territories of the United States and Canada. Blanca Tovías engages with this rich literature, always respectfully, in particular highlighting the views of cultural brokers or organic intellectuals, and Blackfoot and other First Nations scholars, so as to foster a dialogue between Blackfoot and non-Blackfoot scholarship. The Blackfoot underwent rapid and multifaceted change during the transition to life on reserves or reservations, but this study emphasises the threads of Blackfoot cultural continuity, so easily lost to view in studies that stress change. They resisted forced acculturation even while they adopted strategies of accommodation, exercising agency in the maintenance of their society and culture. Blanca Tovías does justice to the Blackfoot and their culture, and their determination to retain the integrity of their culture while navigating decades of radical transformation.

UNIVERSITY OF NEW SOUTH WALES, AUSTRALIA, *March 2011*

Acknowledgements

This volume was prepared during my tenure as a University of Sydney Postdoctoral Research Fellow. Sydney University has provided a rich, vigorous and collegial environment in which to pursue the comparative and interdisciplinary history of the Americas. It has also provided me with generous funds to further my research and attend conferences. My special thanks go to Michael McDonnell, Dirk Moses, and Robert Aldrich who have provided feedback and encouragement. Robert Aldrich spent much of his valuable time reading chapters and made excellent suggestions. It is a pleasure to record my debt of gratitude to the members of the American History Reading Group, who gave me timely feedback on the first section of the book. Ann Curthoys, John Docker, and Judith Keene have generously shared their wider intellectual concerns with me.

The research for this volume was initially undertaken as a doctoral dissertation at the University of New South Wales. The readers of my dissertation — Bob Hodge, Michael McDonnell and Susan Schroeder — provided sound advice on how best to turn my research into a monograph. It owes much to the encouragement and support of many colleagues and friends, especially my supervisors at UNSW, David Cahill in the School of History and Philosophy and Sue Kossew in the School of English, Media and Performance Studies. This book could not have been written without David's unconditional support. He has provided intellectual stimulus and mentored me beyond the call of duty. He has also shown unrivalled enthusiasm for my work, and has provided wise counsel and untiring editorial and proofreading labours. I am forever in his debt. Sue Kossew always had constructive advice as I endeavoured to find a balance between the disciplines that inform my research. Generous funding from the UNSW Faculty of Arts and Social Sciences allowed me to undertake research in Canada and the United States. I wish to record my appreciation to Martyn Lyons, former head of the Research Committee.

It would be near impossible to cite all those who gave me practical advice and moral support during this project. My ideas were tested during frequent discussions with colleagues and friends. I warmly thank Fernanda Duarte for being my role model and sounding board. During my overseas research travels I received invaluable assistance from Janine Gasco and Jerry Moore, who opened their house to me, fed me, encouraged me, and gave me valuable feedback. Mike Hruska and Evelyn

Acknowledgements

Ellerman were tremendous hosts in Edmonton. Evie first kindled my interest on the Blackfoot Sun Dance, which led me to focus my dissertation on Blackfoot history and literature. Vanessa Escudero and her parents also received me warmly in their home during the initial stages of my research and provided practical assistance.

It is a pleasure to record my appreciation for excellent discussions with the members of the Indigenous Studies Group at UNSW, especially Martina Horakova, Ben Miller, Hallie Donkin, Pia Solberg, Johanna Perheentupa, and David Fonteyn. My heartfelt thanks go to the late Chicka Dixon for opening his home to our group and for frank discussions, and I thank his niece Liz Mayer for her friendship. During the preparation of my dissertation I shared an office with Heather Moritz. Heather generously provided unsurpassed critical and proofreading skills, and I cherish her continued friendship.

I received timely advice from members of the H-AmIndian discussion group. I am especially obliged to Rod Thomas for a copy of his draft article on "Native American Women Warriors". Roland Bohr shared advance passages from his research in progress, and Kenneth Lokensgard gave me useful hints to make the best out of my 2005 research trip to Canada and the United States. Yale Belanger and Mary Scriver welcomed me in their homes in Lethbridge and Valier, respectively. I am greatly indebted to the scholars who have paved the way for my study through their own work on the Blackfoot, especially the early Blackfoot and non-Blackfoot ethnographers who strove to document Blackfoot knowledge, and whose names I cite throughout this study. Hugh Dempsey, author extraordinaire whose many publications on the Blackfoot inform this book, was supportive of my project when he generously came to meet me at the Glenbow Archives in Calgary during my 2005 research trip. In Montana, Rosalyn LaPier provided me with contact numbers and welcomed my enquiries. In the unrivalled intellectual environment of the American Society for Ethnohistory's annual conference, Alice Beck Kehoe shared ideas as I sought to navigate my way through the shoals of ethnohistorical practice.

My research was kindly assisted by many librarians and archivists. Gerald Conaty was of great assistance at the Glenbow Archives, providing me with access to invaluable materials. At the Glenbow, both Patricia Molesky and Jim Bowman helped guide my research. The staff at the Library and Archives of Canada, Provincial Archives of Alberta, Montana Historical Society, and the National Archives and Records Administration in Denver allowed me access to documents and responded to my enquiries. I am also grateful to the librarian at the Medicine Springs Library, Blackfeet Community College, for access to the Library's Special Collection. My gratitude also goes to the Glenbow Museum and Archive, the Smithsonian American Art Museum, and the Joslyn Art Museum for

Acknowledgements

allowing me to publish reproductions of photographs and artworks from their collections.

My friends and family played a significant part in the completion of this volume. Phillip Plaisted gave me enormous support; he has not only been my IT specialist, cook, carpenter and house painter, but at times has also been my financier, driver, photographer, and many things besides. My children Pedro, Adelina, and Pablo challenged me to continue learning in order to keep up with them. Adelina's assistance with the preparation of my bibliography was timely. My parents taught me to value knowledge and instilled in me the curiosity that has guided me throughout my life. My father, Rómulo Tovías, has always made me feel special; my mother, Dolores Guajardo, did not live to see the completion of this book but was proud of me always. My sister, Adelina Tovías de Miranda, and my brother, Mario Tovías Guajardo, have been unfailing in their love and affection.

My gratitude goes foremost to the Blackfoot past and present, those who shared their knowledge to be passed on to the new generations. I salute them for their dedication to documenting Blackfoot knowledge, and for embracing writing in order to document Blackfoot cultural heritage. This book seeks to honour them by recognizing their contribution to knowledge.

Introduction
The Threads of Continuity

This is a book about continuity, about the ways in which the past wove itself into the new lifeways forced upon the Blackfoot of present-day Alberta and Montana by Canadian and American westward expansion. The effects of the Blackfoot encounter with Europeans began to transform their practices long before the Blackfoot had direct and sustained contact with the traders who spearheaded the westward advance of colonization. The full effects of American and British influence in Blackfoot domains began in the second half of the nineteenth century and continue to this day. This study focuses on specific processes of cultural transformation that draw the threads of continuity binding the non-sedentary era to the radically changed environment of reserve life.

The autonomy and heterogeneity of the Blackfoot First Nations — the Siksika, North Pikuni, South Pikuni, and the Kainai — leaves little room for generalization. Each of these First Nations was formed from bands (*gens* or *gentes*), each bearing a distinct name. In the late nineteenth century George Bird Grinnell — a naturalist and amateur ethnographer who spent many summers with the Blackfoot — compiled a list of eight Siksika, thirteen Kainai, and twenty-four Pikuni bands. He noted that the bands were "a body of consanguineal kindred in the male line", although they "often received outsiders."[1] Europeans coined the term Blackfoot Confederacy to refer collectively to the Blackfoot First Nations that "have now developed a formal political alliance."[2] The Blackfoot had two minor allies who shared their territory: the Tsúùt'ínà (Many People or Every One (in the tribe)) or Sarcee; and the At-séna (also Atsina, Gros Ventre or "Entrails People"). Around 1862 the latter became enemies of the Blackfoot,[3] although their close association by then had already created familial ties that would continue to be maintained.

Among the Blackfoot, the organization of band affairs was the purview of a *Ninnaa* ("leader [. . .] lately tribal Chief or Councilor"). *Nina* was a leader who no longer went to war, a recognized warrior who had no further need to acquire deeds of courage.[4] This leader, together with a variable number of distinguished men (minor chiefs or councillors) guided the band's movements and looked after the needs of his followers. Leaders gained respect on the basis of their war achievements, the acquisition of Sacred Bundles (or other sacred items considered *natoyi* or "Medicine"), and through their generosity.[5] The prestige of some leaders transcended the sphere of their bands,[6] but decisions such as joint war actions were made by consensus. As was the case at inter-tribal level, there were no mechanisms, other than persuasion, to compel the different bands to adhere to collective decisions. The bands gathered every summer during *Ako-katssinn* ("the time of all people camping together", often shortened to "circle encampment"). During this time, they hunted buffalo and prepared for their central sacred rite, Ookaan, which Europeans dubbed the Sun Dance. Each division held a separate circle encampment, which featured visitors from other divisions and other First Nations.[7]

The Blackfoot participated in sodalities collectively named *I-kun-uh'-kah-tsi* (all-comrades societies). Membership was age-graded and cut across the different bands of each division. Wissler explained their functions thus:

> to preserve order in the camp, during the march, and on the hunt; to punish offenders against the public welfare; to protect the camp by guarding against possible surprise by an enemy; to be informed at all times as to the movements of the buffalo herds and secondly by inter-society rivalry to cultivate the military spirit, and by their feasts and dances to minister [. . .] social recreation.[8]

To gain entry into a society required that existing members retire and ceremonially transfer their membership to a new cohort. The new members paid in kind for the privilege. Societies provided a hierarchy for advancement that commenced in childhood and culminated in the most powerful, respected and feared of all societies: the Horns. Each society had a distinct function; for example, the Crazy Dogs Society (or Mad Dog Society) enforced discipline, acting as "police" within the camp and during the hunt. Some societies, like the Horns, did not admit single members but required both man and wife to join the society together.[9] Members of the societies took part in the bands' decision-making processes, acting as councillors. This Blackfoot-specific meaning of society should not be confused with the common application of the term to define a community. In this study, society always refers to the *I-kun-uh'-kah-tsi*.

Historical Antecedents

Blackfoot culture, along with those of other First Nations peoples of the Plains and Prairies, was radically transformed by the acquisition of European goods, including the horse, firearms and metal tools, first through intertribal networks during the very early eighteenth century, and subsequently by direct participation in the fur trade.[10] The incorporation of these goods into First Nations lifeways ushered in a period of cultural florescence. During the so-called golden age of the "Plains Indians" (1750–1875), the Blackfoot alliance dominated a territory extending from the Elk (Saskatchewan) River to the Yellowstone River. Until the middle of the nineteenth century this territory was considered off-limits to whites and enemy First Nations.[11] The Blackfoot attacked and destroyed trading posts on several occasions. In 1810 thirty whites were killed when a war party attacked a trading fort at the mouth of the Big Horn River established by trader Manuel Lisa; and a party of Kainai burnt Fort Piegan in 1833.[12] However, those who followed the right protocols and came in peace were well received by the Blackfoot, which is evident from the experiences of fur traders (such as Henday and Cocking) in the eighteenth century. The opposite occurred when eight young Pikuni met and camped with American explorer Meriwether Lewis and some of his men in 1806. The meeting ended in bloodshed when the Pikuni attempted to steal guns and horses from the explorers. Relations between Americans and the Blackfoot took a long time to recover from the incident. During conversation, Lewis had announced to the Pikuni that he intended to sell guns to the different western tribes, Blackfoot enemies included, a prospect that the Blackfoot fiercely opposed.[13]

Blackfoot influence straddled both sides of the forty-ninth parallel or international boundary, which in 1846 created an artificial division between kindred Blackfoot bands.[14] In time, it resulted in the permanent separation of the Pikuni, now divided between the Blackfeet Reservation in Montana and the Piegan Reserve in Alberta. The chronological context for this study extends back to a time when Blackfoot bands moved freely between both sides.

In geographical terms, Blackfoot participation in the fur trade was conducted on the periphery of their territory, wherein British (Hudson's Bay Company, henceforth HBC) and Canadian (Northwest Company) trading posts were operating by 1794. The Blackfoot travelled northwards to trade at these posts. They traded wolf and fox skins as well as fresh and preserved provisions, and even horses (which were indispensable for traders to hunt and transport goods). In return, they obtained axes, kettles and knives; luxury items like vermillion, beads, blankets, tobacco and liquor; and guns and ammunition for both the hunt and to defend their territory from enemies.

American posts on the Missouri River drew significant Blackfoot trade from the early 1830s. However, trading at distant posts meant that Blackfoot lifeways remained autonomous, albeit increasingly dependent on European goods. The remoteness of Blackfoot territory from large population centres in the East allowed them to continue their erstwhile

INTRODUCTION

lifeways without undue pressures from settlers until well into the nineteenth century. Gradually, however, the Blackfoot world had to contend with the compounding effects of colonial expansion that forced eastern First Nations westward. One result was to increase the number of intertribal rivals competing for ever-diminishing resources. On the British side, the depletion of pelt animals in the East accounted for the gradual westward movement of First Nations peoples. Similar conditions applied in the United States, where forced removal of entire First Nations in the early decades of the nineteenth century in order to make way for American colonists increased the competition for resources west of the Mississipi. Wars between the United States and First Nations refusing to relinquish their ancestral lands also had deleterious effects. Violence in Montana was greatly increased by the so-called Sioux Wars, when the U.S. Army was deployed in order to force them onto reservations. The demographic pressures resulting from these wars were felt by First Nations such as the Blackfoot, who faced yet more competition from bands escaping westwards from the Army.

Competition for Blackfoot trade between the British and Canadian companies ended in 1821, when they joined forces. However, they were soon facing competition from American trading companies. From 1830, the Blackfoot began trading a substantial number of buffalo robes at American Fur Company's posts along the Upper Missouri.[15] The process of establishing the fur trade with the Blackfoot was protracted and at times violent. Despite these differences, mutual interest served to maintain a trade from which both sides profited and created what historian Richard White termed the "Middle Ground," a period of Indian–white relations characterized by accommodation[16] when "whites could neither dictate to Indians nor ignore them. Whites needed Indians as allies, as partners in exchange, as sexual partners, [and] as friendly neighbors."[17] Mutual dependence made the middle ground: "a place in between: in between cultures, peoples, and in between empires and the nonstate world of villages [. . .] the area between the historical foreground of European invasion and occupation and the background of Indian defeat and retreat".[18] The middle ground disappeared with the bison herds: without commodities for exchange, what remained was a relationship of dependency that left the Blackfoot little room for manoeuvre. Henceforth, settlers saw the First Nations peoples of the Plains as obstacles to be removed from their path, either peacefully or by force.

SOURCES

This volume relies on five sets of primary documentation: (1) early traders' and travellers' accounts; (2) published and archival records by amateur and professional ethnographers, government officials and missionaries; (3) documentation pertaining to the administration of reserves; (4) Blackfoot-authored texts, including translated and transcribed oral stories, transcriptions of pictographic records ("year counts" or "winter counts"), testimonies, memoirs, and (5) contemporary fictional representations of Blackfoot subjectivity by Blackfoot authors.

Traders, travellers and, later, amateur and professional ethnographers, began documenting the Blackfoot in 1754–1755, when trader Anthony Henday of the HBC recorded meeting them briefly on two occasions and failed to persuade them to send young men to conduct trade at the HBC's factory at Fort York. Similar failures met his successors, Henry Pressick (1760–61) and Matthew Cocking (1772–73).[19] The trading journals that provide early glimpses of the Blackfoot were kept by traders as a condition of their employment. As anthropologist Gerry Conaty notes, David Thompson's journal (1784–1812) contains the first "good description of early Blackfoot culture". A trader with the Northwest Company who came from a prominent New Jersey family, Alexander Henry The Younger, also left a journal of his trading experiences (1799–1814), which was published together with that of Thompson by Elliott Coues.[20] Among the travellers who met with the Blackfoot are the painter George Catlin, who produced the earliest known portraits of the Blackfoot during his stay at Fort Union in 1832, together with ethnographic descriptions.[21] The travels in the Upper Missouri in 1833–1834 of Prussian Prince Alexander Philipp Maximilian of Wied-Neuwied in the company of Swiss artist Karl Bodmer also produced invaluable paintings of Blackfoot as well as the related journal by Prince Maximilian.[22]

After these early sketches came the writings of amateur ethnographers (including missionaries) who became acquainted with the Blackfoot when they still pursued their autonomous lifeways.[23] Once the Blackfoot settled onto reserves, it became easier for professional ethnographers to live among them and to secure access to informants. Then, interest in documenting cultures that were believed to be on the verge of extinction, through the practice of "salvage" ethnology,[24] fuelled the production by professional ethnographers of several texts recording Blackfoot knowledge. During the first half-century of reserve life, the foundations of canonical Blackfoot history were established. Salvage ethnologists, like the traders and travellers who preceded them, relied on Blackfoot organic intellectuals and bilingual collaborators. Five foundational "salvage" volumes by George Bird Grinnell, Clark Wissler and David C. Duvall, Walter McClintock, Christianus Cornelius Uhlenbeck, and James Willard Schultz, are fundamental to this study.[25] These are key works widely cited by scholars, except possibly for Uhlenbeck, who is included here because he provides the only early bilingual collection of Blackfoot Stories, which are "literally" translated and therefore retain more of the Blackfoot language than other translations. A diary kept by Wilhelmina Maria Uhlenbeck-Melchior, his wife, is instructive because it provides detailed descriptions of his methodology and identifies his informants.[26] Duvall was the earliest Blackfoot ethnographer. He possessed mixed ancestry, his mother being a Pikuni. However, although he spoke the Blackfoot language, he relied for information on knowledgeable Elders as much as non-Blackfoot ethnographers did.

Whatever their shortcomings, these texts are valuable resources and the first point of departure for Blackfoot and non-Blackfoot researchers. Early chroniclers of the Blackfoot wrote about their own experiences and supplemented their observations with the contributions of Blackfoot informants. However, failure to integrate the interconnections between stories, ritual, and everyday practices has left unacknowledged in colonial texts the existence of a viable epistemology that ensured the transmission of Blackfoot knowledge.[27] This problem has begun to be redressed in the more recent work of Blackfoot scholars themselves, whose advances inform this study.

This study profits from a rich vein of unpublished documentation in Canadian and United States archives collected during the early reserve era. During 2004 and 2005, I consulted the archival holdings at the Library and Archives of Canada in Ottawa, the Glenbow Archive in Calgary, the Provincial Archive of Alberta, Edmonton, the Montana Historical Society Research Centre in Helena, and the Special Collection at the Medicine Springs Library, Blackfoot Community College, Browning. A visit to the Museum of the Plains Indian, Browning, was instructive for its collection of traditional Blackfoot clothing. However, written records pertaining to the reservation formerly held at the Museum have been relocated to Denver and were unavailable for consultation. My research also benefited from consulting the Special Collections of the Mackimmie Library, University of Calgary, and the Mansfield Library and Archive, University of Montana, Missoula.

The work of Blackfoot intellectuals is vital to this study, above all to incorporate, through their work, an emic perspective into the analysis of cultural transformation, thus enabling a dialogue between Blackfoot and non-Blackfoot scholarship. Among these, from the early reserve era, I refer particularly to Bull Plume, Natosi Nepe-e, David C. Duvall, and Crooked Meat Strings.[28] Among contemporary authors, I refer, among others, to Mike Mountain Horse, Percy Bullchild, Woody Kipp, Reg Crowshoe, Beverly Hungry Wolf, Nimachia Hernandez, Betty Bastien and Audrey Weasel Traveller. I also draw upon Fraser Taylor's biography of Kainai "Grandfather of Sacred Horn Society", Nii'ta'kaiksa'maikoan (Pete Standing Alone).[29]

In revisiting the foundational texts of colonial history, the intention is not to provide a totalizing view of Blackfoot history. Such a comprehensive approach has already been produced in ethnohistorian John C. Ewers's *The Blackfeet: Raiders on the Northwestern Plains*, an invaluable resource for this study. Eminent historian Hugh Dempsey has also contributed greatly to the writing of Blackfoot history. His numerous publications span the genres of history, biography, ethnography and literature. Most valuable for the purposes of this study are his biographies of Chiefs Isapo-Muxica (Crowfoot) and Mekasto (Red Crow), two Blackfoot leaders who played significant roles during the signing of Treaty Seven with the Dominion in 1877.[30] They were two of the principal Blackfoot negotiators with white officialdom during the early reserve era. Dempsey's position as chief ethnologist at the Glenbow Archives and Museum in Alberta, and his personal ties to the Blackfoot, having married a Kainai, provided him with a perspective rarely afforded a non-Blackfoot researcher — his interpreter was none other than Akay-Namuka (Many Guns) or James Gladstone, the first member of a First Nation ever to have been elected to the Canadian Senate (1958),[31] and who was Dempsey's father-in-law. This study builds upon the work of these Blackfoot and non-Blackfoot scholars.

In my research for this book, I have sought to engage with Blackfoot and non-Blackfoot scholarship with a view to analyzing cultural continuity within processes that have hitherto not received sufficient attention. This methodological strategy aims to dispel simplistic generalizations regarding cultural loss and the locating of First Nations authenticity in a distant, irretrievable past, by picking out the threads of continuity within a tapestry of cultural change. Such an approach has required a close reading and close analysis of micro-historical aspects, resulting in the four case studies.[32] Although these processes are viewed separately, they are deeply interconnected, and these connections are made explicit throughout the volume. The interconnectedness between the sacred and the secular in the Blackfoot worldview — and, therefore between the stories, the ritual, and the everyday — dictates that Ookaan take precedence as the first case study. Blackfoot customs, beliefs, identity, and individual and communal values all intersect (then as now) in Ookaan, and it was a significant site of both Blackfoot accommodation with, and resistance to, the full onset of colonial rule.

Note on Nomenclature

Multiple names have been applied to the Blackfoot-speaking First Nations, the Kainai, Siksika and Pikuni. The most common in the documentation of interest to this volume are Blood, Northern Blackfoot or Blackfoot proper, and Piegan or Peigan, respectively. In recent times, Blackfoot scholars themselves have reversed naming trends by using ethnonyms, the names that First Nations peoples use to refer to themselves. In 2001, the Blackfoot Gallery Committee, comprising members of each of the Blackfoot First Nations, published self-identifiers, including the collective terms Niitsitapiksi (Real People) and Nitsi-poi-yiksi (speakers of the Real Language).[1] The names for each First Nation are:

Kainai: (translates as "Many Leaders"), also called Blood, Bloods, Aapaitsitapi Kainah, Kainawa and Akainawa.
Siksika: (translates as "black-footed people") also called Northern Blackfoot or Blackfoot Proper.
Pikuni: (translates as "a people that possessed poorly dressed or torn robes"). Also called Pikani, Piikani, Pikunii, Piegan, Peigan. The Pikani are now divided in two autonomous First Nations. In Montana they are called Blackfeet, Piegan, South Pikani, or Amsskaapipikani; and in Canada they are called Peigan; North Pikani: Aputosi Pikuni, Apatohsipikani, or Skinnii Piikani.

"Archithinue Natives", historian John Ewers argues, might have been used to refer collectively to "the Blackfoot tribes and their Sarsi and Gros Ventre allies".[2] In 1772 Mathew Cocking, a trader with the HBC, recorded the following names for the "four Tribes, or Nations" (Kainai, Blackfoot, Pikuni and Tsúùt'ínà or Sarcee): "Mithco-Athinuwuck or Bloody Indians, Koskitow-Wathesitock or Blackfooted Indians, Pegonow or Muddy-Water Indians & Suxxewuck or Wood Country Indians." Cocking named the Gros Ventre "Powestic-Athinuwuck", i.e. "Water-fall Indians."[3] In 1787–8 David Thomson referred to the Blackfoot divisions as "the Peegan, called Peeaganakoon, the Blood Indians (Kennekoon) and the Blackfeets (Saxeekoon)."[4] By mid-twentieth century, the spelling had been standardized to Blackfoot for the entire alliance, and Piegan (or Peigan), Blood, and Northern Blackfoot for the three Blackfoot-speaking

Note on Nomenclature

divisions. From 1855, when representatives of all the Blackfoot divisions signed a treaty with the United States of America, their official name below the Forty-Ninth Parallel became Blackfeet.

Even among Blackfoot scholars, a clear consensus on the most appropriate spelling of these names is not reflected in practice. Throughout this volume "Blackfoot" is used to refer to all the Blackfoot-speaking First Nations. "Blackfeet" is only used when citing from another text, or when referring specifically to the South Pikuni, whose reservation in the United States is called "Blackfeet Reservation".[5] For each First Nation, I use "Pikuni", "Kainai", and "Siksika" to indicate singular and plural, even though forms such as "Pikunis" abound in the documentation. Although a third-party reference for a single Blackfoot noun requires the "–wa" suffix, and the plural the "–iksi" suffix, these suffixes are not used here.[6]

By the early twentieth century, many Blackfoot used their Anglicized names in their dealings with non-Blackfoot. The names of the Blackfoot signatories to Treaty Seven with the Dominion in 1877, for example, appeared in both the Blackfoot and English languages, but only the translated names appear in subsequent official documents. Personal names in the original language are acknowledged in this volume, where available. During the non-sedentary era, it was common for a Blackfoot man to undergo several, sometimes up to eight or ten, name changes in his lifetime. Women also changed their names, though less frequently. One of the most respected Siksika leaders who signed Treaty Seven, Crowfoot, had been known throughout his life by the names of Astoxcomi (Shot Close), Kyiah-sta-ah (Bear Ghost), Istowun-eh'pata (Packs a Knife), Isapomuxica (Crow Indian's Big Foot) — the last often being misquoted as "Chapo-Mexico". Apart from the difficulties created by the same person being known by different names at different times, there is the added confusion created by the adoption of deceased relatives' names, not to mention different spelling conventions and even plain errors due to language misunderstandings. Naming practices were modified by the colonizers during the reserve era through the treaty rolls upon which annuity payments were based, but Blackfoot names bestowed in the traditional fashion continued to be used internally.[7] The challenges of Blackfoot nomenclature for English speakers act as a reminder of the difficulties inherent in cultural translation.

THE LEGACY OF COLONIAL MISNAMING

Nomenclature difficulties arise from the (mis)naming of the First Nations peoples of the Americas, which began with what Umberto Eco magnanimously calls serendipity and Paul Chartrand calls Christopher Columbus's "naming fiasco." Columbus's mistaken belief to have made landfall in the

Note on Nomenclature

Indies in 1492 was perpetuated in the misnomer "Indian" being ascribed to the totality of the inhabitants of what was named "America."[8] In current use "America" and "Americans" have come to refer exclusively to the United States and its citizens, no longer to the continent extending from Alaska and the North West Territories to Tierra del Fuego, which is herein referred to as the Americas. Many Canadians refuse to identify as "Americans", a term they do not see as having pan-American coverture.[9] Terms such as Euro-American, Euro-Canadian, Native American, and Native Canadian are used in order to disentangle history in terms of the border between Canada and the United States, often referred to as the "Medicine line" by First Nations peoples such as the Blackfoot, whose domains were artificially divided by the Forty-Ninth Parallel.[10] Here, citizens of the United States will be referred to as "American" in preference to awkward neologisms such as "Unitedstatian", following the widespread convention, notwithstanding its patent inaccuracy, given that this is a narrowing of a term that historicaly applies to the inhabitants of the Americas.

The term Indian homogenizes a complex and heterogeneous world and reinscribes myriad indigenous subjectivities, by taking the place of the names that First Nations peoples had for themselves in their own languages. As Anishinaabe scholar Gerald Vizenor argues, "the *Indian* is a simulation and loan word of dominance". Yet, despite this awareness, the longevity and extensive use of some imposed names makes it practically impossible to avoid them, not least because many were adopted and subsequently used as self-identifiers by First Nations peoples themselves. Pikuni ceremonialist Percy Bullchild, for example, refers to himself as a "Blackfeet Indian." Articulating the "naming fiasco" is simpler than escaping its grip. Yet, as Vizenor notes, grappling with these problems of nomenclature is helpful to "understand the problems of identity among tribal people who are burdened with names invented by the dominant society."[11] I have opted for using "Indian" without quotation marks throughout this volume in recognition of the wide use of the term, but have used ethnonyms wherever possible. Despite the pejorative connotations progressively accumulated in the term Indian, it is ubiquitous during the historical period addressed here, being entrenched in the language through terms such as "Amerindian", "Plains Indians", "Indian Country", "Indian Agents", and "Indian Dances". Consequently, its use in one guise or another is unavoidable, even though it has been more recently replaced by terms such as First Nations peoples, Aboriginal peoples, Indigenous peoples, Native Americans, and Native Canadians. The preferred term in Canada is First Nations, while in the United States it is Native American. "First Nations peoples" is used here in preference to Indians, but chapters 9 to 11 employ "Indian", for reasons that are explained therein.

Conversely, the European, Euro-American and Euro-Canadian colo-

Note on Nomenclature

nizers were also subsumed under the collective noun "whites," used in everyday language by both First Nations peoples and whites themselves. The name in the Blackfoot language is Napikwan (Old Man Person). For the fur trade era, the documentation makes a distinction between the English traders from the Hudson's Bay Company, their (French–Canadian) rivals, and the Americans. Rather than reflect the origins of individual traders, these distinctions related to the companies themselves. During an era of competition there was a practical reason, because each offered their customers different trading terms. Likewise, when colonization arrived in the North Western Plains, home to the Blackfoot First Nations, it followed different paths under the leadership of the Great Father (the President of the United States) and the Great Mother (The Queen). The term "whites" or "white" is used throughout this study wherever more specific terms are impractical.

Some instances of misnaming have been the result from genuine confusion and the language difficulties faced by early chroniclers; others have been deliberate. For example, First Nations peoples applied derogatory names to refer to their enemies. This negative stereotyping was part of a process of "Othering" peculiar to the North Western Plains. The Blackfoot name for the Cree was "Lying People" or "Liars", and for the Assiniboine (Nakoda) "Cutthroats". The Kutenai called the Blackfoot *Sahantla* (Bad People).[12] The newcomers documented some of these derogatory exonyms based on the information of their guides. As a result, some of these exonyms and their translations into English and French have been perpetuated in the historiography. As they are gradually replaced, multiple names for the same group coexist in the documentation.

PART I

The Blackfoot Sun Dance

Resistance and Persistence, 1877–1920

1

The Sun Dance
Invoking the Sacred

The complex of ritual activities that comprised the Blackfoot Ookaan, commonly referred to as the "Sun Dance,"[1] marked the highest point in the Blackfoot ceremonial calendar. During the time when the Blackfoot still relied on the buffalo hunt for their livelihood, Ookaan provided the climactic finale to the Circle Camp gathering, *Ako-katssinn*. As the name indicates, the Blackfoot bands would camp together, their lodges forming a great circle within which each band occupied a predetermined place. The Circle Camp took place in summer, when a communal buffalo hunt supplied ample meat and the saskatoon berries, an important food component of the Blackfoot diet, were ripe and plentiful. Food abundance and the proximity of bands that travelled separately during the rest of the year provided opportunities for feasting and renewing acquaintance. Thanks to this propinquity, the Blackfoot could engage in social, cultural, and political activities that reaffirmed, reproduced, and revitalized Blackfoot culture. Although the Pikuni, Siksika, and Kainai each formed their own Circle Camp, visitors from other divisions and even from other First Nations were welcome at these gatherings, camping outside the circle of lodges. Most importantly, proximity of the bands provided opportunities for the conduct of rituals and ceremonies separate from Ookaan, which added to the importance of the Circle Camp. One example is the transfer of Bundles, which had to be passed across bands at set intervals via the requisite initiation rites. Sacred Bundles, as was the case with sacred objects and also with ceremonial functions, circulated in accordance with an economy of transfer that resulted in the sharing of sacred knowledge among the different bands. Inductees received ownership of sacred objects and the instructions necessary for their care and maintenance from the previous owners, reciprocating with a payment in kind. In light of this rich cultural context, the anthropologist Clark Wissler described the Blackfoot Sun Dance (including *Ako-katssinn*) as a "true tribal festival, or demonstration of ceremonial functions in which practically every important ritual owner and organization had a place."[2]

PART I — THE BLACKFOOT SUN DANCE

FIGURE 1.1 *Piegan Sun Dance camp* [1889], Glenbow Archive, Calgary, Canada, NA-118-16.

In the latter part of the nineteenth century, once the Blackfoot had been forced to settle due to the destruction of the buffalo herds on which their livelihood had been dependent, officials in both Canada and the United States sought to persuade them to curtail or eliminate their traditional practices, most especially sun dances. These attempts were congruent with assimilationist policies that had a long pedigree in the New World. Officials, as was the case with missionaries, deemed the sun dances practiced by First Nations of the Plains and Plateau, together with the Potlatch of the Pacific First Nations, to be the principal obstacles along the path to Christianity and civilization. These official efforts at forced acculturation began in earnest once hitherto non-sedentary First Nations settled on reserves and reservations. Their attempts were facilitated by First Nations' dependency on government food rations in the aftermath of the buffalo's demise. Official threats to withdraw this vital assistance became commonplace, in order to compel compliance with regulations. On the three Blackfoot reserves in present-day Alberta, and the Blackfeet Reservation in Montana, Ookaan played a pivotal role in the continuing vitality of Blackfoot culture at a time of dramatic change. A sketch of the significance of the ceremony, therefore, will precede the analysis of the effects of the prohibition. The present chapter anatomizes this significance, while the succeeding two chapters respectively analyze the official endeavours to suppress or curtail its performance, and the corresponding Blackfoot responses to this iconoclast campaign. These chapters necessarily reflect the uneven availability of records pertaining to the suppression of sun dances at specific locations. The documentation in respect of the Siksika (Blackfoot Reserve) and the Kainai (Blood Reserve) in Alberta, provides a richer perspective than that of the Piegan Reserve in Alberta or the Blackfeet Reservation in Montana.

Cultural Centrality of Ookaan

The centrality of Ookaan, the Blackfoot Sun Dance, resides in the fact that the ceremony maintains the links between Natosi (the Sun) and the Blackfoot. The offerings made during Ookaan serve to renew the relationship between the Blackfoot and the Above Beings (Natosi, his wife Kokomi-kisomm (the Moon), and his son Ipiso-Waahsa (the Morning Star)), who assist them in times of need. Reciprocity for benefits received accords well with the Blackfoot worldview. According to this worldview, in which the sacred and secular are interrelated, every Blackfoot activity can be linked to a wider realm wherein animate and inanimate beings impart knowledge and share their power with humans. More broadly, the Blackfoot ceremonial life strengthens the relationship between themselves and their helpers, the Naa-to-yi-ta-piiksi (Spirit Beings), who "changed themselves into human form and taught [the Blackfoot] ancestors the ceremonies and songs that [they] could use to call on them for help".[3] In other words, the conduct of ceremonies followed these teachings, which were constantly being passed to new custodians through ritual transfer.

Among the Blackfoot, to build a Medicine Lodge to Natosi required that a married woman, whose virtue must be beyond reproach, make a public vow to become the Holy Woman in the Sun Dance and thereby also the "Mother" of her community.[4] The vow was both a request for assistance and a promise of reciprocation, as in the case of a woman who prayed for her son's health thus: "Listen, Sun. Pity me. You have seen my life. You know that I am pure. I have never committed adultery with any man. Now, therefore, I ask you to pity me. I will build you a lodge. Let my son survive. Bring him back to health, so that I may build this lodge for you".[5] Once Natosi granted such a request, the promise could not be broken. In order to fulfil her promise to preside over a Sun Dance, the vower had to acquire the "Natoas Bundle" by transfer from the current owner, that is, from a woman who had previously become the Holy Woman during Ookaan. The Natoas's significance resides in that, as recorded in the Blackfoot Stories, it was first handed down to the Blackfoot by Elk Woman, whose standards of modesty and purity provide the model that generations of Blackfoot women have been encouraged to emulate.[6] The vower and her husband incurred a great deal of expense, not only in order to reciprocate for the transfer of the Natoas, but also in connection with other aspects of the ceremony that required reciprocation in kind, including horses, Hudson's Bay Company blankets, or other highly valued goods.

Anthropologists have documented some eighteen kindred ceremonies of the North American Plains and Plateau[7] to which the descriptor "Sun Dance" came to be applied. This misnomer, Leslie Spier notes, possibly derived from *"wiwanyag wacipi"*, a ceremony of the Dakota also known as the "sun-gazing dance."[8] However, Spier recognized that the Blackfoot Sun Dance is unique, although sharing some characteristics with other ceremonies.[9] D. B. Shimkin compiled this taxonomy of the common characteristics of sun dances and kindred ceremonies:

> (a) initiation as a result of a vow; (b) ceremonial approach to the site of the ceremony; (c) formation of a Circle Camp and pitching a tipi for the vower and sponsor inside the circle; (d) erection "with great formality" of a [. . .] forked tree as the centre pole; (e) ritual construction of a Medicine Lodge around the centre pole; (f) "dancing, fasting and thirsting" for several days and nights; (g) recounting of war deeds and the giving away of property and; (h) self-sacrifice by those who had vowed to "have themselves pierced through the pectoral muscles".[10]

Shimkin's taxonomy applies generally to the Blackfoot Ookaan. During the buffalo days, the central rites of Ookaan lasted four days, although the sacred rites pertaining to the ceremony began months before the formation of the Circle Camp, itself lasting several weeks. The camp moved four times before arriving at the definitive site of the ceremony. Once there, a forked tree was ritually felled, transported and erected at the centre of the Medicine Lodge, the structure purpose-built for Ookaan. This tree or "Sun Dance Pole" represents the *axis mundi*. Before its erection, supplicants would place upon it goods of value as offerings to Natosi. However, notwithstanding the shared aspects among sun dances, as Shimkin acknowledged, noteworthy differences exist in the specific way in which each First Nation conducts the ceremony.[11] Such differences include the way in which the respective oral stories of different First Nations narrate the origin of the ceremony. The specific connections between the ceremony and the practitioners' worldviews can also be quite distinct, as is the case with how the people of each First Nation view themselves vis-à-vis the wider world. Therefore, while Shimkin suggested 1700 as the possible date for the beginning of the Sun Dance in the Great Plains, First Nations who practice the ceremony explain its origins by reference to their respective sacred stories. Scholars often refer to these narratives, handed down orally from generation to generation, as mythologies. Yet, for First Nations such as the Blackfoot these narratives comprise true records of the distant past. That such a conflict of views exists, however, is peripheral to the forced acculturation debacle that unfolded from the late nineteenth and the early twentieth centuries. Attention here will centre on those aspects that had a bearing on the attempts to curtail the practice, on the one hand, and on the effects that such efforts had for the practitioners, on the other.

According to the Story of Paii (Scarface), Natosi himself instructed this Blackfoot ancestor on the manner in which Ookaan should be conducted. In contrast with the Enlightenment ideology of human mastery over nature, in the Blackfoot view there is a need "to sacrifice in order to receive knowledge."[12] Accordingly, the culture hero Paii underwent sacrifices before Natosi agreed to remove the scar from his face whence his name derives. A fuller version of the Story of Paii appears on chapter 9, suffice for now to note that the sacrifices the Blackfoot offer during Ookaan follow Natosi's teachings to their ancestor. The shape of these offerings has not remained static. It has been transformed in the way that all cultures transform in response to intercultural influences and material circumstances. What remain unchanged are the Blackfoot principles of sacrifice, generosity, and reciprocity embedded, *inter alia*, in the Story of Paii. These principles find expression during Ookaan in myriad ways, not least in the gifts that the Blackfoot offer to Natosi at this time. During the early reserve era, the period of interest here, such offerings ranged from a valuable item of clothing, a sacred object, or a white buffalo robe, to the gift of a person's own flesh through the enactment of self-mortification rituals. During Ookaan, the Holy Woman sacrificed by fasting and praying for four consecutive days, at the conclusion of which those present shared a sacramental meal featuring buffalo tongues. One hundred of these had to be ritually obtained from freshly slaughtered beasts and preserved in preparation for Ookaan. After the demise of the buffalo herds those of cattle became a substitute. Dictated by necessity, Ookaan underwent modification from time to time. However, during the early reserve era government officials in both Canada and the United States, intent upon erasing all vestiges of First Nations' cultures, embarked on a course of exerting pressure with the ultimate aim to extinguish sun dances.

SACRIFICE, RECIPROCITY AND CULTURAL REPRODUCTION

The detrimental effects of regulations against sun dances consist in their attack on the practices of sacrifice, generosity and reciprocity that pervade the Blackfoot worldview and which featured in manifold ways during the Circle Camp and Ookaan. Although the specific regulations and their implementation will be explored thoroughly in chapter 2, for present purposes it should be noted that gifts or "giveaways" became one of the principal targets of the prohibition, together with the self-sacrifice rites through which a small number of warriors reciprocated for Natosi's assistance at times of great danger. Taking into account the cultural significance of activities marked for extinction from the perspective of the practitioners, it becomes evident that much more is at stake than mere transfers of property. While property exchanges were ubiquitous during the time when the Blackfoot bands camped together, these giveaways sought to uphold the principles of generosity and reciprocity indispensable to fulfil community obligations and thereby to attain the respect of the community. The self-mortification rituals were also indispensable in order to renew the relationship between the Blackfoot and Natosi. In other words, when officials sought to prevent these actions from taking place, they imperilled the continuation of Blackfoot cultural reproduction: the practices that gave meaning to the Blackfoot.

The most significant transfers in terms of the value of goods exchanged relate to Sacred Bundles (including highly revered Beaver Bundles and Medicine Pipes), and induction into the *I-kun-uh'-kah-tsi* or age-graded societies. The premium placed on sacred items such as Beaver Bundles and Medicine Pipe Bundles was commensurate with the high regard in which these sacred objects and their owners were held. Sacred Beings gave these bundles to the Blackfoot, together with valued knowledge, including songs and rituals necessary to fulfil their owners' reciprocal obligations. These can be quite onerous to observe, including daily routines and taboos associated with their care. In the Blackfoot worldview, Gerald Conaty points out, the spiritual power attached to Medicine Pipe Bundles and Beaver Bundles increases their owners' prestige. During times of need, their owners act as intermediaries between sacred beings and the Blackfoot, opening the Bundles in order to request assistance from the sacred realm. Conaty notes that a "[a] 'chief' had, as a rule, owned and transferred to someone else two Medicine Pipe Bundles and often looked after a Beaver Bundle."[13]

Some sacred objects had to be transferred within specified time limits, and in accordance with established protocols.[14] For example, according to Siksika Old Bull, a Medicine Pipe Bundle had to be transferred outside the band of the current owner every four years. The current owner and his assistants would physically "catch" the would-be new owner in a ritualized manner. After being touched with the pipe, the candidate would be physically carried to the current pipe owner's tepee wrapped in a blanket. Refusal to acquire the Medicine Pipe Bundle by going through the required initiation and making the requisite payment in kind to the previous owner could bring bad luck and even death to the one caught or his immediate family.[15] The Blackfoot disliked being "caught", because the previous owner of a Medicine Pipe could pick from among the new owner's horses, those that he would take as reciprocation. Such practice meant the new owner stood to lose his favourite horse in exchange for the Bundle. The rule that such a transfer should be made outside the band of the current Bundle's owner made the Circle Camp the ideal time for such transfers. However, after settlement, when the bands lived within close proximity, transfers could occur at other times.

A similar circumstance applied to induction into the *I-kun-uh'-kah-tsi*, or age-graded societies. Membership began in childhood and culminated in the most respected of all societies, the Horns. The members of a society would "buy" membership into another society as a collective, which required current members to retire and transfer their regalia. Retiring members transferred their rights to new inductees, who reciprocated with payment in kind. In turn, retiring members would buy into another society, always moving up one step within the societies' hierarchy. Again, as society membership cut across band membership, the Circle Camp provided the ideal space for such transfers to take place during the non-sedentary era. For example, the *Ma'toki* or Motokix (Old Women's Society or Buffalo Women's Society) always held their secret meetings during the Circle Camp, inducting new members at that time. Their meeting concluded with the members performing a public dance.[16] Although separate from Ookaan, the transfer of Bundles and societies' meetings added to the significance of the Circle Camp. *Ako-katssinn* thus encompassed a veritable palette of ritual activities in which property changed hands in accordance with principles of generosity and reciprocity. Any attempt to curtail or prohibit these activities would necessarily have widespread impact upon the Blackfoot social organization.

There were other instances where "giveaways" featured during the Circle Camp. *Naamaahkaani* ("counting coup"), the public recounting of feats that elevated a Blackfoot individual in the estimation of the community, preceded many Blackfoot rituals. During the buffalo days these recitations of self-achievement recounted feats such as touching an enemy before striking him the deathblow, capturing enemy weapons, shields, bonnets or other objects deemed to possess sacred power. During the historical period, counting coup additionally featured the capture of horses, guns, or enemy scalps. Counting coup played a part in cultural reproduction by impressing upon the young a desire to emulate such heroic deeds. One of the junctures at which *Naamaahkaan* takes place during Ookaan is prior to the ritual lighting of the sacred fire. Honouring the cherished Blackfoot ideal of generosity, the person counting coup ends with a distribution of gifts to those present.[17] It would be difficult to document the many acts of generosity and reciprocity that take place during the Circle Camp, each and every one of which enhanced the social position of the giver, opening up the possibility of attaining leadership. While the Circle Camp was the perfect venue for displaying wealth, which can be a sign of possessing sacred power,[18] only through acts of generosity, including feasting and gifts, could aspiring leaders gain prestige and current leaders increase their following.[19]

Marriages counted among those activities occurring during the Circle Camp that featured gifts as an intrinsic component. When the bands travelled separately, most marriages were arranged and took place at this time. Aspiring grooms could win favour from their prospective fathers-in-law by hunting on their behalf.[20] To validate a marriage, prospective in-laws would send horses and other valued goods to a groom's family and receive equally valuable gifts in return.[21] It seems that property was constantly changing hands during the Circle Camp, whether after counting coup, when transferring Sacred Bundles or other sacred objects (tepee designs, shields, headdresses and weasel suits), joining societies, making marriage arrangements, honouring visitors, or feasting followers. These acts that attached respect to the giver in Blackfoot society transgressed white notions of thrift and were judged by officials and missionaries to be a cause of poverty among First Nations. Consequently, these giveaways were targeted for eradication. Generosity, notwithstanding its consonance with Christian teachings, was condemned when practiced by the Blackfoot in accord with their traditions. Agents and missionaries constantly complained against the lack of provision for their future needs by the Blackfoot, which placed a burden on public coffers that officials sought to limit.

However, no component raised more objections than the self-sacrifice ritual or "piercing" that was a common feature of Plains sun dances, including Ookaan. This piercing simultaneously repelled and attracted whites. The offering, also known as "taking the cut" or the "making of braves", was in reciprocation for the favourable outcome of a warrior's vow, when seeking aid from Natosi at times of life-threatening danger. Between two and five pledgers underwent the ritual each year during Ookaan. Cuts were made "through the right shoulder blade and [. . .] on each side of [the supplicant's] breast then running a sharpened stick through the skin [. . .] A shield was fastened to the stick in his shoulder blade while two ropes were fastened to the two sticks on his breast." After embracing the centre post, the supplicant "backs off until he comes to the end of the rope and starts to dance [. . .] trying to break the skin which the ropes are fastened to".[22] Those who took part in this rite did so on their own undertaking, and without coercion, although during the early reserve era Indian Agents and missionaries complained that whites with "an appetite for the sensational and novel" provided financial assistance for the ritual in exchange for being allowed to witness it. In 1889, for example, the duration of the Sarcee Sun Dance was lengthened "at the special request of the white people, who had given them lots of money to do so."[23] A misconception gained currency that the reciprocation ritual signified a rite of passage to become a warrior, therefore, in the official documentation of the era, "taking the cut" is often referred to as the "making of braves."[24]

Other, less conspicuous self-mortification rituals that took place during sun dances included the cutting of a portion of a finger (sometimes offered as reciprocation but also part of Blackfoot mourning practices); and the cutting of very small pieces of flesh, to be buried around the Sun Dance Pole.[25] The documentation seldom mentions these practices, perhaps owing to their lesser public profile. Overall, it seems to have escaped the notice of those who passed moral judgments and recoiled at First Nations peoples' rituals that Christian praxis does not preclude self-mortification. Alluding to this parallel, Grinnell compared "piercing" to a penance, not unlike acts of self-denial "in our own centres of enlightened civilization."[26] Walter McClintock in his *Old North Trail* drew similar connections, naming a chapter on the origins of Ookaan "Legend of Poïa, The Christ Story of the Blackfeet."[27] Official attitudes were less understanding. Missionaries and officials uniformly decried the self-sacrifice ritual as a sign of savagery, a heathen practice that could threaten the security of settlers by inspiring Indians to revert to their savage ways.

The foregoing sets the scene for a better understanding of the effects upon the Blackfoot of regulations seeking to curtail or eradicate sun dances. The importance of sacrifice, generosity and reciprocity can best be appreciated from a perspective that takes into account the threads binding Blackfoot ceremonial, ritual, and cultural practices to these principles. Rather than an exhaustive description of the Circle Camp, Ookaan, and the activities pertaining to Blackfoot cultural reproduction taking place therein, I have sought to establish the importance of sacrifices that, ranging from the giving away of material goods to the offering of a person's own flesh, were performed at every juncture of *Ako-katssinn* and Ookaan. Community standards encouraged the Blackfoot to strive in order to observe ideals of sacrifice, generosity, and reciprocity. Those able to uphold these ideals could become leaders. Conversely, those who failed to live by these standards would be reduced in the estimation of their community. During the early reserve era, cultural change was driven by circumstances, particularly the lack of resources attendant upon the destruction of the buffalo herds in the early 1880s. Without the buffalo hunt, highly valued buffalo tongues were substituted by beef tongues, obtained from government rations. Adaptation took another guise during the early reserve era, when officials in both Canada and the United States sought to curtail or, wherever possible, eliminate sun dances. To this end, they enacted and implemented regulations calculated to put an end to this central ceremony in order to advance official assimilationist agendas.

2
Colonial Conceits and Indictable Offenses

The prevalent belief that, in order to become civilized, First Nations peoples in both the United States and Canada needed to surrender their beliefs and ceremonies, is ubiquitous in the official documentation pertaining to the first half-century of Blackfoot life after settlement (beginning in the late 1870s and early 1880s). Less is known about the relentless nature of assimilationist measures implemented as part of the civilization efforts on reserves and reservations in Canada and the United States, respectively, where the all-too-familiar process of forced assimilation harnessed long-standing ideologies of European superiority to a gradually increasing capacity to legislate over the lives of First Nations peoples. With the opening of the West to white settlers, colonial dominance extended to First Nations whose geographical isolation had shielded them from the advances of settlement until well into the nineteenth century. This was true of First Nations such as the Blackfoot, who exerted dominance from the Upper Missouri to the Saskatchewan River. Three events paved the way for the colonization of the Blackfoot in the second half of the nineteenth century. The first was the discovery of gold in Montana in 1862, the second was the advent of railways in 1881, and the third, shortly thereafter, was the destruction by over-hunting of the bison herds on which they depended for their livelihood. During the 1862 summer, between 500 and 600 prospectors passed through Fort Benton, a town that had grown around a trading fort established — with Blackfoot acquiescence — in the 1840s to capture the Blackfoot trade in buffalo robes, the name for the tanned buffalo hides that were exchanged for European commodities.

By 1864 the Blackfeet Agent, Gad E. Upson, reported to his superiors in Washington that the entire population of Montana was "no less than thirty thousand". He also claimed the mountains were full of prospectors, and settlers occupied valleys and streams for the purposes of agriculture. Montana, he boasted, yielded much gold dust, and new placers and lodes were being discovered weekly.[1] Except for a few Kainai who lived in Montana, the Kainai and Siksika territory was north of the boundary line.

Colonial Conceits and Indictable Offenses

As conflict with settlers escalated, these bands crossed into Montana only to conduct trade or raid their enemies. The railways arrived in Montana in 1881, in time to give the *coup de grâce* to the already dwindling bison herds, providing an efficient means for the transportation of robes to industrial centres. The historian Michael Punke claims that in 1882 "the Northern Pacific Railroad alone shipped 200,000 hides to eastern processing facilities, an amount that filled an estimated 700 boxcars." The following year, the railroad transported only 40,000, and by 1884, "the total harvest fit in a single boxcar."[2] The railway provided settlers with fast access to the West, and encroached upon the buffalo grazing areas. It bridged the distance that had allowed the Blackfoot to maintain their relative autonomy while engaging in the fur trade and adapting European goods into their lives consistent with their own interests. From the 1830s onwards when the Americans established trading forts within reach of the Blackfoot First Nations, in competition with the existing British and Canadian posts north of the line, the Americans attracted a great proportion of the Blackfoot trade in buffalo robes. Blackfoot bands travelled great distances in order to exchange their tanned bison robes for guns, ammunition, kettles, blankets, items of clothing, beads, paint, and a variety of manufactured goods. Those Blackfoot living north of the boundary were first to suffer famine when fires were lit to prevent the buffalo herd from moving into Canada in 1880. Those able to do so went south, remaining in Montana until the last of the buffalo had been hunted and the buffalo herds had been eradicated.

European goods obtained through the fur trade, together with ownership of horses, which the Blackfoot first obtained through intertribal networks, had contributed to a florescence of Blackfoot culture in the early nineteenth century. However, by the 1880s, starvation forced them to settle. The South Pikuni occupy the Blackfeet Reservation in Montana, and the North Pikuni, Kainai and Siksika occupy the Peigan, Blood, and Blackfoot reserves, respectively, in current-day Alberta, Canada. There, they became subordinate and dependent on government rations for survival, and subject to official interference in every aspect of their lives. Although the administration of Indian Affairs in each country did not always follow the same path, both pursued long-standing goals of assimilation. These had begun in the United States with the Indian Trade and Intercourse Act of 1790.[3] Canada continued similar policies of "civilizing the Indian" to those pursued by Britain since 1815.[4] Even though in the late nineteenth century efforts to curtail or eradicate First Nations' cultural practices were unevenly implemented across the reserves and reservations where the ceremonies were practiced, officials and missionaries often expressed a desire for the complete eradication of so-called Indian dances, which they blamed for preventing the acceptance of Christianity and civilization by First Nations peoples.

Part I — The Blackfoot Sun Dance

Settlement afforded opportunities for officials and missionaries to coerce the Blackfoot into giving up the long-held values, beliefs, and practices that shaped their identity, but which contravened European values. Confined within geographically demarcated spaces, they were expected to become Christians and adopt "agriculture and pastoral pursuits" under the tutelage of Indian Agents and the Farming Instructors provided in Canada by the Department of Indian Affairs (DIA), and in the United States by the Bureau of Indian Affairs (BIA).[5] Missionaries were charged with educating the young to prepare them to reject their cultural inheritance so that, as the older generations passed away, ceremonies such as sun dances would disappear.[6] In benign terms the goal was "to have the Indian educated out of them",[7] or, in the oft-cited words of Captain Richard Pratt, founder of the Carlisle Indian School in Pennsylvania in 1879, to "Kill the Indian in him, and save the man."[8] Residential schools were favoured because they prevented children from participating in what officials viewed as "the contaminating influences of camp life", including hunting, sporadic raiding for horses, and sun dances.[9] The students were forced to communicate in English, and only through subterfuge could they speak in their own languages. Canadian schools followed the American model. In 1895, a North-West Mounted Police (NWMP) report exposed the residential schools' illegal practice of locking-in children at night to prevent them from running away and returning to their families.[10]

The settlement of First Nations on reserves provided opportunities for the missionary enterprise that had not been available during the time when the bands followed the seasonal movements of the buffalo, although, against all odds, Protestant as well as Catholic missionaries had from 1840 occasionally managed to proselytize among the Blackfoot. The Jesuit Pierre-Jean De Smet was a pioneer, baptizing the first Blackfoot on American territory in 1841, a chief who was baptized on Christmas Day, and received the name of Nicholas.[11] De Smet became a firm friend of the Blackfoot. In 1851 he prepared the official map defining, *inter alia*, the boundaries of Blackfoot territory at the signing of the Fort Laramie Treaty, between the United States and several prairie First Nations, which the Blackfoot did not attend because they did not receive sufficient advance notice. However, despite the early connections established between the Catholic missionaries and the Blackfoot, in 1875, when reservations were divided among different denominations under President Ulysses S. Grant's Peace Policy, a Methodist minister, John Young, was appointed as Blackfeet Agent (1876–83).[12] Consequently, the Jesuits were forced to continue their mission from an off-reservation base. The rivalry between Catholics and Protestants continued. In 1882 the Agent banned the Jesuit Father Peter Prando from the Blackfeet Reservation.[13] This competition for souls was not exclusive to Montana. It was also a feature of missionary work north of the boundary line, where pioneer missionaries had made extraordinary sacrifices in order to make early contact with the Blackfoot bands. Robert Rundle, a Methodist, spent eight years working out of Fort Edmonton (1840–48), within reach of the Blackfoot bands. Albert Lacombe, a Catholic priest, spent part of the winter of 1865–66 among them.[14] North of the Forty-Ninth Parallel, the Oblate missionary Constantine Scollen built a hut on the Elbow River in 1873. From this mission house, he baptized sixty-seven Blackfoot during his first summer among them. Upon the arrival of the NWMP in 1874, Scollen built a second mission house on the Bow River.[15] His growing influence among several First Nations is evident in his presence at the signing of Treaty Six between the Dominion and the Crees in 1876, and Treaty Seven with the Blackfoot, Sarcee, and Stoney in 1877. Missionaries who ministered to the Blackfoot during the buffalo days held few expectations of being able to persuade them to abandon their ceremonial and ritual practices, but their expectations grew apace after the bands abandoned their non-sedentary lifeways.[16]

Although some missionaries showed tolerance towards First Nations' beliefs, most were opposed to the continuation of their rituals. In Montana, the Jesuit priest John B. Carroll declared Blackfoot sacred practices to be "devil worship",[17] while in Alberta, the Reverend J. Huggonard — then principal of the Red Deer Industrial School — complained that "sun dances and kindred ceremonies had a very unsettling effect on the Indians and confirmed them in all practices adverse to Christianity and civilization."[18] However, not all missionaries were as intolerant as Carroll and Huggonard. The Methodist John Maclean, who worked among the Kainai during the 1880s, accommodated the beliefs of his congregation, hoping to win followers for Christianity in the long term. Overall, missionaries' conviction of the superiority of Christianity and civilization overrode any misgivings as to the prize that First Nations had to pay to acquire their benefits. Among the deleterious effects of white contact, for example, John McDougall denounced the "demoralizing and decimating" effects of liquor. In adulterated form, bootleg whiskey, distributed liberally as an incentive to trade, was to blame for many deaths among the Blackfoot.[19] Prostitution was another practice attributed to white contact. Moreover, better than anyone else, missionaries witnessed the catastrophic effects of virgin soil diseases among First Nations' populations. However, what they saw as the heathen beliefs of First Nations peoples, and what they perceived to be the benefits of Christianity, far outweighed any other considerations. Christianity, civilization, and assimilation were intrinsically related in late-nineteenth century Canada and the United States, and ceremonies such as sun dances were seen as obstacles standing on their path. Missionaries who actively opposed sun dances blamed them for the lack of success in their conversion efforts. In their view, not only did sun dances prevent acceptance of Christianity, but they also incited lust and unsettled marital relations.[20] These missionaries condemned the ceremonies in their sermons, lobbied the government to eradicate them, and stirred public opinion through press pronouncements.

Official attitudes to sun dances also differed, a common complaint being that they exercised "a demoralising effect".[21] However, while both missionaries and officials often couched their objections in terms of a concern for the welfare of First Nations, they might have also feared the potent combination of religious fervour and rebellion that gatherings such as the Circle Camp could unleash. The welcoming of relatives and visitors from afar at sun dances could provide opportunities for alliances against the colonial order to emerge.[22] The United States Army's violent repression of the Ghost Dance religion between 1887 and 1895 illustrates both the potential of religious ceremonies to unite disparate peoples and the worst excesses stemming from fear of such phenomena.[23] The white mythologies that provided the ideological basis for the colonization of the First Nations of the Americas — "salvation" and "civilization" — were a prelude to subsequent regulations designed for their forceful acculturation. For the most part, these white myths concealed the self-interest of the colonizers.

Civilizing Myths and White Interests

After Columbus stumbled upon the shores of what became San Salvador in 1492, the introduction of Christianity provided the fundamental justification for European conquest of the Americas. By the early reservation era in the United States and Canada, Christianity was viewed as the first step towards imparting the benefits of civilization among First Nations peoples there. Although this white mythology no longer has the force it possessed before the detrimental effects of industrialization and progress were recognized, it remained a truism during the last decades of the nineteenth century. In the ethnocentric perspective of government officials, the lifeways and worldviews of First Nations peoples held little value. Lieutenant-Governor Alexander Morris reflected the prevailing settler ideology in 1880, when he referred to his role, on behalf of the Dominion, in securing the signing of the so-called numbered treaties with First Nations. Morris claimed to have secured "the good will of the Indian tribes [. . .] opening up to them a future of promise, based upon the foundations of instruction and the many other advantages of civilized life."[24] That treaties secured lands for the benefit of settlers, thereby diminishing First Nations peoples' means of survival, is a subtext of this promising future. In practice, the latter became conquered peoples, their status being that of wards of the State with no citizenship rights.[25]

The Baptist Minister and then United States Commissioner of Indian

Colonial Conceits and Indictable Offenses

Affairs Thomas Jefferson Morgan articulated a similar white myth in 1889, when explaining the benefits of his Bureau's program of Indian education. It will bring them, he claimed "into fraternal and harmonious relationship with their white fellow-citizens [. . .] the sweets of refined homes, the delight of social intercourse, the emoluments of commerce and trade, the advantages of travel, together with the pleasures that come from literature, science and philosophy, and the solace and stimulus afforded by a true religion".[26] What Morgan called the "irregularities of camp life" must give way to "the methodical regularity of daily routine."[27] Absent from the rhetoric of benefiting First Nations — which the historian Francis Prucha attributes to "patriotic Americanism" — is any acknowledgement that First Nations peoples possessed rich and complex cultures, maintained trade and diplomatic networks, enjoyed the pleasures of travel and social life, and derived great benefits from their relationship with the animate and inanimate world through their rituals and ceremonies.[28]

Lofty promises made at treaty signing did not materialize. Instead of advantages, the first half-century of reserve life was characterized by population decline, which afflicted the Blackfoot on both sides of the boundary line. This decline, at a time when their lives were subjected to unprecedented official control (see Appendices 1–4), points to the sordid side of official neglect and corruption, which appears to have reached its apogee in the administration of reservations on the American side.[29]

FIGURE 2.1 *Piegan (USA) encampment, Montana* [c.1890s], Glenbow Archive, Calgary, Canada, NA-1463-1.

Dependence on government rations during this period gave officials leverage to dictate correct behaviour, allowing their charges little room for manoeuvring. In Morgan's words, "This civilization may not be the best possible, but it is the best the Indians can get. They can not escape it, and must either conform to it or be crushed by it."[30] Rather than a rhetorical flourish, his bellicose language is consistent with the history of violent conflict between Americans and First Nations peoples. The Blackfoot in Montana felt the force of the US Army's brutality when, in 1870, forces commanded by Brevet Colonel Eugene M. Baker massacred Heavy Runner and his followers at their winter camp on the Marias River. The attack was planned and authorized, respectively, by two Civil War generals, Lieutenant General Philip Henry Sheridan, and General William Tecumseh Sherman, President Grant's Chief Commander of the Army.[31] Historians who have turned their attention to the Army's attack on Heavy Runner's band concur that what Sheridan called Baker's "fight with Piegan Indians" was in fact a massacre.[32]

Another myth that was used to strengthen white beliefs of the superiority of civilization over First Nations' lifeways was the long-held view among the colonizers that First Nations peoples were destined to become extinct. Despite lacking any empirical basis, this assumption first gained currency in the 1780s. In the United States it had been mooted to justify the Removal Act of 1830, which sanctioned the forced resettlement of First Nations peoples from their eastern lands to areas west of the Mississippi River, a removal justified by the need to preserve them from "'total extinction' at the hands of the advancing tide of white population."[33] This was accomplished through forced marches during which many lives were lost. Yet Elbert Gerring, the second Superintendent of the Bureau of Indian Affairs, touted removal as "the only 'humane' policy" for postponing "total extinction."[34] By the late nineteenth century, once the bison herds had been exterminated by over-exploitation in which settlers, First Nations peoples, and traders from American and European concerns all played a part, the imminent demise of First Nations peoples became an unquestionable truth in the white consciousness, with as much currency in the United States as it had in Canada.[35] A professed friend of the Blackfoot, George Bird Grinnell, a naturalist and editor of *Forest and Stream*, a New York publication dedicated to the outdoor life, rationalized the ineluctable demise of the Indian in 1907 as "nothing more than the operation of the inexorable natural law that the weaker must perish while the fitter shall survive." Perhaps, he mused, "it is best that the Indians should fade away as we [have] seen them fading to-day."[36] This fatalistic belief went hand-in-hand with the conviction that assimilation was the only path to survival. In the words of the historian Robert Berkhofer Jr., "the Indian as stereotyped had to face extermination through acculturation, if not through genocide."[37] This was clearly expressed, for example, in the words of Hiram Price, US Commissioner of Indian Affairs (1881–85), who argued: "one of two things must eventually take place, to wit, either civilization or extermination of the Indian."[38] Well into the twentieth century, the elegiac colonial discourse of a dying race continued to condition the relationships between Ottawa and Washington, on the one hand, and First Nations peoples, on the other. It is against this backdrop that the suppression of sun dances began during the early reserve era. This myth of the disappearance of the Indian prevailed even after the trend of diminishing populations that had characterized the first half-century of reserve life shifted direction in the 1920s and 1930s.[39]

However, back in the late 1880s, the destitution of the Blackfoot, added to that of other First Nations in the United States and Canada, had come to exemplify what was commonly referred to as "the Indian problem". Having reached this point, First Nations' own uncivilized lifeways were blamed for their destitution. Once treaties had secured settlers' access to First Nations' lands, governments came to view the expenses associated with the maintenance of treaties as onerous, more as largesse than as fair compensation. In the official view, solving the Indian problem required the assimilation and absorption of First Nations peoples into the body politic of the colonizers, so that their separate collective identities would cease to exist.[40] As a prerequisite, sun dances, the wellspring of the reproduction of these collective identities, had to disappear.

While missionaries decried sun dances as conducive to immoral behaviour, officials were more concerned with what they viewed as its "demoralizing" effect on work practices. The Canadian Commissioner for the North West Territories in 1892, Hayter Reed, argued that "by the Indians congregating in this way [. . .] they lose at least from four to six weeks [. . .] in which they should be at work, repairing their fences, and breaking new land, and summer fallowing: besides which it unsettles them from steady work for a longer period."[41] Frequently, complaints against sun dances concerned the loss of working days and the fact that the ceremony materially interfered "with the progress of the work". The success of Indian Agents was measured in terms of the progress towards civilization at their respective reserves, including increases in agricultural production, the number of permanent homes built, attendance of children at school, and the absence of conflict between the reserves' residents and settlers. Some agents blamed sun dances for impeding their efforts to achieve these goals. For example, in 1885 Siksika Agent Magnus Begg referred to the ceremony as "an unmitigated nuisance". In 1914, W. J. Dilworth, the newly appointed Agent at the Blood Reserve, suggested to his superiors that the duration of the annual Circle Camp be shortened to two weeks.[42]

Although no evidence has emerged that prohibiting sun dances was intended as a step towards the physical eradication of the practitioners, the spectre of cultural genocide is raised by the systematic and state-sponsored nature of efforts to eradicate these ceremonies. Official attitudes were characterized both by prohibition, aimed at eroding the maintenance of a culture distinct from that of the colonizers, and the avowed official aim to replace First Nations peoples' beliefs with Christianity. It was tantamount to removing a crucial mechanism for cultural and social reproduction, an essential means of transmission of cultural heritage to the young. Moreover, these attempts at forced acculturation took place during a critical juncture, when the very physical survival of the Blackfoot was dependent on government-supplied rations.

There is no doubt that some altruistic, albeit misconceived motives underlay the prohibition of First Nations peoples' ritual practices and their replacement with Christianity and white values. However, other weighty matters also fuelled governments' desire to accelerate the transition of First Nations — no longer able to subsist from hunting and gathering — into self-sufficient agriculturalists and ranchers. Their assimilation into colonial society and ultimately their becoming citizens would bring about the phasing-out of the treaty obligations that burdened the public coffers. In Ottawa, Hayter Reed, who by 1893 became the Deputy Superintendent General of Indian Affairs, succinctly expressed the rationale for eradicating indigenous cultures:

> The problem which confronts the department in the territories is a most difficult one: to redeem from a state of partial savagery a horde of Indians dominated by tribal law and aboriginal customs and to transform them into competent agriculturists, ranchers, or mechanics. [. . .] and, if the progress continues as steady in the future, it will not be long before the Indians of the North-west Territories will be able to provide themselves with the necessaries of life.[43]

Reed's ethnocentric bias aside, he patently believes in the benefits of civilization, even though, in the process, as E. Brian Titley has argued, in the 1990s Reed — who as Indian Agent received the sobriquet of "Iron Heart" — had encouraged conditions on the reserves that bore "uncanny resemblance to serfdom."[44] Officials in both Canada and the United States believed that if individualism could be instilled into First Nations peoples their advancement towards civilization would accelerate. However, although in Canada officials decried what they viewed as communistic activities on the reserves, DIA officials like Reed still wanted to keep First Nations peoples confined on the reserves, rather than sent out into the outside world where, in his own words, they would be "downtrodden and debauched."[45] In the United States, as Berkhofer argues in his seminal book *The White Man's Indian*, tribalism was incompatible with the ideals

Colonial Conceits and Indictable Offenses

of individualism first expounded by Alexis de Tocqueville in the 1830s, when he posited that American liberalism led to equal opportunities to achieve material success.[46] These ideas had little application to First Nations peoples throughout the nineteenth century and part of the twentieth. Equality would have been unthinkable as applying to those whose very humanity remained in doubt among the American public throughout that era. Moreover, the myth that Indians lacked individuality rests on shaky grounds. On the basis of her studies of the Kainai society (Blood Reserve) in Canada, the anthropologist Esther S. Goldfrank has challenged that stereotype. During the buffalo era, she has argued, the Kainai had been highly individualistic and competitive, characteristics that, in her view, had remained during the reserve era.[47] Notwithstanding Goldfrank's argument, when viewed through a Christian lens, Blackfoot practices of generosity and reciprocity should have been lauded rather than condemned. In the final analysis, missionaries and officials employed impressionistic and at times contradictory perspectives to devalue the world of the colonized.

Canada and the United States each had a vested interest in seeking to destroy what they regarded as the communitarian lifeways of First Nations peoples, an objective that, *inter alia*, would open reserve lands to private ownership. This can be surmised from the expedient that citizenship status was tied to the abolition of common ownership of reserve lands. The territory surrendered by treaty had not quenched settlers' thirst for further releases. In the United States, the 1887 General Allotment Act (the Dawes Act) provided a new way for the carving-up of reservation lands by conferring citizenship on allottees. President Theodore Roosevelt called it "a mighty pulverizing engine to break-up the tribal mass." On the Blackfeet Reservation, however, the effects of allotment were delayed until 1917, when the Office of Indian Affairs submitted their Allotment Schedule for approval.[48] Successive Canadian governments also viewed the reserves as transitory.[49] In 1920, during deliberations of a bill for the compulsory enfranchisement of "civilized Indians", meant to apply only to Eastern First Nations, Duncan Campbell Scott, poet, essayist, and Deputy Superintendent General of Indian Affairs, described his goal thus: "I want to get rid of the Indian problem. I do not think [. . .] that this country ought to continuously protect a class of people who are able to stand alone [. . .] Our objective is to continue until there is not a single Indian in Canada that has not been absorbed into the body politic, and there is no Indian question, and no Indian Department."[50] Rather than a future in which Indians could share the benefits of civilization as posited earlier by Alexander Morris in his treaty manifesto, Scott's desiderata allude to freeing the Dominion of responsibility for the welfare of First Nations. In 1920, First Nations such as the Blackfoot were a long way from being seen as equal in Canada or the United States. In the former, inequality was enshrined in the Indian Act, while in the latter, as Berkhofer notes, despite the ethic of equality spoused by society, neither white reformers nor society at large accepted racial equality and cultural pluralism.[51] Even at a time when the enfranchising of Indians was contemplated, debates in both countries attest to the discourse of white superiority being deeply ingrained.

The prohibition of First Nations' ceremonies within such a context of inequality points less to a concern with their welfare than with settlers' interests. Insofar as officials perceived First Nations' beliefs and rituals as leading to the perpetuation of practices such as warring and horse raiding, eradicating the former was deemed a pre-requisite for discontinuing the latter. North of the Forty-Ninth Parallel, settlement was more gradual and less violent. Blackfoot warring and raiding for horses there began a slow but steady decline following the arrival of the Mounted Police in late 1874, although small raiding parties continued to cross the international boundary more than a decade later, albeit sporadically.[52] However, in 1874, the realization that the buffalo days were ending placed a premium on the relationship between the Blackfoot and the Mounted Police; those who continued to go on the warpath did so against their leaders' wishes. The ensuing common poverty of the bands, as one white official suggested, might have softened old enmities. However, revenge parties continued to be mustered against traditional enemies when dictated by the Blackfoot honour code.[53]

In Montana, the propinquity of the Blackfoot and white settlers and miners erupted in sporadic but violent episodes throughout the 1860s. Consequently, those Pikuni who remained south of the boundary line were placed in the worst possible negotiating position during their transition to settled life. Following the 1870 massacre of Heavy Runner's band, and the reduction of their population caused by a smallpox epidemic that same year, famine struck the Pikuni bands during the 1883–84 winter. Between one-quarter and one-third of the Pikuni population in Montana died of starvation. Some observers blamed catastrophe on neglect from the Indian Agent and Washington.[54] The Department of Indian Affairs placed responsibility on Washington "*directly* and *entirely*" for delaying the appropriation of funds for the Agency by three months, and for appropriating a lesser amount than that requested.[55] Pikani Almost-a-Dog was "said to have kept a record of each death as it occurred by cutting a notch in a willow stick", reaching a total of 555.[56] A more humanitarian approach kept the death rate low on the Canadian reserves during the same period, but even there the Blackfoot population spiralled downward, a trend not reversed until the 1920s.[57] Contrary to the purported benefits of settlement, unsanitary conditions on the reserves increased illness and death rates. These vicissitudes made imperative the need for divine assistance and therefore for ritual and ceremonial activity. As the buffalo days

Colonial Conceits and Indictable Offenses

FIGURE 2.2 *The Blackfoot Treaty (Treaty 7), 1877, Crowfoot speaking,* Glenbow Archive, Calgary, Canada, NA-40-1.

ended, the Blackfoot faced new challenges: physical survival was the overriding priority, but given the interrelatedness of secular and sacred realms in their worldview, the reproduction of a distinct Blackfoot culture and identity relied upon the continuation of ceremonies such as Ookaan, at the very time when officials were determined to curtail or eliminate them.

Legislating the Sacred

Upon signing Treaty Seven with the Dominion in 1877, the Blackfoot became subject to the Indian Act of 1876 as wards of the State.[58] This Act and its subsequent amendments rendered them dependent, legally incompetent, and subject to arbitrary decree in all aspects of their economic, political, and spiritual lives. While missionaries influenced the process of assimilation by exercising pressure through such means as denying baptism to the non-conforming, the Indian Act defined legal limits for their ritual and ceremonial practices, including sun dances.[59] However, in 1884, despite official animosity, a total ban on sun dances was deemed to be both premature and a security risk. Legislation therefore fell short of total prohibition.[60] Instead, subsection 1 of section 149 of the Indian Act stipulated:

Part I — The Blackfoot Sun Dance

> Every Indian or other person who engages in, or assists in celebrating or encourages either directly or indirectly another to celebrate any Indian festival, dance or other ceremony of which the giving away or paying or giving back of money, goods or articles of any sort forms a part, or is a feature, whether such gift of money, goods or articles takes place before, at, or after the celebration of the dance or who engages or assists in any celebration or dance of which the wounding or mutilation of the dead or living body of any human being or animal forms a part or is a feature, is guilty of an indictable offence and is liable to imprisonment for a term not exceeding six months and not less than two months; Provided that nothing in this section shall be construed to prevent the holding of any agricultural show or exhibition or the giving of prizes for exhibits thereat.[61]

Generosity and reciprocity being the *sine qua non* for every conceivable activity during the Circle Camp and Ookaan, it is manifest that implementation of the regulation would have far-reaching effects. Adhering to the letter of the law would entail an overhaul of Blackfoot practices of sacrifice, generosity, and reciprocity observed "since time immemorial." It is notable that the wording of the legislation fails to mention sun dances *per se*; instead, the loose term "Indian dance" allows for its broad application. Moreover, the wording of the prohibition against the "wounding or mutilation of the dead or living body of any human being or animal" by implication debases the acts of self-mortification through which the Blackfoot maintained their reciprocal obligations with their sacred helpers. Lastly, the exemption of agricultural shows and exhibitions underscores a double standard applied to First Nations peoples *vis-à-vis* white settlers. Matters were little different in the United States, where similar prohibitions were in place under the Court of Indian Offenses (established in 1882), which decreed:

> Any Indian who shall engage in the sun dance, the scalp dance, or war dance, or in any other similar feast, so called, shall be deemed guilty of an offense, and upon conviction thereof shall be punished for the first offense by the withholding of his rations for not exceeding ten days or by imprisonment for not exceeding ten days [. . .] Any Indian who shall engage in the practices of so-called medicine men, or who shall resort to any artifice or device to keep the Indians from the reservation from adopting and following civilized habits and pursuits, or shall adopt any means to prevent the attendance of children at school, or shall use any rites and customs, shall be deemed to be guilty of an offense, and upon conviction thereof, for the first offense shall be imprisoned for not less than ten nor more than thirty days.[62]

The Canadian regulation specified "giveaways" and "mutilation", and imposed harsh penalties: imprisonment of not less than two months and no more than six months. Conversely, the rules under the US Court of Indian Offenses were broader in scope, including any activities that would prevent complete assimilation, but imposed more lenient penalties: imprisonment of not less than ten days and no more than thirty days. In 1904 the US Department of the Interior gave these measures the force of law, which would remain in place until 1935.[63] Having established the legislative framework to curtail or eliminate what were viewed as the "demoralizing and barbarous"[64] practices of First Nations peoples, implementation of the measures was placed in the hands of Indian Agents who, in tandem with missionaries, formed the vanguard of colonialism. Agents, who controlled the distribution of food rations, used them as a lever to press for compliance with their directives. Where necessary, they could seek assistance, in Canada from the Mounted Police, who exercised "military, police, and civil governmental functions",[65] and in the United States from the Army, civil militias, and the Indian Police.[66]

The colonizers' conceit of the superiority of civilization prevented them from appreciating the benefits that First Nations peoples such as the Blackfoot derived from their ceremonial and ritual practices. Official documents abound with condemnations of sun dances without ever adverting to their significance in maintaining the well-being of the practitioners. This well-being derived from the renewal of links to the sacred realm, whether through Ookaan or through the transfer of Sacred Bundles, or other items deemed sacred. It also stemmed from renewing acquaintance with distant relatives and friends during the Circle Camp, and from the social recognition that accrued to those able to adhere to Blackfoot ideals of sacrifice, generosity, and reciprocity.

A Canadian Saga of Assimilation and Blackfoot Resistance

The security of settlers and the State alike was an important consideration as the battle lines were drawn for the campaign against "dances" in the Dominion. Canadians had made it their overriding priority to avoid costly wars such as those that took place in the United States, especially during and after the Civil War. Insofar as the sudden repression of sun dances might have increased the likelihood of rebellion, *sub rosa* directives circulated to Indian Agents effectively softened the thrust of the regulations. In 1889, Commissioner Reed reassured his superior in Ottawa that he had emphasized to the Sarcee Agent, who had alerted the Mounted Police to halt a Sun Dance, that "the Department would never sanction the adoption of force to prevent the repetition of Sun Dances, and recommended dissuasion as being the means most likely to be successful."[67] However, Ottawa periodically extended and strengthened the regulations that could

Part I — The Blackfoot Sun Dance

potentially be applied to repress sun dances, or to curtail the ability of First Nations to congregate for such purposes.

Such were the effects of the infamous Pass System, designed and introduced by Reed in order to prevent travelling by those who lived on reserves, allowing for the prosecution of infractors under the Vagrant Act. Although the Pass System violated treaty rights, Reed's superiors in Ottawa approved it *ex post facto* as a militarily expedient measure during the Riel Rebellion of 1885. Although the Blackfoot did not join the rebellion and even offered to assist the Mounted Police to suppress it — an offer that the Police declined — they were not exempted from the hardships caused by the Pass System. Extra-judicially, Ottawa encouraged Indian Agents to employ "such means as exist for marking [. . .] displeasure towards those who leave without first having obtained passes."[68] We can only speculate what those means might have been, but the vague wording of the instruction suggests that Indian Agents enjoyed some scope for informal punitive measures.

The Pass System attempted to segregate First Nations peoples from settlers' towns, and to prevent them from visiting relatives on other reserves, especially during sun dances. This occurred even though the DIA and the Mounted Police were aware that there was no "legal right to arrest any Indian unless he [. . .] committed some offence". Mounted Police officials feared that any person illegally arrested might end up in Court, whereupon the law would find for the defendant, a disastrous prospect for their "prestige with the Indians."[69] In 1888, some three years after the two arms of the service began colluding to create the impression that the Pass System had legal force, Superintendent Deane warned that some Indians "seem to be aware that in point of law they have as much right to roam about the country as white men, and that confinement to a reserve was not one of the provisions of their treaty."[70] Contrary to the NWMP's vaunted fairness, they enforced this illegal measure, which was still in use in 1917. Keeping First Nations peoples in ignorance of their rights appears to have been routine practice. The NWMP were in an unenviable position, because settlers were opposed to "Indians being allowed to roam the country"[71] and looked to the Police to stop them.

In theory, the Pass System could have prevented visitors from joining sun dances that were held outside their own reserves. However, even when agents opposed such visits, travelling parties would set out at night so as to avoid detection. Moreover, evidence confirms that Indian Agents exercised their own judgment and signed travelling passes for large groups of their charges. For example, among the "upwards of 250" tepees erected at the Kainai Circle Camp in 1902, a report identified Siksika, Pikuni and Sarcee visitors, all of whom "had passes signed by their Agents." The same occurred at the Peigan Reserve that year.[72] The Peigan Agent's Annual Report for 1917 indicates that he was of the view that visitors could attend sun dances as long as they did so as observers, and did not participate in the ceremony. He noted that the "scout and police have always been instructed to watch for strange Indians taking part which is forbidden", adding that "no notice of visitors has been taken if they are there as sightseers only."[73] To judge by the equivocal implementation of the Pass System, the letter of the law was merely an opening gambit, complemented by *sub rosa* directives and extra-judicial pressure, with mutual accommodation between Indian Agents and their charges also coming into play. Indeed, many Blackfoot continued to travel to attend sun dances at other reserves or merely to visit relatives.

Yet another measure introduced in 1890 increased the power of Indian Agents over their charges, and hence their capacity to enforce policies restricting sun dances. Each Indian Agent became an *ex officio* Justice of the Peace "with the power and authority of two justices of the peace". This meant that, in cases where the law stipulated that two Justices of the Peace countersign a directive, Indian Agents had no need to seek a second signature.[74] In 1892, Ottawa thought that the time was right for adopting "more energetic measures" against sun dances without compromising safety. Additional regulations followed in 1895.[75] The following year, the new Minister of the Interior, Clifford Sifton, reorganized the Department of Indian Affairs, replacing the then Deputy Superintendent General Reed with James A. Smart, who also had responsibility for the Department of the Interior. While austerity dictated Sifton's changes, historian D. J. Hall has argued that the Sifton era brought into the administration of Indian Affairs men who had little sympathy for Indians.[76] Hall notes that in 1902, the Governor General, Lord Minto, "took up the issue of the sun dance, which he believed was unreasonably prohibited." His efforts found no sympathetic hearing among Indian Affairs or Mounted Police officials. The reasons that Comptroller F. White adduced in favour of continuing the campaign against sun dances reflect the changing circumstances on the reserves. Whereas earlier sun dances had been blamed for "the atrocities practiced by the Indians", White argued that, in this new era, the reasons for prohibiting sun dances had more to do with "the evil influences of the Whites and Half breeds who attend the dances and corrupt the poor Indians."[77] In the end, Minto's efforts failed, although the old official line that sought merely to discourage the practice remained in place.[78]

Prohibition was not the only strategy deployed against sun dances. Since 1886, Reed had encouraged Indian Agents to sponsor competing events such as agricultural fairs ("harvest homes"), a picnic, or a racing day, with the Department providing as inducement a steer for a feast.[79] These efforts seem to have met with some success. However, measures to curtail First Nations peoples' cultural practices during the first two decades of the twentieth century indicate that some optimistic reports forecasting the abandonment of ceremonies had more to do with Agents' desire to reassure their superiors than it did with the realities of the reserves.

The official determination to eradicate Indian dances was in 1914 extended to encompass any public displays of First Nations' distinctive cultural practices. The new curbs were aimed at shows and exhibitions in settlers' towns, such as the Calgary Stampede, and "Wild West Shows", most notably that of Buffalo Bill Cody. In the United States a directive to stop these performances had been issued in 1890, although Cody's show, which began in 1883, ran for three decades unimpeded. In Canada, seeking to attract larger crowds, organizers of the Calgary Stampede offered payment and food provisions in order to entice sufficient numbers of Blackfoot to bring their lodges and horses to the Stampede grounds, where they proved to be highly popular. The DIA opposed such displays, which nurtured practices they were intent upon eradicating. Consequently, in 1914 Section 149 of the Indian Act was amended to proscribe First Nations peoples' participation at such public events, and Indian Agents were advised as follows:

> Any Indian in the Province of Manitoba, Saskatchewan, Alberta, British Columbia or the Territories who participates in any Indian dance outside the bounds of his own reserve, or who participates in any show, exhibition, performance, stampede or pageant in aboriginal costume without the consent of the Superintendent General of Indian Affairs or his authorized Agency and any person who induces or employs any Indian to take part in such dance, show, exhibition, performance, stampede or pageant, or induces any Indian to leave his reserve or employs any Indian for such a purpose, whether the dance, show, performance, exhibition, stampede or pageant has taken place or not, shall on summary conviction be liable to a penalty not exceeding twenty five dollars or to imprisonment for one month, or to both penalty and imprisonment.[80]

The provision conveys the extent of official efforts to curb the display of Indian culture.[81] Often, their attempts were out of step with popular sentiments. The white population's curiosity towards the horses, costumes and performances of First Nations peoples ensured the financial success of events in which the latter participated. In 1917, the Blood Agent summarized the harm that, in his view, such activities caused to the assimilation program:

> I might say that these fairs depend largely on the Indians, for their racing events. It seems as if the Directors of local Fairs are of the opinion that no fair would be a success, unless there were full attendance of Indians, with their race[-]horses. This procedure, is detrimental to the progress of the Indians [. . .] The interest enlivened amongst these Indians, in Broncho [sic] busting,

Horse racing, etc at the Stampede and Fairs from 1912 to the present, has worked great harm to them. The fact that Tom Three Persons, a Blood Indian won the belt and championship at the Calgary Stampede in 1912, has been responsible for the condition, that every boy on the Blood reserve between the ages of 17 and 23, wishes to be [. . .] Tom Three Persons, and all they think about is saddles, chapps [sic], silver spurs, Race and bucking horses, etc a full equipment of the above accoutrements makes him a hero in his own eyes, and in the eyes of the admiring young women on the reserve.[82]

Inconsistency prevailed in the attitudes of officials and the general population towards the cultures of First Nations peoples. Policies and regulations sought their eventual assimilation, but the Indian Other held a fascination for the white population. This attraction contributed a modicum of pride to First Nations peoples. The stream of high-ranking visitors to the reserves, who came fully expecting to be entertained with displays of the Indian culture so maligned in the Indian Act, points up official ambivalence. In September 1889, the Governor-General visited the Blood Reserve, where he was received in "the usual manner" (these occasions were not rare): "A large number of Indians assembled to do him honour. A pow-wow was held and a sham fight was given, showing the Indian method of warfare, which was highly interesting."[83] This anecdote illustrates the simultaneous valuing and devaluing of First Nations' cultural practices characteristic of the assimilation era.

Regulations seeking to prevent First Nations peoples from earning public admiration for their abilities and craftsmanship were unnecessarily harsh. As Indian Agent turned chronicler George Gooderham noted, Indians loved "parades, fairs and stampedes,"[84] which allowed them to exhibit skills from their hunting days. Agents were left to implement unworkable restrictions in the interstices between indigenous pride and the enjoyment of the white patrons. Moreover, the Department of Indian Affairs itself granted exemptions when pressed to do so by the organizers of such events.[85] It is precisely due to this discrepancy between regulation and practice that the effects of the assimilationist measures were ameliorated.

However, despite this accommodation, the regulations against sun dances continued to be periodically reinforced and extended. In 1918, the Indian Act was amended to make "the giving away and mutilating features [. . .] summary instead of indictable offences." In other words, the right to a trial by jury was removed. Agents had by this time magisterial powers "to try Indians, whites or others" for these offences.[86] In 1921 the Indian Act was again amended to impede further sun dances, Potlatches, and other rituals. Indian Agents and the Mounted Police received instructions "to stop formation of large gatherings and break up pagan camp meetings."[87] Prohibition appears to have gathered its own bureaucratic momentum in Ottawa, with lawmakers being quite oblivious to the accommodation that existed on the reserves. With Ottawa having embarked upon extirpation of the dances, it was of little moment that, according to the DIA's own reports, First Nations peoples were advancing steadily toward civilization. By the 1920s many Blackfoot had become profitable ranchers. Indeed, in 1917, a report claimed: "agricultural and stock raising industries among [Prairie] Indians have met with such a measure of success that rationing is now practically a thing of the past, except in the case of those who are aged or invalids, and therefore unable to support themselves."[88] Increasing self-sufficiency went hand in hand with increased confidence to negotiate with Indian Agents, and to resist measures that violated what the Blackfoot considered the "moral economy"[89] of reserve life.

Ottawa was clear in its desire to see the end of sun dances, but Indian Agents were expected to avoid using force: eradication was the goal, but the directive remained to avoid confrontation, and to use "extreme caution as to arrests and none should be made if dance begun."[90] This attitude remained constant throughout the several reorganizations of the DIA, although it did not prevent some overzealous officials from applying undue pressure against the holding of sun dances. Some agents became crusaders against the ceremony. One notable hardliner, William Morris Graham, served as Indian Agent (1897), Inspector (1904), and later Commissioner for Greater Production for the Provinces of Manitoba, Saskatchewan, and Alberta (1918–32). His autocratic style earned him the sobriquet of "Kaiser of the West." In these roles, Graham conducted a protracted, though unsuccessful campaign against sun dances, lobbying his superiors to take a harder line against their continuation.[91] Graham complained against allowing "those of the Hobbema, Blood and other Alberta Agencies to make the [Sun Dance] an annual practice [because] Indians of other Bands will probably wish to follow an example which we should not allow."[92] He was assuredly correct in his view that an even implementation of proscriptive measures was required were sun dances to be stopped, but Ottawa's attitude of moderation remained firm.

United States Opposition to Sun Dances

The legislative efforts against sun dances in the United States obeyed the same rationale as that of Canada. Commissioner Price drafted the rules to abolish "rites and customs so injurious to the Indians" that the Court of Indian Offenses, established in 1882, drawn-up in 1883, proscribed "participation in certain dances, plural marriages, the destruction of property by mourners, and the purchase of wives and concubines." The so-called Medicine Men, a derisive appellation to describe ceremonial leaders, "were not to engage in their 'usual practices' or use their influence to subvert the civilization program."[93] Commissioner Thomas J. Morgan strengthened these measures in 1892 as part of a series of regulations entitled "Punishment for Crimes and Misdemeanors Committed by Indians" in order to oppose the perpetuation of "Indian dances, polygamy, and activities of medicine men".[94] Participating in the Sun Dance could be punished with the withdrawal of rations or imprisonment.

Unlike the more specific prohibition of "giveaways" and "mutilation" in Canada, the American measures left no room for accommodation, effectively targeting not only sun dances but also any activities presided over by the Grandfathers, as the Blackfoot refer to their ceremonial leaders. The Secretary of the Interior, Henry M. Teller, justified the legislation with a tirade against "the savage and barbarous practices that are calculated to continue [the Indians] in their savagery". Moreover, he claimed, despite the efforts of "missionaries, teachers and agents",

> Yet, a few non-progressive degraded Indians are allowed to exhibit before the young and susceptible children all the debauchery, diabolism, and savagery of the worst state of the Indian race. Every man familiar with Indian life will bear witness to the pernicious influence of these savage rites and heathenish customs [. . .] These dances, or feasts, as they are sometimes called, ought, in my judgment, to be discontinued, and if the Indians now supported by the Government are not willing to discontinue them, the agents should be instructed to compel such discontinuance [. . .] A great hindrance to the civilization of the Indian is the influence of the medicine men, who are always found with the anti-progressive party. The medicine men resort to various artifices and devices to keep the people under their influence [. . .] steps should be taken to compel these impostors to abandon this deception and discontinue these practices, which are not only without benefit to the Indians but positively injurious to them.[95]

Teller resumes several discourses familiar from the Canadian example: white superiority, civilization and progress versus savagery and degradation, Christianity versus diabolism (or heathenism) and debauchery, and finally, the accusation of self-interest against the Grandparents, the keepers of sacred knowledge.[96] The rules under the Court of Indian Offenses were printed under Article 4 of the Regulations of the Indian Office and took effect in April 1, 1904, but enforcing assimilation had begun earlier. For example, in 1881 Commissioner Price advised Blackfeet agent John Young: "It is the policy of this Department [. . .] to discourage by every judicious means, all barbarous Indian dances, feasts, and savage customs, and to encourage the Indians to relinquish them as rapidly as possible." In 1887, the Blackfeet Agent, Major Baldwin, ordered the

Indian Police to stop Ookaan, with force if necessary, and demanded that individuals who received a brood mare from the government abstain from participating in the ceremony. Ookaan did not take place in 1888, but Baldwin's removal gave a reprieve to the Pikuni, though not for long. In 1892 Steell refused permission for activities such as "the medicine lodge, bundle openings, and dancing" because they were time-consuming and kept the Pikuni from work. In 1894, a new agent, Captain Lorenzo Cook prohibited not only sun dances, but also "Indian mourning, beating the tom-tom, gambling, and wearing Indian costumes."[97] In 1898, Robert J. Hamilton, a Pikuni educated at the Carlisle Indian School, was sacked from his position as interpreter to Thomas Fuller, the Blackfeet Agent. Hamilton had been promoting the training of "young men in the Sun Dance and for older men to pass down oral traditions" in a house that Fuller — at Hamilton's behest — had designated for learning English and reading American literature.[98] Extant photographs of Pikuni sun dances held in 1899 and 1900 in Montana attest to the resilience of Ookaan.[99]

Wishing to erode interest in sun dances, agents south of the Forty-Ninth parallel tried "to induce the Blackfeet to observe the Fourth of July instead."[100] Their strategies mirrored those used by their Canadian counterparts, the most salient being the provision of food and prizes for alternative sports days and the withdrawal of rations for participants. As the historian Howard Harrod notes, by the turn of the century the Blackfeet were celebrating the Fourth of July with "traditional celebrations, often including a sun dance", much to the dismay of the Catholic priest, John B. Carroll. In 1910, Carroll published an article titled "The Fourth of July Dishonored" in which he articulated the dangers this practice posed for the Christianization and civilization enterprise:

> It animates the Indians with the spirit of dancing, belief in Indian medicine, a passion for painting and dressing in heathen fashion, and strengthens their inborn disposition to be superstitious [. . .] It certainly does retard advancement in Christianity and true civilization. It converts the blessings of civilization into moral evils to hedge in and make more desperate their situation in the realm of darkness, to make them more blind and obdurate, so as not to perceive the light of true civilization.[101]

Despite his negative attitude, Carroll indirectly expressed the vitality of the sun dances when he complained that the Blackfoot imagine "that their ways are as good for Indians as white people's ways are for white people". Likewise, when he accused the Blackfoot of thinking "that their own heathen customs are just as good as civilized customs, and even more venerable", Carroll expressed a Blackfoot perspective that rarely saw the light of day. Finally, Carroll also railed against the whites who flocked to the Sun Dance, because they confirmed in the Blackfoot "the idea that their holy medicine is powerful."[102]

While this chapter provides ample evidence of the relentless efforts of officials and missionaries in the United States and Canada to eradicate sun dances, it also provides the context that constituted the backdrop for such attempts. Clearly, some accommodation took place between Indian Agents and the Blackfoot. This combined with the inconsistent implementation of assimilationist measures to allow some latitude for Ookaan to continue, albeit with periodic disruptions. It is also evident that in order to understand the mechanisms employed during the first century of life on reserves in Canada, we need to be aware of the attitudes that prevailed within the Department of Indian Affairs *vis-à-vis* those that prevailed among the Mounted Police. These two arms of the government did not always work in unison. In Montana, the actions of Robert Hamilton, who promoted the continuation of sun dances under the Indian Agent's nose, making use of facilities provided for the assimilation of those resident on the Blackfeet Reservation, serves as an overture for the chapter 3, which analyses Blackfoot responses to official measures against their sacred practices.

3

Honouring Creator Sun and Praying for Good Crops

Scholars have argued that the very process of forced assimilation paradoxically strengthened the separate identities of First Nations peoples as they resisted absorption into the colonizer's culture.[1] This observation applies with some force to the Blackfoot who, despite the asymmetrical power relations of the early reserve era, were not passive receptors of the colonizers' desires. Within a context in which officials in charge of Indian Affairs could "dictate correct behaviour to a subordinate group"[2], their disapproval of sun dances elicited Blackfoot resistance, both in Canada and in the United States. At times this resistance went hand in hand with accommodation dictated by the need to ensure the well-being of the community.

Blackfoot attitudes towards Christianity might have been indifferent or lukewarm during the early reserve era, but irrespective of their degree of conversion, many Blackfoot welcomed missionaries, and firm friendships between individual Blackfoot leaders and "Long Robes" (Catholic), and "Short Robes" (Protestant) have become legendary. It follows then that many Blackfoot did not see Christianity as being irreconcilable with their own sacred practices, in contrast with the views of the missionaries. The Blackfoot did not immediately accept missionaries' demands for the abandonment of long-observed practices. For example, missionaries demanded that those who sought baptism should renounce polygamous marriages, even though there was no agreement about which wives should leave the marriage, or about the status of the "semi-widows" or "abandoned" wives and their children. Dissolving enduring conjugal arrangements imposed much hardship on all those involved, and the Department of Indian Affairs recognized polygamous marriages hoping for the practice to be abandoned voluntarily. The practice took a long time to disappear. In Montana, some Blackfoot remained faithful to their customary marriage practices into the 1920s.[3]

A similar resistance met efforts to curtail Ookaan, although the Blackfoot were pragmatic in their response to regulations and embraced some curbs they considered beneficial. However, although they compromised in order to secure the continuation of the Circle Camp and Ookaan, they rejected giving up the practice altogether. For example, there are no records of overt resistance to the prohibition of the "piercing" ritual. On the Blackfoot Reserve, Siksika leaders cooperated to its anti-climactic end, as recorded in the 1889 report of Magnus Begg, their agent: "Last July during the sun dance the Indians were preparing to have some braves made in the usual way by torture. When the Rev. Mr. Tims and myself arrived [. . .] I explained to the chiefs that it was against the wishes of the Department [. . .] and asked them to do away with that part of the performance, which they agreed to at once.[4]

This outcome was touted as a victory for the civilizing project. The Superintendent General of Indian Affairs, Edgar Dewdney, attributed the phasing out of the offending ritual to the cooperation of Siksika Chief Crowfoot, whom he knew well. Two years earlier, in 1887, the Department had erected a "good house" for Crowfoot, "On account of his willingness in helping the Indian Department officials in their work amongst the Indians."[5] Crowfoot's cooperation with the agent in phasing out the "piercing" ritual should not be read as implying that he had become acculturated. He had never given up his multiple wives and, despite his friendship with priests, Crowfoot placed his Blackfoot beliefs "over anything the white man had to offer".[6] He always took his place in the Circle Camp with his Moccasin Band — although he did not join in the sacred rites of Ookaan — and he always observed Blackfoot mourning practices, dressing in rags even while he received visiting dignitaries.[7] It is possible that Crowfoot opposed self-mortification altogether. His biographer, Hugh Dempsey, notes that Crowfoot told his wives during his last days that "there should be no severing of fingers and scarring of their flesh when they mourned his passing."[8] By 1889 the respected leader was ailing, after his passing his favourite horse was shot to accompany him to the Sand Hills in accordance with Blackfoot beliefs. That his priest friends and the authorities overlooked Crowfoot's "uncivilized habits" demonstrates the two-way workings of accommodation during the early reserve era.

There are alternative explanations for the Blackfoot surrender of the piercing ritual. In 1911, Big Bravo told David Duvall, the Pikuni–French amateur ethnographer who collaborated with Clark Wissler, that those who underwent the self-torture ritual "generally die shortly after they have done so, not right soon, but a few years after they have done so". People attributed their passing to their having undergone the ritual, which was "the same as if they had made an offer of themselves to the Sun."[9] Wissler suggested yet another reason: that the practice had been borrowed from the Arapaho, and had not "thoroughly adjusted to its place" when it was discontinued.[10] Notably, in 1885 no Siksika "candidates for the torture act" presented themselves,[11] although Agent Begg reported that in

1892 three men "wanted to be brave", a euphemism for undergoing the piercing ritual.[12]

It appears that other First Nations followed suit, and the "piercing" ritual did not survive among First Nations in the Dominion. George Gooderham, who was the Indian Agent at the Blackfoot Reserve (Siksika) for twenty-six years (1920–46), and later became a chronicler, claimed that in 1895, as a six year-old, he had witnessed the last "making of a brave" at Piapot's Cree reserve in the Qu'Appelle Valley, where his father, John H. Gooderham, was the sub-agent.[13] In the United States, the Lakota ritual "piercing" survived in South Dakota by going underground.[14] The Blackfeet in Montana discontinued the ritual.

The Blackfoot also welcomed the phasing out of "catching", a practice they were not fond of. As mentioned earlier, "catching" was a customary means to force an individual to become the new owner of a Medicine Pipe Bundle. "People hated to be 'caught'", and a man who saw the Medicine Pipe owner coming might hide to avoid him. The reason for this avoidance resided in that the Pipe's owner would take the new owner's finest horses in exchange for the Bundle.[15] During the Siksika Circle Camp in 1921, Corporal Harper reported witnessing the practice, but by 1937 it had stopped. Conversely, the Pass System was an unacceptable constraint resisted by the Blackfoot, for it impeded visits to their distant relatives and attendance at sun dances outside their reserves. In 1897, the Kainai head chief Mekasto (Red Crow) lodged a complaint with the local Mounted Police Superintendent against the Agent for, *inter alia*, refusing to sign passes for the Kainai to visit their Pikuni relatives in Montana.[16] In 1916 the Siksika retaliated against the Pass System by withdrawing their children from school, arguing that they did "not do any more dancing than their white neighbours and that they see no good reason why they should be singled out in this particular."[17] By drawing attention to the cultural double standard, the Blackfoot signalled their refusal to inhabit a subservient role. Their persistent refusal to accommodate the desires of the colonizers to curtail their travel — not just a cherished experience, but also a way of life for those who were born before the reserve era — and the circumstance that the Pass System had no legal validity, meant that many Blackfoot continued to attend sun dances away from their reserves.

In regard to the prohibition of "giveaways" in the Indian Act, it is somewhat ironic that in 1896 missionaries encouraged Indian children at the Regina Industrial School to give away money earned by working under an outing system to support "religious work."[18] After all, the Indian Act forbade Indians from giving away their wealth. The double standard of these actions was not lost on the Blackfoot, but their voice is seldom heard in the documentation. However, in 1915, Pikuni leader Bull Plume wrote to the DIA arguing that giving presents to friends was no different than "the present we gave to King George and Government of the sixteen hundred dollars in the year 1914" (a donation to the war effort). Bull Plume further claims that only "Indian made goods" were to be given out as presents, including "coats, pants, moccasins, beaded belts, neck beads, stone pipe tobac[c]o, pocket knife, handkerchief, a blanket that we can do without". In regard to valuable items such as "wagon, harness, rig s [sic] saddle, horses, cattle, furniture", he declared that they were "pleased" that the Department had stopped them from giving these away.[19] Rare letters such as this illustrate the currency among the Blackfoot of discourses appropriated from the colonizers. Bull Plume was able to deploy these discourses to defend the rights of the Blackfoot to exercise generosity toward their own community. Resistance here had a hidden transcript, since Bull Plume's letter omits that, despite the prohibition, transfers of sacred Bundles involving exchanges of property had not stopped on the reserve.[20]

In 1897 the Siksika wrote to the Indian Commissioner in Regina requesting permission to hold a Sun Dance. Although the original request is not extant, the response is illuminating. Surprisingly, in the midst of a regime of prohibition, the Commissioner allowed the dance to go ahead. While he declined to provide material assistance towards the ceremony, he offered that there would be "no interference therewith on this occasion", provided the Siksika met certain conditions: the ceremony would last only five days; it would not be compulsory; no torture or giving away of property would take place; there would be no interference with workers "before, during or after the dance"; children would not be taken away from school; and the Siksika would "engage to fill the existing Schools to their full capacity."[21] These conditions provide a succinct map of the goals of assimilation, at the same time that the Commissioner's suggested arrangement illustrates the existing gap between the regulations and actual practice. Since officials had no discretion to broaden the limitations of the Indian Act along the lines the Commissioner prescribed, it is unclear what avenues he could have taken to pursue compliance. Repeated as a mantra in official documents, the directive was to stop sun dances by dissuasion, with legal means being a last resort. This policy conveniently avoided judicial scrutiny of the methods employed. For example, as noted earlier, a supply of beef tongues was indispensable for the rites of Ookaan. Given that these items formed part of the rations distributed by the agency, in 1898 Siksika Agent, G. H. Wheatley, refused to provide the necessary "beef tongues and paunches", causing the Sun Dance to move from July to August, a delay that Wheatley attributed to the chiefs' impression that he "would relent" and supply them with the indispensable beef tongues, which he refused to do.[22] The Agent had secured a contract for five hundred tons of hay, and in his view the "working Indians" had "no time to waste on dances." There is no record of how the beef tongues were obtained, but the ceremony went ahead. However, there were no residual ill feelings because, in September of that same year, Wheatley organized the first "Blackfoot fair," which was opened by Commissioner A. E. Forget.

Chief Weasel Calf's White Savages

In 1921, with a view to enforcing new regulations against "pagan gatherings", Agent Gooderham and NWMP Inspector Jim Spalding proceeded to the Circle Camp where the Siksika had congregated in preparation for Ookaan. Chief Weasel Calf asserted their right to practice their ceremony, reportedly arguing that "They only wanted to live in Peace and they met this way once a year in a friendly way to pray to the Unseen God of the Sun for their sick, for good crops and that they might be happy. In this he said, they were only carrying out what had been taught them by their Fathers and which had been the custom of his tribe for the past 500 years."[23]

It is worthy of remark that Ookaan was revitalized through the incorporation of prayers for "good crops". More interesting is the colourful account Gooderham published thirty-eight years later. Together with Spalding, he noted, he was invited to sit on a "democrat [a horse-drawn carriage] chair" with a large canvas erected over it to cover the sun, which had been set up on the edges of the camp. Weasel Calf told the two officials that "this was a religious camp which was the Indian[']s way to worship his God before the whiteman came [. . .] it would remain at all costs and [. . .] no white savage would be allowed in the camp."[24] Spalding's report did not mention "white savages", but he added that, as a group of women approached the gathering, several of the "old Indians" turned them away "in no uncertain manner", adding that it "was quite apparent that these fellows do not sympathize with women's suffrage."[25]

Gooderham and Spalding agreed to allow the ceremony to take place "on condition that no whites were allowed to enter" — although two white men were present. With Weasel Calf's assent, Spalding deployed Constable Banks and Corporal Harper to remain at the camp and report on the proceedings. Given that they spoke no Blackfoot, two Siksika men served as interpreters. Banks and Harper kept away from areas barred to whites, such as the vower's lodge. However, they witnessed the transfer of a Medicine Pipe, including the "catching" of David Bull Bear, who paid two horses as reciprocation to Little Light, the previous owner. Although Harper's report circulated widely within the Mounted Police and the Department of Indian Affairs in Ottawa, no consequences followed the catching or the payment.[26] This *laissez-faire* attitude demonstrates that despite the continuation of legislative efforts against sun dances in Ottawa, implementation of the measures followed a more pragmatic path.

Honouring Creator Sun and Praying for Good Crops

Judging by the previous anecdote, and the scant number of members of the Police Force in attendance, it is evident that sun dances could only be prevented with the cooperation of First Nations peoples. The ceremonies were not illegal, provided the forbidden features did not take place. But even if they did, the two officials would have been unable to stop them. This is clear from Gooderham's quip: "Frankly, they were two against many [four hundred according to Spalding[27]] and even in the [1920s] men of Weasel Calf's calibre were not to be trifled with on such a serious matter as freedom of religion!" Gooderham did not record his ever having stopped other sun dances; on the contrary, he appears in some photographs flaunting the DIA's rules, escorting white visitors to the ceremony. Gooderham seems to have had a cordial relationship with the Siksika. He recorded, for example, having attended a social dance at the reserve during the winter of 1921, an example of his tacit tolerance towards Blackfoot cultural practices.[28] Gooderham was made an honorary chief of the Siksika in 1931, and devoted his later years to writing about the Blackfoot.

The measures against sun dances encountered sustained resistance on the Blood Reserve. A controversy arose in 1889 when Justice Macleod dismissed charges against two Kainai men — Calf Robe and Prairie Chicken Old Man — whom the Police had arrested during a Sun Dance held off their reserve. The Comptroller's report indicates that "the judge severally censured the Police for making an arrest during a Sun Dance and declared

FIGURE 3.1 *George Gooderham, Honourary chieftanship ceremony, Blackfoot reserve, Alberta* [1931], Glenbow Archive, Calgary, Canada, NB-1-2.

it illegal to arrest an Indian without a warrant." During the trial, the Kainai Agent, William Pocklington "took a very strong stand against the Police, in all his actions, and left no stone unturned to show them in the wrong."[29] In dismissing charges of obstruction against five Kainai men — Crop-eared Wolf, Big Wolf, Little Pine, Day Chief, and Sleeping on Top — who had prevented the Police from arresting the two accused, Macleod observed that the Police "were in the wrong in attempting the arrests, and that they were trespassers and got no more than they deserved." The actions of the Police, he said, were "as bad as attempting to make an arrest in a Church, and that had they attempted to arrest a white man at some religious festival they would probably have been handled still rougher."[30] There was consternation among the Police, not only because this precedent attempted against their practice of arresting First Nations peoples without warrants — a practiced that continued thereafter[31] — but also because Macleod had dismissed the serious charges against the two men deemed to have been wrongfully arrested.[32] The significance of Macleod's judgement resides in his public acknowledgement of religious rights, likening the right to hold sun dances to the religious rights of whites. After all, the Indian Act never forbade sun dances *per se*, but only specific activities associated with them. Some officials had seen fit to exceed the limits of the legislation, but Justice Macleod's ruling provided a timely corrective.

The zeal with which Macleod and Pocklington conducted themselves during the court case was unprecedented. Before becoming a judge, Macleod had been the Mounted Police Superintendent in the district — the town of Macleod in Alberta is named after him — and must have been well aware of the methods employed by the Mounted Police. In 1889, however, there were special circumstances that called for diplomacy. Commissioner Reed had been anxious to secure from Mekasto, the Kainai chief, the surrender of a portion of the reserve without expense to the government. Ottawa had mistakenly "sold" the land to a white rancher, and would be liable if the Kainai insisted on removing him. In December of that year Macleod and Pocklington persuaded Mekasto to sign the surrender without the issue of compensation being raised.[33] Although a detailed analysis of the circumstances surrounding this episode lies beyond the scope of this chapter, it serves to illustrate the multi-layered nature of negotiations between First Nations peoples and the Dominion, as it suggests that Macleod acted in the interests of obtaining Mekasto's signature.

While Pocklington stood firm against the police for interfering with the Kainai ceremony, F. C. Cornish, his counterpart at the Sarcee Reserve, was doing exactly the opposite. The Sarcee, like their allies the Blackfoot, were signatories to Treaty Seven. The Sarcee had not gathered for a Sun Dance in 1888, and in 1889, when they attempted to do so, their agent asked the Mounted Police to intervene. It later transpired that a large contingent of whites had made a donation to Bulls Head, the Sarcee chief, to persuade him to enact the forbidden ceremony of "making of braves" for their entertainment. However, rather than support Cornish's efforts to suppress the ceremony, Reed distanced himself from his subordinate's actions. In a letter to Ottawa, Reed claimed: "I have pointed out to [Cornish] that the Department would never sanction the adoption of force to prevent the repetition of Sun Dances, and recommended dissuasion as being the means most likely to be successful."[34] This rebuff encapsulates the *sub rosa* directive that agents should avoid using the legislation to stop sun dances. First Nations peoples were never privy to this policy, which casts a different light on the proscription of the ceremonies.

As regards the Kainai, they utilized any means at their disposal in order to continue their ceremonial practices, including taking advantage of the competing interests of Catholic and Protestant missionaries. In 1891, during a meeting that Samuel Trivett, an Anglican missionary convened to persuade the Kainai to give up the Sun Dance and to send their children to the Anglican school on the reserve, the Kainai head leader Mekasto agreed to give it up, with the explanation that "it was the same as Christmas and New Years [*sic*] among the whites". The other leaders assembled also offered to send their children to Trivett's school, if he would only secure the release from prison of one of their men, "Good Young Man". White Calf promised the missionary that "if he got 'Good Young Man' out of the Guard Room he would believe in God". Paradoxically, as noted by NWMP Superintendent Steele, "the reason the Indians were anxious for his release is, that he is required to put up the lodge if they are to get up a Sun dance this year."[35] This coincidence calls into doubt the sincerity of the Kainai leaders' undertakings.

The Kainai might have felt justified in employing any available ruse in order to resist the relentless pressure from their Agent to stop their ceremonies. James Wilson, the Indian Agent who had replaced Pocklington, was another anti-Sun Dance crusader. Despite the precedent set by Macleod in 1889, upholding the right of religious observance, Wilson set out to eradicate sun dances during the 1890s. In his biography of Mekasto, Hugh Dempsey narrates the yearly confrontations between the Agent and the Kainai in a chapter he aptly named "The Sun Dance War". Commissioner Forget reported triumphantly in 1895 that no sun dances had taken place at the Blood Reserve for "two seasons."[36] According to Dempsey, this was not strictly correct. The Kainai had gathered in a Circle Camp in 1893, but had omitted "most of the sacred part of the ceremonies."[37] In 1894, on the pretence of having to go away by himself to make an offering to Natosi, Running Wolf, a minor chief, tricked Agent Wilson into giving him six whole beef tongues. These allowed Running Wolf's wife to fulfil her vow to build a lodge to the Sun that year. In retaliation, Wilson cancelled Running Wolf's contract to undertake freighting work for the agency. Such a course of action once again illustrates the extra-judicial strategies available to Indian Agents.

In 1895 Wilson's instruction to render any beef tongues unusable for the Sun Dance by having them cut in half paid dividends. Without the indispensable sacramental tongues, there was no Ookaan. Wilson sponsored alternative celebrations on Dominion Day (1 July). In his report, Commissioner Forget claimed that, having visited the three Blackfoot reserves "in connection with the efforts being made to repress the sun dance", the Pikuni and the Kainai had agreed "to substitute Dominion Day sports for the objectionable dance." The Siksika, he rued, were "more obdurate and the dance went on, though stripped this year of nearly all its former glory [. . . but he did] not anticipate its recurrence next year."[38] His prediction in respect of the Siksika did not come to pass. The Kainai, lacking the indispensable beef tongues, might have unwillingly given up their ceremony in 1895, but their capacity to resist had not been exhausted. Reserve life allowed opportunities for caucusing and planning ways to defeat the Agent.

In 1898, Wilson, the Blood Agent, extended his opposition to encompass all "giveaway dances". That year, Mekasto intervened to obtain an exemption for Singing Before, one of his wives, to give fifteen horses in reciprocation for the Medicine Bundle she required in order to join the *Ma'toki* Society. She had vowed to buy the Bundle during the illness of the venerable leader, and now that he had recovered, she had to fulfil her vow. In view of Wilson's intransigence, Mekasto sought assistance from Superintendent Deane of the NWMP. Deane disliked Wilson and disagreed with his stance. Moreover, Deane was concerned with a rumour spread among the Kainai that their great chief was to be arrested. Seeking to defuse their animosity, Deane informed the Kainai that provided no giveaways other than the exchange of horses occurred during the ceremony "no court would hold that the Indian Act had been infringed". He extracted a promise from the Kainai that this would be the case, and that no Sun Dance would be attempted that year. Mekasto took this to be approval for transferring the Bundle, and sent Police Scouts to spread the news and gather the bands. Deane later denied that he had given approval, and alleged that he had merely offered to write to Wilson to request his permission on behalf of the Kainai. By the time his letter arrived it was too late. The next year, on the strength of this precedent, the Kainai gathered again, this time for the "Horn Society to transfer memberships."[39] Emboldened by these successes, the Kainai determined to have a Sun Dance.

In 1900 Wilson lost the final battle to eradicate the Sun Dance. Deane was instrumental, approving "eleven days of ceremonies". Wilson refused to provide the beef tongues, whence "arrangements were quietly made for the [Kainai] scouts, who received their rations directly from the Mounted

Police, to take their meal allotment in whole tongues." Wilson made a last-ditch effort by threatening to withdraw rations, but he relented when Mekasto, whose prestige was at stake, made a threat of his own. He would "kill his whole herd, if necessary, to feed the camp."[40] The ceremony went ahead. The Kainai had won a significant battle, but opposition to sun dances continued.

Deane's conciliatory attitude, despite his expressed belief that the ceremony served no useful purpose, points to the overriding need to maintain peace with the Blackfoot. Conversely, even at a time when some Blackfoot — like Mekasto — were successful ranchers and no longer reliant on rations for survival, the collective well-being of the bands still required accommodation with Indian Agents. Sun dances represented only one front on which such negotiations took place. The Mounted Police were quick to sound the alert when agents became too forceful in their demands. This was patent in 1905, when Superintendent Primrose wrote to his superiors in Regina at the request of Day Chief, Mekasto's successor. Primrose averred: "I do not wish to be an alarmist, but one of these Indians could cause us a whole heap of trouble if he wished, which would be intensified if he happens to have a following." The letter followed a dispute between the Agent, Robert N. Wilson, and Day Chief over reduced rations and the pasturing of cattle belonging to the Mormon community of the town of Cardston. The agent insulted Day Chief "and threatened to take his medal away and to degrade him from the position of Chief, and make him an ordinary Indian." Day Chief asked the Mounted Police Superintendent to inform his superiors of the Agent's actions.[41] While agents were constantly berated from Ottawa to reduce the cost of rations, their position in charge of resources belonging both to the government and to their charges, made them susceptible to corruption, an allegation almost impossible to substantiate, especially when their wards were illiterate.[42]

However, conditions at each reserve varied. The Blackfoot suffered less interference in their ceremonies than some of their Cree neighbours.[43] While the Mounted Police were able to detain Crees and Salteaux without a warrant, they earned a judicial rebuff when they took similar actions against the Kainai. NWMP Superintendent Steele noted: "You will see that while we must have a warrant" to arrest a Blood (Kainai), "it is not in the opinion of the Indian Commissioner required for the weaker bands of Indians." It appears that the Blackfoot were aware that so long as no self-torture, giving away of property, or alcohol consumption occurred during Ookaan, the agent could not disallow it. In the notebook in which he recorded his Winter Count *circa* 1910, Bull Plume noted: "Duncan Scott [Deputy Superintendent General of Indian Affairs 1913–32]. He told me that dancing was not forbidden."[44] The Kainai professed their compliance with the limitations and, in 1914, their agent concurred with their view:

PART I — THE BLACKFOOT SUN DANCE

"No drinking or other immoral conduct has been indulged in. The grounds have been competently policed at all times day and night. No white visitors have been allowed. The duration of this dance has been the shortest time known to all the old timers; another feature there has been no horses sold as against 208 last year."[45]

In the light of such reports, ongoing harassment of sun dances seemed unjustified; yet it continued. In 1914, after more than two decades of legislated prohibition, the new Agent at the Blood Reserve, W. J. Dilworth, complained: "The Sun Dance has been held here yearly *no obstacle has been put in its way.*"[46] Indeed, the DIA's annual reports record that Ookaan continued to be held on the Blackfoot reserves. Christianity slowly gained followers, but it lived cheek-by-jowl with traditional beliefs, and it would seem that most of those who embraced it, did so superficially.[47] Even leaders deemed to be "progressive" invariably maintained multiple wives and, when gravely ill, sought comfort in their traditional beliefs, not in Christianity. Siksika Weasel Calf, for example, lived with his two wives, appearing in public with the younger of the two as man and wife, and declaring the older wife merely as residing in the home of the married couple. This was common knowledge, but the arrangement remained unchallenged.

In 1921 Kainai Chief Shot in Both Sides telegraphed the DIA when their Agent tried to force them to hold the Sun Dance after the payment of treaty monies. Shot in Both Sides justified his opposition to his agent's directive. His followers, he claimed, "would waste treaty money on dance".[48] This request serves as a reminder that some aspects deemed beneficial by the colonized may readily be incorporated while simultaneously others are rejected. DIA officials could not always dictate either when or how Blackfoot practices should transform.

A clear understanding of the centrality of Ookaan in Blackfoot culture is crucial for assessing the potential impact of its prohibition. It appears that the regulations aimed at its eradication continued to be strengthened regardless of Blackfoot advances towards self-sufficiency.[49] This suggests that the expressed rationale for the attack on Ookaan was a mere subterfuge, and that the true objective was eradicating Blackfoot culture so as to pave the way for Christianity and eventually full assimilation. In Canada, eradication of sun dances was viewed as a pre-requisite in order to fulfil Duncan Campbell Scott's desiderata, *inter alia*, "no Indian question, and no Indian department."

Forty-three years after the Blackfoot settled on reserves, whites' familiarity with their lifeways and those of other First Nations had not enhanced intercultural understanding to any degree. Scott's words echo the "vanishing Indian" discourse of the early nineteenth century. Once whites had possession of First Nations' lands, the cost of treaty promises became a burden. The fulfilment of Scott's desiderata demanded full

Blackfoot integration into the body politic, and therefore their disappearance as a separate people. Ookaan presented an obstacle to this goal, hence the ongoing harassment of the practice and its votaries.

In Canada, despite presenting public opposition to sun dances, the DIA was biding its time, expecting the practice to disappear of its own accord as white observers so often predicted. During the early reserve era, the consensus of officialdom was that it was just a matter of time before those Blackfoot who knew and lived the buffalo days would die, and their religious beliefs with them. This at least is what officials and missionaries hoped for, but they were to be disappointed in the long run. Resistance seems to have been strengthened, rather than weakened, by the regulations. The reach of the Canadian laws prohibiting aspects of the Sun Dance and curtailing travel, added to the uneven approach to implementation, which provided the Blackfoot with grounds for manoeuvre, certainly absolve the legislators from any charge of cultural genocide. However, the pertinent DIA correspondence amply demonstrates that Indian Agents were encouraged by their superiors, where possible, to go beyond the legislation to prevent sun dances. A personal letter to Indian Commissioner David Laird (Winnipeg) from the NWMP Controller Fred White (Ottawa) stated: "We all agree that the 'Sun Dance' ought to be suppressed."[50] In the final analysis, this *de facto* if not *de jure* prohibition had the potential to harm Blackfoot culture. That such an outcome was averted is testimony to Blackfoot determination, but also to the circumstance that official machinations were unequal to the challenge of obtaining and deploying sufficient resources and manpower for the full implementation of the restrictions. Two speeches by a North Pikuni and a Montana Pikuni, respectively, illustrate the depth of Blackfoot opposition to the prohibition. The first is by Natosi Nepe-e (Brings-down-the-Sun) (1905):

> The white race have always cheated and deceived us. They have deprived us of our country. Now they are trying to take away our religion, by putting a stop to the ceremonial sacred to the Sun. Our religion was given to us by the Sun and Moon, and we will never give it up, while the Sun and Moon last. The white people have given us no good reason why they wish to take away our religion. We do not fight, nor drink whisky at our ceremonials, and there is nothing harmful that can come from them. We have been struggling to keep up our religion, in order that our people may be happy, and that they may lead better lives. When I began preparations for a Sun ceremonial this spring, in accordance with the vow, made by one of our women for the healing of her sick son, the agent shut off our rations. He would not allow my family to receive the food, upon which we are dependent. Because of these things my heart has become bitter, and I have made a vow, that I will have nothing more to do with the white race.[51]

Part I — The Blackfoot Sun Dance

Natosi Nepe-e refutes the superiority of civilization and labels whites as "cheaters and deceivers", epithets that often were levelled at Indians. First Nations peoples interpreted treaties differently to the ways in which officialdom did. They saw rations as payment for the land, and their withholding as a form of cheating. Whether intentionally or not, the terms of Natosi Nepe-e's speech echo Christian practices: "We fast and pray [. . .] to lead good lives and to act more kindly towards each other." The parallel draws attention to the double standard in the demands imposed on First Nations peoples. The second speech, by Stock-stchi (1910), also draws attention to the prevailing double standards:

> We know that there is nothing injurious to our people in the Sun-dance. On the other hand, we have seen much that is bad at the dances of the white people. It has been our custom, during many years, to assemble once every summer for this festival, in honour of the Sun God. We fast and pray, that we may be able to lead good lives and to act more kindly towards each other. I do not understand why the white men desire to put an end to our religious ceremonials. What harm can they do to our people? If they deprive us of our religion, we will have nothing left, for we know of no other than can take its place.[52]

Stock-stchi repeats word for word one of Natosi Nepe-e's sentences; the repetition draws attention to the role of the transcriber, Walter McClintock. Whether the two Blackfoot men used the same expression, or whether the repetition is a product of McClintock's translation, it is evident that the latter felt compelled to record Blackfoot dissatisfaction with the prohibition of sun dances. McClintock attended Ookaan during his sojourn with the Blackfoot, indicating that the prohibition had been ineffective. For all that, McClintock disparaged Blackfoot beliefs, which were to his mind superstitions that kept them in a "mental and spiritual slavery."[53] McClintock's ambivalence, recording a defence of Ookaan while condemning Blackfoot beliefs, is an example of common white attitudes towards First Nations.

In the United States, the prohibition of sun dances was finally lifted in 1934, when the New Deal administration of Franklin D. Roosevelt, with John Collier as Commissioner for Indian Affairs, restored freedom of religion and gave First Nations the right to revive their cultures through the *Indian Reorganization Act* (also known as the Wheeler–Howard Act).[54] Even the "piercing" ritual eventually was permitted, if this had no effect on the Blackfoot, who had abandoned the ritual permanently, it allowed the Lakota in South Dakota to bring into the open a ritual they had maintained secretly. According to Lakota ceremonialist Fools Crow, in 1952 they were given written permission to include the previously forbidden ritual in the Lakota Sun Dance.

Honouring Creator Sun and Praying for Good Crops

Insofar as the Blackfoot are concerned, they were unequivocal in their refusal to give up the Circle Camp and Ookaan. If anything, their resistance to acculturation was stimulated by the demands placed on them by government officials. Confronted with overzealous agents such as James Wilson, they exploited the tensions between DIA officials and the Mounted Police. Having compromised by eliminating some forbidden practices, they then asserted their right to continue to practise their ceremonies. While the Many Guns Winter Count records that, with few exceptions, the Siksika continued to gather for Ookaan during the first four decades of the twentieth century,[55] Goldfrank reported that "the Kainai Sun Lodge has been raised annually since 1910, sixteen women vowing it, sometimes two of them jointly."[56] By mid-century, a new Indian Act was promulgated in Canada, and "most of the provisions for aggressive civilization and compulsory enfranchisement were deleted."[57] John C. Ewers, who lived in Browning between 1941 and 1944, noted that, with few exceptions, most of the Pikuni in Montana had become Christians, and the great majority had become Catholics. Behind the museum of which Ewers was a curator, those Pikuni who continued to observe the ceremony gathered with their painted lodges in 1942 to observe their rituals and recount their sacred stories.[58] The transformation of First Nations' ceremonial life was then proceeding in accordance with their changing needs, rather than as a result of outside interference.

The foregoing chapters provide a wide perspective of the workings of assimilation efforts and the responses that such efforts elicited among the Blackfoot, in particular with reference to the proscription of sun dances

FIGURE 3.2 *Blackfoot house and tipi, Blackfoot (Siksika) reserve, southern Alberta* [c.1908], Glenbow Archive, Calgary, Canada, NA-3322-12.

Part I — The Blackfoot Sun Dance

in Canada and the United States. They present a view of the Blackfoot that complicates blanket claims of victimhood, which, by their very nature, obscure or deny Blackfoot actions that served to shape their own cultural transformation during the early reserve era. The Blackfoot that emerge from this case study did not see themselves as victims, and were able to deploy a wide repertoire of contention in order to maintain cultural continuity during an era of rapid transformation.

PART II

The Grammar of Blackfoot
Leadership Dress, 1830–1920

4

Dress, Sacred Stories, and Worldviews

Interpreting Blackfoot dress as an indicator of changing social and political phenomena and, in particular, as an indicator of intercultural social relationships is valuable because the study of bodily representation allows us to "address human processes for constituting the social self, social organization, and shared notions of authority and value".[1] Dress transformations within a community over time can be related to social and political change, especially when such changes are associated with the encounter between Europeans and indigenous peoples during the colonization process. The analysis of Blackfoot dress attendant upon the advance of colonialism that occupies this and the following two chapters will encompass two periods: the fur trade era (*c*.1820–1870); and the era of transition to life on reserves in Canada and reservations in the United States (*c*.1870–1920). However, since Blackfoot history did not commence with the white encounter — even if written history did — due attention must be paid to Blackfoot worldviews, in order to link dress to power and leadership. This study thus links dress to the social order and relates dress protocols to local (or band) perspectives of gender, power, and politics. It focuses on the political and gendered semiotics of dress worn by Blackfoot elites to signify their position both within their own bands and within relations with other First Nations peoples or with Europeans and later with their descendants, principally Euro-Americans and Canadians.

Self-fashioning through dress by the Blackfoot elites from the time when travellers and traders wrote their first reports, embodied a fluid identity. In particular, Blackfoot ethnogenesis during an era of economic and political turbulence correlated with the transformations and continuities of the dress that elites displayed in public arenas. From the 1750s, the fur trade ushered in a period of cultural florescence in the Plains, providing access to an array of materials that First Nations peoples eagerly sought and adapted to their respective dress practices. The Blackfoot acquired European goods initially through Cree and Assiniboine middle-men, and eventually by taking their pelts and furs to trading posts established within their reach.² Emerging intercultural alliances between Blackfoot leaders and European, Canadian and American traders exercised a transformative effect on the customary power structures of these First Nations. Such alliances, often cemented by familial ties, gave leaders who brought their followers to the trading forts access to sumptuary goods. Leaders distributed among their followers liquor and tobacco received from traders thereby fulfilling their reciprocal obligations and buttressing their authority over their followers. The diplomatic ties established during the fur trade often laid the groundwork for eventual treaty negotiations between the Blackfoot and the United States (1855) and the Dominion (1877); trading allies became treaty facilitators and negotiators. Dress played a significant role in these diplomatic transactions.

Many of the earliest representations of First Nations peoples took shape at trading posts. The early historiography is informed by the journals kept by employees of trading companies. Moreover, trading posts were a hub for white visitors from faraway places, who came West eager to observe a way of life that — they believed — was destined to disappear. These travellers — including naturalists, ethnographers, and artists — produced texts, photographs, and paintings whose value as early historical records is of great significance. These provide a glimpse of the importance of dress as a marker of status, and as a source of personal and communal pride among First Nations. Early representations nevertheless paid little heed to women, focusing on the male warrior and buffalo hunter.

The variety of dress designs in the extant record — documents, photographs, paintings, and surviving items of dress — provides evidence of the heterogeneity of subjectivities available to Blackfoot persons, who could achieve status by following a number of paths. Focusing on their dress practices as a dimension of local and intercultural relations lends complexity to Blackfoot history. The materiality of sartorial choices as individual and collective projections of identity speaks its own language. If we depart from McLuhan's dictum that "the medium is the message", it is possible to "read" dress as a text in order to appreciate, not only the complexity of the Blackfoot worldview, but also the capacity for adaptation and the vitality of their culture. The analysis here does not aim to search for an essentialist perspective on Blackfoot dress practices, but focuses on the way in which dress reflects a changing world.³ The Blackfoot bands eagerly embraced European goods, including items of dress, but at the same time continued to observe dress codes whose reason for being pre-dated the European encounter.

Blackfoot dress over the two periods of interest here reflects not merely changing material conditions, such as the availability or scarcity of the materials utilized, but also the existence of networks and the workings of cultural appropriation, what Stephen Greenblatt termed "self-fashioning". Greenblatt argues that "the power to impose a shape upon oneself is an aspect of the more general power to control identity — that of others at least as often as one's own."[4] A study of the dress of the First Nations is particularly apposite because of its capacity to signify to a wide audience the personal qualities and achievements of the wearer. It is useful to signal here the extensive use of dress as a gift in Plains intertribal diplomacy. Dress exchanges that occurred in diplomatic encounters, and the fluidity of Plains cultural practices, contributed to the spread of dress traits and, ultimately, to the hybridity of dress. However, Blackfoot dress remained sufficiently distinct and identifiable by friends and foes, particularly because of a "preference for large triangles, hourglasses, and diamonds" usually set against a background of soft tanned and whitened (with white clay) elk, deer, mountain goat and antelope skins fashioned into shirts, leggings and dresses.[5] Decorations included dyed porcupine quills, animal skins (such as otter and ermine), shells, hooves, elk teeth, and even human hair. This outfit was supplemented with a plain or painted buffalo robe, or a robe decorated with dyed porcupine quills. Necklaces and earrings incorporated a variety of animal skins, feathers, claws, bone carvings, shells and wood. Feathers and pelts could indicate status, or be used as adornment, and for warmth in winter.[6] The design of Blackfoot dress altered according to individual circumstance. Garments could be acquired as trophies or war, or be fashioned following designs received in dreams.[7] The Blackfoot adorned their bonnets with ermine skins, for they admired the ermine's aggressiveness.[8] Three bonnet styles predominated: "the straight up bonnet", the "straight up bonnet with the boss ribs", and the "horned bonnet". Eagle tail feathers adorned the first two, and a pair of horns and a fringe of ermine strips the third.[9]

Blackfoot dress constituted a system of signs that, like other semiotic systems, was complemented by a "linguistic admixture."[10] Independently of language, however, the *signifieds* of Blackfoot dress could be interpreted by cultural insiders, those with an emic view. The origins of dress are encoded in Blackfoot oral stories, and the early writings of fur traders and travellers. The painter George Catlin and Prussian Prince Alexander Philipp Maximilian of Wied-Neuwied, in the company of Swiss artist Karl Bodmer, travelled among the First Nations of the Upper Missouri in 1833–34. The portraits of First Nations peoples by Catlin and especially Bodmer offer a rare view of material culture from that era.[11] Furthermore, in the late 1800s ethnologists paid a great deal of attention to Plains dress, although viewing change as "contamination", thus running the risk of objectifying dress as a relic.[12] Yet, dress transformation *per se* provides a useful indication of broader changes in power relations. Blackfoot dress encodes sacred and secular meanings, making it desirable to begin this study by drawing its links to their sacred stories.

Part II — The Grammar of Blackfoot Leadership Dress

The Sacred Dimension of Male Dress

Dress, as other cultural, political, and social practices of the Blackfoot, connects with a sacred realm whose links to the present are constantly renegotiated. The meanings of dress are contained in the Blackfoot Stories, the repositories of their identity and worldviews, the shared notions of what it means to be Blackfoot.[13] This link is manifest in the story of Scarface (Paii or Poïa), from the Star Stories cycle. Scarface was a poor ancestor who lived for a time with Natosi (the Sun), his wife Kokomi-kisomm (Night-Light, the Moon), and their son, Ipiso-waahsa (Morning Star, Venus).[14] The narrative is set in the dog days, an era that ended when the Blackfoot acquired the horse through intertribal trade in the early decades of the eighteenth century.[15] During his quest to have a scar removed from his face — a condition imposed by the woman he wished to marry — Scarface killed seven cranes that were attacking Morning Star. After this act of courage, Natosi removed his scar and gave Scarface instructions on how to conduct Ookaan (the Sun Dance). The Star Beings gave Scarface gifts before he returned to his people, including a buckskin suit, consisting of elk shirt and leggings. The suit symbolized the killing of the seven enemies.

In Three Bears' version of the story, narrated to David Duvall in 1910, a plate of porcupine quills, representing the Sun, decorated the front and back of the shirt given to Scarface.[16] Strips of quills between three and four inches wide covered the seams on the outside of the shirt's sleeves and leggings. The sleeves and leggings were also fringed with hair locks, "representing the scalps of the cranes Scarface killed."[17] When Scarface returned to his people, his dress denoted that he had become *akáinauàsiu* or *akainawa'si* ("full grown in age"), often translated as "chief".[18] Though it is not certain whether Scarface's story (with no parallels in the stories of other Plains First Nations)[19] reflects Blackfoot practice, or *vice versa*, it does inscribe the underlying dialectical relationship between dress and power within the Blackfoot worldview in the pre-settlement era, and underlines the link between secular power and the sacred realm.

Three Bears' description of the quilled disk on Scarface's shirt fits the design of the shirt that Stu-mick-o-súks (Buffalo Bull's Back Fat, or The Buffalo's Back Fat), the head chief of the Kainai, wore for his 1832 portrait by Catlin, one of several portraits of Blackfoot dignitaries that the artist painted during his sojourn at Fort Union (see Figure 4.2 CP).[20] According to Catlin, the full attire of the Blackfoot leader consisted of the following:

> a shirt or tunic, made of two deer skins finely dressed [. . .] the seams running down on each arm, from the neck to the knuckles of the hand; this seam is covered with a band of two inches in width, of very beautiful embroidery

of porcupine quills, and suspended from the under edge of this, from the shoulders to the hands, is a fringe of the locks of black hair, which he has taken from the heads of victims slain by his own hand in battle. The leggings are made also of the same material; and down the outer side of the leg, from the hip to the feet, extends also a similar band or belt of the same width; and wrought in the same manner, with porcupine quills, and fringed with scalp locks. These locks of hair are procured from scalps, and worn as trophies [. . .] And over all, his robe, made of the skin of a young buffalo bull, with the hair remaining on; and on the inner or flesh side, beautifully garnished with porcupine quills, and the battles of his life very ingeniously, though rudely, pourtrayed in pictorial representations.[21]

The robe worn over his shirt by the leader, which Catlin did not reproduce, belongs to a well-documented "autobiographical" pictographic genre. Warriors decorated these robes with figures that symbolized their war deeds, which accounts for their being known as "story robes" or "brag robes" (see Figure 4.1 CP). Emphasis on keeping true records of war achievements made these robes ubiquitous in the Plains, where a warrior's reputation was as important to protect as his very life.

Taking into account that the Scarface story originated during the dog days (before c.1700), the similarity with both Catlin's painting and Three Bears' version of the sacred narrative, narrated in 1910, is notable. Such correspondences across two centuries, however, raise some questions. Was this disk design already in use during the dog days, or perhaps earlier? Or, was it in vogue during the nineteenth century, soon to be replaced by the advent of European glass beads available through the fur trade? Maximilian claimed that the "round rosettes" on the front and back of Blackfoot shirts — similar to those worn by the Assiniboine — were "a foreign fashion, and the genuine Blackfoot costume ha[d] no such ornament."[22] Adding to Maximilian's claim, Clark Wissler noted that such circular designs on the breast and back, common among the Blackfoot in the 1830s, were also widespread among the Assiniboine and a few other First Nations of the northern Plains.[23] While Catlin painted portraits of Nez Perces, Mandan, Assiniboine, and Blackfoot warriors wearing shirts with the disk design, this adornment did not feature in Bodmer's Blackfoot portraits painted a year later.[24] In Bodmer's portrait of Stu-mick-o-súks, the Blackfoot leader wears a hair-fringed shirt made of red trade cloth with painted buckskin sleeves (see "Chief of the Blood Indians", Figure 4.3, CP). His face is painted red, a colour associated with the Sun, and with sacred power.[25] A strip of blue and white trade beads is superimposed where the sleeve joins the body of the shirt, and a strip of white trade beads borders the collar and continues over the shoulders. The shirt attests to the incorporation of trade materials by the 1830s, but also to the way in which the new materials were fashioned into existing designs and became part of Blackfoot costume. The continuity of design in this shirt can be appreciated in the nineteen black horizontal lines painted on the sleeves (only the left is fully visible), which the Blackfoot painted to mark the number of attainments of the wearer (*coups*). According to one version of the story of Scarface, displaying achievements in this matter also came from Natosi. The suit given to Scarface had one line painted for each of the birds killed, although according to the story, the lines were painted on the leggings, not on the shirt. Natosi instructed Scarface to tell his people that they "shall wear black stripes on their leggings when they kill enemies".[26] The disk design, unlike the *coup* marks, is not to be seen in the red trade cloth shirt worn by Stu-mick-o-súks.

Taking into account Maximilian's claim regarding the "Assiniboine" ornament, it is of interest to note the description of the disk design in Three Bears' version of Scarface, a story set in the ancient days when the Blackfoot still used dogs as beasts of burden. The only plausible explanation is that, at some unknown point, the story was reworked in order to incorporate a "foreign fashion" into the Blackfoot universe. If this was the case, however, the story was not reworked to include horses or guns, which during the nineteenth century effectively functioned as extensions of dress as signifiers of power and status. I will return to the incorporation of dress designs from neighbouring First Nations to discuss diplomacy and war in chapter 5. For now, it is pertinent to pursue further the relationship between the story of Scarface and Blackfoot dress. The disk design, whether "foreign" or not, would have been the prerogative of few individuals, an elite which, like Scarface, gained respect through deeds of courage.

Another correspondence between the Scarface story and dress is the Blackfoot practice of decorating shirts and leggings with the hair of their slain enemies, a practice that continued as long as wars did. The elite Blackfoot whom Catlin, and Maximilian and Bodmer met in the 1830s decorated their shirts in this manner. The ideology that exalts war achievements, according to the story, originates in the sacred realm, where the Star Beings live parallel lives to those of the Blackfoot. It is part of the teachings that Natosi imparted to the Blackfoot through Scarface. Moreover, when Ipiso-waahsa (Morning Star) visited the Blackfoot, he wore a suit similar to that given to Scarface. Therefore, when the Blackfoot whitened the tanned hides for their buckskin suits, they did so in memory of their close relationship with Ipiso-waahsa and Natosi.[27]

The story of Scarface imbues the buckskin suit with symbolic power derived from the prestige associated with martial prowess.[28] This is consonant with the collective goal of defending Blackfoot sovereignty and territorial integrity amid strong intertribal challenges in the era preceding settlement on reserves. The sacred and secular realms thus blend in the buckskin suit. In the same way that the hair locks on the sleeves and leggings of Scarface's suit represent the scalps of the cranes he killed,[29] it was appropriate that those who emulated the culture hero should dress in the finest elk or deer shirt and leggings, richly quilled (later beaded) and fringed with highly prized ermine tails or hair locks from enemy scalps. These suits are themselves a sacred "bundle", requiring ritual initiation of the would-be wearer.[30] The story attributes the practice of scalping to Natosi's teachings. Although the origins of scalping enemies cannot be dated, wearing locks from enemy scalps was described in 1833–34 as commonplace among the Blackfoot, the taking of an enemy scalp rating higher than the taking of an enemy's horse, although lower than other deeds such as taking an enemy's gun, bow, shield, war bonnet, shirt, or ceremonial pipe.[31]

The sacred realm also defined the boundaries of dress, delineating prohibitions and taboos. Markers of power such as suits fringed with human hair could usually be worn only by those who had slain an enemy in battle, although band leaders who had attained at least one deed of valour could acquire them, even if they had never killed an enemy. The red-winged woodpecker's feathers, Bullchild noted, were reserved for the sole use of "Creator Sun", whose clothing was fringed with these feathers — "no one else was entitled to use them."[32] Indeed, some dress taboos had to be observed, although receiving a dress design in a dream would entitle the dreamer not only to wearing the design, but also to transfer it ritually to another person while continuing to hold the rights to it—a copyright entitlement of sorts. As the incorporation of the Assiniboine disk in the story of Scarface demonstrates, new designs could be incorporated into the Blackfoot universe and into the Blackfoot stories, which need to be read in context, rather than as immutable narratives.

BAND LEADERSHIP AND DRESS

The Blackfoot mechanisms to attain leadership follow a logic consonant with Blackfoot worldviews. These perspectives can be useful to appreciate Blackfoot history as being more than the history of their contacts with Europeans or Euro-Americans. Their sacred stories and ritual provide an inside perspective of the way in which elite dress symbolized power at different points in their history and therefore dress practices illustrate one of the guises of cultural continuity. Blackfoot decision-making during the buffalo-hunting days devolved upon a number of well-respected band members (minor chiefs or councillors) led by a headman or chief, who was the "most respected able-bodied man" in the band.[33] Respect for these leaders stemmed from their achievements in war, acquisition of Sacred Bundles (and other sacred items considered *natoyi* or "Medicine"), and generosity.[34] Band autonomy meant that decisions that affected all the bands had to be reached by consensus. However, western perspectives of leadership emphasized the role of band "chief". These attitudes had some bearing on white expectations that chiefs should speak for all the bands of their respective First Nations, and in the case of the Blackfoot, at least for all the bands of each division (Pikuni, Kainai, Siksika). Women's did not become band leaders, although Running Eagle, a Pikuni woman, became a war leader. A few Blackfoot women, who achieved war honours, are known to have participated in band decision-making. However, information on these women and the roles they played is sparse. Female power therefore needs to be discussed separately in terms of sacred and secular practices that specifically provide women with a path to attaining respect.

The *I-kun-uh'-kah-tsi* (age-graded societies) provided a means for social advancement among the Blackfoot. Membership into the societies started in childhood and culminated in the most respected of all societies: The Horns, "said to have life and death power." Membership of some age-graded societies, including the Horns, required husband and wife to join together, thus sharing the prestige involved.[35] The dress and regalia worn by the members of each society was distinct and recognizable to the whole community, they could only be obtained by purchasing the rights from previous owners, which often meant that a whole society would transfer its rights to an incoming cohort at the same time. Each Blackfoot society played a specific role, and within each society members also occupied positions within an established hierarchy, reflected on their dress.

Dress traits functioned as a language, as in the case of the suit Natosi gave to Scarface. One of the principal tropes had to do with success in war, which the Blackfoot measured via a hierarchy of deeds generically recognized as *coups*. During warring times the Blackfoot recognized as a *coup* the killing or scalping of an enemy, and the capture of valued items, including shields, bows, arrows, guns, war bonnets, war shirts, medicine pipes, and guns.[36] Some war trophies were retained, but more often, they were distributed in accordance with established reciprocity protocols. Successful warriors shared their spoils of war with those who aided them (i.e., by providing food, moccasins, or prayers for their success). Assistance might come from the band's leader, or from the warrior's own family. Within a social context in which generosity accrued honour, and stinginess scorn, a quilled or beaded buckskin suit, fringed with ermine strips, marked its owner as a person of distinction. War deeds provided a means to acquire wealth and to attain prestige regardless of social origin, and dress appropriately reflected these achievements. Pictographs on warrior's story robes served to display their achievements. Although not always politically motivated, dress provided irrefutable proof of the wearer's status. A stark distinction separated everyday dress from that worn during ceremonies, societies' meetings, and war. While the hunt required minimal dress, the best dress was displayed during peace meetings, rituals, and ceremonies. Warriors carefully transported personal items imbued with power (Medicine) when raiding enemy camps. Even when circumstances did not allow them to don these garments into battle, their owners felt protected just by carrying them along.

The ceremonial agenda of *Akokatssinn* (the Circle Encampment), and Ookaan provided myriad opportunities to display a person's worth. For example, during meetings of the *I-kun-uh'-kah-tsi*, and during ceremonial transfers of sacred objects such as Beaver Bundles and Medicine Pipe Bundles, everyday dress gave way to highly valued items of dress and regalia.[37] Within the former, initiation rites — which often took place during the Circle Camp — included the bestowal of the society's dress and the accompanying instruction via prayers, songs, and face painting. Each society had distinct raiment, and within each society the dress of leading members bore distinct features to mark them out.[38] For example, among the Kainai, the leader of the All Brave Dogs Society wore "a coyote skin with his head thrust through a slit in its middle, [. . .] a weasel-tail or hairlock suit, and war bonnet". He always had "a blanket across his left arm and [. . .] his rattle in his right hand." His nose, mouth and chin were covered with red paint ("Coyote painting").[39] Red paint is always associated with the sacred. A red-painted dress and red moccasins, for example, served to distinguish the owner of a Medicine Pipe, a most prestigious possession — ownership being a prerequisite for aspiring band leaders — that was collectively the property of a married couple, who jointly cared for it.[40] Again, the precedent for this practice is that, as Bullchild affirms, "Creator Sun" himself wore a "red-earth-painted white buffalo robe around his shoulders", while his whole body, including his hair, was also smeared with red paint.[41] Alexander Henry the Younger, whose trading journal provides glimpses of life on the prairies in the early contact era, was repelled by the Blackfoot habit of smearing red earth on their hair and bodies. Siksika women, he bemoaned, "are a filthy set".[42] Their hair was "never combed except with the fingers". It was "worn loose about the neck and always besmeared with the red and lead-coloured earth." This, he continued, "gives them a savage countenance, though the features of many of them would be agreeable, were they not so incrusted with earth." Henry's reaction highlights the gulf that divided the Blackfoot perspective from that of the newcomers.

The Sun Dance was an occasion for the display of finery, especially at key moments such as immediately prior to raising the holy tree, and before lighting the sacred fire, when distinguished leaders counted *coup*. Moreover, the Circle Camp also provided the best opportunities for aspiring leaders to dispense generosity and attract followers. As in the precedent of the suit given to Scarface by Natosi, dress gifts were highly valued. Buckskin suits circulated through an economy of transfer in accordance with an emic logic based on principles of generosity and reciprocity.

Part II — The Grammar of Blackfoot Leadership Dress

Restrictions applied to specific items of dress. Social derision and even tragedy would befall those who failed to comply with scrupulous standards of veracity and the appropriate ceremonial transfer required to wear such garments (e.g., those associated with societies, the keeping of sacred objects, or the acquisition of deeds of valour).[43] These transfers served to reproduce Blackfoot institutions; they were a rite of passage and not a mere gesture, providing the initiate with knowledge in the form of prayers, songs, and apposite face painting. The property exchanged as reciprocation for these transfers, as noted earlier, contributed to wealth redistribution and the maintenance of a social hierarchy based on the pursuit of common goals.

Viewed from these perspectives, dress signified power within a holistic context in which the secular and the sacred are interwoven. The power inscribed in dress cuts across both domains, with material success attributed to possession of strong Medicine, and with Medicine ownership being "a property distinction" because any woman or man must possess substantial property in order to acquire sacred objects deemed to be "medicine."[44] The power that could be read in a person's dress was not only a marker of past achievement but could be a harbinger of future gain. A war leader who possessed strong Medicine was more likely to lead his followers to success.[45] Peacetime or civil leaders also required strong Medicine to ensure good outcomes for themselves and their bands. Their generosity in redistributing their wealth enhanced their status and attracted followers — a measure of their stature. McClintock observed that a Blackfoot leader "must be kind-hearted and open-handed, ever ready to share his food supply with the poorest of his tribe. His tipi must always welcome the stranger, and it devolved upon him to entertain generously the visiting chiefs and delegations from other tribes."[46]

Generosity always earned respect for the giver, and generosity, prestige, and possession of the most ostentatious dress were inseparable in the Blackfoot worldview. A *minipuka*, the favoured son or daughter of a wealthy family, embodied this combination. The prestige of a *minipuka* was measured by his/her parents' "ostentatious distribution of property made in the name of the favored child."[47] A gift presented to the *minipuka*, for example, would be reciprocated with a much more lavish gift. The *minipuka* continued to exercise generosity to those in need in his or her band even after the parents died.[48] *Minipuka* children were not expected to exert themselves (their parents waited on them) or go to war, but as adults they could become leaders whose role was to provide for the less well off. From childhood, *minipuka* wore the best items of dress, marking their status as *istuisanaps* (others respect them), and above their peers, including their own brothers and sisters.[49] This is another instance where, before settlement in the late nineteenth century, leadership positions were open to those capable or willing to exercise generosity. The existence of *minipuka* among the Blackfoot serves as a reminder that band authority was not vested in one person, but was exercised simultaneously by several leaders who came to attain respect via different paths. These paths invariably marked the dress worn by Blackfoot elites.

Women, Dress and the Sacred

According to a Blackfoot story of "The First Marriage", men were poorly dressed before they lived with women. They wore rawhides because they had no knowledge of how to tan skins or sew. Instead of moccasins, they "wore the gamble-joint of the buffalo".[50] Blackfoot dress was the product of women's labour, with quillwork a sacred occupation requiring ritual initiation. The introduction of large "pony" beads through the fur trade supplanted to a great extent, but did not discontinue the use of the more laborious quillwork. A Siksika quilled suit exhibited at the Glenbow Museum in Calgary, for example, has been dated to the early 1900s, one century since the introduction of beads in the northwestern Plains.[51]

The earliest reference to quilling on a Blackfoot woman's dress is probably that of Alexander Henry. In his 1808 journal, he noted that some women cleaned their coverings "with white clay, and when trimmed with fringe and quillwork look[ed] tolerably well."[52] In 1832, when Catlin painted a portrait of Eeh-nís-kim (The Crystal Stone), one of Stu-mick-o-súks's "six or eight" wives, he mentioned that her dress was "made of skins" but did not elaborate on its decorations (see Figure 4.4 CP).[53] In her portrait, a band of blue beads runs along the neckline, continuing over the shoulder and finishing at the cuff. Buckskin beaded pendants also adorn the visible part of the dress. Thus, while her husband posed for Catlin wearing a quilled shirt, Eeh-nís-kim's dress illustrated a change in Blackfoot dress, from quills to beads.

Whereas ermine and hairlock fringes were highly desirable in men's dress, elk teeth were the most highly prized adornment on Blackfoot women's dress, a preference shared by other Plains women, including the Crow. The incisor teeth of the elk were placed in rows, a few centimetres distant from each other around the entire yoke area of the dress. Imitation teeth made from bone and cowrie shells, and brass bells were sometimes used as alternatives. However, elk teeth remained a prized item into the twentieth century — in 1903 Walter McClintock photographed a young girl wearing a dress profusely decorated with elk teeth. He reported having seen dresses with three hundred teeth, then valued at one dollar each.[54] The high value that Blackfoot women placed on this adornment is explained by their sacred stories. In particular, the ornament provides a link to Elk Woman, the guiding example for the conduct of Blackfoot women.

Part II — The Grammar of Blackfoot Leadership Dress

Those women who followed the example of Elk Woman reached the zenith of their prestige by vowing to honour Natosi with a Sun Dance, thereby becoming the Holy Woman, mother of her people. However, during the ceremony, neither quillwork nor elk teeth adorn her dress. She wears "a very plain robe, given by the mythical Elk Woman [. . .] and headdress [Natoas] with moose hooves and crow tail feathers". This attire symbolizes chastity and modesty, two ideal qualities of a Blackfoot woman.[55] In fulfilment of her vow, during four days of confinement, prayer, and fasting, the Holy Woman appears humble, bearing "an expression of great sadness and suffering" with her hair "down and red-ochred."[56] Her modesty, Alice Kehoe argues, "is a sign of her *intrinsic* power: she is so secure in it that she need not flaunt her role."[57] That power, adds Kehoe, derives from women being "the intermediary or means through which power has been granted to humans", as illustrated in the story of the Woman Who Married a Star (see below). Women's intermediary role is evident in manifold ways, of which Ookaan is but one. Through their intercession, the Blackfoot received two of their most sacred bundles (The Beaver Bundle and the Thunder Pipe Bundle), handed down to "human women" according to the Blackfoot Stories. It follows that women are indispensable in transfers of these objects whose ownership is the *sine qua non* for attaining leadership.[58]

The Story of a Woman Who Married a Star illustrates how, through the intercession of human women, sacred beings have established and renewed their links to the Blackfoot. This story, and others associated with the Sun Dance, narrate the origins of the Holy Woman's dress.[59] According to Brings-Down-the-Sun, So-at-sa-ki was a Blackfoot ancestor who became Morning Star's wife and lived with the Star Beings, during which time she bore him a son. Despite her husband's warnings, she dug a large turnip and, through the hole it left in the ground, she saw her people and became homesick. She returned to her people with her son, both wrapped in an elk skin. On her head was the Natoas — the sacred bonnet named after the turnip — and she also brought back the digging stick. She was lowered from the sky with a buffalo rawhide rope. These sacred items were passed on to the Medicine Lodge Woman, the Holy Woman in the Sun Dance.[60] During the Sun Dance a rawhide rope is attached to the Sun Dance pole. The power inscribed on the plain robe handed down to the Blackfoot and worn by the Holy Woman during the Sun Dance is associated with the purity of Elk Woman, from whom the robe originates. When her husband pursued her to punish her for adultery, Elk Woman proved that the accusation was not true. She challenged her husband to knock down a tree, which he failed to do. Elk Woman's power proved to be superior and she felled the tree — this power is embodied in the Holy Woman. Elk's assistants in pursuing his wife, a Moose and a Crow, gave Elk Woman hooves and feathers as tokens of recognition. The high regard for

Elk Woman resulted in elk teeth becoming the most valued decorations on a Blackfoot woman's dress.[61]

Women's chastity, like men's bravery, accrued prestige to the individual, her family, and her people. The Holy Woman's pledge to hold Ookaan secured divine protection for her whole community. An unchaste woman, like a warrior who betrayed his comrades, risked being killed by her own people. Those who were unfaithful to their husbands usually had their noses or ears, or both, cut off for the first offence, and were killed either by the husband or some relation, or by the *I-kun-uh'-kah-tsi* [the all-comrades societies] for the second.[62] On the basis of their research among the Siksika in Alberta, ethnographers Lucien Hanks and Jane Richardson Hanks noted that some women were punished through "society rape fests", a euphemism for pack-rape perpetrated by the *I-kun-uh'-kah-tsi*. Such punishment, they argued, derived from the fact that "women were credited with the initiative in love." Despite such brutal punishment, the Hanks found that, among the Siksika, the number of women "ineligible to vow the Sun Dance bespeaks the frequency of these illicit affairs."[63] Diamond Jenness wrote that the Blackfoot "seemed to have encouraged their young men to practice seduction, and then scorned the women who yielded to their advances."[64] However, women who followed the example of Elk Woman, like men who followed the example of Scarface, gained respect.

The models that the Blackfoot stories define for men and women to attain honour should not be interpreted as restricting either men or women to those models, but as antecedents that pervaded Blackfoot lifeways during the dog days and the buffalo era. Wider possibilities for understanding the links between Blackfoot women and power emerged from the research of professional ethnographers during the first half of the twentieth century, and in the more recent work of Alice Kehoe, who proposed a contrasting interpretation of the workings of power in Blackfoot culture, arguing that power was open to all persons.[65] What follows is an attempt to engage with the various ways in which power was open to Blackfoot women, and how these paths intersected with dress.

The Power of Women's Business

A broader appreciation of First Nations women's roles and the manifold ways in which women could acquire and exercise power is often absent from early colonial representations. A gulf separates the portrayal of men as powerful and fearless warriors and that of women as unattractive drudges held in slave-like conditions by their husbands. Yet Blackfoot women, and more so elite Blackfoot women, were not without power. Foucault noted that individuals "are always in a position of simultaneously undergoing and exercising" power, and are neither "its inert or consenting target" nor "its points of application."[66] When the circulation of power in Blackfoot culture is viewed through the prism of their dress practices, the generalized view of women's abjection begins to crumble.

Women's absence from key events of the colonial encounter can be revealing of their social position within their own culture, but also of the ethnocentric and gender biases of the authors of the ethnological documentation.[67] White women did not arrive with the first fur traders, being considered too frail for a life in which their indigenous counterparts thrived. This stark difference demonstrates the need to analyze Blackfoot women's experiences through culturally specific perspectives. I will therefore engage with the arguments proposed by anthropologists familiar with the Blackfoot, and the manifold ways open to Blackfoot women to acquire power. In particular, I will refer to Alice Kehoe, whose approach is grounded in the Blackfoot sacred realm and is backed by extensive ethnographic research. While these perspectives do not provide the view available to insiders of the culture, they do provide alternative perspectives to counterbalance the early, male-oriented, Blackfoot historiography.

Among the buffalo-hunting First Nations, the adoption of horses during the eighteenth century reduced women's role in the hunt, including their sacred role in attracting the buffalo. However, women's traditional occupations still contributed significantly to their families' well-being and wealth. They were the principal butchers and processors of pemmican, a mixture of dried meat, fat and berries that was the main nutrient of the Plains First Nations and a prized exchange commodity. Moreover, by performing specialized services as midwives, healers, tanners, and manufacturers of lodges, clothes, and moccasins, including quillwork and beading, women enhanced their individual prestige. These activities allowed them to accumulate wealth, a key marker of power among the Blackfoot. Women who provided warriors with moccasins to take on the warpath, which could amount to ten or fifteen pairs per journey, were rewarded handsomely. Dempsey notes that after a successful raid at enemy camps during the early 1850s, Red Crow, the celebrated Kainai chief, sent a horse to the woman who had made his moccasins.[68]

Blackfoot women owned the tepees in which they lived as well as their contents. When moving camp, therefore, it was women who pulled down the tepees and loaded them onto pack animals. When these were not available, women carried the loads themselves. Upon arrival at a new camp, they erected the tepees, collected wood, started the fires, and prepared meals. When compared with men's spectacular hunting and warring, these prosaic tasks might have created the impression that women's roles were devalued. An example of how First Nations women's contributions were seen within their own communities indicates that this was not the case. Matonabbee, a Chipewyan chief who was part Cree, and who accompanied explorer Samuel Hearne on a thousand-mile trek on foot from Prince of Wales Fort to the mouth of the Coppermine River in 1770–72, urged that women should be part of the expedition because:

> When all the men are heavy laden, they can neither hunt nor travel to any considerable distance; and in the case that they meet with success in hunting, who is to carry the produce of their labour? Women were made for labour; one of them can carry or haul, as much as two men can do. They also pitch our tents, make and mend our clothing, keep us warm at night; and, in fact, there is no such thing as traveling any considerable distance, or for any length of time [. . .] without their assistance.[69]

Matonabbee's affirmation of the worth of women's work was expressed to counter the Hudson's Bay Company's decision to send a male-only contingent on the expedition, deemed too harsh for women to undertake. For Matonabbee, men were at a disadvantage without the assistance of women. Clark Wissler similarly emphasized a positive view of women's roles:

> In pre-reservation days a woman was judged by the number and quality of skins she had dressed, the baskets she had woven, or the pottery moulded; and her renown for such accomplishments might travel far. When by chance you met a woman who had distinguished herself, it was proper to address her in a manner to reveal your knowledge of her reputation, as "Grandmother, we are happy to look upon one whose hands were always busy curing fine skins."[70]

Through their activities, Blackfoot women honoured their nation, contributed to social reproduction, and gained wealth and prestige. Their achievements, however, do not feature as prominently as those of men in the year counts or winter counts, the pictographic records on which Blackfoot *his*torians recorded one salient event each year. One remarkable exception is the Many Guns Winter Count, compiled in the first decade of the twentieth century, a compilation of oral stories in the public domain dating back to 1831. For the years following the cessation of warring, this winter count recorded the names of Holy Women who vowed to put-up the Sun Dance.[71] As a genre, however, winter counts are more concerned with the martial deeds of men; when they mention women, it is mostly to record their being killed, often by their own husbands. Bull Plume's Piegan winter count (1770–1923), for example, only mentions a woman in the entry for 1880, the year "When 'Holy Milk' killed his wife." The rest of the winter count is occupied with *his*tory (my emphasis). In similar fashion, Big Brave's Winter Count only mentions women (three entries) to record their being killed, two at the hands of their own husbands.[72]

PART II — THE GRAMMAR OF BLACKFOOT LEADERSHIP DRESS

Violence against women as recorded in winter counts appears to have been an accepted norm. George Bird Grinnell, an American naturalist who became a friend of the Blackfoot and recorded their oral knowledge in his pioneering *Blackfoot Lodge Tales*, noted:

> The man had absolute power over his wife. Her life was in his hands, and if he had made a payment for her [to her father], he could do with her about as he pleased . . . women who behaved themselves were well treated and received a good deal of consideration. Those who were light-headed, or foolish, or obstinate and stubborn were sometimes badly beaten.[73]

Other observations of women's position *vis-à-vis* their husbands agree with this view. In 1832 Catlin described them as "slaves of their husbands"[74]; and according to McClintock (*c*.1896), "Of necessity women took the place of servants in the capacity of wives."[75] Reading Blackfoot women's dress as reflecting their status is instructive because it reveals the heterogeneous social positions occupied by women. It throws into relief the existence of a social hierarchy of women that precludes their being homogenized and reduced to a common denominator. Moreover, there is evidence, most apparent in the internal contradictions within the extant documentation, that the positions open to Blackfoot women were fluid and complex. These contradictions, and comparisons between different sources, enrich the portrayal of Blackfoot women during this era.

The sacred domain was not the only realm in which Blackfoot women could gain respect. Blackfoot social stratification provided advantages for elite women. Daughters of wealthy families entered into politically significant marriage alliances and brought important connections to their husbands and parents. To be worthy of such a woman, a man required wealth and prestige. She would likely become his *o'totamin.ai* (Sits-beside-him wife, or principal wife).[76] According to Grinnell, when receiving visitors a wife was expected not to talk, but merely listen and attend to the fire.[77] However, as he noted, the Sits-beside-him wife was "allowed at informal gatherings to take a whiff at the pipe [. . .] and to participate in the conversation." She also exercised control over secondary wives and would not take part in lowly tasks.[78] She would preside over food preparation, but would only serve distinguished visitors. Other evidence suggests that a principal wife was free to express her opinion, even when in opposition to that of her husband, something that lesser wives could not do.[79] In his journal for 1794–95, Duncan M'Gillivray claimed that "notwithstanding the boundless authority of the men, — a few of the other sex wear the Breeches."[80] We can surmise that favoured daughters (*minipuka*) of elite families, who were not expected to participate in menial work while growing up, would have featured among the privileged few. There is little documentation to explain why some women, were called *nina.ki* (chief woman), except that they were "treated like a man."[81] At the other end of the scale, wives ranking lower in the hierarchical order worked harder and had fewer privileges, especially those who might have been taken from enemy camps by force and who would occupy the most abject positions within their adoptive bands.

Apart from the foregoing possibilities for women to wield power within the Blackfoot worldview, women played an important, albeit scantily documented diplomatic role in intertribal peace treaties. In 1871, the Bad Guns band led by Siksika chief Agwmaxkayi (Many Swans) met with the bands of four Cree leaders, including head chief Sweetgrass, to smoke the peace pipe. While the story as recounted centres on Many Swans, his principal wife, Akai'niskimyaki (Many Buffalo Stones Woman), emerges as the principal Siksika advocate of the treaty. After a missionary delivered the initial gifts of tobacco to her husband, she persuaded him to agree to the treaty. Moreover, she travelled unarmed to the enemy camp, and holding aloft the Union Jack, led the four Cree chiefs and many of their followers back to her band's camp. The flag, obtained from the HBC, functioned as an intertribal peace symbol. We can assume that for such an important occasion Akai'niskimyaki would have worn her best dress, but only her husband's dress merited description. It was a military-style uniform (red coat with brass buttons and gold braid), recently presented to him during a visit to an HBC trade post.[82]

Interrogating historical records on the experiences of women is complicated by a dearth of information. As is evident in the previous paragraph, women are silenced in the documentation. Often they are merely referred to as someone's wife, or someone's daughter.[83] Whilst leading men received lavish gifts from traders, including military-style uniforms, women were given nothing of the sort. One informant claimed that women only received "buttons" as presents from traders.[84] Yet, Kehoe claims that Blackfoot women exercised power in ways that were not understood, and therefore not reported, by the overwhelmingly male chroniclers on whom we rely for early information of the Blackfoot. The extent to which women's contribution to their communities became devalued as a result of contact with whites has been the subject of much speculation. Having explored some of the ways through which Blackfoot women earned respect and status in what could be considered typical women's occupations, what follows focuses on Blackfoot women's acquisition of status in spheres that challenge common stereotypes.

There was no law to prevent Blackfoot women from going on the warpath and many are known to have gone on raids, while others achieved prestige through defensive action under enemy siege.[85] Pikuni women were known for their war exploits, while according to Imiten.a, Siksika women were "all cowards".[86] During the nineteenth century, Pi'tamakan (Running Eagle), a Pikuni, became the only known Blackfoot woman to have attained the status of war chief. She is credited with leading several successful horse raids on the Flathead herds west of the Rocky Mountains. According to Abenaki author and storyteller Joseph Bruchac, Running Eagle Falls in Glacier Park marks the place where Running Eagle sought "to gain the power of a vision". This occurred after enemies killed her husband. She returned from her vision quest ready to become a war chief.[87] Pi'tamakan was first named Weasel Woman as a child. In recognition of her achievements, she later received the honour of a male name (Pi'tamakan),[88] bestowed during Ookaan when she counted *coup* after "going twice into the enemy's camp and taking six horses."[89] Among the Blackfoot, no other woman is known to have led war parties, and no female images have emerged to counterbalance that of the iconographic male warrior on horseback. According to Weasel Tail, who narrated details of Running Eagle's life to John Ewers, during raids, her dress consisted of "men's leggings, a sort of undershirt doubled over like a diaper, a woman's dress and a blanket coat."[90] The comparison of the undershirt with a diaper conveys a less-than dignified image, one hardly befitting a leader of war parties. The source of the story is a man who went with her on raids. He is credited with narrating the details to Weasel Tail, John Ewers' Kainai informant. In his historical novel about the life of Running Eagle, James Schultz simply notes that she wore "men's clothing when on a raid" and women's dress at home. All accounts agree that Running Eagle achieved distinction in war, a field of endeavour in which not many women participated. In Schultz's narrative, she counts *coup* three times, including for the taking of "a gun from the man she herself killed."[91] Although no description of the dress and regalia she wore when counting *coup* is extant, it is to be expected that it would have rivalled those of her male counterparts who had achieved similar honours.

Other women who did not court warring were not exempt from engaging with the enemy through defensive action.[92] In her study of captive women in the Canadian West, Sarah Carter notes that, when very young, Calf Old Woman, a Siksika, earned the honour to "sit as a warrior in Blackfoot councils". She had been captured by her father's killer: "While they were riding together she stabbed him with his own knife, tossed his body from the horse's back, scalped him, cut off his right arm, picked up his gun and rode back to her people [. . .] chased most of the way, she returned with the three greatest trophies a warrior can wrest from an enemy."[93] She went on to marry Old Sun, a respected leader. Actions such as those of Calf Old Woman would have given her the right to count *coup* and to wear a hair-fringed suit. Viewed against stereotypical roles, women's participation in war may appear to be transgressive. However, it is easy to understand why women would engage in war when their own survival was at stake. Moreover, as Kehoe argues, Blackfoot practices provide for "autonomy" to be exercised by any living being, and "Competence is the outward justification for the exercise of autonomy."[94]

This is demonstrated by the existence of a category of women among the Blackfoot known as *ninauposkitzipxpe* (manly-hearted women), which ethnographers Oscar Lewis and Esther Goldfrank in 1939 documented among the Pikuni in Montana and the Kainai in Alberta, respectively. This social category survived colonization and its attendant cultural transformations.[95] According to Lewis, manly-hearted women were mature, married, and wealthy women who possessed traits such as "aggressiveness, independence, ambition, boldness and sexuality". The term "manly", Lewis argued, "does not refer to masculinity of appearance or sexual behavior". On the contrary, manly-hearted women, he claimed, were "passionate women". Some of them had been *minipuka* (favoured children) and became *ninauposkitzipxpe* (manly-hearted women) in their later years. Lewis notes that they "excelled in feminine occupations", as tanners, seamstresses, and beaders. He also notes that at the time of his study "the six most important medicine women on the reserve [were] all in the manly-hearted group." Four of these women, he added, were also *minipuka*. Manly-hearted women exercised economic power independently from their husbands and possessed an "ability to control social situations." They were set apart from other women by virtue of the fact that "they wore well-tanned skins, expensive buckskin dresses decorated with elk-teeth, and fine leggings embroidered with porcupine quills". Lewis argued that manly-hearted women were viewed by the Piegan as "deviants" because of their lack of compliance with the established standards of female behaviour, which "laud meekness and docility and require women to relegate themselves to the background of Piegan social life."[96]

Lewis's contention that manly-hearted women were deviants was refuted by Ruth Benedict, who supervised the studies of Lewis and Goldfrank. Benedict argued that the Blackfoot ethos Lewis described placed a strong emphasis on self-assertiveness. She claimed that expecting "women reared in such an atmosphere to be mild and submissive is too great a demand to make — and so you get [. . .] manly hearted women."[97] In other words, Benedict did not see manly-hearted women as being transgressive, but rather she saw Blackfoot worldviews as being conducive to such behaviour.[98] Lewis's contention has the effect of denying the very premise that his evidence establishes — his study demonstrates that manly-hearted women were not outcasts, their role evidently being within the parameters of Blackfoot practices. However, Lewis remained convinced that the important social, economic and religious roles played by Pikuni women did not prevent the Pikuni from placing "a premium on masculinity", encouraging "male dominance". He argued that this dominance was evident in the "bride price, preferred patrilocal residence, the double standard and wife beating, the formal age grades and institutionalized friendship relationships that exist only for men, the exclusive participation of men in the tribal government and the channelization of prestige to the men."[99] However, as he himself noted, manly-hearted women also exercised power and gained prestige, although they did not occupy positions within the tribal government.

Lewis, like many of his white male predecessors, identified ways in which male power was exercised to the exclusion of women. His generalization, however, required him to explain the existence of the group of manly-hearted women. He solved this challenge by claiming them to be "deviants". Nevertheless, manly-hearted women possessed personal power that transcended local and even western notions of gender difference. That they should have stood out through the finery of their dress restates the importance of dress as a marker of power. Blackfoot women's dress, like that of their male counterparts, appears to signify power within a system of values that recognized multiple paths to achievement for both men and women, and thence to wealth and prestige. These specific examples of the opportunities open to women in Blackfoot culture indicate that those depictions of women as mere slaves of men fall far short of presenting a reliable perspective.

These contrasting views of Blackfoot women's experience need to be more fully researched before a clearer picture emerges. Mourning practices, for example, are revealing: men would cut some of their own hair, "going without leggings, and for the loss of a son [not for a wife or daughter, they would] sometimes scarify their legs". By contrast, women would cut their hair short to mourn all relations, and for their husbands, sons and other males in the family — but not for a daughter — they would sometimes cut a portion of a finger "and always scarify the calves of their legs".[100] The disparity in these practices tells its own story, but one that eludes interpretation by outsiders. Could it be that women did not require special sacrifices to reach their destination after death? Or, could it be that their loss was viewed as less significant? Despite contrasting and sometimes incomplete accounts, the existence of the noun *nina.ki* to designate women as chiefs, plus the ready acceptance by the Blackfoot of the authority of Queen Victoria as the "Great Mother", suggests that perhaps, as Kehoe has argued, "anyone can aspire to becoming more powerful." In light of this, we should strive for a better understanding of the ways in which women gained access to power, a difficult task given the inbuilt bias and the many erasures of Blackfoot women from the extant documentation.

The dress worn by Blackfoot elite men and women could be read by insiders of the culture as inscribing the achievements of the wearer across sacred and secular realms. The Blackfoot origin stories explain the ideologies encoded in dress and define the prerequisites for wearing certain markers of distinction. While according to the sacred stories there is a stark contrast among the characteristics that the Blackfoot most appreciated in men and women — bravery *versus* chastity and modesty — dress practices lead us to other categories beyond this dichotomy. Two examples are the categories of *minipuka* (favoured son or daughter), and *ninauposkitzipxpe* (manly-hearted women), both distinguished by the finery of their dress.

The restrictions that applied to the dress of the Blackfoot societies, the *I-kun-uh'-kah-tsi*, whereby leaders of each society were set apart from lesser members through markers inscribed on their dress, demonstrates its capacity to encode messages and meanings for those able to interpret them. Although male dress dominates the documentation of these societies, it is well to remember that in order to join the most respected of all societies, the Horns, it was a precondition that a couple (usually, but not exclusively, husband and wife) should be initiated together.

Dress prohibitions also tell a story of social stratification based on achievement that is defined according to a hierarchy of deeds, and not according to gender. When women such as Running Eagle achieved war feats, these were measured in accordance with the same standards that applied to their male counterparts. However, less information is available on women who achieved in "womanly" occupations. Apart from "Medicine women", whom Lewis described as belonging to the manly-hearted category, we are left thirsting for more information on the lives of women, especially the opportunities that might have been open to them to exercise power within their communities.

5
Fur Trade, Success, and Dress

Another dimension needs to be added to the meanings attached to Blackfoot dress in accordance with their stories: the adoption of dress traits due to intertribal exchange. As Maximilian noted in the 1830s, Blackfoot men's shirts had incorporated the Assiniboine disk, even though, according to the story of Scarface, the design had been handed down from Natosi, the Sun. These circumstances reveal the mechanisms whereby dress traits could be appropriated and become "Blackfoot" — if not in the literal view of outsiders such as Maximilian, at least according to the Blackfoot perspective. As Benedict Anderson argued in his pioneering *Imagined Communities*, nations construct their imaginary so as to establish their uniqueness; the Blackfoot stories served that purpose, but dress itself also played a part. Dress exchanges in intertribal encounters showcased the artistry of women, but they also served to disseminate techniques and designs widely. One of the Blackfoot painted by Bodmer in 1833, for example, was clad in a Navajo blanket and wore a silver cross (see Figure 5.1 CP: the man, wearing a blanket with blue and white stripes, stands in profile behind a group of dogs). The man had been living among the Hidatsa in the Upper Missouri so that he could have acquired his prize blanket from traders who brought it to the Hidatsa village or by travelling south himself. Apart from diplomacy and trade, during which participants exchanged gifts, including items of dress, war captures also account for the shared characteristics between Blackfoot dress and that of other First Nations. The meanings attached to Blackfoot dress thus reflected a history of intertribal diplomacy and war that set the basis that would later regulate their exchanges with European, Canadian, and American fur traders, who observed the established precedent, adjusting their trading protocols to First Nations practices predating European contact.[1]

The sartorial aspects of intercultural diplomacy provide a material trail that reflects ongoing intertribal negotiation and contestation, even though the precise circumstances in which each specific trait was adopted are missing from the record. The Blackfoot buckskin, in particular, affords us a view of continuity within an overall context of cultural transformation; it continues to be used in a ceremonial manner to this day. This chapter views dress transformation attendant upon Blackfoot–white contact during the fur trade era as an extension of Blackfoot intertribal diplomacy predating it. It utilizes the materiality of dress in order to analyze continuity within the transformations attendant upon these intercultural encounters. Rather than viewing the adoption of European dress as a sign of acculturation — or flow of hegemonic practices in one direction — it proposes that this process of transformation is more apt to be described as transculturation,[2] whereby both sides of the encounter undergo adjustment.

Many terms have been coined to refer to these cultural borrowings, including, as Peter Burke notes: "appropriation, exchange, reception, transfer, negotiation, resistance, syncretism, acculturation, enculturation, inculturation, interculturation, transculturation, hybridization (*mestizaje*), creolization and the interpenetration of cultures."[3] This multiplicity of terms, Burke argues, reveals "a new conception of culture as *bricolage*, in which the process of appropriation and assimilation is not marginal but central."[4] It is worth restating that despite their heterogeneity, cultures maintain a coherence not easily threatened by cultural borrowings, what Burke calls "the creativity of reception and the renegotiation of meanings." The redeployment of borrowings — in this case European materials and items of dress — to a new context (e.g. the Blackfoot bands) gives them different meanings to a degree that dispels the notion that "what was received was the same as what was given."[5]

INTERTRIBAL DIPLOMACY AND WAR

Intercultural exchange in the northern Plains did not begin with white arrival. Walter McClintock titled his book on the Blackfoot *The Old North Trail*, after a horse and travois trail that ran from Calgary to the south, "inhabited by people with dark skins", and narratives of Blackfoot travellers have them visiting as far as Taos towns.[6] The Blackfoot also traded at the Mandan earth-lodge villages on the Upper Missouri. As Ewers notes, evidence of trade there was first documented in 1738 by Pierre Gaultier de Varennes, Sieur de la Vérendrye. He reported that the agriculturalist Mandans were not only exchanging their produce for the product of the chase of buffalo-hunting First Nations; they were also trading in "guns, powder, ball, knives, axes, and awls" from the Assiniboine. It was from the Assiniboine that la Vérendrye had first heard of the Mandans. By the time Lewis and Clark and the Corps of Discovery ascended the Missouri River and spent the 1804–5 winter with the Mandan, their trade network had expanded to include Europeans and Euro-Americans. Traders from the North West Company and the HBC, as well as businessmen from St. Louis had penetrated the villages' networks, adding their presence to that of the Crows, Assiniboines, Cheyennes, Kiowas, and Arapahoes. Intertribal rivalries, which the captains recorded at length, placed a premium on guns and ammunition, which Lewis and Clark promised to deliver by trade.[7]

The Great Plains had always been a contested terrain whose occupiers often spoke more than one language and, when required, communicated through sign language, their *lingua franca*.[8] The visual messages encoded in their dress, like sign language, could be recognized beyond tribal boundaries.[9] The use of hair locks to adorn shirts and horned headdresses, for example, marked those who had earned the right to wear them in accordance with the ideologies of each community. However, their wear was circumscribed to those who had attained the right through deeds of courage and daring. The complex meanings encoded in dress, although specific to each First Nation, would have been available to those with an insider perspective, or emic view, which not only friends possessed, but also enemies who could distinguish the stature of a warrior through his dress. Dress featured as the gift of choice during trade, visiting, peace-treaty meetings, and even during meetings with enemies at times of truce, horses being also highly regarded in similar contexts. As the story of Scarface illustrates, presenting a worthy visitor with a buckskin suit reflected the host's generosity, which elevated the social stature of the giver.

Among the Blackfoot, the acquisition of war shirts and war bonnets as trophies of war was considered a *coup*, to be publicly recounted at key moments during rituals and ceremonies. These captured items encoded power and were as dutifully cared for as their local counterparts. These acquisitions increased the complexity of dress that was already the product of myriad combinations and permutations of shape, colour and design, all of which bespoke the cultural and geographical specificities of each First Nation. Manufacturing techniques and decorative patterns thus spread beyond tribal boundaries.

Intertribal kinship established through "capture, marriage, and adoption" would have increased the spread of dress traits.[10] When women from enemy tribes were captured and taken as wives by their captors, they brought with them manufacturing and design techniques that would have been inserted into their new locales. In their historical novel *Sun God's Children*, Schultz and Donaldson include a dialogue between two Blackfoot men, one of whom, aware that captured Blackfoot women live among their Crow enemies, wonders if these women would be happy. His comrade responds: "Had we not in our tribe Crow women, Snake women, Kutenai women, Cree Women and Women of the West-Side tribes, whom our warriors had captured, and with their children, plenty of food, good clothes, were they not happy?[11] This fictional portrayal rings true. The cross-cultural presence within the two men's band speaks volumes of the fluidity of Plains identity, and thus, of Plains dress. To complicate this picture further, intermarriage that did not involve forceful capture was another means to enlarge cross-cultural exchange. There is a lacunae in the scholarship on intermarriage within the different First Nations of the Plains, voluntary or otherwise, for its contribution to the fluidity of Plains cultures, which is generally obscured in homogenizing tribal-centred histories.

Blackfoot men and women are known to have travelled far from their domains in search of adventure — a cherished pursuit for them. The little-known (and perhaps apocryphal) Blackfoot vignette "How the Blackfeet got the Pinto Ponies"[12] narrates how two youths went to the Southwest, spent more than a year away from their camp, and earned seats at the tribal council after returning with the first "spotted ponies" ever seen by their people. They had stolen these ponies, together with "beautiful wooden saddles decorated with high horns and silver, and silver-encrusted bridles." According to the story, they also stole *sombreros* embroidered with silver thread, one of which was ceremonially offered to the Sun during Ookaan (Sun Dance). This narrative illustrates both the workings of cultural appropriation and the adaptability of material culture. According to this account, horses, saddles, and hats were re-inscribed with Blackfoot meanings by attaching value to their acquisition and incorporating them into Blackfoot practice as signifiers of status. Moreover, by offering a *sombrero* to the Sun, the appropriation transcended the secular domain, attaining the status of a sacred offering. It is evident from this narrative that the acquisition of non-Blackfoot items of material culture was highly prized and not seen as contamination. This further explains the hybrid nature of material culture throughout the Plains. The common view of war trophies — including dress items — as symbols of power, which the vignette illustrates, provided a mechanism for the incorporation of non-Blackfoot items of material culture into Blackfoot practice without incurring a loss in cultural coherence. Guns were treated in similar fashion, and the Blackfoot considered obtaining them through war an achievement of the highest order. Whether Blackfoot networks extended to the Southwest — and other stories suggest that they did — intertribal networks carried trade items far from their places of origin.

Trade with, *inter alia*, Cree and Assiniboine bands during the early eighteenth century first provided the Blackfoot with an array of European items that increased the complexity of their dress designs, including glass beads, brass tacks, bells, stroud (coarse woven cloth), blankets, and hats.[13] More significantly, the Blackfoot obtained their first firearms through these middle-men during an era when they refused to undertake the perilous journey to Fort York themselves. Survival depended on their readiness to incorporate new technologies. Armed with guns and provided with horses (also obtained through intertribal networks), the Blackfoot were able to defeat their Shoshone enemies and to drive them south, having previously been unable to resist their northward advance.

The cultural transformation attendant upon the spread of horses illustrates better than any other example the spread of cultural hybridity in the Plains. Among the Blackfoot, horses became the most conspicuous markers of status and a means for social advancement regardless of birth, measuring wealth and, by extension, their owners' power. Consequently, they were highly coveted war trophies. The Spaniards, who first introduced horses to the Southwest, limited the right to ride on horseback to those considered of noble status. In the hands of First Nations peoples of the Plains, horses became a leveller of social difference. Moreover, among the Blackfoot, horses were absorbed into an economy of the sacred that followed Blackfoot worldviews; they became signifiers imbued with Blackfoot meanings. For special occasions, horses were caparisoned with elaborate costumes including feathers, beaded cruppers, and martingale chest ornaments (used mostly by women).[14] Some horses were also painted with symbols that recounted the owner's war feats. Thus they complemented the war shirt and the story robe as records of achievement.[15] European goods contributed to the complexity of Blackfoot dress even before they gained direct access to the fur trade.

Fur Trade Captains

The era ushered in by the fur trade is generally considered to be a high point of Plains cultures, a period of florescence. This is particularly evident in the adornment of Blackfoot dress. For the Blackfoot, who first obtained European goods through Cree and Assiniboine middle-men, direct access became available when British (HBC) and Canadian (Northwest Company) posts were established within their reach during the late eighteenth century.[16] The conduct of the fur trade at these trading forts was conditioned by competition between the two companies, and from 1830 onwards — when they joined forces — by competition from American traders.[17] In 1831, the Americans built a post on the Missouri River, where the Blackfoot began trading buffalo robes, dry provisions, and horses.[18]

Even though they coveted firearms and other European goods, the Blackfoot at first reacted violently to the establishment of trade posts within their territories. Intertribal trade could provide these goods without trespass on their territory. Preventing enemies from obtaining firearms through trade was another key consideration. Although this dual imperative rarely obtained in practice, alliances between First Nations such as the Blackfoot and traders eventually blossomed. Traders often secured customers by entering into familial relationships with headmen who could secure them the trade of their followers, a common aspect of the European fur trade that Sylvia Van Kirk documented in her pioneering *Many Tender Ties: Women in Fur Trade Society, 1670–1870*.[19] The networks that elite First Nations women opened up to their fur trader husbands served to create a context of cooperation and mutual benefit for which Richard White coined the term "middle ground". This middle ground, White argues, was best documented in official encounters, but it originated from daily encounters that required solution to immediate problems revolving "around basic issues of sex, violence, and material exchange."[20] The middle ground also operated as a catalyst for cultural transformation for both parties in the encounter. Of interest here is the relationship between dress and power within this middle ground.

As White notes, besides the mutual benefit of fur traders and their customers, conflict might arise at any moment at trading posts. It could erupt between the posts' occupants and their customers, or between enemy First Nations encountering one another at a trading post. Fur traders living in small numbers in remote locations from European settlements could fall prey to bands resenting their presence within their domains or from groups with grievances against the traders. Moreover, fur traders depended on their customers, not only for profit, but also for their very survival. Apart from pelts and furs, First Nations supplied them with horses for travelling and hunting, and also with provisions. Pemmican, a dry compound of meat, berries and fat, sustained traders during long trips and during the winter months when fresh buffalo meat became scarce near their posts.[21] Moreover, since it was in the interest of traders to avoid disruptions of trade occasioned by intertribal conflict, they mediated to keep the peace between their customers. In 1831, Kenneth McKenzie, a "northern" trader who later joined the American Fur Company, brokered a formal peace between the Blackfoot and the Assiniboine that made it possible for the former to trade at Fort Union, inside Assiniboine territory. Such a truce was temporary. The Blackfoot-speaking First Nations and the Assiniboine shared a history of broken treaties. Many lives, not to mention profits, would be placed in jeopardy when peace accords either were not in place or failed to be honoured. It was also in the interest of First Nations peoples to secure access to the fur trade. They had come to depend on European goods, especially guns and ammunition, indispensable to avoid becoming the victims of better-armed enemies. Moreover, items such as kettles, knives, blankets, and even glass beads and paints gradually replaced traditional materials that required more time and effort to produce.

Competition maintained the middle ground by forcing traders to offer better products, prices and conditions. Elaborate trading rituals observing indigenous reciprocity practices were a means to attract trade, and became normative prior to trade taking place.[22] The leaders of trading parties presented fort factors with gifts of horses and manufactured items, including items of dress.²³ Traders reciprocated with gifts of liquor, tobacco, and military-style suits, the latter reserved for leaders of large trading parties. Traders expected that band leaders would prevent their followers from taking their furs to their competitors, to ensure that they traded in peace, and to guarantee that they repaid any cash advances received from the traders. When these expectations were not fulfilled, the gifts were held back.²⁴ In 1833, the Pikuni head chief Mehkskeme-Sukahs (Iron Shirt) presented the trader David Mitchell of the American Fur Company with a scarlet uniform that English traders had recently given him, in order to signify to the Americans his preparedness to favour them with his trade in future.²⁵ In such manner, whites were drawn into the economy of transfer — acculturation flowed in two directions. The military uniforms were readily incorporated as markers of Blackfoot status. Leaders were quick to adopt them, but to those who expected Indians to look like the stereotyped Indians, the military uniform represented a sign of acculturation. John Ewers posits that Maximilian directed Bodmer to paint his portraits of First Nations peoples wearing native dress, in preference to the military-style uniforms given to them as gifts by fur traders.²⁶ Between August and September of 1833, Bodmer executed a panoramic view of the encampment of the three Blackfoot First Nations that had come to trade at Fort McKenzie (see Figure 5.1 CP).

Recorded encounters between First Nations peoples, explorers, and traders often describe the normative giving away of presents consisting of items of dress, among other gifts. Thus, a coat and a gun counted among the presents that Henry Kelsey presented to the leader of the Naywatame poets in 1691.²⁷ When they formalized a peace treaty with the Mandans, Lewis and Clark acknowledged "one chief of each town" with a gift of "a flag, a medal with the likeness of the president of the United States, a uniform coat, hat and feather." They gave so-called second chiefs medals "representing some domestic animals, and a loom for weaving"; and "third chiefs [. . .] medals with the impressions of a farmer sowing grain".²⁸

Presenting gifts of dress to their customers was a well-established ceremonial in the fur trade. In 1763, a typical HBC's "Captains' Outfit", reserved for "far away Indians" who came to trade at York Factory, comprised the following items:

> A coarse cloth coat, either red or blue, lined with baize, with regimental cuffs and collar. The waistcoat and breeches are of baize: the suit is ornamented with broad and narrow orris lace of different colours; a white or checked shirt; a pair of yarn stockings tied below the knee with worsted garters; a pair of English shoes. The hat is laced and ornamented with feathers of different colours. A worsted sash tied around the crown, an end hanging out on each side down to the shoulders. A silk handkerchief is tucked by a corner into a

loops [sic] behind; with these decorations it is put on the captain's head and completes his dress.[29]

The military uniform was a *faux* copy; lieutenants received an even more "inferior suit". These gifts can be read in terms of a European desire to impose their practices and values, or to see their own image mirrored in the "savages". In respect of the US Government, Viola links the gifts of clothes bestowed during diplomatic meetings to the desire to turn Indians into whites.[30] From another perspective, these sumptuary goods served a symbolic function that recognized local band hierarchies, their bestowal being concordant with long-standing intertribal diplomatic practices.

These well-documented rituals began with the earliest encounters between explorers and First Nations in the East.[31] Within the context of the fur trade, their grammar reflected power hierarchies on both sides of the encounter, with pride of place being accorded to fort factors on one side, and trade captains on the other. Although profit, rather than politics, was the driving force of the fur trade, elaborate trading rituals, as James Miller argues, "demonstrated European adjustment to Aboriginal ways."[32] Despite the manifest inappropriateness of stockings, silk handkerchiefs, and English shoes, the military dress of trading leaders contained some potency. It was recognized as a signifier of status that bridged the intercultural divide.

Alexander Henry the Younger described a trading visit by the Pikuni in 1810 that commenced with the fort factor greeting the arriving bands, who were led by the principal man or band chief, followed by others in order of "rank or precedence, derived from the number of scalps taken in war."[33] The trade captain presented one of his best horses and some buffalo robes to the factor as a gift. In reciprocation, it was customary for factors to give trade captains flags, military double-breasted jackets, and top hats decorated with eagle plumes.[34] These gifts — not readily available to non-elites — were henceforth incorporated as part of the sartorial trappings of a Blackfoot elite. Pre-existing mechanisms for adopting foreign components into Blackfoot dress practices paved the way for the adoption of the trade captain's uniform. Exchanging gifts, especially buckskin suits, during friendly intertribal meetings and peace treaty parlays was a long established custom. With increased white contact, the gift of a military uniform followed this pattern.

It would nevertheless be misleading to assume that traders routinely recognized power hierarchies among their customers. Gifts of dress items, spirituous liquor, and tobacco were an incentive to trade. Consequently, they could be bestowed on those who could supply the desired supply of furs, whether chiefs or not. A fur trader from the Northwest Company complained that "after making the father a chief [by giving him presents before trade], you are sometimes obliged to do the same thing with his son in order to secure his hunt, for the former has not the power to secure it for you."[35] This journal entry indicates that First Nations were adept at negotiating with traders, and that traders were willing to present the sartorial trappings of a chief according to their business needs. Such an attitude was perhaps a portent of things that would follow the imposition of full white hegemony. That traders referred to the bestowing of uniforms as "making a chief", incorrectly suggests that band authority was subject to traders' approval. Lewis and Clark used the same language when presenting leaders with gifts during their epic voyage. An entry for 29 October 1904 records a list of "chiefs who were made-to-day". The gifts given to the principal Mandan leader, however, disappointed his followers who had expected "large presents" from the explorers.[36]

It was earlier noted that trade rituals had the potential to bolster the authority of band leaders by giving them access to goods they could distribute among their followers, and thus to fulfil their reciprocal obligations. As such, fur trade alliances did have an effect upon the internal politics of their customers. However, white favouritism could also backfire. In 1833, a dispute arose after traders presented Bear Chief, a Pikuni leader, with "a double-barreled shotgun [. . .] a beautiful new uniform and a red felt hat". Irate that their leaders were not equally treated, the Kainai trading at the post killed Bear Chief's nephew in retaliation.[37] Likewise, when traders presented a chief's uniform to a lesser leader, they could bring the scorn of the bands to bear upon the recipient. In 1866, Isapo-muxica (Crowfoot), then a minor Siksika leader, saved a group of traders from impending death at the hands of Big Swan (another Siksika leader) and his followers. In gratitude, when Crowfoot next visited their fort, traders presented him with "a British flag, a chief's uniform of scarlet cloth, and other presents"[38] — gifts customarily reserved for head chiefs. Crowfoot's friendly relations with traders would play a role in reserving a privileged position for him in years to come. In 1877, during negotiations with the Dominion leading to the signing of Treaty Seven, Crowfoot was accorded an unprecedented position as head negotiator. His name took precedence over other head chiefs on the treaty document.[39]

The custom of presenting military uniforms to leaders was still observed in 1870, when two Siksika chiefs (including Agwmaxkayi or Many Swans), were persuaded to trade at the Hudson's Bay Company's post at Fort Edmonton, rather than at the American Fort Whoop-Up, receiving, among other gifts, "complete uniforms — red coats with brass buttons and gold braid, pants, shirts, and silk top hats decorated with red and blue plumes".[40] Notably, by 1871 these uniforms had become standard dress at intertribal peace meetings. That year, Many Swans embodied the workings of transculturation as he rode to negotiate a peace agreement with four Cree leaders and their followers. On the hide of his white horse, he displayed his war deeds, drawn in red paint "loot, gun-loot, deeds, men killed". He wore on this occasion the military uniform that traders in Edmonton had given to him the previous year (see Figure 6.1 for a reserve era example of the military uniform).[41]

The adoption of Western items of clothing and decoration so evident in photographs of the late nineteenth and the early twentieth centuries reflects a kaleidoscope of individual tastes and imagination.[42] The Blackfoot adapted European garments and modified them to become "Indian"; vests were beaded with intricate patterns; hats were decorated with feathers; HBC blankets were turned into capotes, a long-sleeved coat; beaded bands were sewn on blankets for decoration; silver peace medals and pocket watches, when available, adorned the ensemble. At one level, the adoption of European dress can be interpreted as a sign of acculturation, or the displacement of Blackfoot dress. At another, it can be seen as the appropriation of European clothing and its re-deployment as Blackfoot dress. The second interpretation would not assume that wearing European dress *ipso facto* signalled an acceptance of European values, and therefore as proof of the much-vaunted "disappearance of the Indian". Such an inference would be based on a myth of authenticity that devalued the present in favour of a romanticized past.

BLACKFOOT WOMEN AND THE FUR TRADE

The fur trade gave Blackfoot women access to dress materials and items of adornment that offered practical advantages. Glass beads obviated labour intensive quillwork, and imitation elk teeth were easier to obtain than the expensive original item. However, Blackfoot women are reported to have been more reticent to adopt European dress than their male counterparts. Rather, they incorporated new fabrics such as calico and trade cloth, and adorned their dress with beads, bells, and brass tacks following traditional dress patterns and designs.[43] Lines of quillwork were replaced by ribbons or beads, threaded so as to reproduce the original visual effect as can be appreciated in Bodmer's 1833 portrait of Stu-mick-o-súks (see "Chief of the Blood Indians", Figure 4.3 CP). Cloth materials such as stroud and wool flannel were also incorporated into existing designs. But there was no female counterpart for the military attire presented as a gift to the leaders of trading parties.

As mentioned, Alexander Henry the Younger's journals are amongst the earliest sources for information of the First Nations of the northwest Plains, including the Blackfoot (Piegan, Kainai and Siksika), Cree, Assiniboine, Sarcee and Gros Ventre. In his 1809 journal, Henry noted trading with two "tribes" of Blackfeet, one under the leadership of Painted Feather, and the other, which Henry names as the Cold Band, under the leadership of Gros Blanc. From the former, Henry invited "30 principal men, [and 40] heads of families" to come in to the trading establishment.[44] It appears that the Northwest Company only received one-third of all the Blackfoot trade, with their HBC neighbours capturing the other two thirds. Henry's journal makes no mention of gifts of military uniforms, although it is evident that he has a great regard for Painted Feather. Instead, twist tobacco and especially diluted "Blackfoot rum" were given as incentives to trade. No women are mentioned in Henry's account of the 1809 trading visit, although in his jurnal he refers to Blackfoot women as "a filthy set". It is not clear whether he refers to their morals or their personal hygiene. Henry noted that the dress of "some" Blackfoot women were "cleaned with white clay, and when trimmed with fringe and quill-work look tolerably well." This is all he has to say about women's dress. He also reported that their tents were kept clean.[45] However, in his assessment of gender relations, Henry declared Blackfoot women to be mere slaves of their husbands. Blackfoot men, he noted, offered their women to strangers "as they would bladders of grease, and often feel offended if their services are not accepted." Henry's comments all but ignore any appreciation of the role of women in the terms articulated by Chief Matonabbee. Although the latter agreed that hard labour was allocated to women, he interpreted that practice as signalling women's strengths, not as a sign, as indicated by Henry, of their being "held in slavery". The hospitality shown to white travellers among the Plains First Nations extended to the sexual realm, an area that most chroniclers acknowledge with some disgust, but that contemporary scholars relate to an "invitation to kinship".[46] As a cultural outsider, Henry was unappreciative of the ritualized nature of such hospitality, and underlined it as proof of debasement. His claim about the slavery of Blackfoot women is repeated in subsequent accounts, and has obscured other aspects of Blackfoot women's experience. Against Henry's view that Blackfoot men pushed their women onto strangers, Wissler argued that the "lending of wives [by the Blackfoot] was looked upon as a disgrace, or at least as irregular"; although he suggested that some women may have occupied abject positions, especially captured women from enemy bands.[47]

Catlin, whose 1832 portraits and letters described Blackfoot male leaders trading at Fort Union in flattering terms, was more circumspect in his comments regarding Blackfoot women. He described them generally as being "not handsome", although he described Eeh-nís-kim (The Crystal Stone), as having a "rather pleasing" countenance, "an uncommon thing amongst the Blackfeet" (see Figure 4.4 CP). Eeh-nís-kim was the youngest among Stu-mick-o-súks's six or eight wives. According to Catlin, she was "the last one taken under his guardianship". The chief smiled upon his young wife "with great satisfaction [and] he exempted her from the drudgeries of the camp [. . .] keeping her continually in the halo of his own person." He "watched and guarded her as the apple of his eye."[48] Women's presence during fur trade encounters does not usually elicit much comment in fur traders' journals. However, it seems remarkable that Catlin should have painted two Blackfoot women, especially when taking into account that he was to paint none other "except such as are decided by the chiefs to be worthy of such an honour". Of his other woman subject, Catlin only mentions her name, "Ah-kay-ee-pix-en, the woman who strikes many", and her dress, which is almost identical to that of Eeh-nís-kim: "a beautiful dress of the mountain-goat's skin, and her robe of the young buffalo's hide."[49] While Catlin contends that Blackfoot women were not handsome, his own portraits of the two Kainai women contradict his contention. In terms of women's power, as the chief's favourite *(ninauake)*, Eeh-nís-kim was treated with a great deal of consideration, and shared with elite men the privilege of being portrayed by Catlin, even if her position was dependent upon being the favourite wife of a powerful man.[50] We are left wondering about the connections of the other woman he painted, Ah-kay-ee-pix-en, The Woman Who Strikes Many. What gave the latter the privilege of being painted by Catlin? Her name certainly indicates that she was no ordinary woman. This, like many other questions pertaining to the roles occupied by Blackfoot women, must remain unanswered.

Blackfoot women, like the women of other buffalo-hunting First Nations, played a key role during the fur trade era. The increase in the number of wives taken by men in the Plains during this era is often related to an increased demand for the product of women's labour, in particular preparing tanned robes for the fur trade.[51] This explains why some Blackfoot men had in excess of ten wives, in a hierarchical arrangement where the principal wife occupied a privileged position in relation to the rest.[52] According to Oscar Lewis, "the native term for a wife lower than third or fourth means slave wife."[53]

Their relative absence from the documentation represents the major obstacle for scholars who attempt to write an inclusive history of First Nations women, and their role in diplomatic exchanges, both intertribal and intercultural. A point of departure can be the recognition that wherever Blackfoot men went, Blackfoot women went with them. Women may well have been excluded from certain political activities, but while men conducted their diplomatic rituals, women had also opportunities for women-exclusive gatherings. Even war was not outside the range of activities that Blackfoot women could embrace.

In relation to dress, and the transformation of Blackfoot dress during the two eras of this study, we are inevitably led to women, for women manufactured Blackfoot dress, and it is through their adoption of new styles and techniques that Plains dress became hybrid. It is therefore through women's labour that we can learn of women's own intertribal networks. Beginning with women's mobility that explorers documented since the early encounters with First Nations of the northern Plains, we can take it for granted that women's kinship ties extended not only beyond their bands, but also beyond their First Nations. The presence of women among peoples considered enemies of their own people speaks of a fluidity that is seldom discussed in band or tribal oriented histories predicated on the premise of homogeneity and distinctiveness. Historians must move beyond such band/tribal oriented perspectives, and embrace this fluidity of experience, which is hinted at in some primary documents, but never fully elucidated.

The first difficulty encountered when seeking to analyze the relationship between Blackfoot women and power in the nineteenth and early twentieth centuries is the scant attention paid to individual women, including elite women, in the extant representations of intercultural encounters. In 1871, when two Siksika leaders arrived to trade at the HBC post in Edmonton, the wife of one (Ninonista), who remains nameless in the documentation, took 100 skins to trade on behalf of a band member who could not make the trip in person. Ninonista's wife conducted her trade directly, and separately from that of her husband.

Moreover, the fur trade introduced a novel and significant intercultural role for First Nations women. Sylvia Van Kirk has emphasized the crucial intermediary roles played by First Nations women who entered into marriages *à la façon du pays* (after the custom of the country) with fur traders. These women brought not only their talents and labour into these partnerships, but also valuable family connections and expert local knowledge. Interracial marriages opened new roles for women as intermediaries or cultural brokers between the two worlds, as well as creating new living spaces (trading posts) where their dress suitably transformed to reflect their bicultural environment.

The figure of Natuyitsixina (Natawista or Holy Snake Woman), a Kainai from an elite family, looms large as the most influential Blackfoot woman within the middle ground of the American fur trade. In her *Frontier Diplomats*, Wischmann has provided an unsurpassed perspective of the life experiences of an elite Blackfoot woman during the fur trade era. Natuyitsixina married chief factor Alexander Culbertson during the early nineteenth century and for the next thirty years acted, now as an advocate for her people and family, now as a diplomat on behalf of whites. Her dress, alternating between indigenous and European styles, reflected her ambivalent position between two cultures.[54]

The ornithologist John James Audubon reported seeing Natuyitsixina, her Indian maid, her husband and two other Americans riding across the prairie "all dressed in Indian garb", including face painting. During the celebrations of a newly located Fort Lewis (to be re-named Fort Benton) in 1850, "Natawista, her fingers sparkling with emeralds and rubies, wore a splendid bright red silk dress purchased in St. Louis". During a ball in

Fur Trade, Success, and Dress

FIGURE 5.2 *Natawista Iksana, Blood woman, Alberta* [n.d.], Glenbow Archive, Calgary, Canada, NA-5014-1.

1851 she wore a gown "fringed and valanced according to European mode." At other times, she combined European dress with buckskin leggings, a clear reflection of her bicultural reality. In May 1875, having divorced her first husband and married another white trader, she wore a dress in "the Dolly Varden style":

> a large figured chintz just short enough to display the gorgeous stripes of balmoral petticoat which in its turn was also just short enough to show two very small feet clade [sic] in moccasins and a pair of leggings beautifully worked in beads. She also had on a heavy black velvet loose-fitting overcoat and over this, a most brilliant striped shawl, the stripes being about three inches broad and alternatively red, blue, green and red, with a narrow line of yellow between each color.

The Dolly Varden character from Charles Dickens' novel *Barnaby Rudge* is hardly the image one would expect to be applied to a Blackfoot woman living in the northwest Plains during the second half of the nineteenth century, even one from an elite family. The allusion illustrates the stock of familiar images against which Blackfoot women were judged.[55] The two worlds could not have been further apart, and yet, for most men who found themselves away from their familiar surroundings, First Nations women provided the only choice of partner. Moreover, Natuyitsixina's outfit, which she wore with beaded leggings and moccasins, illustrates the fluidity of dress during the fur trade era. It places high European fashion on a par with Plains dress, as one complementing the other, neither superior nor inferior, perhaps an indication of the operation of the middle ground. Natuyitsixina's bicultural experiences provide proof of the possibility and capacity of women to achieve power. She pushed the boundaries of both Blackfoot and white cultures and exerted influence on both sides of the cultural divide. Against the common allegation that First Nations women were thrown into the arms of traders in exchange for goods, her husband underwent as much scrutiny as that endured by Blackfoot husbands-to-be, and had to fulfil his obligations to her family before he was allowed to marry her according to tribal custom.[56] Years later, their marriage was confirmed by a Catholic wedding. Natuyitsixina secured for Culbertson the rich profits of her relatives' trade in buffalo robes. Moreover, she facilitated his success as an appointed special government agent to the Blackfoot by travelling with him among her own people. Natuyitsixina's trajectory stands as proof that lineage played a defining role in the achievement of status among the Blackfoot. For her services to the Commissioner of Indian Affairs, she received no gifts of clothing but rather a silver cup "lined with gold and engraved 'To the Second Pocahontas.'"[57] While this compliment might now be considered a dubious honour, given its allusion to a woman credited with aiding white colonizers, the gift unequivocally points up the importance of Natuyitsixina's ambassadorial role.

The diversity and complexity of elite Blackfoot dress and its dynamic transformations and individuality cannot be contained within a totalizing view. The specific deployments outlined above exemplify the nuanced meanings it conveyed to those with an emic view of Blackfoot culture in the intercultural arena. The creative and pragmatic appropriation of European dress codes by Blackfoot elites was a gradual process because of their relative isolation from major European settlements. This allowed them some space in which to absorb and redeploy new technologies and new items of dress in accordance with existing intertribal diplomatic practices The donning of military uniforms obtained as fur trade gifts should be seen as a continuation of intertribal observances, rather than as a sign of acculturation *per se* — that is, as an outgrowth of a long-established tradition of exchange that fostered dress hybridity. Blackfoot leaders coveted European dress in the same way that they coveted war trophies, and deployed it strategically to reclaim authority in the eyes of two constituencies: their trading partners and their followers.

Moreover, European garments that offered practical benefits were readily incorporated and often remodelled to suit local requirements. European technologies that improved on indigenous ones were likewise quickly adopted. The hybridity of Blackfoot dress resulted from the established practice of incorporating non-Blackfoot items that were deemed to be, not only more practical, but also aesthetically pleasing. On these terms, European dress widened the sartorial repertoire of an elite whose dress had already been hybridized through intertribal exchange. Rather than constituting a rupture, this acceptance can be interpreted as being concordant with the fluidity of pre-established dress practices.

Blackfoot dress was transformed in creative and pragmatic ways through intercultural networks, while remaining true to existing political relations and mechanisms for the acquisition of prestige among the bands. The reserve era posed different challenges. The increasing presence of traders in First Nations domains heralded the arrival or large numbers of settlers in the second half of the nineteenth century. The building of the railways brought about the demise of the bison herds. With this form of transportation, buffalo robes found their way into industrial uses. The scarcity of buffalo, whose fur was used for robes and moccasins, placed increased pressure on other sources of food and dress materials, such as deer and mountain goats. Scarcity of these traditional materials accelerated the transformation of Blackfoot dress. A new era of bureaucratic rule over the everyday life of the bands brought renewed demands for Blackfoot assimilation. As in previous stages of social and political change, dress can be analyzed in order to read Blackfoot responses to their new political environment.

6
The Longevity of Buckskins

By the closing decades of the nineteenth century, the wearing of European clothing by the Blackfoot was becoming commonplace on the three reserves in Alberta and the reservation in Montana. The scarcity of traditional clothing materials in the aftermath of the demise of the buffalo herds placed pressure on other game, especially elk, the skins of which were sought after materials for dress manufacture. Without the buffalo, Blackfoot self-sufficiency came to an end; their increased dependence on government rations and clothing handouts conspired with white efforts to accelerate their acculturation into white lifeways. The contact zone of the reserve as defined by treaty gave the colonizers unprecedented control over the everyday lives of the Blackfoot, and in time the ability to reconfigure tribal politics by exercising influence on leadership choices. Leadership positions, which before settlement followed established patterns gradually became subject to approval by the colonial administration.[1] The remoteness of Blackfoot territory had only delayed the imposition of colonial rule advancing westward in both the United States and Canada. In tandem with the rapidly changing political landscape, the complex semiotics of Blackfoot dress underwent transformation. However, this chapter argues that although colonial processes wrought many changes to the fluid *modus vivendi* of First Nations peoples of the northwestern Plains, the symbolism of the buckskin suit remained a constant, a thread linking the Blackfoot buffalo days with the changing tapestry of life on the reserve.

The dress of Blackfoot leaders acquired a new layer of meaning with their forced settlement on reserves. This was the most dramatic episode of the imposition of colonial rule and marked the end of the middle ground phase of the colonial encounter. It owed less to military defeat than to destitution. Even after signing treaties the Blackfoot bands had continued their erstwhile non-sedentary lifeways, but from 1879 the bison no longer crossed into Canada, deer soon was not to be found either. The Blackfoot ate skunks, porcupines and gophers, but by July of that year twenty-one Blackfoot deaths by starvation had occurred.[2] Canadian officials gave urgent relief, Commissioner Edgar Dewdney travelled to the agencies distributing treaty payments and food.³ Canadian officials encouraged the able-bodied to cross the border into Montana in pursuit of the last remnants of the herd. They returned destitute two years later. During their absence, a Farming Instructor had begun planting and was caring for cattle, and old people, who had remained behind, had settled in huts near the ration house.⁴ The Blackfoot, who had enjoyed dominion over a vast territory and had been a source of provisions for fur traders in the mid-nineteenth century, became reliant on government-issued rations and gifts of used clothing for their survival.⁵ According to Grinnell, until "1887 it was rather unusual to see a Blackfoot Indian clad in white men's clothing; the only men who wore coats and trousers were the [Indian] police and a few of the chiefs."⁶ However, between 1887 and 1892 most men changed to citizen's dress-coat and trousers (as European clothing was described). Power shifted to the State and the authority of Blackfoot leaders became subject to bureaucratic approval, which was henceforth encoded in the gold-braided military-style uniforms, the silver medals, and Winchester rifles presented at treaty signing, which became their insignia of office.⁷

Military Uniforms in the Twentieth Century

The military uniform worn by Blackfoot leaders during the early reserve era was freighted with ambivalence, reflecting their liminal position as brokers between their followers and the white bureaucracy, whose decrees they were meant to enforce. Within the reserve it distinguished leaders from their followers; within bureaucratic circles, it was interpreted as signalling their acquiescence to a higher power. The language of diplomacy was steeped in the language of mother–child or father–child relationship between the colonizers and the colonized, whereby the British Monarch was "The Great Mother" and the President of the United States "The Great Father". In practice, as Viola argues, such language became a "diplomatic device rather than an expression of subordinance".⁸ Blackfoot leaders were consummate diplomats and well aware that survival depended on their ability to negotiate successfully with the colonizers, represented by the Indian Agent.⁹ Agents found, however, that despite the hardships of their new life, twenty-five years of reserve life had not tamed the "proud and imperious spirit" of the Blackfoot.¹⁰

Official meddling with Blackfoot leadership positions began from the moment of treaty signing and increased gradually. United States treaty commissioners invested authority by presenting the military uniform to a number of leaders, but not to all leaders, a precedent set by Lewis and Clark in 1804–1806.¹¹ The commissioners sought to deal with a single supreme leader for each First Nation, treating others as "minor" leaders, which was at odds with traditional leadership mechanisms. Undeterred, when a maximum leader was not put forward, the commissioners took it upon themselves to make the appointment. They continued the fur traders' practice of "making chiefs" by presenting head chiefs with military uniforms and gilt swords. The same attitude prevailed in Canada. Dealing with several leaders for each separate band was expensive (minor chiefs and head chiefs received larger annuities and more benefits than the rest of the reserve population) and administratively onerous. However, during the crucial early reserve era the reduction in the number of recognized Blackfoot leaders was accomplished by attrition.[12] The governments of Canada and the United States followed a similar strategy of indirect rule through Blackfoot leaders. In Canada, validating an individual as leader by presenting him with a "chief's jacket" and medal created an obligation to assist the Agent to implement measures designed to "civilize" those on the reserve. At times, leaders' obligations to their people placed them at odds with bureaucratic expectations. At the same time, these leaders could only gain respect by exercising generosity to their followers, an obligation that could be fulfilled by their symbolic presence at the distribution of treaty benefits.

Leaders who did not receive or who rejected the military uniform continued to exercise authority over their followers, which resulted in two tiers of authority functioning at the same time. Some leaders rejected outright the symbols of white authority and white insignia, deeming them worthless.[13] The epithet "white chief" was coined to describe those whose authority was invested by colonial administrators and not according to Blackfoot practice.[14] However, living in peace was a condition of the treaties, thereby removing war as one of the mechanisms for attaining leadership in the time-honoured fashion. Blackfoot warring days began to ebb — although sporadic horse raiding continued for more than a decade — and with them, the *raison d'être* of a hair-fringed suit, which could only be worn by those who had killed an enemy.[15] During the reserve era killing an enemy and capturing horses became a punishable crime by law. The only Blackfoot who could wear the fringe of human hair at this time had gained that honour previously; they became legends in their own lifetime.

In Canada, the authority of the Agent on the reserve included the prerogative to remove uncompliant leaders. An 1895 amendment to the Indian Act of 1884 "allowed the Minister to depose chiefs and councillors" deemed "to be resisting the innovations of the reserve system and the Government's efforts to discourage the practice of traditional Indian beliefs and values."[16] Chiefs were expected to co-operate with the Indian Agent to advance Blackfoot assimilation.[17] The significance of the chief's uniform as a sign of authority during this era is evident in George Gooderham's recounting of the removal from office of minor chief Joe Calfchild by the Agent, saying that he had "lost his 'coat'".[18] When Agent Wilson had a dispute with Day Chief in 1905, he threatened to remove

The Longevity of Buckskins

his medal, which *ipso facto* would make Day Chief an "ordinary Indian."[19]

Indian Agents exercised authority with little outside supervision, and Blackfoot leaders had no avenues to seek redress when disputes arose. Regional inspectors visited the reserves annually, but officials maintained a united front in their dealings with their charges. The Indian Agent's control of food rations was sufficient to coerce compliance with his directives. In Canada, the Mounted Police were called to support the Agent when required, and the Indian Police played a similar role in the United States. However, on the Blackfoot reserves and reservation most of the day-to-day negotiation occurred between Blackfoot leaders and their Agents. Blackfoot leaders maintained a good relationship with the NWMP, and on several occasions asked Mounted Police officers to forward complaints against their Agent to Ottawa, although the *status quo* was largely maintained without Police intervention.

As before, the political authority attached to the office of chief remained closed to women, although it did not follow that women were subordinate in other respects. In 1938, a woman owned the largest horse

FIGURE 6.1 *Red Crow, head Chief of the Bloods*, Glenbow Archive, Calgary, Canada, NA-668-53.

Part II — The Grammar of Blackfoot Leadership Dress

FIGURE 6.2 *Crowfoot, during tour of eastern Canada* [1886], Glenbow Archive, Calgary, Canada, NA-182-2.

herd on the Blackfoot (Siksika) Reserve (200 horses), while two other women were listed as owning fifty horses apiece. This suggests that some women could wield sufficient economic power to earn them respect and influence in tribal affairs.[20] However, negotiations between the Blackfoot and whites remained an all-male affair.[21]

Siksika Crowfoot and Kainai Red Crow became two of the best-documented leaders of the early reserve era, thanks to Dempsey's excellent biographies. Red Crow, seen in Figure 6.1 holding a pipe, wears his chief's uniform and several medals, the largest of which is his treaty medal. Crowfoot, Figure 6.2, was photographed during a tour of eastern Canada wearing buckskins, a beaded top hat, and his treaty medal. Both leaders won prestige on the warpath and through deeds of outstanding courage, and both played significant roles during treaty negotiations.[22] Crowfoot's reputation as a diplomat and mediator between the Blackfoot and the white worlds earned him an unprecedented position as principal negotiator on behalf of the entire Blackfoot bands, leading to the signing of Treaty Seven in 1877 with the Dominion. Thereafter he became the most influential Blackfoot leader, gaining a reputation as favouring the whites. However, his crucial role in the treaty did not lend him any authority over bands other than his own Moccasin Band.[23] He negotiated on behalf of the Blackfoot First Nations to allow the railways to cross their territory, and he received a medal entitling him to unlimited transportation in appreciation. Moreover, a cheque for $70 arrived for the chief every month, which only came to the attention of his followers after Crowfoot's death.[24] The distinctions accorded to Crowfoot created tensions, and the pejorative "white chief" label was attached to the venerable leader by disgruntled followers.[25] Other leaders likewise parlayed their trade relationships into diplomatic ones during treaty signing. Alliances forged during the fur trade era prepared the ground for the later signing of treaties. Crowfoot's nomination as leading negotiator did not confer any lasting authority, yet, as the first leader to sign the treaty, he was placed, together with Old Sun, above other Siksika chiefs, thereby formalizing a new hierarchy outside Blackfoot custom.[26]

CULTURAL TRANSFORMATION AND MIMICRY

In his essay, "Of Mimicry and Man: The Ambivalence of Colonial Discourse", Homi Bhabha articulates the view of mimicry as a "discourse constructed around an *ambivalence*", and as a "sign of a double articulation; a complex strategy of reform, regulation and discipline, which 'appropriates' the Other as it visualizes power." Bhabha's main concern is the possibility of disrupting the colonial discourse through a "double *vision*" that turns mimicry into a *"menace"* to colonial authority. The military-style dress that was used by whites to distinguish Blackfoot elites may well have embodied the wish of the colonizers to replicate their own image in the colonized, to a degree that, as Bhabha argues, was *"almost the same, but not quite"*.[27] Canadian legislation, for example, clearly stipulated the manner in which Indians were to imitate whites. Washington's desire to turn Indians into whites, argues Herman Viola, accounts for the gifts of military-style clothes bestowed during diplomatic meetings with First Nations' leaders in that capital.[28] The wish for the colonized to be *"almost the same, but not quite"* could well have been expressed in the military-style dress — not quite a real uniform. The question that remains open is, how did the Blackfoot of the early reserve era respond to this colonial desire for a recognizable Other?

It would be simplistic to interpret the adoption of items of European dress as imitation[29] or mimicry, or as expressing a desire by the Blackfoot to become white or even to look like whites. To do so would be tantamount to affirming that during the early reserve era, Blackfoot lifeways centred on white concerns and white actions, the opposite seems to have happened. The Siksika derided the first few of their number who turned to gardening, asking the reasons for their wishing to "act like whites".[30]

Part II — The Grammar of Blackfoot Leadership Dress

Given that many Blackfoot disrupted efforts to turn them into farmers and Christians, the opposite seems to have been the case. However, the reserves were characterized by a division between "progressives" and "traditionalists", some Blackfoot seized the opportunities to become successful ranchers, others rejected some innovations but embraced others, and yet another group focused on Blackfoot traditional ways and sought to maintain them. While life on the Alberta reserves and the Montana reservation relentlessly transformed, the buckskin dress remained a thread binding the past with the Blackfoot present, an emblem of national pride.

During the first decades of life on reserves, however, Blackfoot leaders' prestige was enhanced by access to the uniform. Material benefits attached to their office that placed them in an advantageous position in comparison with "ordinary" Indians. Housing, travel, higher treaty payments, and even officials and missionaries turning a blind eye to their practicing poligyny were some of the benefits of those wearing the uniform and medal. Self-interest and a readiness to comply with official demands, however, should not be equated with a desire to become "white". Moreover, during the early reserve era Blackfoot chiefs continued to discharge their reciprocal obligations to their followers, their lifeways had transformed, but leaders' responsibility for the well-being on the bands remain a constant.

This was a difficult time at which the Blackfoot feared being absorbed into the colonizers. While the Blackfoot readily adopted Western technologies deemed to improve their lives, such as guns, and later embraced a whole array of technologies and white education, there is anecdotal evidence that they looked down on some of the (bad) habits of whites. During his last days (early 1890), Chief Crowfoot admonished his followers: "My children do not act like a white man even if you look like a white man [. . .] never try to be a white man you will never be one be proud of being an Indian stay an Indian as the Great Spirit made you an Indian and he was right."[31] White habits such as whipping children or refusing to feed them between meals appeared callous to the Blackfoot; a Blackfoot woman who did not to feed her children on demand was scornfully called "a white woman."[32] The Principal at the Industrial School at Qu'Appelle explained Blackfoot unwillingness to send children to school on the "old reason [. . .] 'that they won't resemble the white people'".[33] This indicates that if the colonizers constructed stereotypes of "Indians", the latter also constructed stereotypes of whites. According to McClintock, Blackfoot children shied away from him because "They had been taught from infancy that white men are dangerous monsters."[34]

Resistance to change extended to the religious sphere, even though many Blackfoot accepted baptism, they adopted Christianity largely on their own terms, which greatly frustrated missionaries whose writings allude to what they considered a "veneer" of Christianity rather than true faith. In respect of Ookaan, efforts to eradicate the ceremony by officials and missionaries failed. It was sufficient for the crops to fail or their horses to die for those who had embraced Christianity to seek solace in their indigenous beliefs and rites.[35] Even white food was at first disagreeable to the Blackfoot, though the loss of the buffalo left them with no other option but to eat beef.[36]

With the passing away of many well-respected leaders, deliberate efforts were made to weaken activist chiefs and to bolster those deemed progressive or well disposed toward assimilation, efforts that created dissension among the bands.[37] In 1903, at the recommendation of Agent J. A. Markle, a minor leader, Yellow Horse, was promoted to head chief of the North faction of the Siksika.[38] He was chosen because he could be relied upon "to support government policy and assist the Agent in carrying it out." Yellow Horse "was always dressed in the official suit of a chief[:] a blue jacket trimmed with yellow braid and brass buttons and grey trousers". His trademark was a silk hat presented by a British visitor to the reserve. However, Yellow Horse never cut his hair short, or abandoned the use of beaded moccasins.[39]

FIGURE 6.3 *Yellow Horse, head chief of the Blackfoot and his wife* [ca. 1910], Glenbow Archive, Calgary, Canada, NA-350-1.

Part II — The Grammar of Blackfoot Leadership Dress

Despite his appearance as a quintessential white chief and his baptism as an Anglican, Yellow Horse, whose body after death was wrapped in the Union Jack, remained steadfast to his Blackfoot beliefs to his last moments. He instructed his relatives that his favourite pinto horse was to be shot in order to accompany him in the afterlife according to Blackfoot custom. Likewise, in the words of the Agent, "his wife returned to her pagan faith" and would not let the coffin lid be closed, in order that his spirit could come and go at leisure.[40] The Christian veneer was perhaps more a tool of diplomacy than true conversion.

Longevity of the Buckskin Suit

Concurrent with the adoption of European dress as everyday wear and the military uniform as the insignia of chieftainship, buckskin suits retained their symbolic value and new avenues for their display emerged, including fairs and pageants. Within the traditional realm, during the first decades of life on the reserve the frequency and value of transfers of sacred items increased. Ceremonial life was revitalized because of the relative propinquity of the bands compared to the distances that had separated them during their non-sedentary days, and because the hardships of reserve life made it imperative to seek divine favour, thus increasing the need for divine assistance.[41] Nevertheless, in different measure at each of the reserves, the authority of traditional leaders was eroded. The *minipuka*'s role all but disappeared, supplanted by the Agent, who controlled the distribution of goods on the reserve. As time went by, cultural transformation, resisted by those who lived during the buffalo days, took its course. The new Blackfoot generations showed little interest or had little opportunity to become engrossed in their old traditions. In 1911, for example, David Duvall reported that "a Medicine Pipe owner is not thought of as so great and they are more common [and therefore] not looked upon as they were in the olden times." While the owner of the Medicine Pipe maintained his traditional dress "well painted up with the red", he mostly went about "dressed in citizen's clothes". In the past, no one would have dared "to go in front or cross in front of [a Medicine Pipe owner] while they were leading camps", but without their distinct dress, they became indistinguishable.[42]

However, although European dress became everyday wear, ownership of buckskin suits continued to be a mark of distinction. Physical proximity allowed for more cultural activities than were possible when the separate bands were constantly moving camp. More intricately decorated goods resulted from having more time available and access to European materials employed in dress production, such as cloth and beads.[43] Buckskin suits remained a crucial marker of a distinct Blackfoot identity, a symbol of a Blackfoot desire to remain different, even though their wear became largely ceremonial.[44]

A great deal of accommodation was required in order for the Blackfoot to ensure not only physical survival, but also cultural survival. Bill Ashcroft refers to transformation "as the consistently effective practice in postcolonial cultural production." In most cases, he argues, resistance is not "a heroic enterprise, but a pragmatic and mundane array of living strategies to which imperial culture has no answer," which manifests itself as "a refusal to be absorbed."[45] This provides a lens to interpret events such as the early twentieth-century transferral of the celebration of Ookaan in Montana to the Fourth of July, and the incorporation of the Stars and Stripes into the proceedings.[46] As bureaucrats on both sides of the border vied to assimilate the Blackfoot, a growing interest among the surrounding white population resulted in their sponsorship of sun dances. This happened much to the chagrin of Indian Agents bent on discouraging the practice, which in their view prevented their charges from embracing the benefits of civilization. Ookaan survived long enough for the right to attend this gathering to be legally recognized, and the practice continues to this day.

While European dress was overwhelmingly the everyday norm, buckskin suits continued to be worn — apart from religious ceremonies — for diplomatic purposes and during public performances for the benefit of whites.[47] One interpretation attributes the popularity among the Blackfoot in the 1890s of a Sioux-style feathered bonnet, dubbed "flowing feather bonnet," to the fact that this bonnet was not looked upon "as a sacred headdress". The prohibitions attaching to horned headdresses did not apply to the Sioux-style bonnet and therefore "anyone could wear one."[48] This adopted headdress was worn when the Blackfoot displayed their regalia on tours outside their reserves; received visits from dignitaries or participated in parades and stampedes.[49]

After 1910, when the Great Northern Railway opened tourist facilities at Glacier National Park, it employed Blackfoot "to camp, dance, demonstrate sign language, and 'be colourful'" for the benefit of tourists.[50] Likewise, First Nations peoples, including the Blackfoot, became a drawcard at the Calgary Stampede from its inception in 1912. These new contexts maintained the demand for men and women's buckskin dress, and placed value on traditional clothing, even if such dress was now deployed in a different context, within the sphere of performance.

During this era, the buckskin suit remained one of the strongest emblems of a separate identity; a symbol of a Blackfoot determination not to be totally absorbed into white culture at a time when radical transformation was required to ensure physical survival. The buckskin dress functioned as a sign that can be read in the light of Angelika Bammer's contention regarding the construction of identities: "The historical terrain

Part II — The Grammar of Blackfoot Leadership Dress

between necessity and choice [is] the place where oppression and resistance are simultaneously located".[51] In the present case, re-deploying buckskin suits in new contexts served to ensure their longevity.

The military uniform of Blackfoot chiefs during the early reserve era was a double-edged marker of leadership that sought to appeal to tribal society, while at the same time gaining the acceptance and recognition of the representatives of the colonial hegemony — DIA officials, missionaries, Mounted Police, and the "seizers" or "long-knives", as US soldiers were dubbed. These elites navigated the bands' transition to sedentary lifeways at a time when their very physical survival was threatened. They were cultural brokers or "framing specialists" who interpreted the culture, ideas and wants of each side to the other.[52] Their liminal if central role between the two cultures found expression in their adoption of the clothing and decorations of their European Other. In the public sphere during this era, Blackfoot women hardly feature, other than through their husbands and fathers,[53] and although Agents recognized women's rights to their husbands' property (previously distributed among his male relatives), treaty payments were paid to men as heads of families, widows being the exception.[54] Women continued to be absent from Blackfoot–white negotiations, but as is evident in Lewis's 1939 study of the Peigan Reserve at Brocket, Alberta, elite Blackfoot women continued to exercise power in ways that were concordant with Blackfoot lifeways. Despite the availability of glass beads since the early nineteenth century, in 1939 manly-hearted women on this reserve continued wearing quilled buckskin dresses.

Poverty during the reserve era and the reduced availability of traditional materials curtailed the dress options of most Blackfoot, but many elite Blackfoot remained wealthy, especially through cattle ownership. In Montana, by the 1940s fewer than forty men (out of a total population of c.5000) living on the Blackfeet Reservation owned quilled or beaded buckskin shirts and leggings. The number of women who owned beaded buckskin dresses was believed to be smaller. Only those Pikuni men and women who made a living entertaining tourists at East Glacier were reported to own a number of such items of dress.[55] In Alberta, during the late 1930s and early 1940s, ethnographers Lucien M. Hanks and Jane Richardson Hanks found that Siksika "clothing [was] of the poorest quality, frequently tattered, and sometimes soiled". They reported that despite having the third highest income among the reserves in Canada, the Siksika lacked adequate clothing to keep them warm in winter.[56] The remark needs to be qualified, because a wealthy elite maintained their privileges into the new era. Sufficient numbers of Blackfoot attended the Calgary Stampede every year since its inception in 1912, extant photographs attest to the continued production of beaded buckskin suits which, rather than decrease with time, seem to have become more richly ornamented as time went by.⁵⁷ This elite maintained a demand for ceremonial transfers and for buckskin suits, according to Hanks and Richardson Hanks, not having to go on the warpath, and with rations of food being issued weekly, the Siksika had time on their hands, and "a veritable epidemic of society dances and ceremonials sprang up", for those able to afford them. Membership in the Horn Society went "from a gun and blanket before treaty to a horse, and from one horse to several horses."⁵⁸ Wissler argued that, despite opposition by bureaucrats, the social mechanisms of generosity and ceremonial participation continued to provide the means for the Blackfoot to acquire prestige during the reserve period.⁵⁹ Participation in war as part of the armed forces of the Dominion enhanced the reputation of Blackfoot in the period after settlement. As earlier noted, buckskin suits were also redeployed in new contexts (e.g. tourist performances at Glacier National Park and the Calgary Stampede) thus ensuring their survival as one of the most powerful emblems of Blackfoot identity. This suggests that identity was itself protean, reflective of the creative adaptation innate to the introduction of colonial rule.

Finally, despite the many bureaucratic efforts aimed at erasing any vestiges of indigenous culture, the Blackfoot practice of presenting beaded buckskin suits to visiting dignitaries has not disappeared and these suits continue to be the foremost gift in Blackfoot diplomacy, considered appropriate for visiting British royalty and Canadian politicians.⁶⁰ The buckskin suit is a classic example of the workings of cultural transformation: its significance was re-inscribed and redeployed in order to adapt it to new uses, an indication that the assimilation of the First Nations peoples of Canada and the United States did not always proceed according to white designs.

PART III

Ethnographic Encounters
Cultural Transactions and Translations

7

Between Orality and Text
The Encounter with "Salvage Ethnography"

Blackfoot knowledge, transmitted orally from generation to generation, was transformed into text, first by travellers, priests, traders, and colonial administrators, and later, during the late nineteenth and the early twentieth centuries, by professional, university-based anthropologists. The collection and transcription for publication of the erstwhile orally transmitted knowledge of the First Nations of the United States and Canada reached its apogee at a time when the imminent "disappearance" of the Indian was taken for granted. This belief decreed that as much knowledge as possible of their way of life should be salvaged before their final extinction. Interest in Blackfoot epistemologies, lifeways, and practices from amateur and professional ethnographers resulted in the production of texts that have in time become canonical history. Five of these texts are explored here in order to focus on their intersection with Blackfoot ways of knowing, aiming to arrive at a better understanding of the Blackfoot informants, the people of knowledge who contributed to the production of five foundational volumes of Blackfoot history: George Bird Grinnell's *Blackfoot Lodge Tales: The Story of a Prairie People* ([1892] 2003); Clark Wissler's and David C. Duvall's *Mythology of the Blackfoot Indians* ([1908] 1995); Walter McClintock's *The Old North Trail or Life, Legends and Religion of the Blackfeet Indians* ([1910] 1992); C. C. Uhlenbeck's *A New Series of Blackfoot Texts from the Southern Piegans Blackfoot Reservation Teton County Montana. With the Help of Joseph Tatsey, Collected and Published with an English Translation by C. C. Uhlenbeck* (1912); and James Willard Schultz's *Blackfeet and Buffalo: Memories of Life Among the Indians* ([c.1878–1915] 1962). Among these, Uhlenbeck's publication alone is bilingual (English/Blackfoot).

Justification for choosing these texts as appropriate to the study of the process of cultural translation is fourfold. First, they had their genesis in collaborations that took place during the first half-century of reserve life.

This was a transitional time when Blackfoot epistemology remained moored in their oral tradition, although undergoing a process of adaptation that began with European contact in the late eighteenth century. This process accelerated with the forced settlement on three reserves in Canada and one reservation in the United States in the last decades of the nineteenth century. Second, these texts have become canonical works for Blackfoot and non-Blackfoot alike.[1] As Blackfoot scholar Thedis Crowe (Ahkiiwa Iyoumako Mistewaw, Sokapiiwa or Good Crooked Stick Woman) noted, "Grinnell's *Lodge Tales* and other non-Indian writings about the Blackfeet have been held as the absolute foundation of Blackfeet history". Therefore, she argues, these early representations are also responsible for "the categorization and stereotyping of the Blackfeet."[2] Third, these texts collectively exemplify the heterogeneous approaches and perspectives of an ethnographic practice that was itself in flux. Fourth, the cross-cultural collaborations that produced these texts provide a sample of the widely fluctuating conditions and power relations attendant upon the encounter between orality and writing.

The analysis here supports the premise that, despite the asymmetrical power relations of colonialism, the Blackfoot sought to shape the representation of their own past. By harnessing the medium of writing to Blackfoot "ways of knowing", they sought to inform their own future generations. Few Blackfoot could read at the time of publication of these collaborations.[3] Those who could, however, might well have felt that they did not need a book to tell them what they already knew. In time, however, Blackfoot and non-Blackfoot scholars have come to defer to the authority of these early anthologies. For example, Blackfoot author Beverly Hungry Wolf notes that the "legends" — a term other First Nations scholars reject — collected in the volume co-authored by Wissler and Duvall "are about the same as legends still told today, but in many cases more thorough."[4] She is not alone in this view, which suggests that fresh scrutiny of the production of texts such as those of interest here is warranted.

I begin by contextualizing the production of the five texts via a survey of their authors' background, disciplinary credentials, ideologies, and approaches to the task of documenting Blackfoot knowledge. I will draw attention to the contribution of those Blackfoot who translated and interpreted knowledge from one culture to another. As this story about stories unfolds, Blackfoot epistemology will be called upon to add hues to a picture wherein Blackfoot genres can be seen to find continuity in a new medium.

The compilation and publication of the five key texts of interest fit along a continuum of an ethnographic practice itself undergoing radical change. The texts by Grinnell, McClintock, and Schultz are the product of amateur ethnography; that of Wissler and Duvall bears the hallmarks of an incipient anthropological discipline in the United States, promoted by the Smithsonian Institution from its foundation in 1846; and Uhlenbeck's text is representative of linguistic salvage endeavours, a subfield of anthropology. A paradigm shift towards the universities and towards anthropology becoming a professional discipline occurred in the first decades of the twentieth century. The foundational ideas for this shift came from Edward Tylor, Lewis Henry Morgan, Emile Durkheim, and Frantz Boas.[5] Boas, a physicist turned ethnographer who pioneered the professional practice of anthropology in the early twentieth century, taught at Columbia University (1896–1936).[6] University-based Boasians generally distanced themselves from non-professionals, scornfully classed as "horse and buggy ethnographers".[7] Boasians discarded the notion that the indigenous cultures of North America were at "a primitive stage in human evolution."[8] They viewed these cultures as having remained static prior to contact with Europeans, and as a result valued the cultural past over the present, which was interpreted as contamination, which fuelled the practice of salvage ethnography.[9] Henceforth, in James Clifford's words, "Intensive fieldwork pursued by university trained specialists, emerged as a privileged, sanctioned source of data about exotic peoples." This development accords well with Foucault's claims concerning the constantly contested and changing ways in which universities constrain knowledge to produce discourses that are "within the true". However, as Clifford himself reminds us, "nothing guaranteed *a priori*, the ethnographer's status as the best interpreter of native life."[10] Although Foucault's and Clifford's perspectives emerged long after the texts studied here were produced, they provide a counterpoint to the "scientific" and authorial claims of the early representations of the Blackfoot.

Apart from the authors of the foundational texts, numerous European and Euro-American travellers, explorers, traders, colonial administrators, and missionaries have written about the Blackfoot, often on the basis of their personal experiences. Generally these authors share a cultural bias, reflecting ideologies current at the time, which placed "civilization" above the "savage" lifeways of First Nations peoples. In her introduction to the 2003 edition of Grinnell's *Lodge Tales*, Blackfoot scholar Thedis Crowe warns readers about the superiority of "white views and cultural values"[11] encountered therein. Indeed, even those who, like Grinnell, professed to have the best interests of the Blackfoot at heart could not escape re-inscribing these ideas. However, the authors of the five texts invested a great deal of their time and effort to document Blackfoot knowledge, an indication that they valued such knowledge.

DOCUMENTING A DISAPPEARING WORLD

The pioneering authors of the five texts sought to fill a void in Western scholarship and in the public domain about the Blackfoot, their worldviews, and their lifeways. These authors were not addressing a Blackfoot audience; Grinnell, McClintock, and Schultz sought to inform the American public, who knew little or nothing about the Blackfoot. Grinnell expressed a desire to dispel negative stereotypes about the "Indian." Ignorance, he felt, contributed to the mistreatment of Indians in the United States, which prevailed because those who legislated about them were "entirely unacquainted with this people or their needs."[12] It is safe to assume that these intended readers saw First Nations peoples through the kind of stereotypes that Robert Berkhofer distilled in *The White Man's Indian*. Co-authors Wissler and Duvall addressed their writing to the readers of the *Anthropological Papers of the American Museum of Natural History*. Wissler established his reputation through publications of his fieldwork among the Blackfoot and various Siouan First Nations of Montana and the Dakotas between 1902 and 1905.[13] Duvall, the son of Pikuni Yellow Bird (Louise Big Plume) and Charles Duvall, a French Canadian trader, had no professional qualifications but possessed literacy in English and spoke the Blackfoot language. In 1903 Duvall met Wissler, who gave up conducting fieldwork *c.*1905, leaving to the bicultural Duvall the task of interviewing Blackfoot elders ("Grandfathers" and "Grandmothers") who possessed knowledge of the Blackfoot past. While these elders spoke in their own language, Duvall recorded the interviews in English. Wissler argued that Duvall possessed "considerable linguistic ability" and had set himself the goal of becoming the "most accurate translator" of the Blackfoot. Uhlenbeck, the only linguist among the salvage scholars, addressed his fellow philologists and linguists of the present and the future, expressing the hope that one day his work would serve as a stepping stone for studies of the Blackfoot language. Having published two collections of Blackfoot texts in 1911 and 1912, Uhlenbeck's Blackfoot Grammar finally came out in 1938.

Like Duvall, who played a key role documenting Blackfoot knowledge during the early twentieth century, literate individuals of bicultural ancestry contributed to expand Western knowledge by collecting knowledge of their own First Nations. Among them were George Hunt (Kwakiutl), James Carpenter (Crow), Francis LaFlesche (Omaha), Arthur Parker (Seneca), and John N. B. Hewitt (Tuscarora).[14] Although their bicultural background might have been an advantage, during the production of the five texts, "mixed-blood" and "half-breed" — the terms commonly applied to these individuals — had pejorative connotations, implying the loss of an essential, pristine quality. Since the arrival of the first Europeans in the Americas categories emerged on the basis of blood quantum that in some contexts were legally binding.[15] However, pejorative terms express negatively what can also be seen in positive terms: the ability to function in two worlds. Malcolm McFee suggested that instead of "half-blood" such individuals should be called "150% man [/woman]". Arguing against the notion that acculturation necessarily denotes a replacement of one culture by another, he proposed recognizing an individual according to competency rather than blood quantum.[16] Indeed, competency in their indigenous language and literacy in English, which bicultural individuals had earlier access to, placed them in an ideal position to act as cultural brokers. Their role in bridging the gap between Europeans, Euro-Americans and their own First Nations emerges from their salience in early historical and literary writing about First Nations.[17] Their bicultural competency also gave them the upper hand in the political arena. On the Blackfeet Reservation in Montana, by 1930 two-thirds of the population had mixed ancestry and by the middle of the twentieth century this group "dominated the Tribal Council".[18]

Out of the six authors, Grinnell and McClintock seem to have had the most in common, both came from wealthy families with powerful connections in the East, and both went to Yale although neither studied anthropology. Grinnell, a naturalist, first travelled West with an expedition organized by paleontologist Otheniel Marsh in 1870. In 1874 he took part in Custer's expedition to the Black Hills, South Dakota, and nearly joined Custer's campaign in 1876, but circumstances prevented him from participating in the ill-fated expedition.[19] The near miss did not lessen his attraction to the West, although initial interest in exploration and hunting eventually shifted when, in the words of the historian Edward Harris III, he "fashioned himself a chronicler". Harris views this transition as a logical step from a preoccupation with the preservation of nature to one of preserving the knowledge of Indians.[20] Grinnell began writing hunting stories for *Forest and Stream*,[21] a New York journal dedicated to the outdoor activities in which he delighted. By 1876 he became the journal's Natural History editor, progressing to joint ownership (with his father) by 1880.[22] Throughout these years, Grinnell's summers were dedicated "to hunt, explore, climb mountains and glaciers".[23] By the mid-1880s, he began compiling "Indian tales, history and ethnography", using sign language to communicate with informants, although relying mostly on paid translators. He witnessed the detrimental effects of western expansion upon First Nations. Prompted by James Willard Schultz, who would later become a prolific author on the Blackfoot, Grinnell lobbied against official neglect of those living on the Blackfeet Reservation in Montana. He raised awareness in the East of the famine that between 1883 and 1884 caused the death of more than one quarter of their population, obtained the removal of the Indian Agent, and successfully lobbied in Washington to improve their condition. By 1889, having published a book on the Pawnee, Grinnell set his sights on a publication about the Blackfoot.[24]

For his part, McClintock's first acquaintance with the Blackfoot occurred in 1896 when, as part of an expedition by Gifford Pinchot, Chief of the Forest Service of the United States, he met William "Billy" Jackson (a.k.a. Sikisikakoan or Blackfoot-Man), who welcomed and guided him through the Blackfoot camps, introducing him to a life that was to absorb McClintock and to result in the publication of two books on the Blackfoot, one opera based on a Blackfoot story, and several articles.[25] Between 1906 and 1940 McClintock presented public lectures at venues across the United States and Europe, which he illustrated with his own lantern slides. Among his audience were men such as Theodore Roosevelt and Andrew Carnegie. In Europe, McClintock presented his lecture to the Crown Prince of Prussia.[26]

Uhlenbeck's linguistic focus sets him apart from the other authors. He came to Montana during the summers of 1910 and 1911 to collect Blackfoot stories that would assist him eventually to write a Blackfoot grammar. He published his 1910 research, collected during the space of three months, in 1911. In 1912 he published the results of his 1911 summer work among the Blackfoot. Apart from the perspectives Uhlenbeck provides in the respective prefaces, the recent publication of Mrs. Uhlenbeck's diary of their 1911 visit to Montana provides many insights into her husband's methods. Like Wissler, Uhlenbeck relied heavily on the assistance of a bilingual collaborator. Joseph Tatsey, of Kainai and Pikuni ancestry, became his "teacher" — as Uhlenbeck referred to him. Thanks to Tatsey's dedication, Uhlenbeck was able to prepare his bilingual (English/Blackfoot) collections of Blackfoot stories, in which he gives credit to Bear Chief, one of his Blackfoot "teachers". Without Tatsey, Uhlenbeck claimed, "it would have been impossible [. . .] to profit by Bear Chief's life-experience, ancient lore, and imaginative power, as this gentleman speaks only the language of his warlike ancestry".[27] Of Tatsey, Uhlenbeck wrote:

> If I should have been the author of a Blackfoot Grammar, I would certainly have dedicated it to my Indian friend Joseph Tatsey, to whom I owe a debt of gratitude for his disinterested teaching and interpreting, and without whose help and affection I could never have succeeded in gaining the confidence and affection of such Indians as were able to tell me everything about the good olden times.[28]

Alas, in *A Concise Blackfoot Grammar*, which Uhlenbeck published in 1938, he gave no recognition to Tatsey. Instead, Dr. J. P. B. de Josselin de Jong, Uhlenbeck's doctoral student who accompanied him to Montana in 1910, and who also published Blackfoot stories, receives credit for assisting in fieldwork and correcting the text.[29] Uhlenbeck did, however, dedicate Appendix I, in his *Patronimics and Proper Names of the Piegans*, to Tatsey and his family, and Appendix III to Bear Chief and his family.[30]

James Willard Schultz was a storyteller rather than an ethnographer, but he possessed an insider perspective of the Blackfoot. He came West in his youth and learnt the Blackfoot language at the age of eighteen. Having married Fine Shield Woman (Mutsi-Awotan-Ahki), a Pikuni, and having spent more than fifty years living among the Blackfoot, Schultz "not only spoke Blackfoot, he *thought* it as well."[31] Schultz, like Grinnell and McClintock, was Blackfoot by adoption, thus having unlimited access to Blackfoot knowledge. Grinnell credited Schultz — whose contributions to *Forest and Stream* first called Grinnell's attention to the Blackfoot universe — with being the "discoverer of the literature of the Blackfeet."[32] This literature consists of a corpus of oral narratives that have been handed down from generation to generation from time immemorial. After 1903, when Fine Shield Woman died, Schultz published some thirty-seven books based on the Blackfoot, including his personal experiences and many Blackfoot stories he had learnt from friends and relatives. He aimed these books at young readers. Keith Seele, who posthumously edited *Blackfoot and Buffalo* from materials prepared by Schultz's widow, Jessie Donaldson Schultz, argues that Schultz "*was a storyteller, but he never set himself up to be a historian or a scientist*". He "undoubtedly took some liberties with factual history", argues Seele, "and yet he *lived* most of the history that he relates".[33] Grinnell gave recognition to Schultz, who was one of three assistants on his payroll, together with George Hyde and George Bent (who was bicultural).[34] According to Grinnell, "A portion of the material contained in *Lodge Tales* was originally made public by Mr. Schultz". Not willing to prepare a book-length publication of the Blackfoot of his own, Schultz gave Grinnell permission to incorporate his own materials into *Lodge Tales*,[35] which paradoxically is consistently valued above Schultz's *Blackfeet and Buffalo*. Schultz's dramatic style earned for his own volume the label of "folksy."[36]

Despite the varying approaches of the authors of the five texts, they were united in one purpose: to document knowledge of First Nations believed to be in the process of disappearing. "Salvage ethnography" is a term laden with imperialist and ethnocentric assumptions that served to justify the colonial enterprise. The project of salvage was influenced by the discourse of the imminent extinction of First Nations peoples, a fate that the colonizers accepted as the regrettable cost of civilization. The task of salvage aimed at describing "not what the anthropologist actually observed, but a reconstruction from the oldest inhabitants of what had been the habits prior to reservation life."[37] The salvage ethnographer sought to capture a world that existed prior to sustained contact with Europeans — an uncontaminated past that could provide links to humanity's primordial era, which only cultural insiders knew. Grinnell wished to record a world that he saw as relentlessly changing, which he described as "the meeting of the past and the present, of savagery and civilization."[38] In the early 1880s, he viewed with nostalgia the end of the buffalo days. He regretted the passing of that time of freedom and plenty, although he saw acculturation as the only way forward, thinking it "best that the Indians should fade away as we seen [sic] them fading to-day". It was, in his view, the "inexorable natural law that the weaker must perish while the fitter shall survive".[39] Fitness in this context does not equate to physical capacity, as Grinnell admired Indian's physical ability. Rather, technologies of war defined European and Euro-American superiority. Grinnell's remarks accord well with scientific theories such as Social Darwinism, and Lewis Henry Morgan's three stages of the human race, which measured advancement according to a linear progression from "savagery" to "barbarism" and ultimately to "civilization."[40] These ideas provided a convenient justification for western expansion in North America during an era of unsurpassed colonization. The imminent threat of extinction also motivated Uhlenbeck, whose aim "was to learn the [Blackfoot] language and to save it from threatened oblivion by recording an accurate description."[41] The timeliness of these endeavours is indeed one of the reasons the five texts attained canonical status. Beyond recognizing the contribution of the authors, however, we are yet to fully recognize the ways in which Blackfoot knowledge animates these texts.

The discourse of extinction also enjoyed currency among the colonized. Double Runner, one of Grinnell's Blackfoot collaborators, expressed it thus: "The old things are passing away, and the children of my children will be like white people. None of them will know how it used to be in their father's days unless they read the things which we have told you, and which you are all the time writing down in your books".[42] Almost two decades after the publication of *Lodge Tales*, McClintock articulated a similar discourse in his *Old North Trail*, describing the reduction in the number of Blackfoot "full bloods" in Canada and the United States as the "pathetic spectacle of a dying race."[43] He framed his efforts to render Blackfoot knowledge into text as follows:

> I realized that there were locked up in the breasts of the old chiefs and medicine men rich treasures of folk-lore, religious beliefs and ceremonials, I saw that the younger generation was indifferent to their tribal customs, tradition and religion. I also observed that they had no written language, and it seemed inevitable that, with the passing of the old chiefs and medicine men, their ancient religion and folk-lore would fall into oblivion. When I discovered that I could obtain the unbosoming of their secrets and that the door was open to me for study and investigation, I resolved that I would do my best to preserve all the knowledge available.[44]

McClintock's self-appointment as savior of Blackfoot knowledge is all the more dramatic because he fails to acknowledge that Grinnell had previously published *Lodge Tales*, of which McClintock — who cites Clark

Wissler's "anthropological papers"[45] — must have been aware. Nor did McClintock dwell on the fact that the information to which he was privy had been transmitted by successive generations of Blackfoot without the assistance of writing. The indifference he perceived in the younger generation persuaded him that only his own "study and investigation" could save Blackfoot knowledge from oblivion. In this regard McClintock was fully in step with the discourse of extinction that informed salvage ethnography. However, even though his contribution to the preservation of knowledge of the Blackfoot was not unique, one century later, there is no doubt as to its great value. Sherry Smith argues that McClintock's photographs of the Blackfoot, published in 2005 under the title *Lanterns on the Prairie: The Blackfeet Photographs of Walter McClintock*, represent his "most important contribution to Blackfeet history and ethnology".[46] The volume includes an essay by Pikuni scholar Darrell Robes Kipp, who argues that McClintock's contribution has increased relevance for the Blackfoot of today.

Another significant achievement of McClintock, noted by Pikuni/Gros Ventre author Sidner Larson in his introduction to *The Old North Trail*, resides in the "much more personal detail about Blackfoot daily life" that McClintock captures, compared with "other sources from that period", despite idiosyncrasies of 'as told to' autobiography that pervade the text. McClintock places himself at the centre of the events he describes — he is the "I" of the narrative voice — but he also records conversations, ceremonies, and happenings, often including gestures and dialogue. Thanks to these writing strategies, he fleshes out the presence of the Blackfoot who guided him, not only through their territory, but also through their knowledge. For his historical novel *Fools Crow* (1986), Pikuni/Gros Ventre James Welch relied on McClintock's book for his representation of Blackfoot subjectivity.[47]

In their *Writing Culture*,[48] James Clifford and George Marcus gathered perspectives on the pitfalls of ethnographic writing. However, at the turn of the twentieth century the prevailing view was one of unqualified acceptance of its "scientific" approach. Although an amateur, Grinnell had full confidence in his ability to represent the Blackfoot. As with his previous book on the Pawnees, his stated intention was "to show how Indians think and feel by letting some of them tell their own stories in their own fashion."[49] There is no reason to doubt his sincerity; such claims to give voice to the voiceless, however, are now harder to sustain, having been discounted by scholars, both within and outside the discipline of anthropology.

The debate on whether the voice of the colonized, subaltern, indigenous "Other" can be represented at all has been extensive. It has run the gauntlet since Gayatri Chakravorty Spivak's celebrated essay "Can the Subaltern Speak?",[50] and the riposte from Edward Said countering that "the subaltern can speak, as the history of liberation movements in the twentieth century eloquently attests."[51] The participation of First Nations scholars in these debates has increased the degree of scrutiny over current and earlier claims that relate to the representation of indigenous knowledge. The gulf separating the two worldviews that converged during the translation and transcription of Blackfoot knowledge at the turn of the twentieth century would have made it impossible to fulfill Grinnell's intention to let the Blackfoot "tell their stories in their own fashion". His goal accords with the stated aims of the genre of "testimonio", an oral narrative by an often-illiterate participant in the events recounted to an intermediary, often an ethnographer, who transcribes and publishes the *testimonio*.[52] *Testimonios*, however, are narrated in the first person to construct a sense of immediacy between the informant and the reader, a strategy that can obscure the ethnographer's intervention as editor of the text. Moreover, using a first person narrator buttresses the testimonialist's claims to truth, based on his/her "being there" when the action took place. Despite Grinnell's avowed wish to let the Blackfoot speak, the "I" of his informants only makes a fleeting appearance in two paragraphs of the conversation between Grinnell and Double Runner in which the latter ruminates over the passing of the old ways, printed as a "note" preceding Grinnell's introduction to *Lodge Tales*.

Although Grinnell meant for his readers to "get a true notion of the man who is speaking [. . .] the real Indian as he is in his daily life among his own people", he did not close the distance between his Blackfoot informants and his readers through direct quotations. Having mentioned the names of his collaborators in his introduction, he then becomes an omniscient narrator/author. Moreover, by adopting the authorial position, Grinnell appropriates Blackfoot knowledge where his own contribution — going by his own explanation — might have been described as "compiler" or "editor". In contrast, Schultz's *Blackfeet and Buffalo* brings the names of his Blackfoot informants onto the printed page alongside the information credited to them, although at times using pseudonyms. Part one of *Blackfeet and Buffalo* contains his own reminiscences, and Part two stories told to him by his friends, Blackfoot and non-Blackfoot, including: Bird Chief, Hugh Monroe (Indian by adoption), White Quiver, Kai Otokan (Bear Head), Raven Quiver (Joseph Kipp, a white trader), Three Suns, Big Brave, Many-Tail-Feathers, Ahko Pitsu (a.k.a. Chewing Black Bone),[53] and Charles Rivois (born in St. Louis). These men related stories, including those of events they had witnessed or participated in. Schultz defers to Blackfoot voices in ways that Grinnell's editorial hand and scientific tone would not allow. This is illustrated in the testimony of the Baker massacre narrated by Kai Otokan, a survivor. Kai Otokan wishes Schultz to record the massacre "for the whites to read; for the whites of this time to learn what their fathers did to us."[54] There are other instances of Schultz articulating the experiences of colonization from a Blackfoot-centered perspective, a characteristic that marks out *Blackfeet and Buffalo* from the other texts studied here. Schultz's life bears testament to the workings of acculturation, except that he traveled in the opposite direction. He learnt the Blackfoot language, married a Blackfoot and was ritually adopted, receiving the name Apikuni (Far-Off White Robe).[55] Schultz's editor, Keith Seele — himself also a Blackfoot by adoption — describes him as "the greatest interpreter of a noble Indian people" because, despite being a white man, "he was also truly an indian."[56]

Columbia-educated Wissler achieved eminent status in the field of anthropology.[57] He directed the combined Departments of Anthropology and Ethnology at the American Museum of Natural History between 1907 and 1942. He had worked as assistant to Boas in 1902, when the latter was curator of ethnology, and eventually succeeded him.[58] Boas had an invaluable collaborator in George Hunt when researching the Kwakiutl. Hunt, whose father was Scottish and whose mother was Tlingit, grew up among the Kwakiutl and spoke Kwakwala, their language.[59] Boas trained Hunt in ethnological field techniques and linguistic transcription. Wissler's interpretation of the Blackfoot ethnographic data incorporates historical documentation and, consistent with the Boasian diffusionist model, comparisons with other First Nations.[60] Like his mentor and predecessor, Wissler also came to depend heavily for his Blackfoot data on Duvall's abilities. Under Wissler's direction Duvall became an excellent ethnographer; Wissler claimed that Duvall's "interest and skill grew so that during the last year of his life he contributed several hundred pages of manuscript." Duvall brought a keen interest to the study of Blackfoot religion, even though he was not "in any sense an adherent".[61] He "brought no ethnological theories", but Wissler planned and directed the research and framed its findings for publication. The identity of his informants is concealed from the published papers, a standard ethnographic practice. However, in her introduction to the 1995 edition of *Mythology of the Blackfoot Indians*, Alice Kehoe ensured that readers would become familiar with their names. From the account sheets in which Duvall recorded the hourly payments disbursed to his informants, and his notations in his interviews, she has provided a comprehensive list of the Blackfoot who shared their knowledge with Duvall. What Kehoe found when comparing these accounts with other documents was a kinship, as well as a geographic connection of individual Blackfoot whose knowledge was valued and, if not handsomely rewarded in monetary terms, at least documented for posterity. Kehoe makes the link between Duvall's informants and the band under the leadership of Mountain Chief c.1869. Connected to this band, Duvall interviewed Big Brave, Mountain Chief's son; Big Brave's aunts, two sisters married to Heavy Gun; Black Bear, who was Heavy Gun's cousin; and Red Plume. As well as Big Brave, in Heart Butte, Montana, he also interviewed Heavy Gun, Owl Top Feathers, and Tom Kiyo, owner of the Head Carrier's Beaver Bundle, who was one of Duvall's most frequent collaborators. Kehoe's listing of the numerous Blackfoot men and women who shared their knowledge with Duvall denotes a widespread willingness to participate in the documentation of Blackfoot knowledge.

Intermediaries and Translators

Duvall became the first Blackfoot to attain authorial status.[62] His interviews are highly valued for his ability to translate not only words, but also ideas from one culture to another. Kehoe argues that between 1910 and 1912, apart from *Mythology of the Blackfoot*, Wissler published as sole author four papers that bore the hallmarks of Duvall's work.[63] Duvall was a "cultural broker", eliciting, collecting, reframing and translating Blackfoot knowledge for a white audience. He performed the tasks of an "organic intellectual", a Gramscian term used to distinguish those who grow up organically within a social group, as opposed to intellectuals in the normative Western sense. Duvall became an asset to Wissler, to salvage ethnology, and in the fullness of time to future generations of Blackfoot.

He might have considered himself a Pikuni. However, during his life, Duvall's bicultural ancestry attached to him the pejorative label "half-breed". In the eyes of his contemporaries, he occupied racially and socially a liminal position, not being fully accepted as Blackfoot or as white. Grinnell, who was sympathetic to the plight of individuals of mixed ancestry, noted: "If they live off the reservation, they are called Indians, and are told to go and live with their own people, while if they live on the reservation the Indians say that they are white people and should go and live with the whites."[64] Bicultural individuals who married Blackfoot women were often labeled "squaw men". In her introduction to *Mythology of the Blackfoot*, Kehoe fleshes out the figure of Duvall. She observes that after his father's death (when Duvall was six years old), his mother, Yellow Bird, remained three more years at Fort Benton, before moving to the reservation. Duvall spent some years at the Fort Hall Indian School in Idaho and, until 1910, ran a blacksmith shop in Browning. He first married a Pikuni named Gretchen, but later separated from her. In January 1911, he married Cecile Trombley.[65] Duvall shot himself the day when, at Trombley's instigation, "the case for the dissolution of his marriage would have been heard in court."[66] Wissler linked this tragedy to Duvall's liminality: "What galled him most was that no one trusted him [. . .] What else could he do?"[67] The statement, probably expressed at a time of grief is not however a fitting way to explain the life of one who found so many open doors among the "full blood" population of the reservation, one who many Blackfoot entrusted with their knowledge.[68]

Serendipity was at work the day Duvall took his own life at Joe Kipp's inn, in Browning. The Uhlenbecks were also staying with Kipp (Mrs Uhlenbeck recorded the incident in her diary entry for 10 July), as were Grinnell and his wife.[69] They had come to town on account of the Sun Dance. Rather than a coincidence, their convergence must have been a familiar sight at this time of year. Their gathering on such a tragic day serves as a reminder that the salvage project had practical effects upon First Nations communities. Blackfoot knowledge had become the commodity of a new trade. Apart from the (usually modest) hourly fee paid to informants such as those consulted by Duvall, ancillary opportunities to profit from interest in all things Blackfoot emerged, not only for specialists such as translators and guides, but also for providers of services that included meals, laundry, and transport. Moreover, interest in the Blackfoot also extended to items of their manufacture. Wissler, notes Kehoe, first collected artifacts and then myths from the Blackfoot. We are yet to quantify the economic impact of the commercialization of "traditional" objects manufactured to meet collectors' demands during the first decades of the twentieth century. According to James Dempsey — referring to painted robes — early demand came from "people with a direct interest in the Blackfoot", while in the 1930s it came from outsiders, including tourists visiting Glacier National Park.[70]

During Uhlenbeck's second trip to Montana in 1911 — when he collected materials for his 1912 publication — his wife's diary describes in detail their interactions with the Blackfoot community. She records the long working sessions during which Tatsey and Uhlenbeck verified and amended notes from Uhlenbeck's interviews. Tatsey, who was paid for his services, did not share authorial credit with Uhlenbeck, but appears in the title of two publications. Mrs Tatsey for her part earned some income preparing meals and washing clothes for the Uhlenbecks, although Mrs Uhlenbeck complained of the steep charges and reverted to doing their own laundry.[71] Uhlenbeck recited stories collected during his previous visit in the Blackfoot language, hoping "for corrections from his audience."[72] The diary records a stream of Blackfoot visitors; they came to the Uhlenbecks's tent to hear the stories, eat treats of candy and "[chocolate] kisses," and smoke the tobacco that Mrs Uhlenbeck dispensed. She recorded their reactions thus: "All the Indians love the *Napi* stories and they are impressed and don't understand how a *White man* can recount their stories in their language, right in their own words."[73] She described her husband's informants as being mostly elders who were paid fees to "teach" him. For his 1911 publication, Uhlenbeck claims that he collected data "from the mouth of many people, mostly boys and young fellows, who were kind enough to allow me in their leisure-hours to interrogate them about intricate matters."[74] Walter Mountain Chief, a young Pikuni, developed such a close relationship with the Uhlenbecks that he borrowed significant sums of money from them in 1911. According to Alice Kehoe, Uhlenbeck's focus on linguistics gave his informants freedom to express the content of their narratives in their own terms, rather than "according to a European blueprint". He was also able to capture a sense of the stories' rhythm in the original language. She suggests that Uhlenbeck's texts should be read as a heterocosm — "a version of reality that helps make the world intelligible and navigable."[75]

Western beliefs that permeated the era provided the foundations for the process of collecting, translating, and transcribing Blackfoot knowledge during the late nineteenth and the early twentieth centuries. The expectation that First Nations peoples would disappear as distinct peoples, added to Enlightenment ideas of the superiority of "civilization", fuelled salvage ethnology projects such as those introduced here. The conditions that allowed for the production of the five texts provide the context for analyzing the manner in which Blackfoot "ways of knowing" became the bedrock of written Blackfoot history and literature. From these early ethnographies, later historians have documented and continue to revisit a transitional era when the Blackfoot, forced to give up their non-sedentary lifeways, settled on three reserves in Canada and one reservation in the United States. It was in the latter era that, under the auspices of the Smithsonian Institution, interest in the "exotic" peoples of the North American Great Plains grew. However, without the willing participation of Blackfoot Grandfathers, Grandmothers, translators, and a number of "organic intellectuals", some of bicultural ancestry, the project of salvage could not have proceeded. Thus, the five foundational texts owe a huge debt to Blackfoot "ways of knowing". However, the authorial function vested in the compilers and editors of these texts has greatly obscured Blackfoot contributions to the transformation of orality into text.

8

Blackfoot Genres into Written History and Literature

The Blackfoot Stories and pictographic genres that served to preserve their history before the acquisition of alphabetic writing bear witness to a preoccupation with the production and transmission of knowledge of their past in ways that guaranteed its truth value. This study surveys the function of oral stories of the First Nations peoples of the Plains generally, and the stories from the Blackfoot oral tradition (Blackfoot Stories) in particular. It examines oral and pictographic genres within Blackfoot epistemology in order to explore Blackfoot mechanisms for the control of knowledge, and processes of appropriation, transculturation, and hybridity attendant upon a new context of sedentary life and cultural transformation during their first half-century of life on reserves. It culminates with a discussion of a "Blackfoot Year Count" in which the old and the new — pictographs and writing — come together in a hybrid genre in order to record salient events of the Siksika band. This year count illustrates the mechanisms of transculturation.

Europeans equated the absence of writing (chirography) among the First Nations of North America with an absence of history and literature. Taking the pursuit of knowledge to be *a priori* a European preoccupation, they dismissed other "ways of knowing" as inferior and therefore unworthy of study. In the title of his seminal book, *A Forest of Time*, Peter Nabokov proposes thinking of history in terms of the Navajo historian Ruth Roessel's metaphor of "a forest of many different and varied trees" wherein "a Euro-American trunk and branches are only one among many."[1] This study aims to provide a clearer picture of the metaphorical tree that represents Blackfoot knowledge, and thereby to link Blackfoot knowledge to written Blackfoot history in the five texts introduced in the preceding chapter.

While it is evident that the authors of the five texts under consideration valued what Blackfoot informants could contribute to the pool of Western knowledge, they often referred to their collaborators in paternalistic terms. The trope of the "neophyte", where not explicitly articulated, is often evoked in other ways. Grinnell, for example, argued that Indians were "merely grown up children." Referring to attitudes to "blood and wounds and death", Grinnell noted: "Some of the sentiments which [the Indian] expresses may horrify your civilized mind, but they are not unlike those which your small boy might utter."[2] Although these sentiments were expressed in specific contexts, they reflect a wider European conceit about the superiority of their own civilization.

A more complex perspective emerges when drawing lines of continuity between textual representations of the Blackfoot and their own ways of knowing. Focusing on Blackfoot ways of recording, transmitting, and valuing knowledge, it becomes evident that they placed a premium on intellectual property and the recording of information that was "within the true." These precedents informed Blackfoot collaborations with those authors who later documented Blackfoot knowledge and parsed it into history and literature, a process that is viewed here as an extension of, rather than a departure from, Blackfoot practices. It is only by placing Blackfoot and non-Blackfoot scholarship into dialogue that a nuanced history of the encounter between orality and text can be arrived at.

Blackfoot ways of knowing (genres) before European contact point to a preoccupation with the preservation of knowledge according to the expectations of Blackfoot epistemology. The building blocks for constructing this perspective are the stories from the Blackfoot oral tradition (Blackfoot Stories). On a wider canvas, these stories fit into a tradition universal among the First Nations peoples of the Americas, for which Gordon Brotherston coined the descriptor, "Literatures of the Fourth World."[3] The Blackfoot Stories have much in common with those of other First Nations peoples of the Great Plains, the Plains Indians or, to the Blackfoot, the *Sao-kitapiisksi*. These stories bind culture to genres imbued with the Blackfoot ideology and philosophy, thereby providing the means for cultural reproduction, and the transmission of a protean culture to succeeding generations that renews and strengthens group identity.[4]

In 1968, during his widely cited speech at the First Convocation of American Indian Scholars, the Kiowa author N. Scott Momaday proposed that telling stories is:

> An act by which man strives to realize his capacity for wonder, meaning and delight [. . .]. It is also a process in which man invests and preserves himself in the context of ideas. Man tells stories in order to understand his experience, whatever it may be. The possibilities of storytelling are precisely those of understanding the human experience."[5]

If we overlook Momaday's gender-exclusive language, his elaboration aptly describes the overall function of the Blackfoot Stories. These narratives should be appreciated for their creativity, the enjoyment to be derived from their re-telling, and their capacity to preserve and transmit knowledge. These Blackfoot Stories — parsed into "Old People Stories" and "Everyday Stories" — pervade the five texts on which this study focuses, encompassing the secular and sacred realms.[6] An appreciation of this oral tradition and its encounter with writing must begin with an understanding of the manner in which the Blackfoot Stories or *Mokakssini* (knowledge) subsume their worldview. To the Blackfoot, who consider spirituality and way of life as indivisible, these stories represent a unified universe or *Nitsitapiisinni* ("Our Way of Life"). They are true in the literal sense: they are a "record of [their] history since the beginning of time."[7] When Blackfoot Grandfathers, Grandmothers, and scholars make these claims, they seek to delineate the boundaries of their experience and reclaim a right to explicate the Blackfoot universe on their own terms. Some among them go so far as to claim that the non-Blackfoot ethnographers who documented Blackfoot knowledge could not have understood aspects of Blackfoot culture only available to insiders.[8] These claims deny non-Blackfoot authors the capacity to know the Blackfoot world, a political stance that needs to be understood as resistance against colonial appropriation. Generic differences and commonalities provide a vantage point from which to view the adaptation of Blackfoot Stories into non-Blackfoot genres. Translation and transcription loom large among the pitfalls that underlie the process of orality into text, what Derrida called the "economy of in-betweenness."[9] The different functions of the Blackfoot Stories and their written versions in the ethnographic text are the point of departure for contextualizing the process of cultural translation.

First, it is manifest that, independently from the ethnographic texts, the Blackfoot Stories continue to be transmitted in the time-honoured manner, and continue to undergo transformation according to their own protean mechanisms. Blackfoot scholar Thedis Crowe expresses it thus: "The stories are a major part of our cultural connection, the strong umbilical cord that keeps us tethered to the Blackfeet world and reminds us of our history."[10] Viewed from another angle, the Blackfoot oral tradition is a crucial means to nurture a separate Blackfoot identity. Second, textual crystallization *per se* does not prevent the published narratives from being re-absorbed into the oral tradition in full or in part at any time. Indeed, those Blackfoot who collaborated in the project of orality into text expected that their contributions, once written down, would inform future generations of their descendants of how their ancestors lived. I mentioned earlier a number of Blackfoot scholars who acknowledge this ongoing relationship between the two modes of transmission. However, despite any liberating or empowering effects that can flow from embracing cultural hybridity, it is undisputed that, despite the realities of their transcultural experiences, First Nations peoples continue to demand to be recognized as distinct, and overwhelmingly reject hybrid imaginaries.

Within the process of orality into text that resulted in the five publications of interest here, the Blackfoot Stories are the threads of continuity: they are knowledge, or, in Peter Nabokov's apt phrase, "forms of remembering."[11] When these stories are incorporated into alien (etic) genres during the process of publication, such genres impose western meanings and limit the ways in which non-Blackfoot readers engage with the stories. Hernandez argues that applying outside categories to the stories is integral to the colonization of Blackfoot knowledge. In terms of function, her two Blackfoot categories of "Old People stories" and "Everyday Stories"[12] match the two generic distinctions that Boas proposed for Native American oral narratives broadly. The "Old People Stories" are not unlike what Boas described as stories that "relate incidents which happened at a time when the world had not yet assumed its present form and when mankind was not yet in possession of all the customs and arts that belong to our period." The "Everyday Stories" match what Boas described as stories that "belong to our modern period." As is the case with most generic divisions, these categories often overlap. Boas warned that characters from one set could cross into the other, making definitive categorization difficult. He further suggested the category of "myth" for the older stories, and "history" for their modern counterparts.[13] However, this myth-history dichotomy is not value neutral.

As Mircea Eliade observed, the significance of "myth" is ambivalent. Its most familiar sense as "fiction" or "illusion" coexists with its meaning as "sacred tradition, primordial revelation and exemplary model". This latter meaning is that employed by early twentieth century "ethnologists, sociologists, and historians of religions".[14] Nevertheless, Blackfoot scholars, with few exceptions, reject the category of "myth" for the Blackfoot Stories.[15] Such concerns are not trivial to First Nations peoples, who regard their stories "as absolute truth".[16] Against the Blackfoot view of the stories from their oral tradition as a "record of [their] history since the beginning of time,"[17] western scholars have regarded Native American genres as "separate repositories for some brand of historicity",[18] but not as History. To illustrate this point, in his *The Use and Abuse of History*, M. I. Finley argues: "Dates and a coherent dating scheme are as essential to history as exact measurement is to physics."[19] Since Finley expressed this relativistic and ethnocentric view, historians and ethnohistorians have become more adept at engaging with non-Western knowledges. However, perspectives such as Finley's are more akin to those that ruled the era that concerns us. Although Blackfoot historic and literary expressions were not articulated in graphemes comparable to alphabetical writing, and did not contain chronological data to satisfy Western conceptions of history, they recorded past events in ways that were culturally appropriate and meaningful.

Cultural misunderstanding has prevented an appreciation of the literary value of First Nations oral narratives. Despite the contradiction implicit in "oral literature", a term the linguist Walter Ong describes as "monstrous,"[20] the want of a better descriptor (scholars have not taken up the alternative term "orature") to describe oral practices that share many of the characteristics of literature has resulted in its widespread application to narratives such as the Blackfoot Stories. The anthropologist and linguist Dell Hymes argues that Ong's study is not relevant to the Americas, because it does not include "a single New World case". Hymes suggests, based on his research on the literatures of First Nations of the North Pacific Coast, that three characteristics distinguish "literary art": "it must be abstract; it must change; it must give pleasure."[21]

In the late nineteenth century Grinnell was already describing renderings of the Blackfoot Stories as literature, and other scholars share his view.[22] If we consider that Homer's *Iliad* and *The Odyssey* are textual renderings of oral stories, and they are viewed as historical as well as literary representations, an analogy can be drawn to the stories from the oral traditions of First Nations peoples of the Americas, except that in the latter case, no coherent all-encompassing narrative of Homeric-proportions was produced.

A passage of the Blackfoot Story of Scarface, taken from Uhlenbeck's literal English translation, is included here in order to illustrate the texture of the story, its rhythm, and its non-conformity with English grammatical conventions. Uhlenbeck added content in square brackets to add clarity for non-Blackfoot readers. His interventions point up the non-prosaic characteristics of the story, even in its English translation. Uhlenbeck presented this passage as one block of text; however, printing one sentence per line allows a clearer view of sentence structure than is possible otherwise:

All ancient Peigans were camped [in a circle].
There was a chief's child, a woman, [that] would not marry.
Everybody wanted to marry her.
She refused [all of them].
There was a young man, [who] had a ridge-scar on his face.
He was called Scar-face [literally: Ridge].
He said to his younger sister: Tell that girl, that I want to marry her.
She said to that girl: My elder brother tells you, that you should marry him.
She said to her: Who is your elder brother?
Scar-face, she was told by [the younger sister].
[The chief's daughter said to her:] I don't refuse your elder brother.
Tell him: When his scar is seen no more, I shall marry [him].

> That girl went home. She wept.
> Her elder brother said to her: Why do you weep?
> She said to him: I am ashamed of what that woman said to me.
> She says: When your scar is seen no more, she will marry [you].[23]

If we compare the foregoing passage with a non-literal translation of the same passage in Wissler's and Duvall's *Mythology of the Blackfoot Indians*, we gain some idea of how the stories can be transformed in order to make them accessible to a white audience:

> Once there was a very poor young man who lived with his sister. He had a chum. In the camp was a very fine girl, the daughter of a chief, with whom all the young men were in love. Now the poor young man was in love with her also, but he had a long, ugly scar on his cheek. One day he asked his sister to go over to the chief's lodge to persuade the girl to marry him. Accordingly, the sister went over; but when the girl found out what she wanted, she said that she was willing to marry Scar-Face whenever that ugly scar disappeared. She made all manner of fun of Scar-Face./ Now the sister returned and told Scar-Face what the girl had said.[24]

No linguistic training is required to appreciate that, unlike the first version, the second follows English grammar and syntax. The contents of the second version do not require contextual knowledge to interpret meaning. The opening line that sets the Circle Camp as the time when the story begins is not included in the second version. The Blackfoot would have known that marriages took place during the Circle Camp, but this information would have been meaningless to outsiders. The second version introduces the "chum" or "partner", while this character appears much later in Uhlenbeck's version. The wish to marry the chief's daughter in the second version is attributed to "love"; and the scar is said to be "ugly", terms that do not appear in the first version. In the second version, the last sentence indicates that the chief's daughter shows contempt for Scarface, but there is no equivalent sentence in Uhlenbeck's translation. Contempt might have been evident in the tone of the oral performance when the chief's daughter replies to Scarface's sister: "Tell him: When his scar is seen no more, I shall marry [him]." This would explain why, towards the end of Uhlenbeck's version, the Morning Star asks Scarface to give him "that woman [that has scorned you]". These obvious discrepancies point to the difficulties of cultural translation. They demonstrate why transcribing and translating oral stories is, by necessity, a reductive exercise. Uhlenbeck's renditions might escape some of these pitfalls, but the need for his additions in square brackets, and the fact that his translation is longer than the Blackfoot text, indicate that meaning in the Blackfoot language is compressed, requiring fewer words than English to convey the same meaning. As Kehoe noted, thanks to Uhlenbeck's linguistic approach we can get a closer sense of the cadence of the story in ways that other authors were unable to capture.

This brief example of the way in which translation can attach extraneous meanings to the narratives demonstrates the need to appreciate the politics involved in the contest for representation attendant upon the production of the ethnographic text. Similarly, the adaptation of Blackfoot stories to fit non-Blackfoot genres, thus reframing Blackfoot knowledge, cannot be seen as a benign or innocuous exercise. It is, rather, one of the mechanisms for imposing the colonizers' perspective of how the world can be apprehended. This process has often resulted in the devaluation of oral stories such as those of the Blackfoot oral tradition.[25] One common flaw of the imposed categories is that they tend to secularize Blackfoot knowledge, which, as many Blackfoot scholars point out, integrates the sacred and the secular. Moreover, even though, as Hernandez argues, the Blackfoot Stories are linked to the shared notions of what it means to be Blackfoot, stories collected by ethnographers were often published as discrete narratives devoid of any cultural context. I seek to redress this lack of attention through a textual analysis of the Story of Scarface in chapter 9, but for now I will explore other ways in which alien categories can attach to transcribed oral narratives.

Grinnell divided *Lodge Tales* into four parts in order to reconfigure Blackfoot knowledge for his intended audience: the North American general public and perhaps the average reader of *Forest and Stream*. The four parts are: "Stories of Adventure", "Stories of Ancient Times", "Stories of Old Man", and "The Story of The Three Tribes."[26] Parts I to III contain translations of Blackfoot Stories rendered in English, with no more than a few editorial notes. Without going too deeply into the content of the individual stories, it is notable that Grinnell starts with "Adventure" stories, perhaps as a means to entice readers avid for such narratives. That the city-bred Grinnell with an office in New York and powerful friends in Washington — most notably, he was a personal friend of Theodore Roosevelt — interpreted these narratives as adventures, points to his personal experience of Blackfoot lifeways as an exotic indulgence, a tonic to counterbalance the pressures of modern life in the East. Wissler and Duvall classified the foundational "Story of Kutóyis" as a "Star Myth", yet Grinnell listed it under "Adventures".[27] In contrast with the first three parts of *Lodge Tales*, in Part IV, "Story of the Three Tribes", Grinnell becomes the ethnographer/narrator, weaving data collected from his informants with his own research of the limited sources available. His subheadings in Part IV reflect tropes from anthropology: "The Past and The Present," "Daily Life and Customs," "How the Blackfoot Lived," "Social Organization," "Hunting," "The Blackfoot in War," "Religion," "Medicine Pipes and Healing," and "The Blackfoot of To-day." Grinnell does not mention the methods that allowed his Blackfoot informants to maintain such an oral "archive".

The book titles chosen by the five authors also attach specific values to the materials contained therein. Uhlenbeck opts for the generic "texts", while Schultz (or Seele, the editor of his posthumously published text), in keeping with the narrative style, utilizes "memories". The remaining three titles contain the terms "mythology" (Wissler and Duvall), "legends" (McClintock), and "tales" (Grinnell) which correspond to what Nabokov calls "the generic myth/legend/folktale trinity of etic narrative forms."[28] The implications of the term "myth" have already been discussed. Folktales have no equivalent genre in Native American oral traditions. Folklorist William Bascom defines these as "secular narratives, commonly occurring outside any specific place or time, involving human and non-human characters, and are regarded as fictional stories with high entertainment (and educational) value."[29] Among the sub-genres he lists are: "human tales, animal tales, trickster tales, tall tales, formulistic tales, and moral tales or fables."[30] The secular character that Bascom attached to these genres is ethnocentric and cannot be applied to Blackfoot Stories because in the latter the sacred and secular are indivisible. Following Bascom, we would ascribe a secular dimension to "trickster tales", yet the Blackfoot trickster, Napiwa (Napi or Old Man), created the Blackfoot world and taught them everything that they needed to know in order to live. The Oldman River in Alberta bears his name, and his home is in the mountains at the head of this river. These are hardly secular matters. Using the label "tales", and defining stories such as these as secular, is manifestly inappropriate. In *Lodge Tales*, Grinnell made no distinction between "The Blackfoot Genesis", a sober account of how Napi created the Blackfoot and their world, and humorous stories in which Napi engages in all sorts of mischief, such as the one in which he tries to steal the Sun's leggings ("The Theft from the Sun"). Wissler and Duvall likewise gathered the Napi stories under one heading "Tales of Old Man". When historians interact with First Nations stories, the classifications they impose, argues R. David Edmunds, denote a misunderstanding and devaluation of non-Western knowledge.[31] The imposition of a secular genre ("tale") to the story of the Blackfoot creation represents a devaluation of their knowledge.

McClintock's preference for "Legends" in the title of his book is no less problematic. I again rely on Bascom's definition of legend:

> prose narratives which, like myths, are regarded as true by the narrator and his audience, but they are set in a period considered less remote, when the world was much as it is today ... more often secular than sacred, and their principal characters are human [...] They tell of migrations, wars and victories, deeds of past heroes, chiefs, and kings, and succession in ruling dynasties. In this they are often the counterpart in verbal tradition to written

history, but they also include local tales of buried treasure, ghosts, fairies, and saints.³²

Whereas genre distinctions tend to be understood as provisional, with exceptions often proving the rule, the definitions of legend and myth demonstrate the unreliability of these labels. In this instance, "Everyday Stories" or "history" as suggested by Hernandez and Boas, respectively, fit best the stories Bascom categorizes as legends. As Foucault argued, order is "that which is given in things as their inner law, the hidden network that determines the way they confront one another", but it is also "that which has no existence except in the grid created by a glance, an examination, a language".³³ In creating such grids in order to view the knowledge of First Nations peoples, outsiders impose their own meanings, altering those of the practitioners of the cultures they describe.

Translating and transcribing oral stories into text is fraught with difficulties, the most obvious being the impossibility of capturing a live performance — gesture, movement, voice and affect — without disrupting the coherence required of a written narrative.³⁴ Clifford Geertz refers to these anthropological writings as "interpretations, and second and third order ones to boot.³⁵ If we add to these difficulties the imposition of English grammatical structures, we cannot but agree with Vizenor's views that the stories transcribed by ethnographers "are 'fragile' immersions of themes and characters 'in a second nature, a second immediacy.'" As he observes, while "The sound of stories in the ear is a sure sense of presence [. . .] The translation of native oral stories is an absence."³⁶ It is worth transcribing a more elaborate paragraph, where Vizenor expands upon these ideas:

> The translation of native oral stories is an absence, never the natural haunt of presence. The transmutation of sound, the voice, and the trace of memories into written sentences is, at best, an artful pose; an aesthetic absence at the instance of the creation of native stories. Surely there are traces of native presence in translations, but the cause of author renditions is both a cultural discovery and a literary enterprise, and poses as a union of memories; the creases on the verso are cultural restriction and dominance. The sound of stories in the ear is our presence, and the other traces of that nature are survivance.³⁷

Here, in a classic trickster pose, Vizenor paradoxically employs Derridean notions of presence/absence to explicate the Native American context, simultaneously and mischievously denying yet affirming presence. Translation is an "absence" he avers, but the traces in translations are a "native presence". Vizenor also claims that Native stories "are the canons of survivance" and "the other traces of that nature"³⁸. He re-signifies "survivance" to claim that "Native survivance [. . .] is more than survival, more than endurance or a mere response; the stories of survivance are an active presence."[39] In such manner, Vizenor the trickster plays with words, confounds his audience, and defers meaning while turning the world upside down, by re-placing the oral above the written, all the while using writing to effect this move. His purpose is not in doubt: to place value on the oral stories and to claim for the Native American a privileged position vis-à-vis the non-indigenous compiler. Vizenor's theoretical position is a form of identity politics, but his intervention is apposite when seeking to contextualize similar claims in regard to the Blackfoot Stories, and seeking to understand the crucial role of the Blackfoot Stories as threads of continuity that bind Blackfoot epistemology to the published narratives.

Blackfoot Ways of Knowing and History

Having discussed some of the meanings that alien structures can impose upon the interpretation of Blackfoot Stories, I now turn to a more Blackfoot-centered perspective of their "ways of knowing". Blackfoot epistemology defined the context and boundaries applicable to the elaboration and transmission of knowledge that complied with truth requirements. The mechanisms for the transmission of "Old People Stories" preclude attaching authorship to narratives that are a collective cultural inheritance.[40] Authorship of these stories is collective and ongoing, rather than individual and fixed for all time. The occasion and the audience may also affect how the story is recounted. Wissler (who refers to these stories as "myths") points out that among the Blackfoot, the stories "are told by a few individuals, who take pride in their ability and knowledge, and usually impress their own individuality upon the form of the narrative [. . .] to say that any one version [. . .] is correct would be preposterous". Wissler recounts the explanation given to him by a Kainai Grandfather, a "venerable old man" who likened these narratives to common ragweed. The various versions of a story, like the parts of the weed, "all branch off from the stem. They go different ways, but all come from the same root."[41] The lack of an authorial figure attaching to the Blackfoot Stories has no doubt contributed to creating a perception that those who created these stories have long since disappeared, and bear no connection to the Blackfoot who continued to tell the stories, who were by implication viewed as incapable of creating them.

The Blackfoot oral tradition encompassed many genres. The claims to truth of some genres were closely scrutinized by the community, as was the case with war records. The knowledge and songs associated with the transfer of sacred bundles is yet another example. Inductees were required to memorize the teachings received when coming into possession of such items, including a rigorous order of motions, prayers, and songs during ceremonies involving the sacred object, as well as the observation of taboos at all times, including the location and orientation that these sacred items require. This kind of knowledge, which would be passed on to new custodians of these objects, allowed little room for creativity.

Knowledge of the more recent past, what Hernandez describes as "Everyday Stories" and Boas called "history", is also subject to rules, but these are different to those involving sacred objects. Blackfoot interest in the preservation and transmission of knowledge of their recent past, their war deeds, their supernatural encounters, and other events of note in the life of an individual or a band were maintained orally, but mnemonic devices sometimes assisted them to remember significant events. The topographical features of their ancestral lands were the Blackfoot's earliest mnemonic tools. They have a sacred and textual dimension, as rivers and rock formations provide the setting for stories of the creation of the Blackfoot universe and historical events, including supernatural occurrences.[42] They include sacred sites such as *Nin-ais-tukku* ("where the Thunder lives" or Chief Mountain), and the Oldman River in Alberta, which bears the name of Napiwa (Old Man).[43] Likewise, *Katoyisiks* (the Sweetgrass Hills) and the Porcupine Hills are populated by the spirits and feats of Blackfoot ancestors; these toponomies, through the Blackfoot Stories, are connected with the maintenance and reproduction of Blackfoot cultural practices and Blackfoot identity. They are places to which the Blackfoot go to "seek visions."[44]

The Blackfoot also used pictographs to record significant events. The key texts dedicated little space to these pictographic genres that were painted on rocks, tanned buffalo hides, or the hides of other animals (elk hides, cowskins and other hides[45]). Perishable materials made it imperative that these records were copied onto new hides from time to time. Events of individual and collective interest of the band were also painted on lodge covers and liners, and other surfaces discussed below under the rubric of War Art. These genres demonstrate Blackfoot interest in preserving relevant knowledge of their past. The existence of these systems of representation refutes the view of the Blackfoot as being without history. Although this is not the place to provide a holistic view of how these genres functioned within an integrated cultural system, I will examine their more overt formal attributes, and ways in which they preserved Blackfoot knowledge.

Blackfoot "*Ai Sinakinax*, Writers of History" kept collective histories of their respective bands, known as "Year counts" or "winter counts".[46] These contain the salient event of each year for a given band. Nabokov notes that a winter count is a translation of the Blackfoot *snaksin* ("picture-writing"), and should not be confused with a census.[47] The characteristics of this genre, which was used extensively by the buffalo-hunting

First Nations, are that they adhere to a chronological order, and consist of a pictograph which denotes the name given to a specific year, and which depicts the most salient or "epitomizing event" of that year.[48] Their contents are not autobiographical, rather, the events recorded are of collective interest to their keepers' bands. The pictographs of winter counts are arranged in a spiral, rather than a linear fashion. A ritual transfer was required when the winter count passed from one owner to the next. Like the professional historian, the keeper of the winter count exercises control over its content, not only by deciding which event deserves to be entered each year, but also when recounting the event in full detail before an audience.

Interest in winter counts and a wider recognition of their historical significance is a relatively recent phenomenon. Linea Sundstrom, for example, used winter counts in her study of epidemic disease, including smallpox outbreaks, in the Northern Plains between the early eighteenth and the early twentieth centuries.[49] Among the extant Blackfoot winter counts is that recorded by Kainai Parkapotokan (Bad Head), the "Bad Head's Winter Count". It covers the period between 1810 and 1883 and was transcribed by Robert N. Wilson, who served in the North-West Mounted Police (1881–84) and eventually became Indian Agent at the Kainai Reserve in Alberta. The contents of Bad Head's Winter Count were the subject of a 1951 article in the *Lethbridge Herald*, and were republished by Hugh Dempsey in 1965.[50] Bad Head was a Kainai leader and, at the time of publication, his was the earliest Blackfoot winter count known. However, in 1979 Paul Raczka published "Bull Plume's Winter Count," which covers the years 1764 to 1924. Four Pikuni men and a white missionary, successively, maintained this winter count for most of their lives. Each in turn passed it on to a new *historian* in order to ensure its continuity.[51]

The longevity of the Bull Plume's Winter Count is unsurpassed among the extant Blackfoot winter counts. Of the consecutive keepers of this winter count, the first has not been identified; the second was Mehkskéhme-Sukáhs (Iron Shirt), who was also known as A-pe-so-muckka (Running Wolf) for most of his life.[52] He was the subject of a painting by Karl Bodmer during the latter's sojourn at Fort McKenzie in late 1833. Mehkskéhme-Sukáhs was a chief of the *Ich-poch-semo* (Grease Melters) Band.[53] When he died in 1850, his son (later also known as Running Wolf), travelled north to live at the Peigan Reserve in Alberta. Here he received the name Natosi Nepe-e (Brings-Down-The-Sun). He was, notes Raczka, the leader of the Lone Fighters Band and a "holy man," and became the third keeper of the winter count. McClintock sought out Natosi Nepe-e to question him about Blackfoot knowledge in 1911, but made no mention of the winter count, even though he also met with the fourth keeper, Pikuni leader and ceremonialist Bull Plume.[54]

McClintock reports that Bull Plume offered to show him very old "tribal records [. . .] handed down by Wolf Child, my grandfather". However, he was unable to see them, because when Natosi Nepe-e found out about Bull Plume's offer, he convinced McClintock to remain in his camp, offering to instruct him in Blackfoot "legends", "customs", and the "worship of the Sun". Natosi Nepe-e had earlier refused to instruct McClintock, having vowed to "have nothing more to do with the white race" when the Indian Agent threatened to withdraw rations to prevent him from leading a Sun Dance. He relented once Bull Plume invited McClintock to camp with him and promised to show him old tribal records, and to allow him to copy them:

> For several years I have endured many things from this Bull Plume. I will no longer be silent, but will now speak plainly. If you desire to go to the camp of this man, I will not hinder you [. . .] I would prefer to have you stay with me, inasmuch as you came first to my camp and I have been preparing myself to relate to you many things that have happened to my people in former days.[55]

Both Bull Plume and Natosi Nepe-e were respected leaders and ceremonialists, the latter occupying a higher position. Bull Plume, who led in the opening of a Medicine Pipe attended by McClintock, was still young to have accumulated as much knowledge as his elder. There is a discrepancy between Natosi Nepe-e's claim that he had received the winter count from his father Running Wolf and later passed it on to Bull Plume, and Bull Plume's claim that he had inherited it from his own father.[56] The rivalry between the two Blackfoot ceremonialists, according to Raczka, was of no consequence; however, it is likely that Natosi Nepe-e deliberately prevented McClintock from viewing the winter count by drawing him away from Bull Plume.

Bull Plume's interest in Blackfoot history is evident in that he secured the winter count from Natosi Nepe-e. Transfer would have involved reciprocation consisting of valuable goods on the part of Bull Plume. It is possible that by the time Bull Plume met McClintock, he had already determined to have its contents transcribed. In 1912 he found a way to do so. He recounted the contents of the winter count, then still kept painted on a hide, to Canon William Haynes, an Anglican missionary, who reproduced the pictographs and recorded Bull Plume's interpretations.[57] Haynes, who at his death in 1937 had spent fifty-six years among the Blackfoot, continued adding to the winter count, recording the last entry for 1924. Clearly, Bull Plume saw the technology of writing as beneficial for the upkeep of Blackfoot history and sought to appropriate it to safeguard the winter count for future generations.

Amidst the dramatic changes forced upon the Blackfoot during the early reservation era, and the scarcity of buffalo hides, it is significant that

Natosi Nepe-e and Bull Plume had continued to maintain the winter count. Here, then, are two Grandfathers recording the past in accordance with Blackfoot ways of knowing during the so-called historical era. Moreover, it is notable that Bull Plume had been eager to collaborate with McClintock in the latter's project to document Blackfoot knowledge, and had eventually ensured the transcription of the contents of the winter count. Blackfoot such as Bull Plume, Natosi Nepe-e, Joseph Tatsey, David Duvall, and many others whose names appear all too briefly in the texts analyzed here, provided the threads of continuity that this chapter seeks to bring to the fore. The stories they contributed were transformed into "history" and constitute the traces of "survivance" that can unsettle the notion of the Blackfoot as a "people without history".

The Blackfoot, like other First Nations of the Plains, used pictographs in order to record past events. An intersection between oral and pictographic genres is evident in the practice throughout the Plains of a public oral performance dedicated to recounting acts of bravery recognized as *coups*. Counting *coup* describes both the act of gaining honour through a deed of courage, and the subsequent oratorical performance whereby the deed is recounted. The oral performance or counting *coup* established the *bona fides* of warriors. During the buffalo days, war feats and sacred knowledge were worthy of *coup* counting. The Blackfoot would count *coup* when they captured from an enemy a "shield, bow, gun, war bonnet, war shirt, or medicine pipe".[58] They publicly recounted their deeds at the beginning of sacred rituals, including the liminal moment just prior to opening Medicine Bundles. Kainai leader Mike Mountain Horse notes that counting *coup* takes place at several key moments during Ookaan, such as before the ritual cutting of the centre-pole, when members of the Horn Society loudly recount the heroic achievements of their youth.

Alvin Josephy has claimed that in the ritualized warfare developed by the Plains First Nations, "the mere touching of an enemy, known as 'counting *coup*', brought higher honour than killing."[59] The specific restrictions attached to counting *coup* varied among the First Nations peoples of the Plains. New modalities of *coup* emerged with the influx of European technology and methods of warfare. For example, in his autobiographical *My People The Bloods*, Mountain Horse (1888–1964) claims that scalps and rifles were the Kainai's most highly prized trophies of war. Mountain Horse became a warrior, serving overseas after having enlisted in the Canadian army in 1916 during World War One. Moreover, he wrote articles for the newspapers, and his autobiography, completed *c.*1936, was edited by Hugh A. Dempsey, and published posthumously in 1969.[60]

The genre of counting *coup*, argues Sidner Larson, was not self-centered.[61] It followed that an intrinsic part of the genre consisted of "witnesses who were encouraged to interject, to authenticate, or to correct if they felt that was necessary". Moreover, a variant of counting *coup* was a collective performance described as a "sham fight" or "pantomimic display of skirmishes."[62] Counting *coup* is thus a clear instance of a polyglossic genre in the sense of this term noted by Bahktin. Attempts to capture the genre in writing are inadequate to convey its meaning fully, hence, according to Larson, what prevails of this genre in the written record, is a "Western conception of autobiography as a story of a whole life."[63]

These war narratives perhaps held most attraction for whites, whose imaginings of the Blackfoot stereotyped them first and foremost as fierce warriors, ignoring other qualities the Blackfoot valued, such as generosity, yet another avenue for the Blackfoot to acquire prestige. Nevertheless, as Mountain Horse points out, becoming a warrior was "the highest calling in the eyes of the Indian male [. . .] To 'run' a herd of stolen horses across the border in early days was considered by the Bloods as not only a profitable occupation, but a feat of gallantry and daring as well."[64] According to Blackfoot epistemology, the need to provide evidence of a *coup* has been intrinsic to the genre. Confirmation may be provided by a witness or by producing material proof, e.g., the goods acquired through the deed. Misrepresenting the facts would incur social disgrace and invite tragedy.[65] It was *de rigueur* during truces with enemy First Nations to exchange information of previous battles and raids; any inconsistencies that disproved the accounts given by protagonists could seriously damage their reputation. This is one demonstration of how Blackfoot epistemology, like its Western counterpart, also possessed what Foucault called "rules of exclusion" in order to control discourse that was "within the true." To enact, and to witness *coup* counting would have contributed to making the Blackfoot adept at remembering their shared past, especially those events that they valued most. Representing truth in these narratives was intrinsic to the genre.

Given that counting *coup* was nurtured by war, Blackfoot who enrolled in the Armed Forces maintained the genre alive. Suitable modern situations for counting *coup*, according to Kainai Pete Standing Alone, include "promotions in the armed forces, strikes at a real enemy in an international conflict, travel to far-off places and doing something special, or rendering some important public service." These new *coup* modalities did not replace their traditional counterparts. For example, as Standing Alone notes "Possession of a number of bundles, in itself an indication that a person is of some consequence, is a traditional coup counting situation that has not changed at all."[66]

Before the Blackfoot had access to the technology of writing, the premium placed on achievements worthy of counting *coup* might account for the existence of mnemonic devices that would assist those whose achievements were too numerous to convey by memory alone. In a recent publication, Kainai scholar James Dempsey links Blackfoot war art between 1880 and 2000 to pictographs from the "Late Prehistoric and Protohistoric periods, c.1600–1750" when "records of war experiences appeared." In his detailed and wide-ranging study encompassing exemplars of Blackfoot "war art" held in public and private hands in the United States, Canada, and several European countries, J. Dempsey draws attention to the materials that have been used as surfaces for the genre, which include rock faces, buffalo hides; and in the aftermath of the demise of the bison herds, cowhides, canvas, and paper. Manufactured items utilizing animal hides sometimes used as surfaces for war art, include items of dress discussed earlier (shirts, leggings and robes), as well as lodge covers and liners. J. Dempsey distinguishes "war tallies" from the scenes of battles using pictographs that were painted on some of these hides.[67] These records established the status of warriors within their respective communities and beyond, attesting to their worthiness as leaders.

Individual achievements recorded on "painted robes" have been pejoratively described as "brag robes."[68] Nabokov asserts that this genre was an exclusively male art form in the Plains, subsequent to the introduction of the horse:

> With horses and intensified intergroup feuding, it became customary for Plains Indian warriors to portray battle exploits with pictographic figures on shirts, robes, and even tipi covers. An early example of these self-promotional "partisan histories" came to light after Lewis and Clark collected a Mandan painted buffalo robe depicting a fight between horsemen believed to have taken place about 1797.[69]

The subject matter of painted robes was not a whole-of-life story. Rather, the robe's owner recorded salient experiences, including *coups*, which sustained his reputation, and supernatural events. Each important deed attained by an individual was to be recounted to that person's last days, regardless of the number of *coups* accumulated. Being highly perishable, painted robes would have been replaced from time to time. However, the scarcity of materials after the obliteration of the buffalo, which similarly caused other game to become scarce, forced the genre to migrate to newer materials, including cowhides, canvas, and paper. The depictions of war art, as Dempsey has documented, could be found on innumerable objects, including bows, quivers, war clubs, spears, staffs, axes, pipes, blankets, shirts, lodge covers and liners, and even on the favorite horse of a warrior.

Until James Dempsey's recent work, scholars did not attempt to record systematically the details of painted robes, or the "language" they share, even though some transcriptions of the meanings of individual robes were extant. This is the case with the "Three Suns' Robe". Schultz notes that it

FIGURE 4.1 Karl Bodmer, Swiss, 1809–1893, *Piegan Blackfeet Man*, 1833, watercolour and pencil on paper, sheet: 12 ³/₈ × 10 in.; 31.4325 × 25.4 cm, Joslyn Art Museum, Omaha, Nebraska: Gift of the Enron Art Foundation, 1986, JAM 1986.49.290.

FIGURE 4.2 George Catlin, *Stu-mick-o-súks, Buffalo Bull's Back Fat, Head Chief, Blood Tribe*. 1985.66.149, Smithsonian American Art Museum. Gift of Mrs. Joseph Harrison, Jr.

FIGURE 4.3 Johann Hürlimann, after Karl Bodmer, Swiss, 1809–1893, *Chief of the Blood-Indians, War-Chief of the Piekann Indians, and Koutani Indian*, 1839, engraving and hand coloured aquatint on paper, Joslyn Art Museum, Omaha, Nebraska: Gift of the Enron Art Foundation, 1986, JAM 1986.49.542.46.

FIGURE 4.4 George Catlin, *Eeh-nís-kin, Crystal Stone, Wife of the Chief*. 1985.66.150, Smithsonian American Art Museum. Gift of Mrs. Joseph Harrison, Jr.

FIGURE 5.1 Karl Bodmer, Swiss, 1809–1893, *Encampment of the Piekann Indians*, 1833, aquatint, engraving, and watercolor on paper, Joslyn Art Museum, Omaha, Nebraska, JAM 43.Tab.

FIGURE 8.1 AF 4702, *Wolf Collar's Story Robe*, 1961, moose skin, pencil, paint, string, 123.5 cm × 118.0 cm, Collection of Glenbow Museum, Calgary, Canada.

was presented to U.S. Captain L. W. Cooke (later Brigadier General), by the acting Blackfeet agent 1893–94. Pikuni war chief Three Suns (a.k.a. Big Nose) painted the robe on an elk skin. Some of the feats described demonstrate the range of subject matter of the genre. Three Suns' Robe contained twenty-two pictographs relating to the life of its owner between 1845 and 1870. Cooke transcribed the events depicted, including some dates, according to Three Suns' verbal rendition. Scene 13 (1875) relates a Blackfoot encounter with four Sioux discovered in a thicket, including location, number of lodges camped, and the parlay between them and Three Suns which led to a peaceful resolution. The Sioux were taken away unharmed by six soldiers who came from Fort Walsh, Northwest Territory. Scene 20 (undated) is starker: "Scalps taken by Big Nose. Some, however, were killed by others — the first to take has the honor."[70] The starkness of descriptions such as Scene 20 might have contrasted with the oral performance of the feat related, which would have provided many details and would have been "performed" during large gatherings by the owner.

Grinnell was presented with "an illuminated cowskin" containing "the most striking events in the life of Red Crane, a Blackfoot warrior, painted by himself." In Grinnell's opinion the pictographs were "very rude", "but sufficiently lifelike to call up to the mind of the artist each detail of the stirring events they record."[71] Swiss artist Karl Bodmer, who travelled up the Missouri River in 1833–34 in the company of amateur ethnographer Prince Maximilian of Wied-Neuwied, painted an unidentified Pikuni man wearing a full-length painted robe, but did not report on the meanings it encoded (see Figure 4.1 CP). However, markings on the robe such as "horse's hooves, bows, rifles, and bleeding adversaries tell tales of personal bravery for all to see."[72]

A more complicated process resulted in the painting of "Wolf Collar's Story Robe", currently exhibited at the Glenbow Museum in Calgary, Alberta (see Figure 8.1 CP). According to J. Dempsey, in 1963, Paul Wolf Collar, the grandson of the warrior whose deeds are depicted on the robe, directed artist George Runner, a Sarcee, to represent his grandfather's exploits. These included supernatural visions, encounters with enemies, and horse raids, all of which took place before the Blackfoot signed Treaty Seven with the Dominion in 1877. For nearly a century, Wolf Collar's descendants retained the memory of his exploits finally depicted on the robe — a gesture that, J. Dempsey notes, was prompted by a request from the Glenbow Archive.

The use of mnemonics demonstrates that "history" and the representation of truth occupied a privileged position within Blackfoot epistemology, even if the predominance of war narratives in the genres discussed is to the exclusion of other knowledge. The proliferation of war art during the reservation era, a time when the events that constituted its principal subject matter had become criminal offences, reflects the availability of time and materials (cow hides), but also a Blackfoot desire to construct their own imaginaries based on a Blackfoot-centered history. Another consideration would have been the financial benefit that could be obtained while engaging in a traditional occupation, now turned into a commodity by non-Blackfoot collectors of Indian artifacts.

Blackfoot Agency or White Cultural Appropriation?

Blackfoot epistemology, like its Western counterpart, contains mechanisms for the control of discourses that are "within the true". Blackfoot storytellers would preface their renditions by providing a genealogy of the stories recounted. Although the stories, as collective memories, had no author to guarantee their claims to truth, those who recounted them adhered to rules regarding the "truth" of the stories.[73] Peter Nabokov argues that "any account of Indian–white relations deserves multiple representations," because stories "reflect contrasting or overlapping vested interests, differing modalities of accounting and interpreting, and culturally divergent senses of what it all meant."[74] These considerations illustrate an ongoing scholarly debate, not only about interpretation and representation, but also about who is allowed to speak for whom.

Given that narrative is a construction that can never capture the fullness of a given event, Nabokov's call for "multiple representations" is justified. However, this approach does not imply that all representations have equivalent claims to truth. Foucauldian notions of power/knowledge cannot but be invoked wherever power and truth are discussed, as they do when Blackfoot oral knowledge becomes written text through the mediation of the white ethnographer. Nor can Foucault's elaboration on the production and control of discourses and the "will to truth" be omitted from a context where claims to truth are pervasive. As Foucault noted, truth is intrinsically related to power.[75]

These ideas help to view better the truth claims of the five key texts, which to a large extent rest on the authority of the Blackfoot informants to articulate discourses that counted as true. To document Blackfoot knowledge, the ethnologists relied on Blackfoot who had acquired knowledge in the time-honoured fashion, through participation in societies and ceremonies, through acquisition by transfer of sacred objects, together with the prayers and songs associated with each. While the ethnographers (except for Duvall) belonged to the dominant colonizer elite, their informants also belonged to an identifiable Blackfoot elite, and were recognized by their community for their knowledge. As such, these informants are akin to "organic intellectuals". Their authority rests on their knowledge acquired according to accepted Blackfoot practices including, but not limited to, initiation in graded societies, the acquisition of sacred objects, and the sponsoring of sacred ceremonies.

Blackfoot epistemology, like its Western counterpart, is subject to the workings of knowledge and power, with "power" being often translated as "Medicine", an inadequate term coined to refer to the manifold manifestations of *natoyi* or sacred power that has been discussed earlier in this volume. At a practical level, all humans are deemed to possess a certain degree of sacred power, relative to the goodwill and protection of beings both from the animate and the inanimate realms, which can be acquired in many ways, including through dreams, especially during vision quests.[76] A person's possession of power is evinced by induction into societies, and the acquisition of Sacred Bundles and other sacred objects. Transfer to a new owner of these sacred objects includes the actions, songs, and prayers (knowledge) required for their upkeep. It is worth re-stating that "Medicine ownership is a property distinction because a man [or a woman] must possess much before he [or she] can own medicine."[77]

Apart from these meanings, Blackfoot Medicine or sacred power is also concerned with healing. However, of particular interest here is the notion of Medicine as knowledge, and the status that possession of certain knowledge can confer. In the same manner that a warrior's status is commensurate with his deeds of courage on the warpath, the status of a person of knowledge is commensurate with the sacred items that have come into his/her possession during his/her lifetime. Independently from the respect attached to the owner of sacred objects, each time they are acquired the knowledge concomitant to their keeping is transferred to the new owner. Knowledge obtained thus was and continues to be highly valued, not least because those in possession of sacred objects can act as intermediaries, requesting divine intervention on behalf of other Blackfoot. During the era on which this study focuses, such services were generously rewarded with valuable gifts (horses, blankets and other goods). Ethnographers were drawn into these Blackfoot practices and were required to show their respect for the knowledge received from "Grandparents" through suitable reciprocation.

Professional and amateur ethnographers sought to vouchsafe the authority of the constructions of "truth" in their salvage texts by ensuring the "authenticity" of their informants. This attitude presupposes a disregard for those who became "contaminated", racially or otherwise, by contact with white culture. Thus, while bicultural individuals were perfectly positioned to act as mediators and translators, informants were preferably sought among "full bloods", thus equating truth-value with blood quantum. Grinnell attributes the stories he compiled "mostly" to "Blackfeet, Bloods and Piegans of pure race", including "Red Eagle; Almost-a-Dog [...] Four Bears [...] Wolf Calf, Big Nose, Heavy Runner, Young Bear Chief, Wolf Tail, Rabid Wolf, Running Rabbit, White Calf,

All-are-his-Children, Double Runner, and Lone Medicine Person, and many others."[78]

None of Grinnell's informants, with two exceptions, is identified with the particular stories they contributed. Miss Cora M. Ross, one of the teachers at the Blackfoot agency, whose ethnic provenance is not mentioned, is credited with providing a version of the Story of the Medicine Lodge (Ookaan).[79] The other exception is Mrs. Thomas Dawson, who is credited with the story of the "Lost Children." Moreover, Grinnell cites the assistance of Pikuni by adoption and "veteran prairie man, Mr. Hugh Monroe and his son John Monroe." Hugh Monroe (a.k.a. Ma-kwi'-i-po-wak-sin or Rising Wolf) was the grandfather of William Jackson, Grinnell's assistant. Monroe Sr. had lived among the Pikuni since 1815, and in 1886 had become a resident of the Blackfeet Reservation of his Pikuni wife. He was, according to the lore of the era, a "squaw man".[80]

It is significant that those who went by non-anglicized names were not given specific acknowledgement for the stories they contributed to Grinnell's text. This appears to relate to Grinnell's ambivalent attitude towards First Nations peoples. On the one hand he extols the human qualities of the Indians with whom he has shared many experiences; he declares, for example, that the stories in *Lodge Tales* are "pictures of Indian life drawn by Indian artists". On the other hand, however, he claims: "The Indian has the mind and feelings of a child with the stature of a man"[81]. These ambivalent attitudes strengthen negative stereotypes, even through Grinnell coevally lauded the positive qualities of Indians.

McClintock's claims to truth, like those of Grinnell, rest on the credentials of his Blackfoot collaborators who provide a sense of "authenticity" to his narrative. Chief among them is Pikuni chief and ceremonialist Natosi Nepe-e. Historian Sherry Smith argues that McClintock purposefully masked the presence of bicultural individuals in his writing by using their Indian names, which she attributes to a desire to romanticize the images he portrayed. Moreover, Smith observes that McClintock, in his extensive collection of photographs, never included modern structures, although his photographs were taken "only yards away from Browning, Montana."[82] Her point is well taken, however, McClintock would have heard these names in his daily intercourse with the Blackfoot, who did not refer to each other by their translated names. The Blackfoot obliged whites by utilizing their translated names in their dealings with them, while their Blackfoot names were used in their dealings with other Blackfoot. Evidently, using a person's name, rather than a translation, implies respect and recognition, and, for the sake of the historical record, the inclusion of the Blackfoot names in *The Old North Trail* is an asset.

The authority of the Blackfoot informants that buttressed *Lodge Tales*' claims to truth is reinforced by Grinnell's claim to have rendered the stories "in the words of the original narrators as nearly as it is possible to render those words into the simplest every-day English language".[83] Although such claims of transparency have long been discounted within the field of ethnology,[84] it is indisputable that Blackfoot knowledge reinforced these texts' claims to truth. It is this presence within the process of transformation of Blackfoot oral stories into text that binds the Blackfoot ways of knowing to *written* Blackfoot history and literature. Paradoxically, once the knowledge of First Nations peoples is expressed in Western terms (writing), it becomes highly valued. The intentions of the informants, although not always made explicit, are important in order to understand that they exercised some power through their collaboration with the ethnographers. Despite belonging to an oral tradition, these collaborators saw fit to disseminate their knowledge through writing, which does not imply a capitulation of their ways of knowing. Rather, it demonstrates their preparedness to expand their cultural capital. Within the context of colonialism, the First Nations informant is often portrayed as exploited, misrepresented and ill-used by the ethnographer, with current notions of "collaborative ethnography" developing well after the time period that concerns us.[85] However, those Blackfoot who participated in the process of writing the Blackfoot knowledge need to be given credit for ensuring that their stories would prevail for future generations.[86]

Documenting the knowledge of what Ong describes as "primary oral cultures"[87] has been a concomitant of colonization. The letters written by Columbus describing the inhabitants of the New World marked the beginning of ethnological endeavours in the Americas.[88] The misrepresentations and misunderstandings prevalent in early chronicles served to construct First Nations' subjectivity through a similar process as that exposed by Edward Said in his seminal *Orientalism*. Blackfoot territory was renamed, not to mention artificially divided by the United States–Canada border. The Elk River became the Yellowstone River, the Bear River was renamed the Marias, the Big River, the Missouri, the Sweet Pine Hills became the Sweet Grass Hills, the list goes on.[89] Grinnell negotiated on behalf of the U.S. Government for the Pikuni to sell a portion of their land in 1895, to have it set aside as Glacier National Park, an achievement jointly credited to Grinnell and Schultz. Both men travelled extensively throughout this part of the Rocky Mountains "naming" glaciers along the way.

Early chroniclers colonized First Nations peoples' knowledge by reframing it to fit European worldviews, and re-deploying it towards European ends, most notably evangelization, trade, and colonization. The concomitant devaluation of First Nations peoples by this appropriation is evident in the way that intellectual property was translated without sufficient recognition, concurrent with the disparaging of First Nations' epistemologies and their oral traditions, viewed by most whites as inferior to writing. These attitudes are evident in Ong's claim that

> Human beings in primary oral cultures [. . .] learn a great deal and possess and practice great wisdom, but they do not 'study'. They learn by apprenticeship — hunting with experienced hunters, for example — by discipleship, which is a kind of apprenticeship, by listening, by repeating what they hear, by mastering proverbs and ways of combining and recombining them, by assimilating other formulary materials, by participation in a kind of corporate retrospection — not by study in a strict sense.[90]

Ong's argument relies upon a Eurocentric definition of "study", and thus is self-fulfilling; its corollary is that knowledge can be assimilated but not created within an oral tradition. Such a proposition is manifestly untenable because it implies that unless knowledge is written down it cannot be imparted or reflected upon. This perspective fails to account for the knowledge base of First Nations peoples such as the Blackfoot, without whom the texts studied here would not have been written. Manifestly, if Western epistemology is to be normative, a devaluation of non-Western epistemologies will ensue. However, this ethnocentric contrast continues to have adherents among anthropologists, most notably Jack Goody, who argues that writing constitutes the key difference between 'us' and 'them', for all that he renounces cultural relativism ("sentimental egalitarianism"):

> Relativism, in its extreme form, is saying that the people in Africa are the same as the Chinese, the Japanese and so on. Well, if they are the same, why are their achievements not the same? So the notion that arose in recent years that all human societies are the same goes against cultural history, I think, because it's not possible to equate the achievements of people without writing to those of peoples with writing. We have to take into account the fact that societies that do not have what I call the technology of the intellect are not able to build up knowledge in the same way as the ones that have. Of course, they have knowledge systems about nature but they cannot achieve the same as the societies that have books, encyclopaedias, dictionaries and all that sort of thing.[91]

In order to view the two-way workings of appropriation and the contribution of Blackfoot "historians" to the writing of Blackfoot history it is necessary to recognize that knowledge of the Blackfoot past shared with the ethnographers was not anecdotal or accidental. Rather, it was the product of systematic record keeping that served well the requirements of Blackfoot epistemology. Having said that, it is evident that, in a time of changing circumstances, sufficient numbers of Blackfoot saw in the technology of writing a useful tool to preserve their knowledge. Patently, while the ethnographer retained editorial prerogatives — for example by excluding from publication what Wissler and Duvall describe as "humorous texts (of which there are a great number, chiefly obscene)"[92]

— the Blackfoot collaborators also control the flow of information, as well as its content.

By framing traditional knowledge through their storytelling, the Blackfoot informants, albeit indirectly, acquired access to representation. Potentially, they were in a position to counter negative stereotypes and popular misconceptions, and to demonstrate the complexity of the Blackfoot worldview. Their presence, although mediated by the translators and ethnographers, is the *sine qua non* that animates the texts — the survivance posited by Vizenor. Blackfoot agency needs to be explored in light of the wishes expressed by Blackfoot participants in the process of transcription and translation of Blackfoot knowledge. Those who collaborated on both sides of the cultural divide belonged to two different worlds, had different motivations and interests, but were nevertheless able to cooperate in this mutually beneficial undertaking. A clear example is Bull Plume's determination to have Blackfoot history transcribed. Whereas for the most part the initiative for the project to transform oral stories into text came from the ethnographers, who travelled long distances to seek out the Blackfoot informants, Bull Plume reversed the trend by approaching McClintock and then Canon Haynes. Clearly, Bull Plume saw the technology of writing as beneficial for the upkeep of Blackfoot knowledge of the past, and sought to appropriate it to safeguard the winter count for future generations. Furthermore, it cannot be discounted that Blackfoot participants in the ethnographic encounter felt privileged to have their perspective of Blackfoot history inform the written text. This became evident by the way in which Bull Plume and Natosi Nepe-e competed for McClintock's attention. The process no doubt added to their prestige as "Grandfathers" who held knowledge that was now valued in two cultures.

Cash payments were another benefit to Blackfoot informants. Siksika Raw Eater, for example, was a highly respected "Grandfather" who kept a painted robe with his war exploits. According to John Gooderham, Raw Eater "had a great fund of folklore". Edward Curtis had sought him as his informant in 1924, when he was compiling his massive study of First Nations. Gooderham claims that Raw Eater charged Curtis "one dollar an hour, and he didn't hurry!"[93] The rate seems high when compared with the "one dollar for each half day" that Lucien Hanks and Jane Richardson Hanks paid their Siksika informants in 1938.[94] Such payments accord with the custom of reciprocation observed by the Blackfoot when knowledge was ritually transferred or, more generally, when the knowledge of a ceremonialist or healer was engaged — an indication of the workings of knowledge and power in Blackfoot epistemology, and an indication of the value placed on the keeping of knowledge by the Blackfoot. By entering into that economy of reciprocation, the ethnographers were being absorbed into Blackfoot practice.

PART III — ETHNOGRAPHIC ENCOUNTERS

From the Blackfoot narrators' perspective, the deployment of writing was not unlike their previous appropriation of European technologies, namely the horse, metal tools, and firearms, which took place in the mid-eighteenth century. The benefits of such appropriations were evident in the transformation of the Blackfoot into a powerful equestrian nation by the mid-nineteenth century. Blackfoot willingness to participate in the writing of their oral knowledge follows this pattern, evident in their demand — enshrined in Treaty Seven with the Dominion — for the provision of teachers to educate Blackfoot children in white ways of knowing.[95]

The ritual adoption of influential whites seems to have been a Blackfoot strategy to obtain powerful allies who could provide know-how in their dealings with the dominant culture. Grinnell, McClintock, and Schultz were Blackfoot by adoption. Grinnell's adoption came after he lobbied in Washington for food relief to be sent to the Pikuni during the 1883–84 famine, for which Schultz, who had written to ask for Grinnell's assistance, gave Grinnell much credit.[96] John Ewers, however, disapproved of "earlier writers" (perhaps alluding to Grinnell) who blamed the Blackfeet Indian Agent, John Young, for the catastrophe during which between a quarter and a third of the Pikuni in Montana died. Ewers is silent on Grinnell's role on behalf of the Pikuni, but other scholars note that Grinnell sent letters to officials in Washington that "saw to it that rations reached the reservation."[97] When Grinnell came to Montana in 1885, Little Dog and Little Plume adopted him into the Blackfoot and made him an honorary "chief".[98] They gave him the name Pi-nut-ú-ye is-tsím-okan (Fisher Hat). Harris notes that during the following years Grinnell used not only *Forest and Stream* as a forum to draw public attention to irregularities in the conduct of Agents (notably Agent Baldwin), but he also published letters in the New York press to rally support for the Pikuni. Grinnell served as a conduit for Pikuni grievances at a time where they had no other means of redress.

According to McClintock, his own adoption by Siyeh (Mad Wolf), a respected Blackfoot, obeyed the latter's desire for "an alliance [. . .] a representative, who had lived sufficiently long among his people, to become familiar with their customs, religion, and manner of life, and would tell the truth about them to the white race."[99] It is possible that McClintock's adoption had been conceived as a strategy by Pikuni leaders, who may have seen in the young man another ally in the Grinnell mould. Siyeh and Double Runner, who had close ties to Grinnell, were key players in McClintock's naming ceremony, whereby he became A-pe-ech-eken (White Weasel Moccasin).[100]

For those who became honorary Blackfoot, the benefits of being regarded as Blackfoot by adoption included access to knowledge as insiders. Smith argues that Mad Wolf's expectations of McClintock ended in disappointment, so much so that the Blackfoot eventually decided "not to adopt more white people into the tribe."[101] How long that injunction lasted is not clear. The Kainai, for example, continue to induct distinguished whites into a symbolic office, the Kainai Chieftainship, which entails the bestowal of a Blackfoot name. In 1977, during the commemoration of the signing of Treaty Seven, Prince Charles was inducted, and was given the name Me'-kay-sto (Red Crow), the name of the principal Kainai leader who signed the 1877 treaty. In 1919 the same name had been bestowed on the first inductee into the chieftainship, Charles's uncle, Prince Edward.[102]

BLACKFOOT APPROPRIATION: THE MANY GUNS' WINTER COUNT

Revitalization of Blackfoot genres and their redeployment in ways that are sensitive to changing cultural imperatives is ongoing. For example, Pikuni artist George Bull Child utilized the painted robe genre *c.*1930 in order to commemorate the 1870 massacre of Chief Heavy Runner's band by the U.S. Army.[103] A different instance of revitalization of painted robes resulted in the creation of a new genre: a Blackfoot calendar titled the "Many Guns' Winter Count". Unlike winter counts such as that of Bull Plume, which contained pictographs arranged in a circular pattern, the Many Guns' Winter Count fused the subject matter of the winter count and syllabic writing. According to Many Guns, during the first decade of the twentieth century (1908) two "old Bassano men", Makúya.to'si (Wolf Sun) and Apináko'tamiso (Tomorrow Coming Over The Hill), resolved to start a calendar because the younger generations were not "learning and remembering things."[104] They compiled relevant stories that were in the public domain, of which the earliest dated back to 1831. New material was added each subsequent year, but in keeping with the winter count genre, the sources of the information were not recorded.

The differences between this calendar and winter counts are blurred. Winter counts are similar to early medieval monastic annals, which according to historian James Westfall Thompson grew out of a practice of jotting events on calendars originally designed to mark the date for religious and ritual events.[105] The calendar, which included more than one event per year, utilized "a word in syllabics"[106] to recall significant events, instead of a pictograph as winter counts did. The calendar's incorporation into Blackfoot practices extended to the sacred domain. It was ritually transferred to Many Guns, together with "the learning" required to maintain it, whence it acquired his name. It is evident that in starting the calendar, Makúya.to'si and Apináko'tamiso sought to deploy the new genre to record the subject matter of winter counts. Thus, they instructed Many Guns to keep a track of "persons and their war parties". Many

PART III — ETHNOGRAPHIC ENCOUNTERS

FIGURE 8.2 *Many Guns and wife, Siksika (Blackfoot) reserve, Alberta* [1919], Glenbow Archive, Calgary, Canada, NC-71-12.

Guns continued to maintain the calendar in 1938, when Lucien Hanks and Jane Richardson Hanks interviewed him.[107] Given that raiding was by then a thing of the past, the calendar had shifted focus, recording *inter alia* information on the annual Ookaan, including the name of the Holy Woman (or Women) who vowed to build a Medicine Lodge each year.

Blackfoot cultural brokers and "organic intellectuals", some with bicultural ancestry, were instrumental in creating a written version of their own knowledge/history that would inform subsequent histories of their nation by Blackfoot and non-Blackfoot scholars and, *ergo*, of the Plains First Nations more generally. This thereby preserved an autochthonous Blackfoot history — "from the enormous condescension of posterity"[108] — for future Blackfoot generations while simultaneously inscribing it within Western historiography. The aim here has been to demonstrate this process of transmission by profiling the intellectual position of the Blackfoot informants; their capacity for agency in the construction of their own history for white consumption; and their relative power to produce discourses "within the true" (in the Foucauldian sense) *vis-à-vis* that of the ethnographers who compiled and edited the five key publications, which have become canonical Blackfoot history. In their relations with the pioneer ethnographers, then, Blackfoot informants underwrote the claims to truth of the compilers/editors of these texts.

The ethnographer's report is not only concerned with the altruistic salvage project, or with enhancing white understanding of the "Other", although it carries with it the potential to dispel existing negative stereotypes. Blackfoot who collaborated with the ethnographers saw in the technology of writing a useful tool rather than a threat to their cultural practices; a means to record Blackfoot testimony as to the richness of the Blackfoot worldview and the complexity of Blackfoot lifeways. Blackfoot such as massacre survivor Kai Okotan also viewed the written stories as a medium to render testimony of the colonizers' transgressions.

The Blackfoot oral stories compiled by early ethnographers attest to the existence of complex patterns in the conduct of social and religious rituals, even when this link was not articulated in the anthologies. A clear example is provided by the Story of Scarface (Paii or Poia), which is further explored in the remaining chapters of this book in order to point up the interconnectedness between the story and Blackfoot ideologies. The maintenance of such a system ensured Blackfoot social cohesiveness and cultural reproduction, as well as contributing to their physical and cultural survival as a distinct nation.

Even though the ethnographers' foremost goal was to inform white audiences (both the general public and professionals), the collaborations that transformed Blackfoot knowledge into texts should not be understood merely as a process whereby Blackfoot culture is appropriated, misunderstood, mistranslated, and misused for the benefit of Western scholarship or to enhance the prestige of the putative authors. The stories compiled owe much to Blackfoot brokerage. The stories recorded in these texts, although hybrid/syncretic, remain a vehicle of cultural revitalization. Most importantly, the written text is insurance that future Blackfoot generations, even those removed by circumstances from traditional practices, will know how their ancestors had lived — the expressed desire of Grinnell's collaborator, Double Runner. In effect, as noted by Crowe in her introduction to *Lodge Tales*, Grinnell's text "influenced not only the world's views about Blackfeet people but [their] own views about [themselves] as well".

History, we are told, is written by the victors, not the vanquished.[109] However, the central aim of a self-conscious ethnohistory is to write history from the vantage point of the vanquished. Blackfoot self-representation through the publication of Blackfoot-authored texts began at a time when those who left their mark on the foundational texts reviewed here had already passed away. A generation later, books with an emic perspective, such as Mike Mountain Horse's *My People The Bloods*, began to appear.[110] These self-representations drew from both the oral tradition and the pioneering ethnologies, built securely on Blackfoot testimonies now become foundational, and hence canonical sources of Blackfoot history, literature, and culture.

PART IV

The Oral Tradition in
Contemporary Native Literature

9
Hero Quests, Sun Dancing, and the Story of "Scarface"

Scarface (Paii[1]) was a Blackfoot ancestor who lived during the era when the Blackfoot were yet to acquire horses. Instead, they used dogs to carry their loads when moving camp. Throughout this book, Scarface and his story have been summoned for their relevance to the Blackfoot universe. According to the Story of Scarface (henceforth "Scarface"), this culture hero embarked on a quest to find where the Star People lived in order to ask Natosi to remove the scar from his face. Ookaan, the Blackfoot central ceremony, is conducted according to the teachings that Natosi imparted to Scarface during his visit. Through the ceremony the Blackfoot are able to maintain a reciprocal relationship with the Above Beings. The suit that, according to the story, the Star Beings (the Sun, the Moon, and the Morning Star) gave Scarface is another aspect that has been explored in chapters 4, 5 and 6. "Scarface" was anthologized in the ethnographic texts discussed in chapters 7 and 8, which *inter alia* analyzed some of the meanings that translation, transcription, and the imposition of alien genres could attach to erstwhile orally transmitted narratives. In this and the ensuing two chapters, the Story of Scarface again comes to the fore, this time as the basis from which to view contemporary representations of the Blackfoot by Blackfoot authors James Welch and Emma Lee Warrior.

Establishing the links between "Scarface" and the Blackfoot subjectivity represented in the contemporary writing of Welch and Warrior adds another dimension to the meaning of cultural continuity that has provided the focus for this book. The strategy in this and the two chapters that follow remains one of maintaining a dialogue between Blackfoot and non-Blackfoot perspectives of Blackfoot history and literature. Building upon these perspectives, this chapter analyzes six versions of "Scarface" in order to emphasize the ethical dimensions of the story. It provides a structural analysis that points to Blackfoot-centred ethical ideals, which will, in turn, be utilized in order to undertake a critical analysis of the contemporary texts by Warrior and Welch.

Blackfoot scholar Weasel Traveller observed that the stories of First

Part IV — The Oral Tradition in Contemporary Literature

Nations' oral traditions contain behaviour guidelines for successive generations of "Real People" (First Nations peoples).[2] The Blackfoot perspectives of what constitutes ethical behaviour embedded in "Scarface" rest on the premise that community takes precedence over the individual and that community is extended to encompass all creation: Earth Beings or Ksahkomi-tapiksi (humans, four-legged animals, plants, rocks and the earth itself); Above People or Spomi-tapi-ksi (among which are the Star People (the Sun, the Moon, and the Morning Star),[3] Ksisstsi'ko'm (Thunder), the sky and many birds; and Water Beings or Soyii-tapiksi.[4] As Blackfoot scholar Betty Bastien notes, the Blackfoot received sacred bundles from some of these beings, including the Thunder Medicine Pipe Bundle and the Beaver Bundle, which, for them, "are a major source of protection through their balancing power." Balance, she argues, is the natural law of Blackfoot "understandings of reality as emanating from Ihtsipaitapiiyopa, The Source of Life". Hence, she argues, "Balance is the mission of the Blackfoot culture, and through the organization of societies, balance is manifested in the values, norms, and roles of the people. Striving for balance becomes the motivation of life and the impetus for all relationships", which include those with "cosmic beings".[5]

In order to keep their universe in balance, the Blackfoot must strive to exercise the principles of sacrifice, generosity and reciprocity with all their relations, both from the animate and the inanimate world. This accords well with Thomas King's views on the specific meaning that First Nations peoples in North America, in their respective languages, give to the phrase "All my Relations". In King's words,

> "All my relations" is [. . .] a reminder of who we are and of our relationship with both our family and our relatives. It also reminds us of the extended relationship we share with all human beings [. . .]. But the relationships that Native people see go further, the web of kinship extending to the animals, to the birds, to the fish, to the plants, to all the animate and inanimate forms that can be seen or imagined. More than that, "all my relations" is an encouragement for us to accept the responsibilities we have within this universal family by living our lives in a harmonious and moral manner.[6]

Hence a common admonition is "to say of someone that they act as if they have no relations".[7] Indeed, core Blackfoot ideals are implicit in the common expression "mind your relations". Pikuni scholar Woody Kipp explains that Blackfoot relationships "with people, with animal nations, with the forces of the world — are established through our Native tongues, through the stories we tell our children."[8] In other words, the stories contain the knowledge required in order for the Blackfoot to mind their relations. To this end, the Blackfoot must observe principles embedded in the stories, which include: Bravery, Generosity, Group Effort/Community

Hero Quests, Sun Dancing, and the Story of "Scarface"

Harmony, Honesty, Knowledge as Power, Perseverance and Strength, Reciprocity, Respect, Responsibility, and Sacrifice. The entire Blackfoot community, Hernandez argues, takes notice of individual adherence to these ideals,[9] which refer, to borrow the phrase from anthropologist Gerald Conaty, to "cultural norms and not exceptional behaviour".[10] Pity and Compassion are also ubiquitous in the Blackfoot Stories, and Kipp explains how these ideals fit within the Blackfoot worldview: "In the Native languages we talked with the animals, who were not animals but nations of very different beings, beings who could, and often did, help the poor pitiful human. There is, at the very core of the language, the mandate of compassion."[11]

"Scarface" provides the model behaviour for those who aspire to lead good lives in accordance with Blackfoot ideals. It should be noted that although this narrative distinguishes bravery as a desirable quality, one that allows the hero to achieve his stated goal of having the scar removed from his face, generosity pervades every stage of the narrative. Generosity is exercised not only by the Blackfoot characters, but also by their sacred helpers, including the Star Beings themselves. An earlier chapter discussed how, until the nineteenth century, generosity was the *sine qua non* for becoming a Blackfoot leader. The Blackfoot imperative for achieving balance requires that reciprocity be shown to those who have been generous. Referring to a Blackfoot Old Man story, Bastien notes that "the natural law of reciprocity" that informs on the way that the Blackfoot maintain their connections with their relations is based on "the observation of nature". Nature, she adds, "always tries to be in balance" so that life might be "strengthened and renewed."[12]

Once the Blackfoot bands were settled on reserves towards the late 1870s and the early 1880s, regulations forbidding acceptable, and indeed indispensable practices of generosity, attest to the disparate notions of proper behaviour of Blackfoot people and government officials. As discussed in earlier chapters, the prohibition of so-called give-aways interfered with Blackfoot practices that served to maintain their world in balance. Officials viewed these Blackfoot ideals in reductive terms, as a propensity not to make provision for their own future needs by the Blackfoot. The corollary here would be that if they did not achieve self-sufficiency, the government would have to spend resources to assist them. Such attitudes failed to appreciate the social imperative to exercise generosity and reciprocity. These ideals did not only have currency in relation to the material world, but also ruled the sacred domain through self-sacrifices as those offered to Natosi during the Sun Dance, most especially through the conduct of the ceremony, which follows the instructions received through Scarface from Natosi himself.

Part IV — The Oral Tradition in Contemporary Literature

Ethical Behaviour in "Scarface"

The teachings derived from "Scarface" served as a model for generations of Blackfoot; they reflect the Blackfoot world from which the story emanates. This narrative, like other Blackfoot Stories, promotes "model behavior that is worthy of being retold."[13] Despite the protean nature of oral stories, which makes each retelling unique, the different versions all contain some core actions of "Scarface". From these common elements we can gather specific behaviours to aid our comparative analysis. It should be noted from the outset that my purpose is not to search for a definitive version of the story. This study is based principally on six renderings of "Scarface", although other extant versions have been consulted. A sequence of units of meaning (ætiological passages)[14] relevant to ethical behaviour has been assembled from the various versions. These will facilitate comparison with the two contemporary texts analyzed in subsequent chapters. The six principal versions were collected in the five ethnographic texts reviewed in chapters 7 and 8. Natosi Nepe-e (Brings-Down-the-Sun) narrated the first version to McClintock in 1905, which the latter titled "Legend of Star Boy (Later, Poïa, Scarface)". This is the only version that begins at the time when Scarface's parents (So-at-sa-ki or Feather Woman, and Morning Star) were married, and relates how Scarface (then named Star Boy) and his mother returned to the Blackfoot people. A scar on his face accounts for Star Boy becoming Paii or Poïa (literally Ridge, Scarface).[15] The other versions begin later, when Scarface is already a youth. Pikuni storyteller Sikochkeka (Chewing Black Bone) narrated the second version to Schultz, who published it embedded within a larger narrative titled "The Faith of *Ahko Pitsu* (Told by *Ahko Pitsu*)".[16] The third, titled "Scarface: Origin of the Medicine Lodge", is a composite published in Grinnell's *Lodge Tales* partly attributed to Miss Cora Ross, "one of the school teachers at the Blackfoot agency."[17] The fourth and fifth versions appear in Wissler and Duvall, *Mythology of the Blackfoot*, and are attributed, respectively, to a "Piegan Man," and a "Piegan Woman."[18] The fifth version is significantly shorter than all the others. Uhlenbeck provides the sixth version, titled "Scar-face", a composite bilingual (Blackfoot/English) rendition, but only the English translation is utilized here.[19] Other versions consulted include one that Blackfoot Mike Swims Under narrated to Hernandez c.1999; another published by Pikani author and ceremonialist Percy Bullchild; and two held at the Glenbow Archives: "The Blackfoot Legend of Scarface", compiled by R. N. Wilson, and "Scarface", compiled by David C. Duvall.[20]

As noted earlier, the story is set during the "dog days," an era when the Blackfoot lived in peace and were yet to acquire horses.[21] It begins by establishing the main character's social standing and what he must do to become worthy. He is poor, and in most versions he is an orphan.[22] He wishes to marry a chief's daughter who has rejected many "rich, handsome and brave" suitors, but agrees to marry Scarface, if and when his scar disappears. In different versions, the chief's daughter can be either virtuous and kindly, or scornful. Where she is portrayed as kind and virtuous, Natosi himself wants her for his wife: "Take heed. You must not marry. You are mine", Natosi tells her. Scarface must convince Natosi to free the chief's daughter from that bond, and to signal his assent by removing the scar.[23] When the chief's daughter does not take "pity" on Scarface, she meets an early death towards the end of the story.

The gender dimensions portrayed in the story reflect a male-centred worldview that places the highest value on women's virtue: "The sun pities good women". They shall live a long time. So shall their husbands and children. Chastity is embodied in the Holy Woman during the Sun Dance. Only a virtuous woman can play an intermediary role between the sacred realm and her community; her virtue has a positive impact on all her relations; her lack of virtue can attract punishment for her and her relations. When the chief's daughter refuses her suitors, her mother despairs at the thought that a child could be born while she is unmarried, which would bring shame to the parents.[24] Compared with her male peers, the chief's daughter plays a passive role. Scarface must travel to the end of the known world to ask Natosi to remove his scar (and to agree to his marriage to the chief's daughter), while she waits for her fate to be decided by (male) others. However, she is not without power, for she had been chosen to become Natosi's wife, and by encouraging Scarface to seek her release from that bond, she has exercised autonomy. Alice Kehoe, who contests early portrayals of Blackfoot women as having little or no power, argues that within Blackfoot society "anyone can aspire to becoming more powerful", power being open to all persons.[25] Nevertheless, as is the case in "Scarface", more often than not male power is associated with bravery and women's power with chastity.[26] Chaste women, however, can exercise a great deal of power by interceding between humans and sacred beings.

In order to fulfil the conditions set by the chief's daughter, Scarface prepares like a warrior about to go on the warpath. Being poor, he relies on the pity of helpers, who are often women. An old woman gives him moccasins and food.[27] In one version he meets four women in succession, who help him. Scarface travels east "where the sun rises" and meets the first woman, who directs him to go beyond what "looks blue [a mountain ridge]." She gives him her moccasins to wear and instructs him: "when you arrive, put them with the fore-ends back", whereupon the moccasins will, on their own, return to the owner. In one version, the old woman meets Scarface before her husband arrives, and when he does, the woman intercedes on behalf of the hero. This intermediary role is re-enacted during Ookaan, which in order to take place requires the vow of a chaste woman who intercedes between Natosi and the Blackfoot. The second, third, and fourth women repeat the actions of the first. However, the fourth woman adds a new twist, and directs him to Morning Star, who will tell him "how you can live." According to Swims Under, the "Old Lady" Scarface meets four times is one and the same: Natosi's wife, the Moon. Scarface returns to the same lodge because "the whole world is the Sun's lodge".[28]

After Scarface meets the fourth woman, the narrative moves to the next phase.[29] Such fourfold cycles are often taken to signify sacred numbers, although linguist Dell Hymes suggests that "so-called sacred numbers" might not be primarily "something of transcendental mystical value". Rather, he suggests, they might have "developed from the aesthetic values of rhythmic repetition"[30]. The functions of repetition, whether sacred or aesthetic, are not, however, mutually exclusive.[31] Many components of Ookaan, the Blackfoot Sun Dance, are repeated fourfold. Aesthetically, drawing out the resolution increases suspense and emphasizes the perseverance of the characters. It is notable that some transcriptions of 'Scarface' are devoid of repetition, for example, the version by a Piegan Woman in Wissler and Duvall.[32] This suggests that non-Blackfoot editors, unable to appreciate merit in this "emic" orature device, might have wished to shorten the narrative for their white readers. The opposite would have been required from storytellers whose role was not only to impart knowledge, but also to keep their audiences entranced.

In other versions, Scarface's helpers are animals (i.e., wolf, bear, badger, and wolverine), from whom Napi, a Creator and Trickster, has taught the Blackfoot to seek help: "if you are overcome, you may go and sleep and get power. Whatever animal answers your prayer, you must listen to him."[33] In Schultz's version, when Scarface reaches the "Big Water," the last obstacle in his quest to find Natosi, Scarface gets discouraged and prepares to die. At that point, two swans (a male and female couple) come to his aid, asking him to "take courage". The swans take Scarface on their backs to Natosi's "island home". In other versions, the light of Morning Star guides Scarface. Either way, the story emphasizes that the success of Scarface's quest is reliant on the assistance of his relations.[34] By the time he arrives at Natosi's lodge, Scarface has overcome danger, pain, and even doubt and despair thanks to his helpers. During these trials, he has shown respect for all his relations whose instructions he has followed, yet further tests await him as he reaches the abode of the Star People.

Parallel Worlds

Scarface is welcomed in Sun's lodge and lives for a time with the Above People, Natosi, Kokomi-kisomm, and Ipiso-waahsa. The Star People live parallel lives to those of the Blackfoot. Their home (lodge), dress, food, and ethical concerns mirror those of their human relations. Thus by observing proper behaviour according to Blackfoot codes, Scarface is able to gain their acceptance. The friendship that grows between Scarface and Morning Star stems from different incidents in the several versions of the story. In the Piegan man's version, Morning Star persuades Scarface to accompany him to a place where dangerous birds live, which Scarface agrees to do after being asked four times. The birds attack the two friends whereupon Scarface kills the birds.[35] In Grinnell's version honesty and bravery are evident. Scarface finds "a war shirt, a shield, and a bow and arrows" that belong to Morning Star. Following his helpers' advice Scarface leaves these items untouched, even though the items are of great value. In this version the killing of "large birds with long sharp bills" occurs later. The significance of bravery in the Blackfoot worldview is evident in that all versions of the story contain the killing of the birds to save Morning Star. Moreover, the contrast between the birds who help Scarface and those who attack Morning Star shows that nature is not always benign. Facing fear with courage on this occasion resulted in Scarface's coming of age.

Grinnell notes the value of courage by the Blackfoot, who taught boys "that to accomplish anything they must be brave and untiring in war; that long life was not desirable; that the old people always had a hard time [...] Much better, while the body is strong and in its prime [...] to die in battle fighting bravely".[36] Scarface's courage and honesty, respectively, make him a worthy *tak.a* (male friend/partner) for Morning Star. As such, Scarface enters into a special relationship that exists between two Blackfoot males from early childhood, who might participate jointly in age-graded societies, warfare, and at times even share a woman.[37] As Morning Star's *tak.a*, Scarface becomes like a son to the former's parents.

The hospitality shown to Scarface as a guest of the Star Beings further illustrates the high regard in which the Blackfoot place generosity, especially when shown to visitors who have travelled a great distance. He receives shelter, food, clothing, and friendship, but most significantly, Natosi agrees to remove the scar after Scarface proves his worth (and frees the chief's daughter so that she can marry Scarface). Natosi removes the scar through four consecutive sweat baths shared by himself, Morning Star and Scarface. After each sweat, Natosi rubs the scar with an eagle tail feather and calls his wife, asking her to point out which of the two boys is her son. Three times she points to Morning Star, the fourth she points to Scarface. Hence, when Scarface eventually becomes a Star Person (Jupiter), he is known as The-one-you-took-for-Morning-Star, or False Morning Star.[38]

When the time comes for Scarface to return to his people, Natosi presents him with two raven feathers to be "worn by the husband of the woman who builds a Medicine Lodge"; and a "cloak"; a "hat," and a "wooden pin".[39] These items constitute the Natoas Bundle, which must be transferred to the woman vower who will become the Holy Woman during the Sun Dance. The "cloak" is Elk Woman's robe, the "hat" is the bonnet worn by the Holy Woman, and the digging stick is that of So-at-sa-ki (Feather Woman).[40] Moreover, Moon made him beautiful clothes, and Morning Star gave him a shield.[41] In the Piegan Man's version, Scarface receives a shirt and leggings on which he paints seven black stripes, one for each of the birds he killed. He is also given songs to go with the suit, to be sung each time this is transferred to a new owner. This is the suit that should only be worn by those who have killed an enemy. When he returns to his people, Scarface gives the suit to his Blackfoot *tak.a*. The suit and the absence of the scar are proofs of his visit to the Star Beings. Scarface also brings back valuable knowledge. Natosi teaches him the manner in which the Blackfoot should honour him through the ceremony of Ookaan, so that he will better hear their pleas for help. He also instructs Scarface on the ritual sweat bath, and teaches him how to prepare a smudge (for cleansing rites), giving him for this purpose "a forked stick, and cedar for the smudge, and some feathers".[42]

In the versions in *Blackfeet and Buffalo* and *Lodge Tales*, Scarface marries the chief's daughter; they live happily into old age; and die without pain. Natosi takes them both back to the sky and, according to McClintock's version, Scarface becomes Mistake Morning Star — the name he received when Moon confused him with her son and the Blackfoot name for Jupiter. In the version where the chief's daughter has been unkind, Scarface throws a piece of sinew into the fire. This causes her death whereupon she joins Morning Star, who, wishing to marry the chief's daughter, had given the sinew to Scarface.[43] In the same way that Natosi surrendered the chief's daughter to Scarface, so does the latter surrender her to Morning Star, even though marrying her was the reason for his quest. Unlike Scarface, who becomes Jupiter, the chief's daughter is not transformed into a star. However, what might appear as punishment — her early death — is also a privilege, since she will become the wife of a Star Person.

Scarface's conduct throughout his journey illustrates the qualities that were most appreciated by the Blackfoot who looked to the story as a repository of knowledge and a guide to lead a moral life. The teachings Natosi bestowed on Scarface define not only the reciprocal relationship between Natosi and the Blackfoot, but also that between the Blackfoot and all their relations. These teachings, Hernandez argues, "reify the strength and continuity of a uniquely Blackfoot way of understanding the world". The hero's quest integrates all the elements within the Blackfoot circle of life, especially the value, among other ideals, of honesty, bravery, perseverance, respect for all creation, generosity and reciprocity. As

Hero Quests, Sun Dancing, and the Story of "Scarface"

Hernandez argues, "the earth-to-cosmos connection confirmed through the stories [. . .] teaches respect of the interdependence of humans, all earth life, and the larger circle of the universe because they are inseparable."[44] This claim of uniqueness underlines the Blackfoot-centred worldview embedded in the sacred stories associated with ceremonies. As Hernandez notes, these ceremonies re-enact "the sacred paths that those who journeyed to or from the sky travelled".[45]

While the ethical ideals taught through the Blackfoot Stories serve to maintain a reciprocal relationship between the Blackfoot and all creation, Ookaan is the most significant ceremony for the maintenance of such reciprocity between the Blackfoot and Natosi. Showing generosity towards Natosi (including gifts of a person's own flesh before prohibition ended the practice) was at times meant to propitiate assistance in coming endeavours, and sometimes to reciprocate for benefits already received. The Circle Encampment that culminated in *Ookaan* was a time for displays of generosity, particularly evident through the feasting of relatives or other visitors. Those who came from afar received special attentions, and received gifts like those Scarface received from the Star People. Those Blackfoot who practice generosity grow in stature in the eyes of the whole community. Although the contemporary texts in the analysis that follows belong to an era that is distant from that represented in "Scarface", these contemporary texts continue to emphasize the need for core Blackfoot ideals. Despite the transformation of the socio-historical context, the ethical ideals from the Blackfoot Stories are a significant component of the Blackfoot subjectivity that Native authors represent in the contemporary narratives analyzed in the chapters that follow. Without being exhaustive, the foregoing analysis provides ample evidence that Scarface's success depends on an ongoing ethical engagement with all his relations.

10

The Blackfoot Hero in James Welch's *Fools Crow*

The contemporary historical novel *Fools Crow* (1986)[1] by Blackfoot/ GrosVentre author and poet James Welch (1940–2003) provides an apposite context within which to analyze Blackfoot subjectivity through the lens of the "Story of Scarface". The ethical ideals of the hero from the dog days are here tested against those of Fools Crow, Welch's protagonist. The overt connection between the ancient story and the novel allows us to view the old narrative and the new as different acts of the same play. The drama properly began when Scarface's mother, So-at-sa-ki, married the Morning Star and lived among the Star Beings. She dug a forbidden turnip and, through the hole it left, she gazed at the camps of her people below, causing her to become homesick. Her transgression results in her being sent back to her people with her son Scarface. In the second act the child of So-at-sa-ki and the Morning Star (Scarface) has become a youth. Natosi Nepe-e alone narrated both the story of So-at-sa-ki and the Story of Scarface as a unit. In other versions of "Scarface", the youth is described as an orphan, with no mention of So-at-sa-ki or her fate. *Fools Crow* provides a sequel to the old narratives, the third act of the same play. Like Scarface before him, Fools Crow, Welch's modern-day hero, undertakes a quest in order to gain knowledge. He meets So-at-sa-ki, whom Welch portrays living high up in the mountains with one only purpose: to be reunited with her husband, Morning Star, and her son, Scarface. Welch begins his narrative with the hero still a mere youth, still going by his childhood name of White Man's Dog. As he reaches maturity as a warrior, White Man's Dog also begins to acquire sacred knowledge from Mik-api, "a great and powerful many-faces man" (p. 8) and, as a grown man, Fools Crow embarks on a quest on behalf of his relations that will take him, not to the Star People, but to a place in-between them and the Blackfoot, the abode of his ancestor, So-at-sa-ki.

Welch sets his novel in Montana in 1870, placing it within a well-documented historical context. Having signed a treaty with the United States in 1855, the Blackfoot bands, especially the Pikuni who formed the southern flank of the Blackfoot alliance, had by then seen large numbers of settlers encroaching upon their lands. By 1870 the Pikuni world was on the cusp of life-threatening change. Plains culture had been radically transformed by the horse and the fur trade, the latter made available a steady supply of guns and ammunition and other European goods. Contact with white traders also brought alcohol-induced violence and devastating disease; most dreaded was smallpox, which in 1869–70 caused c.2200 Blackfoot deaths, one thousand of these among the Pikuni.[2] Yet White Man's Dog believes that by acquiring a much coveted repeating rifle from the traders "he could bring about his own luck" (p. 4).

In *Fools Crow*, Blackfoot dependence on European goods is one of the causes for the predicament in which they find themselves. Ironically, as critic Mary Jane Lupton remarks, the long-term consequences of white arrival far outweighed the benefits of the fur trade.[3] Fur traders spearheaded colonization in the West, exacerbating the already fierce intertribal competition for ever-contracting resources. The availability of guns promoted intertribal and Blackfoot–white violence. There is little left of the middle ground that allowed trading forts on the Upper Missouri to thrive from the 1830s. By 1870 traders' profits derived from new customers: the settlers and prospectors attracted to Montana in search of riches throughout the 1860s. Despite fears that the herds were reducing in size and forecasts of their demise, demand for buffalo robes resulted in over-hunting from Indians and non-Indians alike. The ecological catastrophe happened earlier than expected.

A tragic event also occurred in 1870. In January of that year the U.S. Army massacred 173 Pikuni from Chief Heavy Runner's band at their winter camp on the Marias River, marking this year as one of the lowest points in Blackfoot history. Welch narrates the escalation of violence between the Blackfoot and whites that culminated in the massacre. He writes about this episode from the perspective of the Pikuni survivors, among them Kai Otokan (Bear Head), whose testimony of the events appeared in James Willard Schultz's *Blackfeet and Buffalo*.[4] Within this volatile environment, the ethical imperatives of Welch's Pikuni characters are tested to their limit. Yet, despite smallpox and the massacre, in 1870 the Pikuni were still able to pursue their erstwhile autonomous existence hunting buffalo. As Louis Owens notes in his apt reading of *Fools Crow*, Welch's Pikuni men and women "know who and where they are", while "the Euroamerican is peripheral and alien."[5]

During the 1870s, the trade in buffalo robes centered at Fort Benton (Many Houses) remained the Pikuni's principal source of by now indispensable white goods. Without guns and ammunition they could neither hunt nor defend their territory from enemies; items such as knives, hatchets, and kettles had long since replaced their traditional counterparts. The long list of goods that the Blackfoot had adapted to their everyday lives demanded a constant focus on procuring tanned buffalo hides (robes) for trade, their most important exchange commodity. Moreover, Blackfoot survival depended on the bison hunt to fulfil their needs for both food and shelter — "only the blackhorn could provide for all the needs of a family" (p. 47).

Fools Crow, Welch's main character, belongs to the Lone Eaters band, one of twenty-four bands that until the late 1880s comprised the Pikuni division of the Blackfoot alliance.[6] Welch's representation of their autonomous existence is familiar from our reading of pioneer ethnographies. Welch acknowledged McClintock's *The Old North Trail* as one of his sources for *Fools Crow*.[7] McClintock quoted Blackfoot speech at length and, from his pages, Welch recovers the voice of his ancestors. Compare the two passages below. In the first, from *Fools Crow*, Mountain Chief speaks after White Man's Dog fulfils his vow to Natosi during the Sun Dance, in reciprocation for his safe return from a horse raid:

> Haiya! Listen, my people, for I speak to you with a good heart. Once again we have constructed the Sun Lodge in the way we were taught by our long-ago people [. . .]. We have smoked the long-pipes together and are at peace with ourselves. Many have left presents for Sun Chief, and some among us have fulfilled vows made in times of trouble [. . .]. Heavy Shield Woman and her helpers have shown our young girls the way to virtue. Our young men have listened to the wisdom of their chiefs (pp. 120–1).

The second passage is taken from McClintock, as he narrates the words of Chief Mad Wolf, at the conclusion of a Sun Dance:

> Hear! my children, for I speak to you with a good heart. It does us all good to assemble every summer around the Sun-lodge. We have smoked the Medicine Pipe, and the rising smoke has carried away all of our bad feelings. Many have given presents to the Sun, and some have fulfilled their vows [. . .]. The young men have listened to the wise counsels of the chiefs, and the young girls have seen the medicine women.[8]

The resemblance between the two speeches illustrates how Welch's dialogues are linked to his sources. The similarity of views expressed in Welch's narrative emphasizes the author's acknowledgement of Blackfoot worldviews, and the importance of ritual in the ongoing construction of a distinct Blackfoot identity. Owens describes *Fools Crow* as an "act of recovery" that seeks to "reclaim the possibility of a coherent identity" for Welch and for his Blackfoot contemporaries.[9] It is during the Sun Dance that young men and women have an opportunity to revitalize their culture, as they learn from the examples set by those who lead their lives in accordance with Blackfoot ideals. The Sun Dance presents unique opportunities to display generosity and reciprocity to all creation, including sacred beings, especially Natosi to whom the Blackfoot reciprocate for benefits that this Above Being has bestowed upon them by offering sacrifices.

Following the Footsteps of Scarface

Some critics have noted the connections between Welch's *Fools Crow* and "Scarface". Bette Weidman's appraisal of the novel and her survey of the existing criticism contains many shrewd observations. Rather than situate the novel using the framework of non-Blackfoot mythological structures and critical perspectives,[10] Weidman credits Welch with being able to transmit to his non-Blackfoot readers "a refreshed idea of the meaning of adulthood, of fidelity, of endurance through the inevitability of change." Weidman considers it an "audacity" on the part of Welch to take "the risk of introducing the myth world into his realistic historical novel." In the end, however, Weidman's interpretation of the novel, like that of other critics, fails to search for an interpretive tool "inside" Blackfoot culture. This might have assisted her to understand that what she sees as two divergent roads are in fact a reflection of a Blackfoot worldview in which the secular and the sacred can never be disentangled.[11] Welch himself made his intention to write from the "inside" very clear, and pointed to white people as "the real strangers" in *Fools Crow*. As Owens notes, there is no disjunction in the novel "between the real and the magical", as "the sacred and the profane interpenetrate irresistibly". He adds: "If the reader can pass through that conceptual horizon, if the reader acknowledges and accepts this reality", then "he or she experiences an Indian world."[12] My analysis focuses on this Blackfoot perspective as I explore the links between the ancient story and Welch's contemporary novel.

From an ethical perspective, the Blackfoot social organization into bands sets a premium on a community focus. Survival depends on the minding of all their relations, particularly their sacred helpers who, often through dreams, provide them with knowledge to lead better lives. The well-being of the bands required securing a supply of buffalo meat and hides; maintaining ascendency over enemy First Nations to ensure territorial dominance; and the acquisition of prestige and wealth through horse raiding that provided the means for youth to make a name for themselves and become *akáinauasiu* (full grown in age).

The character of Welch's hero develops into a quintessential warrior and epic hero, but also a family man, a devoted husband and a proud father. He is introduced in the novel as White Man's Dog, when he is about to join in a horse raid against the Crow. He is yet to prove his courage and ability in order to earn for himself an adult name. He is also yet to acquire sufficient wealth to be worthy of a wife so that his friends will stop calling him "dog-lover" (p. 4). Before venturing on his first raid, White Man's Dog observes the rituals necessary to propitiate his sacred helpers. He seeks help from Mik-api,[13] who instructs White Man's Dog and prays for him to succeed when he faces the enemy (p. 8). Throughout the novel the hero is portrayed as maintaining reciprocity with his animal helpers, Raven and Wolverine. Attending to his sacred relations is as vital as attending to his Blackfoot relations, and to this end, aware that his life will be in danger, the warrior in the making vows to Natosi "that if he was successful and returned home unharmed, he would sacrifice before the medicine pole at the next Sun Dance" (p. 27). The raid brings success, and White Man's Dog returns with sufficient horses to share with Mik-api in reciprocation for his strong Medicine. As White Man's Dog character develops he grows in stature not only as a warrior but also as a person who is knowledgeable in the sacred ways of the Blackfoot. Fools Crow embodies the attributes of one who leads an ethical existence according to the Blackfoot worldview. He is honest, generous, compassionate, and respectful of all his relations. He renounces personal comforts in order to help his fellow creatures and does not hesitate to follow the instructions of his sacred helpers, whom he trusts with his life.

In a subsequent raid White Man's Dog earns for himself the name Fools Crow by killing Bull Shield, a respected and feared Crow Chief. The name Fools Crow derives from the hero's perceived ability to fool the enemy. However, the name has extra-textual connotations as well. Frank Fools Crow was a respected ceremonial leader among the Lakota at the Pine Ridge reservation in South Dakota. He was a staunch defender of Lakota traditions, especially the Sun Dance.[14] These connections apart, the character in Welch's narrative is apprehensive about exaggerated accounts of how he had fooled the Crows by pretending to be dead. He had protested, but in the eyes of his companions White Man's Dog had returned from the revenge party raid as a man who possessed strong Medicine (p. 151). He would now have to live up to the expectations raised by his new status. Owens argues that while some of the characters in *Fools Crow* are depicted in a "fully human detail seldom allowed to Native Americans in literature by Euroamericans", this is not available to Welch's character whose role, which "demands that he represent the Blackfoot world more completely", requires him to "act more rigidly".[15]

Welch portrays the Pikuni as a heterogeneous community. The autonomous bands respond to outside threats in accordance with what they perceive to be in the best interests of the band. His principal characters are members of the Lone Eaters band, but show concern for other bands.[16] Welch portrays the Lone Eaters as they go about their family affairs, and respond to intratribal events, intertribal wars, and conflict with whites. Blackfoot recognition of an individual's autonomy allows for a range of responses that covers a continuum between diplomacy and outright violence. The heterogeneity of Welch's Pikuni characters and their everyday activities provide a multidimensional picture of a close-knit band whose known world and very survival are threatened. Rather than the fearsome warriors of the white imagination, the characters are fathers, mothers, wives, sons, band members, and proud Pikuni, many of whom are apprehensive about war. They view their warring as unavoidable: a necessary means for individuals to gain respect and sufficient wealth for youth to gain independence from their families. Moreover, within the competitive environment of the Plains, war is a mechanism for maintaining the respect of their enemies and to discourage them from making incursions into Pikuni territory.[17] Some Pikuni deal better than others with the vicissitudes that survival entails, in a world of fierce competition for diminishing resources.

In choosing to write within the historical novel genre, Welch takes on a challenge that most contemporary Native authors avoid. According to Thomas King "The literary stereotypes and clichés for which the period is famous have been [. . .] a deterrent".[18] This choice makes the narrative dependent upon historical documentation, mostly written by non-Blackfoot, which Welch then enlarges with his own experience as a member of the Pikuni Nation. Moreover, the weight of the history of colonization borne by the Pikuni has to be dealt with. In order to create his work of fiction, Welch used the ethnographic texts examined in earlier chapters, each of which contains a version of "Scarface".[19] Applying his creativity to historical accounts, Welch reconstructs the voice of his ancestors in order to represent a vision of history that privileges the Pikuni perspective. While McClintock, Schultz, Grinnell, and their white contemporaries represented civilization as superior to the Native worldview, Welch's Pikuni characters articulate a view from the opposite side. Owl Child, a member of Mountain Chief's band, who has chosen to fight the colonizers, describes whites as "devils" who will push the Pikuni "into the Backbone (the Rocky Mountains) and take all the ground and the blackhorns for themselves." Owl Child's murder of Malcolm Clarke, a trader turned rancher, precipitated the massacre of Pikuni in 1870. This character serves as a foil for Fools Crow.

Honouring Community

The concept of "all my relations" as articulated by King is embedded into the narrative of *Fools Crow*, in which the Lone Eaters band looks askance at those who deviate from honouring the ideals encapsulated in this concept, while those who uphold such ideals earn respect. Owl Child, as the historical character, "had turned away from his own people"; he lived with his own band of desperadoes, stealing horses and killing settlers.

Many Pikuni disapprove of Owl Child, who has transgressed their own ethical imperatives, but respect and even fear his strength and power. Perhaps some Pikuni admire Owl Child's outrages against whites. However, Owl Child's actions violate Blackfoot ideals because they bring hardship, as the bands are collectively tainted by his murderous actions. In contrast, Fools Crow, who kills a white hunter, does so following a plea for help from his relations. The "Napikwan" kills animals for sport, rather than as a source of food. I fear — Raven tells Fools Crow — that "he will kill us all off if something isn't done" (p. 164). Fools Crow gets over his initial reluctance and kills the hunter for the sake of "his brothers, the four-leggeds and the flyers" (p. 165). His actions restore balance in nature, which the wanton killing of the hunter had disturbed.

The requirement for the Blackfoot to mind their relations, especially their sacred helpers, is cast in the novel as vital. In the same way that Scarface must follow his helpers' instructions in order to succeed, the characters in *Fools Crow* are rewarded or punished according to their behaviour towards their sacred relations. Thus, when Yellow Kidney leads a war party again the Crow, Fast Horse, one of the members of the war party, is instructed by Cold Maker (who brings the snow and the winter) to locate a spring from which Cold Maker likes to drink from, and remove a rock that has blocked it:

> if you do this for me, I will make your raid successful. As you drive the Crow horses home, I will cause snow to fall behind you, covering your tracks. But you must find my spring and remove the rock. If you don't, you must not go on, for I will punish you and your party. Either way, because I offer my help you must bring me two prime bull robes for my daughters during the helping-to-eat moon. It will go hard on you if you do not do this. (p. 14)

When the party fails to find the spring, the party leader, Yellow Kidney, decides to continue the raid (p. 21). Although the raid is successful and the party manages to take "one hundred and fifty horses" (p. 34), Fast Horse is late in rejoining his colleagues, and Yellow Kidney is missing. Fast Horse has a second encounter with an angry Cold Maker, who takes him to look at his shivering, eyeless daughters. Cold Maker gives Fast Horse a second chance: "I will let you rejoin your friends, but you must promise me this: When the helping-to-eat moon is full in the sky, you must not only bring my daughters two prime robes but red coals for their eyes" (pp. 37–38). Fast Horse, who behaves like a changed man after the raid, fails to make his promise good to Cold Maker. He refuses White Man's Dog offer to hunt with him to get the prime robes (p. 49). From this point onward Fast Horse becomes alienated from Cold Maker, and from the Lone Eaters. He leaves the band to join Owl Child and his renegades.

Like Owl Child, Yellow Kidney and Fast horse are foils for White

Man's Dog, who minds his relations. He has behaved admirably during the raid. He gave Mik-api five of his best horses in reciprocation for his prayers. White Man's Dog's generosity extends to Yellow Kidney's family, whom he supplies with meat, since they have lost their only hunter (pp. 47; 53). As White Man's Dog begins to assist Mik-api in his routines, he travels to the "Backbone" (Rocky Mountains) to rescue a "four-legged" caught in a white man's steel trap. Raven, who pities the trapped creature (Skunk Bear or Wolverine), tells Mik-api "If you send this young man I will teach him how to use this creature's power, for in truth only the real-bear is a stronger power animal" (p. 52). Raven guides White Man's Dog through this second journey, less than half a day away from his camp. When he stops to eat, White Man's Dog places a small piece of meat "in the fork of a tree" before beginning his meal (p. 54), a sacrifice which indicates his respect for all his relations. As he negotiates a ridge he slides four times (p. 55) but he perseveres. When Raven talks to him, White Man's Dog falls to his knees: "Oh, pity me, Raven!" At this point Raven gives him a lesson regarding the interdependence of all beings, "I am one of great power [. . .] but my power is not that of strength [. . .] In all of us there is a weakness" (p. 56). Indeed, as Natosi tells Scarface, "the raven" is the smartest of all animals "for he always finds food".[20] After requesting some real-meat (buffalo) for Wolverine and for his wives, Raven transfers to White Man's Dog the "magic of Skunk Bear": "You will fear nothing, and you will have many horses and wives. But you must not abuse this power, and you must listen to Mik-api, for I speak through him, that good many-faces man who shares his smoke" (p. 58).

The meaning of "all my relations" is expressed thus, as the Pikuni and their two-legged and four-legged relations care for one another. It is in this spirit that Heavy Shield Woman, Yellow Kidney's wife, vows to build a lodge for Natosi, should this Above Being return her husband to her (p. 44). Of the sacrifices a woman can undertake, becoming the Holy Woman during Ookaan is one of the most onerous. Heavy Shield Woman's prayers are answered. However, the Crow, who captured Yellow Kidney, have cut off his fingers. Lupton associates the missing fingers with frostbite, and hence with punishment from Cold Maker.[21]

The Quest

While Fools Crow, like Scarface, is never deprived of assistance from his sacred helpers, like his ancestor Scarface he must undertake a quest. Following instructions from Nitsokan (Dream Helper), Fools Crow dresses as a beggar and rides for three consecutive days and nights without stopping (pp. 315–18). The fourth day, near his destination, he walks through a thick patch of red willows; their slapping branches stinging his face. A broken-off branch cuts "a long bloody scratch on his cheek", an unmistakable allusion to Scarface (p. 320). After meeting a woman who welcomes him to her cabin, Fools Crow falls asleep and, in his dream, his journey continues. Three times he tries to wade a stream and, like Scarface before him, he gives-in to despair (p. 324). It is then that Wolverine appears, and Fools Crow follows him through a tunnel. The four-fold cycle repeats itself, echoing similar passages in "Scarface". At the fourth attempt, Fools Crow leaves winter behind; he emerges in an immense valley, a "summer land" where there are no birds, or animal herds, but no hunger either (pp. 326–28). There he finds the woman wearing a plain doeskin dress and her dog. She has grey hair, which has been cut short, a sign of mourning among the Blackfoot. When the time comes, the woman reveals her identity to Fools Crow: she is So-at-sa-ki (Feather Woman), Scarface's mother (p. 350). She recounts her story to Fools Crow, in words that closely follow Natosi Nepe-e's version. But she goes beyond the story's ending in order to explain her presence in the "green sanctuary between earth and sky" (p. 360), a place where Sun has taken her "to live in mourning." Now, she tells Fools Crow, Sun "sends my husband and son here each dawn to remind me of my transgression" (p. 350). Thus it is that when the Morning Star and Mistake Morning Star appear in the sky, she wails and begs them to take her back.

In his sequel of So-at-sa-ki's story, Welch combines the image of his Blackfoot ancestor with that of Eve. Morning Star once told So-at-sa-ki: "You have brought upon yourself misery — and misery to your own people." Even So-at-sa-ki speaks of her "sin" being the source of Pikuni suffering, which can only end when her husband agrees to take her back (p. 352). It is then So-at-sa-ki who must show Fools Crow the dark future awaiting his people. It unfolds like a film on a yellow skin he had seen her painting. Looking into the yellow skin, Fools Crow sees smallpox afflicting the Lone Eaters, he sees the soldiers (seizers) leaving their fort with their scout Joe Kipp (p. 355), but he does not see their destination, Heavy Runner's Camp. He assumes that their target might have been Mountain Chief's band, as the soldiers believed they were harbouring the renegade Owl Child. Fools Crow does not see that attack on Heavy Runner's village. Worse still, gazing into the yellow hide, Fools Crow saw the Pikuni country, but noticed no buffalo there "as if the earth had swallowed up the animals" (p. 356). He also saw "the starvation of the Pikunis" (p. 358) which occurred in the 1883–84 winter, when more than a quarter of the Pikuni in Montana would die.[22] For the first time, Fools Crow thinks of the Above Ones "as cruel spirits" for allowing Feather Woman to suffer so, and for allowing "what he had seen." It is the future that awaits his people (p. 359). These catastrophic events cannot be accommodated within the image of a Blackfoot world in balance, but Fools Crow does not learn why the Napikwans are being favoured at the expense of the Pikuni. Perhaps Fast Horse feels the same way and that is the reason for his refusal to honour Cold Maker.

Fools Crow, however, rejects anger, although he grieves — he tells So-at-sa-ki — "for our children and their children, who will not know the life their people once lived" (p. 359). Thus Welch alludes to the words of Double Runner, the Pikuni who told Grinnell: "The children of my children will be like white people. None of them will know how it used to be in their father's days unless they read the things which we have told you, and which you are all the time writing down in your books."[23] Like his ancestor Scarface, Fools Crow has undertaken a perilous journey during which he has been given knowledge so that he might prepare his people for the future. He cannot prevent the events shown on the yellow hide from occurring, but there is some consolation in the fact that the new generations will know that their ancestors did not break the covenant with their sacred relations. So-at-sa-ki foretells that "'Much will be lost to them,' [...] 'But they will know the way it was. The stories will be handed down, and they will see that their people were proud and lived in accordance with the Below Ones, the Underwater People — and the Above Ones'" (pp. 359–60).

Thus, Welch links *Fools Crow* to the Blackfoot Stories, creating a sequel to the stories that ensures their continuity into contemporary times. As Owens notes, "the role of the storyteller is crucial to cultural and individual psychic survival, for stories confer meaning and identity in the Indian world."[24] In *Fools Crow*, the protagonist refuses to become angry (p. 359). He could not understand why So-at-sa-ki and the Pikuni were being punished. Her "only sin was one of loneliness"; while the Pikuni have "always lived in harmony with their sacred beings. Always they had performed the ceremonies to the best of their ability. They sacrificed often and without stinting. And yet they were being punished" (p. 360). Fools Crow saw So-at-sa-ki smiling and her eyes shone brightly as she farewelled him (p. 360). Fools Crow's visit had brought new energy to So-at-sa-ki, who had been disconnected from the Pikuni. Her story, in turn, is also renewed through Welch's narrative, casting fresh light upon an ancient story, narrating a sequel worthy of the Blackfoot oral tradition.

As Fools Crow returns to his people after his journey to the "summer land", the images he saw on the yellow skin become real. The Lone Eaters are afflicted by smallpox, for which they have no cure. Worse still, news of the massacre of Heavy Runner's people reaches Fools Crow while on a hunting trip. He gallops to the site of the massacre, and is confronted with the destructive power of the seizers, the U.S. Army. Few among Heavy Runner's village have survived to tell the horror of the attack that surprised them while they nursed those among them who were afflicted by smallpox. Among the survivors is Bear Head, who recounts the frenzied attack that has left him without a family. His mother, and three other wives of his late father, his "near-mothers", as well as "four sisters and a brother" have all been killed (p. 382).

Welch's authorial ethics have been tested as he represents his Blackfoot ancestors in ways that, while remaining true to history, do not replicate the pejorative stereotype of the "disappearing Indian" of the white imagination. On the contrary, Welch ends his narrative by re-stating the resilience of the Lone Eaters who, having survived the 1869–70 winter, respond to the first rumble of Thunder Maker in the time-honoured fashion. Mik-api opens the Medicine Pipe Bundle, and his assistants pray to the "Above Ones, the Below Ones, the Underwater People". Pikuni continuity is also symbolized in the birth of "Butterfly" (the Bringer of Dreams[25]), the son of Red Paint and Fools Crow. The baby brings the promise of new dreams that will assist the Pikuni in the road ahead. Welch emphasizes Pikuni resilience and their will to prevail within the hostile world that surrounds them in 1870 — a resilience that is evident in the spirit in which the Lone Eaters welcome the end of winter.[26] Although "fewer than in previous years [. . .] the drumming and singing seemed louder, as though they sought to make up in enthusiasm what they lacked in numbers (p. 389). Fools Crow concludes with the image of plenty, as "the rivers of great animals moved [. . .]. The blackhorns had returned and, all around, it was as it should be" (p. 391).

11
Ethics in Emma Lee Warrior's "Compatriots"

While Welch's novel makes overt connections with the Blackfoot world represented in oral stories such as "Scarface", Emma Lee Warrior's "Compatriots" appears to be moving in a different direction. Warrior's main Blackfoot characters have become disconnected from their ancestral traditions, and only recently have begun to participate in the Sun Dance. A heavily pregnant Lucy, the protagonist, is introduced while in the outhouse (p. 48), an image reminiscent of Molly Bloom sitting on the chamber pot in James Joyce's *Ulysses*. In the same way that Joyce represented Molly as a symbol of Modern womanhood, Warrior represents Lucy as symbolic of the contribution of modern Blackfoot women in upholding the Blackfoot community. First Nations women have often been neglected in male-centred historical and literary representations, but in recent times have become visible, especially, although not exclusively, in the writing of women, including First Nations women.

Warrior departs from well-rehearsed Indian stereotypes by creating a female protagonist (Lucy) who is part of a kinship network of women, which includes her aunt Flora, and another, unnamed aunt from "Badger". The heroism of these women consists of upholding Blackfoot ideals of generosity, reciprocity, and community focus through everyday acts. Lucy provides a contrast not only with Scarface, but also with the Indian stereotype in historical writing and popular culture. Reading the short story as an allegory of the hero quest, but at the same time as an antidote for the male "warrior", requires readers to value the everyday as heroic. However, far from homogenizing the Blackfoot community, or Blackfoot women, Warrior's narrative is also populated by Blackfoot who fail to live by Blackfoot standards.

The German compatriots, after whom the short story is named, are Helmut Walking Eagle and Hilda Afflerbach. Helmut is the author of a book on Blackfoot traditions titled *Indian Medicine: A Revival of Ancient Cures and Ceremonies*. He is also a self-styled ceremonialist spearheading the re-introduction of the Sun Dance at the Peigan Reserve, where

Blackfoot who have grown up as Christians are trying to reconnect with the ceremony of their ancestors. Helmut has shed his cultural heritage in order to style himself as an Indian, not a modern-day one like those who live on the reserve, but an Indian from the buffalo era. Helmut's dress reminds Lucy "of the Plains Indian Museum" in Browning (Blackfeet Reservation in Montana). Helmut complements his anachronistic attire by wearing "his hair in braids", and "round, pink shell earrings" (pp. 50 and 57). But the most peculiar characteristic of this self-styled Indian, is that he refuses to communicate in other than the Blackfoot language. Helmut's link to the Blackfoot community is Elsie Walking Eagle, his Pikuni wife, and "the source" of the Blackfoot knowledge that fills the pages of his book (p. 58).

More than unflattering, Warrior's characterization of Walking Eagle turns him into a caricature. The connotations of his name, as Renate Eigenbrod points out, ridicule his stereotyping of Blackfoot culture.[1] Indeed, a flightless eagle can hardly be seen as an Above Being *(Spomi-tapi-ksi)*.[2] Eigenbrod alerts us to the broader connections between Indians and Germans in the real world. She compares Walking Eagle, not with Englishman Archie Belaney of Grey Owl fame, as Ann McKinnon suggests,[3] but with someone closer to the Blackfoot: Adolf Hungry Wolf, the Swiss — but often described as German — husband of Kainai Beverly Little Bear, nee Hungry Wolf.[4] The name "Hungry Wolf" was given to Adolf when he was adopted into the Kainai community. Adolf and Beverly Hungry Wolf are both prolific authors of books on Blackfoot subjects, including two volumes on Blackfoot women by the latter.[5] The Hungry Wolfs have chosen to live without some of the comforts of modern life (telephone and electricity) and to follow a Blackfoot-oriented path. They have been past owners of Medicine Pipe Bundles, which gives a measure of Adolf's acceptance into the Kainai community.[6] However, despite his participation in the ceremonial life of his wife's Kainai community, by virtue of his non-Blackfoot ancestry, Adolf Hungry Wolf, like the fictional Walking Eagle, occupies a liminal position among them.

Blackfoot scholars often express reservations of outsiders who write books about the Blackfoot.[7] Edward Said coined the term *Orientalism* to describe a process of (mis)representation through travel and scholarly texts that, as he points out, tell us more about European yearnings than about the Orient. Warrior alludes to a similar process of appropriation and (mis)representation of Blackfoot knowledge in her characterization of Walking Eagle. Through his book, he not only defines the Blackfoot to outsiders, but, as Eigenbrod notes, "defines and objectifies" their culture for the Blackfoot themselves.[8] However, we need to take into account that many Blackfoot saw benefits for their future generations in the production of books based on their knowledge, and willingly (not naively) participated in such processes of cultural translation. Hence, while

Warrior has not given Walking Eagle any redeeming qualities, it cannot be assumed that this character necessarily alludes to Hungry Wolf, merely because the origin of the latter is mistakenly assumed to be German.

Warrior's characterization of Hilda Afflerbach, the young German character "studying about Indians" (p. 49), is not as harsh as that of her compatriot. Hilda has some redeeming characteristics. She is appreciative of Lucy's cooking, and shows solidarity with her host, playing with her children and helping to wash dishes. However, like her compatriot, and like the "salvage" ethnographers of yore, Hilda glorifies the Blackfoot past and has no interest in their present. She yearns to meet the timeless Indians of Helmut Walking Eagle's books — the burden of authenticity imposed by white (mis)representations. Hilda is disappointed that Lucy does not attend Sun Dances (p. 51). Her higher regard for Helmut as a source of Blackfoot knowledge underscores the exclusion of Blackfoot voices from textual articulations of Blackfoot subjectivity. "Compatriots" revolves around Hilda's arrival on the reserve, hoping that Helmut will give her something she can take back to Germany, where people "are really interested in Indians", so much so that "They even have clubs" (p. 50). There is a stark difference between Warrior's Blackfoot characters and the compatriots, who, as the only non-Blackfoot characters, represent the "White" world in the narrative. Analyzing the elements that signal that difference takes us back to the realm of ethical behaviour embedded in Blackfoot stories such as "Scarface."

Everyday Heroines Building Community

Although the Piegan Reserve of "Compatriots" is far removed from the setting of "Scarface", Warrior demonstrates that core Blackfoot ethical ideals such as generosity, reciprocity, and community orientation, have not been obliterated by forced acculturation. She portrays unsympathetically characters lacking these qualities. In contrast, Lucy touches the lives of her relations, not through extraordinary deeds, but through everyday gestures, including practicing reciprocity. Flora calls on Lucy to ask her to look after Hilda, whom Flora met at the Calgary Stampede and is taking to the Sun Dance after work. Lucy "knew she was boxed in" because "Flora had done her a lot of favours" (pp. 48–49). According to the Blackfoot worldview, reciprocity is fundamental to keep the world in balance. Lucy apologizes to her uninvited guest for her limited resources: "I've got no running water in the house. You have to go outside to use the toilet." What she has, however, she generously shares "even though it was only the usual scrambled eggs and fried potatoes with toast and coffee". Lucy's hospitality — one of several instances in the short story where Lucy is mindful of her relations — is the more remarkable since she "didn't relish having a white visitor" (pp. 49–50). The discomfort is shared by Bob, Lucy's dog, who barks furiously as Flora and Hilda approach: "I don't know what's wrong with Bob; he never barks at me" — says Flora. Lucy surmises that Bob, who is not used to white people, is barking at Hilda, whose irruption into Lucy's space can be read allegorically as akin to white arrival in Blackfoot territory. They came uninvited, they were well received, they imposed their own views of reality, and they disparaged the practices of their hosts as compared with their "civilization".

In view of the circumstances of the Blackfoot characters in "Compatriots", the promises of a better future through civilization and Christianity made at treaty signing ring hollow. Social disadvantage, accrued during more than a century of colonialism, sets Warrior's Blackfoot characters apart from their non-Blackfoot counterparts. Warrior's characters are far removed from the Blackfoot elite. In "Compatriots", poverty, unemployment, alienation and alcoholism stretch the resources of those Blackfoot (mostly women) who strive to uphold Blackfoot ideals despite outside interference. While government officials and missionaries are absent from the narrative, their legacy is palpable. Outsiders continue to define the boundaries of what it means to be Blackfoot — colonization is ongoing. Flora now has to "punch in" at work: "Can't travel on Indian time anymore (p. 49)." Sonny begs a lift from Lucy to leave town because he is scared that the police "might beat [him] up". Lucy "believed the cops did beat up Indians, although none was ever brought to court over it" (p. 52). Critics have explored Warrior's representation of the German compatriots almost to the point of neglecting the Blackfoot characters.[9] In order to place these characters at the centre of our enquiries, we need to view their cultural continuities and cultural disconnections within the context of the history of colonization, which weighs heavily on the narrative, even though not specifically articulated.

Lucy lives in substandard conditions and eats unhealthy food. Even the ham and sausages that she must wait until payday to acquire (p. 50) are processed foods that could never compare with the wholesome diet of her ancestors (buffalo meat, berries and roots). She manages, however, to buy "hamburgers, fries and lemonade" for lunch from the local Cafe (pp. 50–51), and "Kool-Aid" from the "Stop-n-Go Mart". Her dinner, courtesy of Flora, is "Kentucky Fried Chicken", which the children "don't know when to stop eating" (pp. 52–55) — such are the benefits of progress.

By comparison, Walking Eagle is wealthy, possessing the trappings of two worlds. He has a Winnebago motor home next to his tepee. The tepee is "stunning", filled with "buffalo hides. Backrests, wall hangings, parfleche bags, and numerous artefacts [. . .] magnificently displayed" (p. 57). The source of his wealth is unspecified, but readers are left with the impression that it is related to his cultural usurpation. We don't learn of Helmut's activities when he is not directing the Sun Dance. What we do know about him is that his outward appearance is not matched by the qualities that the Blackfoot he seeks to imitate valued most. Helmut fails to observe hospitality to his own compatriot, as well as to Lucy and Flora, two members of the community into which he has forced his way. His "jaw twitched with resentment" when his compatriot asked him if he knew Weisbaden, her hometown. The pleasure of feasting neighbours and visitors who came from afar to renew acquaintances was cherished during the Circle Encampment during the times that Helmut is trying to bring back. As Bastien stresses, the purpose of Blackfoot ceremony and the observance of ideal Blackfoot behaviour seeks to maintain a balance. This principle is missing in Helmut's impersonation. Elsie Walking Eagle is forced to translate her husband's words as he refuses to speak other than in the Blackfoot language in the presence of Hilda, Flora and Lucy. Elsie's embarrassment signals that she is aware of the inappropriateness of her husband's behaviour, but seems powerless to question his authority. As the three women chat with Elsie on their way out, Helmut loudly summons her and Elsie dismisses the visitors, "I don't have time to visit. We have a lot of things to do" (p. 58).

Although the short story avoids overt didacticism, there is no mistaking that those who transgress Blackfoot ethics are portrayed unsympathetically. Flora's cousin, Delphine, is mean to the point of begrudging giving a cup of water to Lucy's son: "'I have to haul water, and nobody pays for my gas,' grumbled Delphine, as she filled a cup halfway with water" (p. 56). Such transgressive behaviour adds heterogeneity to Warrior's portrayal of Blackfoot subjectivity, but is marginalized by being enacted by a minor character. Unlike Delphine, Lucy and Flora are constantly honouring their relations.

Warrior's portrayal of gender relations in "Compatriots" shows women as the backbone of the community while men flounder. In Warrior's narrative, there is a gulf between women like Flora and Lucy and dysfunctional males such as Bunky, Lucy's husband, and Sonny, her uncle. Considering the freezing temperatures of the Alberta winter, having no running water or plumbing must cause Lucy's family great hardship. Yet, while the house lacks basic facilities, Bunky can afford to get drunk with his friends; his job is in jeopardy because of his hangover-induced absenteeism, yet he only goes to work to avoid being in the house while Hilda is there (pp. 48–49). Sonny, for his part, goes on a binge "as soon as he got money"; he "wouldn't quit drinking till he quit living." Alcohol dependency transcends generational differences. Sonny, however, is mindful of his relations. He helps Lucy carry the washing, because she is "not supposed to be carrying big things around in [her] condition". Even though "the effort of lifting the bags was clearly too much for him" and he dropped them "several times before he got to the car", but Sonny stays firm in his wish to do this for his niece (p. 52). His actions may be simple acts of common courtesy, but if read allegorically, as well as in the light of the ethical ideals embedded in the Blackfoot Stories, they are as significant to the maintenance of the Blackfoot community as the more spectacular feats of Scarface. There is a reciprocal bond between Lucy and Sonny. When he comes to her suffering from alcohol withdrawal, she buys him soup and drives him to her place, to protect him from the police (pp. 51–52). In contrast, Lucy refuses to help her husband's relative, "An unkempt Indian man [who] dogged them, talking in Blackfoot". She feels justified in refusing him, because: "I used to give him money, but he just drinks it up" (p. 51). Indeed, what this man wants is for Lucy to procure him some vanilla essence, a substance that the store will not sell to alcoholics.

Navigating the Present

"Compatriots" is a multi-layered text that, apart from the underlying narrative of colonization and loss, also represents Blackfoot resilience and survival. I would argue that Warrior depicts her Blackfoot characters at different stages of a journey, which some are able to navigate better than others. Kinship ties between Lucy and her aunts point to women as the culture bearers in charge of building community. Their strengths reside in their capacity to exercise Blackfoot values that have transcended colonization and forced acculturation. Generosity, reciprocity, and community focus persist among these Blackfoot women, who share what little they have, even with insensitive outsiders such as Hilda. The Blackfoot women collectively provide shelter, food, transportation, and a great deal of their time to this stranger. In contrast, her compatriot refuses Hilda even a few words.

Paradoxically, although "most of the Indians wished Helmut would disappear" (p. 50), many Blackfoot are camped in readiness for the Sun Dance at which he is the ceremonial leader. Interest in "traditional beliefs" is of recent coinage for many of those in the large Circle Encampment, the vision of which makes Hilda gasp in amazement. Some, like Delphine and George Many Robes, have already found their place within the circle; others, like Flora, are still searching. Lucy has no interest in the ceremony, which she dismisses as "just a big mess" over which "mixed-up people" quarrel. Some want to use "Sioux ways" in the practice, "others use Cree" (p. 51). Such disconnections between the Blackfoot characters and their traditional practices are not surprising, given their forced acculturation in the aftermath of settlement on the reserve. However, in "Compatriots" there is a flow of Blackfoot who, having grown-up as Christians, are now re-connecting with the practices of their ancestors. Flora's interest in "exploring traditional beliefs" had started recently, having grown up a

Ethics in Emma Lee Warrior's "Compatriots"

Catholic (p. 56). She has learnt about the Sun Dance from books. Flora has no qualms about the *bona fides* of Walking Eagle's book as a means for cultural revitalization. In Flora's view Elsie is "the source" for the knowledge therein.

That these Blackfoot are prepared to revitalize their culture by relying on the likes of Helmut Walking Eagle points to a need to find ways to strengthen a Blackfoot identity in order to avoid the homogenizing effects of contemporary life. Walking Eagle's ethnographic salvage might well revitalize Blackfoot culture by promoting, to borrow the term from Beverly Hungry Wolf, a "spiritual reawakening".[10] Warrior's unsympathetic characterization of Walking Eagle while simultaneously portraying his large following may be an indictment of Blackfoot attitudes towards their own ceremonies, allowing Walking Eagle to taker over.

The representation of the compatriots as "Others" within a Blackfoot-centred narrative turns the world upside down in relation to colonial representations of Indians. The partnership formed by Elsie and Helmut blurs the boundaries between insiders and outsiders, with the result that Helmut becomes a catalyst for the revitalization of Blackfoot ceremonies. His role in the revival of the Sun Dance can be attributed to Blackfoot indifference. However, Blackfoot like Flora find no reason to reject him, which indicates that even his impersonation might have real utility for those seeking to avoid being absorbed into the mainstream, and who are looking for a space where their different identity as Blackfoot can be strengthened. The significance of the Circle Encampment and the Sun Dance during the buffalo days resided in their relevance to Blackfoot lifeways. For the non-sedentary bands such a gathering provided unique opportunities for cultural reproduction, with the Sun Dance providing a forum for the display of the qualities most appreciated by the Blackfoot. For the revitalized Sun Dance to be relevant, it will likewise have to respond to the needs of contemporary Blackfoot who, despite the cultural transformations undergone since settlement, wish to perform their separate identity.

Warrior avoids portraying her Blackfoot characters as caricatures by representing them as a heterogeneous community, including some characters such as Delphine who fail to mind their relations even in the most basic manner. Warrior's irony targets the compatriots in particular. Walking Eagle believes that he can become Blackfoot by adopting the outward appearance of a museum figure and by speaking the Blackfoot language. However, his adoption of a Blackfoot persona is only superficial, because he fails to uphold the most basic Blackfoot ethical ideal: he fails to mind his relations. Moreover, both Walking Eagle and Hilda are arrogant enough to believe that Blackfoot culture is what is written in books, and not the everyday actions and relationships of current-day Blackfoot people.

Part IV — The Oral Tradition in Contemporary Literature

Warrior addresses more than ethical stances from both the Blackfoot characters and the compatriots. She points to the social disparity that is a legacy of colonialism. She also points to social problems such as alcoholism. The women in "Compatriots" are in different ways involved in upholding the Blackfoot community. Even Delphine — who has yet much to learn about the Blackfoot ideal of generosity — is seeking to revitalize Blackfoot culture and to recover the connection with the Blackfoot past. Although Lucy is not taking an active part in this revitalization, her generosity and the manner in which she minds her relations serve to uphold the Blackfoot community in such a way that her ancestors would have been proud of her. Lucy's behaviour is motivated by ethical ideals of generosity, reciprocity, and community focus that, without being overtly emphasized, provide the foundations for those Blackfoot who strive to lead moral lives.

Literary criticism is sensitive to context. Having earlier set a context from which to view Ookaan as a locus of resistance and a site for the reproduction of Blackfoot culture, the last three chapters in this volume have bridged the disciplinary boundary between history and literary criticism in order to seek the threads of continuity between the Blackfoot oral tradition and the contemporary writing of Native authors such as Welch and Warrior. The purpose of this analysis has sought to reverse the trend to view the contemporary literary production of Native authors purely as a response to colonialism. For all that most versions of "Scarface" that have guided this analysis were first written down during the era of the full implementation of colonial rule, the purpose here has been to seek through the story a point of reference that predates colonialism. The colonial influence on Native literatures is only too evident, above all through the adoption of the language and the several genres introduced as literary templates by the colonizers. Nonetheless, an explicit goal throughout this book has been to seek out cultural continuities, which is the justification for comparing the story of Scarface with the contemporary narratives of Welch and Warrior.

Indigenous identity continues to be a contested terrain in fictional as well as in non-fictional representations. Despite the fragility of representations of identity as distinctive in a world that homogenizes human experience, Blackfoot claims to a separate identity from that of the colonizers can be nurtured through more inclusive and creative re-interpretations of history as much as through fictional representation. The latter is a site *par excellence* for cultural revitalization, above all because of its capacity to imagine a world in which First Nations peoples become the subjects, rather than the objects of representation.

Literary representation has played a part in the creation and maintenance of derogatory stereotypes of Native Peoples, the colonizer's "Other". It is therefore to Native literature, in the first instance, that we can look to reverse the gaze, by directing it towards the colonizers. Welch and Warrior fulfil the expectations of a Native text by representing a world that, like the Blackfoot Stories, is Blackfoot-centred, a world in which the Blackfoot characters articulate a Blackfoot perspective of Blackfoot history. As is clear from the comparative analysis between the Blackfoot Stories and the contemporary texts, the ethical dimension functions as a metalanguage that links the old with the new.

The renderings of Scarface analyzed here represent the Blackfoot world in ways that contradict colonial negative stereotypes that generally constructed First Nations peoples as Others. The story illuminates how the Blackfoot chose to represent themselves. The two contemporary narratives by Welch and Warrior likewise represent Blackfoot subjectivity as heterogeneous, thereby lifting the burden of authenticity imposed by colonial representations. They simultaneously constitute a vindication and a revitalization of Blackfoot culture, its values, and lifeways.

Conclusion

Western expansion in the nineteenth century in both Canada and the United States transformed the lifeways of First Nations peoples of the northwestern Plains, who, until the middle of the nineteenth century, had remained relatively undisturbed by a burgeoning white presence in the East. Geographic distance allowed First Nations peoples who, like the Blackfoot, were able to continue their non-sedentary lifeways until the late nineteenth century, to incorporate European technologies into their practices on their own terms. From the middle of the nineteenth century, the increasing presence of whites and white technology correspondingly increased the pace of cultural transformation of First Nations peoples of the Upper Missouri. The destruction of the buffalo herds left those First Nations whose livelihood depended on this resource unable to continue their erstwhile existence. Settled on reserves in Canada and a reservation in the United States, the Blackfoot-speaking bands began a radically different existence. From the early 1880s, this transformation took the guise of forced acculturation, encompassing the secular and sacred realms. The purported benefits of "civilization," in the case of the Blackfoot, translated into a loss of autonomy, a marked decrease in population numbers, and a subservient position in the United States as well as in Canada, as "domestic dependent nations" and "wards of the state". Within this historical context, the portrayal of Blackfoot history has been subordinated to the narrative of change. This study has sought to emphasize several strands of continuity that are pointed reminders that Blackfoot history does not commence with European arrival, and is not merely a response to the newcomers.

The case studies that comprise this volume support the conclusion that Blackfoot cultural transformation throughout their contacts with Europeans and later with their descendants cannot be taken to be entirely a response to this encounter. Nor did it proceed always in accordance with white desires. The threads of cultural continuity are evident in the persistence of Ookaan, the continuity of ceremonial dress practices, the acknowledgement of the Blackfoot contribution to the project of documenting Blackfoot knowledge, and thereby to Blackfoot history and literature. Moreover, the links between the Blackfoot Stories and the writing of Blackfoot authors such as Emma Lee Warrior and James Welch attest to the way in which the written oral stories continue to inspire

Conclusion

contemporary Blackfoot. The stories of continuity that emerge from each case study broaden and enrich our view of the possibilities open to colonized peoples to resist absorption into the colonized Other.

By viewing Blackfoot cultural transformations via these threads of continuity, this volume has cast light on processes that hitherto have been viewed as incidental to a larger picture. By applying this approach to the circumstances surrounding the attempted eradication of the central ceremony of Ookaan, Blackfoot actions that led to the continuance of the practice come into sharper focus. Much work remains to be done in this respect. The notion that a ceremony such as Ookaan should remain faithful to a specific model in order to be authentic is yet to be discarded. An understanding of the function of ceremony through the ideologies reflected in stories such as "Scarface" serves as a reminder that, to remain meaningful, ceremonies will change to reflect the needs of their practitioners. Official attempts to subvert the ceremony failed to take into account the needs of the Blackfoot bands.

The history of prohibition that threatened Ookaan once the Blackfoot bands settled on reserves and reservations challenges the notion that prohibition and eradication are two sides of the same coin. Legislation needs to be viewed against the many Blackfoot acts of resistance and the myriad reports of the continuation of the practice. In the current study, this approach has paid dividends by demonstrating how Ookaan's continuity was ensured due to Blackfoot actions, despite the best efforts by officials and missionaries to eradicate the practice, and despite the progressive strengthening of legislation to that end. It demonstrates that the history of prohibition must be examined in its heterogeneity, and that broad claims regarding the prohibition of sun dances and kindred practices must take into account the "hidden transcripts" of both the colonizer and the colonized. Even within the asymmetrical power relations of the early reserve era, the unequivocal resistance of the Blackfoot to official and missionary efforts to eradicate Ookaan, their central ceremony, serves to revalorize their survival strategies as a mixture of accommodation and resistance, rather than compliance with official regulation.

Similarly, tracing Blackfoot dress practices during a century (from c.1830) of steadily mounting contact with whites demonstrates clearly that the "middle ground" that had been created during the fur trade era was more than a mere conduit for the exchange of commodities. Trade and treaties were inextricably linked, and defined leadership in the subsequent inter-racial political developments during the first decade of reserve life. Blackfoot–white alliances forged during the fur trade established hierarchies that resulted in the conferral of authority to some Blackfoot leaders, such as Crowfoot, over and above the authority attendant upon their traditional leadership role. Blackfoot "loyalty" to their white allies can better be appreciated against the backdrop of such pre-existing alliances, most notably during critical moments such as the threatened war of extermination against whites by Sitting Bull and his followers, and during the crisis of the Riel Rebellion in 1885. Hugh Dempsey's contribution to the history of these alliances, through his biographies of Red Crow and Crowfoot, demonstrates the diplomatic and oratorical capacity of Blackfoot leaders during the early life on the reserves. It also underscores their political manoeuvring and refusal to accept a subservient role. Adroit leadership was crucial to Blackfoot success in navigating the colonial encounter, above all in the forced transition from their traditional lifeways to the radically different realities of reserve life.

The power relations that come to the foreground when seen through the lens of dress semiotics likewise throw light on the adoption of Western military-style uniforms by Blackfoot leaders. Such displays of European dress can be interpreted as continuous with intertribal protocols established long before white arrival, and not as evidence of a desire by Blackfoot leaders to become "white". The analysis of Blackfoot dress is particularly useful to question and even refute stereotypical representations that homogenize Blackfoot women as powerless, because the symbols of women's status can be inferred from their dressing practices. Within a context of changing circumstances women's dress practices tell a story of Blackfoot women as exercising different kinds of power through womanly activities, elite status, and economic strength. This demonstrates that their erasure as actors in the historiography masks women's capacity to exercise power, both in the secular and the sacred realms. Importantly, the study of Blackfoot dress opens a window onto the manner in which, from their transition to life on reserves, Blackfoot people in general, and Blackfoot leaders in particular, continued to "imagine" their own subjectivity through the strategic deployment of buckskin dress. More studies are required that emphasize the manifold ways in which First Nations peoples themselves deployed the buckskin suit, rather than the usual emphasis on the appropriation of this most potent symbol in mainstream popular culture.

The chapters in Parts I and II of this volume highlight two manifestations of the viability of Blackfoot cultural practices and the significance of Blackfoot worldviews within the rapidly transforming environment of the early reserve era. Both the continuation of Ookaan and the continuation of dress practices link the Blackfoot present to the Blackfoot Stories that have transmitted the Blackfoot worldviews to successive generations from "time immemorial". These stories provide the foundations of Blackfoot epistemology, and their preservation and transmission as written history and literature is the subject of Parts III and IV. The chapters therein are concerned with the guises of continuity within the realm of written representation, whether in history or literature. The imposition of Western epistemologies and thus Western ideas of history and literature ushered in

Conclusion

by colonization was integral to the "civilizing" mission of colonialism — to wean the colonized from their own ideas of historical time, place, cosmology and causation, preparatory to infusing their cultures with Christianity and Enlightenment ideas of progress and modernity. Jack Goody has charged that this Eurocentric project involved, and involves, the "theft of history".[1] Pre-colonial cosmologies and sense of a people's origins are lost to view or devalued by the "civilizing" process. Such histories are thenceforth reclassified as myths, and are collected and transcribed by the colonizers with an almost antiquarian interest in documenting the knowledge of First Nations peoples — the task of "salvage ethnology". However, when the production of the texts of "salvage" is viewed from another angle, it becomes evident that the Blackfoot Grandfathers and Grandmothers provided the backbone for the production of these early texts by non-Blackfoot authors. When the existence of a complex Blackfoot epistemology with its own coherent mechanisms for the construction of "truth" according to the Blackfoot worldview is taken into account, the contribution of Blackfoot knowledge can be put in perspective. While the pitfalls of representing the Other have been amply explored in the historiography, we still know very little about those organic intellectuals whose knowledge was documented and later incorporated into historical texts on the Blackfoot. Different views expressed by these intellectuals also deserve to be analyzed and questioned.

The reinterpretation of the Blackfoot past is ongoing, especially in the works of Blackfoot scholars whose work informs this volume. Blackfoot epistemology, like its Western counterpart, possesses its own complex dynamics for reproducing "truth". Scholars are increasingly aware of the power/knowledge relations that provide the foundations for colonial histories such as those written about the Blackfoot. However, apprehending the ways in which Blackfoot knowledge was transformed into the early texts of Blackfoot history demonstrates that, despite the prevailing asymmetrical power relations that provided the context for the writing of such texts, Blackfoot organic intellectuals contributed greatly to this history. Their role has not yet been sufficiently recognized. This is one of the contributions that this book has attempted to make: to emphasize the significant part played by Blackfoot intellectuals in the writing of early Blackfoot history and literature.

Quite apart from the conditions surrounding the writing of the early texts based on orally transmitted Blackfoot knowledge, the Blackfoot Stories that have been documented in early texts have here been linked to the contemporary writing of Blackfoot authors Emma Lee Warrior and James Welch. Stories such as "Scarface" can explain much about the Blackfoot world, their ideologies and ethical ideals. This is evident in that each of the chapters in this study bears some connection to "Scarface." Native literature is thus part of the normative History of First Nations

Conclusion

peoples. Stories such as "Scarface" should not be viewed as unchanging narratives of a distant past. It is evident from the way that this story can be connected to history and literature that this protean narrative, like Blackfoot culture, remains meaningful to successive generations because its meaning speaks to core Blackfoot behaviours that continue to provide ideals for those wishing to live a moral life. The histories encoded in stories such as "Scarface" reveal themselves in such ethical imperatives as that of "minding" one's relations, a concept that does not refer only to the extended family, but to the family of creation. This ethical sense, a kind of moral economy of identity, is inscribed within (in the Western sense) normative as well as pre-colonial literature and history of the Blackfoot, and are reaffirmed in Ookaan, which ritually and cyclically encodes and reaffirms a protean Blackfoot identity that remains separate to that of the colonizers.

The perspectives gained through Blackfoot history provided the ideal grounding for a critical appraisal of the role of literary representation as a major site for decolonization, in particular through James Welch's historical novel *Fools Crow*, and Emma Lee Warrior's short story "Compatriots". Establishing firm links between the Blackfoot Stories and these contemporary representations goes some way towards revalorizing as literature the stories from the Blackfoot oral tradition. George Grinnell realized the intrinsic literary worth of these stories and was one of the first scholars who referred to them as "Blackfoot literature." However, his interest did not extend to the relationship between the stories and the contemporary Blackfoot worldview, even though his knowledge of Blackfoot culture must have afforded him an appreciation of the interconnectedness between the stories, the ceremonies that re-enacted the stories, and the Blackfoot worldview. It is only through the more recent work of Blackfoot scholars that we have now increased access to these links, but the documentation of the stories through the "salvage ethnologies" discussed in Part IV is crucial for the building-up of this scholarship. In a sense, Blackfoot Grandfathers fostered a connection between Blackfoot and non-Blackfoot scholarship, and this connection continues in the present. This study has sought to create bridges between these two strands, the emic and the etic, which are demonstrably both complementary and mutually beneficial.

The study of Blackfoot literature is as yet to receive the scholarly attention that Northwest Coast literatures have attracted, in particular from the groundbreaking studies of linguist Dell Hymes. The continued compartmentalization within studies of First Nations literature, which leaves the stories from the oral tradition to anthropology or ethnohistory, creates an artificial boundary (as Thomas King points out) that negates the links between the stories from the oral tradition on the one hand, and contemporary Native writing, on the other. This volume spans discipli-

Conclusion

nary boundaries in order to represent a more nuanced history and a more comprehensive interpretation of literature that strikes a balance between continuity and change, by infusing both genres with insights drawn from the Blackfoot worldview and Blackfoot epistemology.

Focus on continuity within rapidly changing cultural environments has served to emphasize the two-way workings of transculturation. More importantly, it highlights that, within the asymmetrical power relationships of the contact zone of the reserve and the reservation, the Blackfoot resisted forced assimilation and exercised considerable agency in defining the pace of their own cultural transformation. The combined product of the foregoing chapters points clearly to the need for comparative studies in order to explore further how distinct First Nations peoples, who as neighbours endured the vicissitudes of colonization processes, could end up having such vastly different colonial experiences. Each of these chapters owes much to those Blackfoot scholars who have articulated Blackfoot epistemology in ways that continue to widen the possibilities for researchers of Blackfoot history and literature. Their writing is making available emic perspectives that add clarity to an interpretation of Blackfoot history and literature from which fresher, more inflected perspectives can emerge. It is evident in the work of scholars such as Hernandez and Bastien that it is possible to create bridges of understanding between Blackfoot and non-Blackfoot scholarship. Deepening scholarly understanding of First Nations peoples' epistemologies not only serves to cast these in sharper relief, but also adds complexity to present and future research agendas.

Appendices 1–4

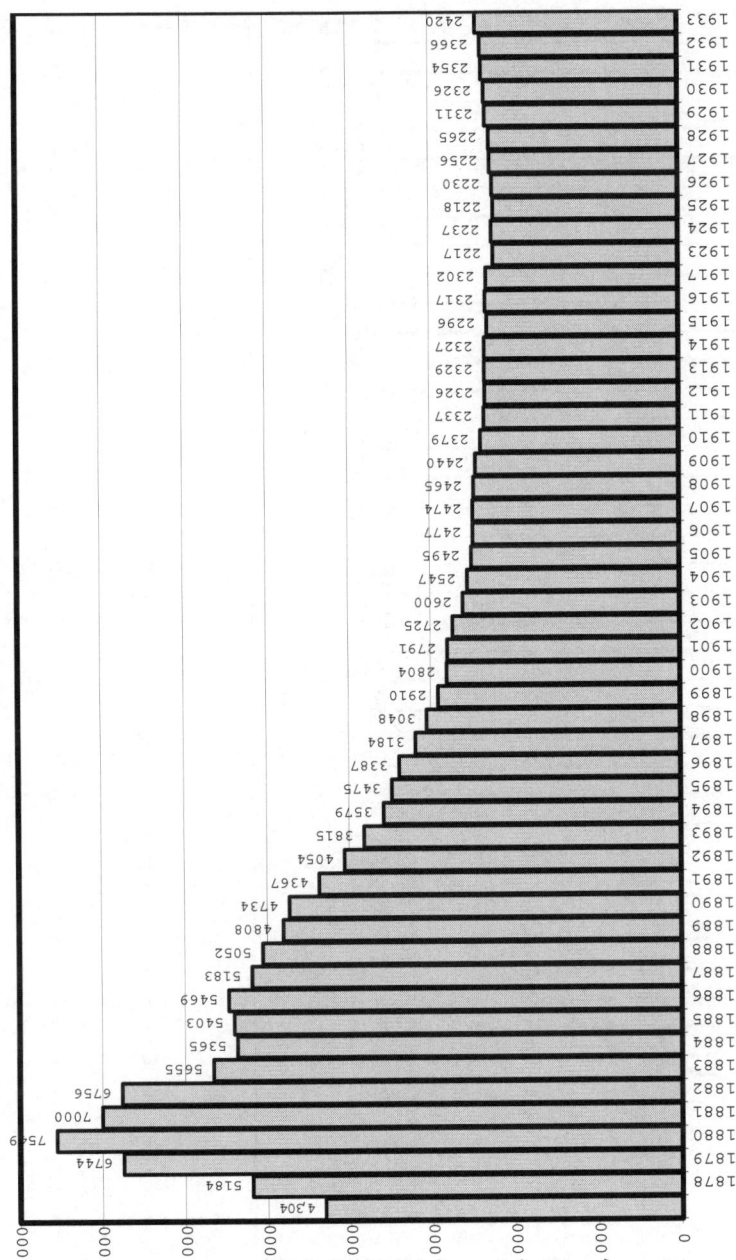

APPENDIX 1
Combined Blackfoot Population in Canada, 1877–1933

Prepared by: Blanca Tovías.
Based on *Annual Reports of the Department of Indian Affairs, Dominion of Canada, 1864–1990*; and Hugh A. Dempsey: 1979, *Indian Tribes of Alberta*.

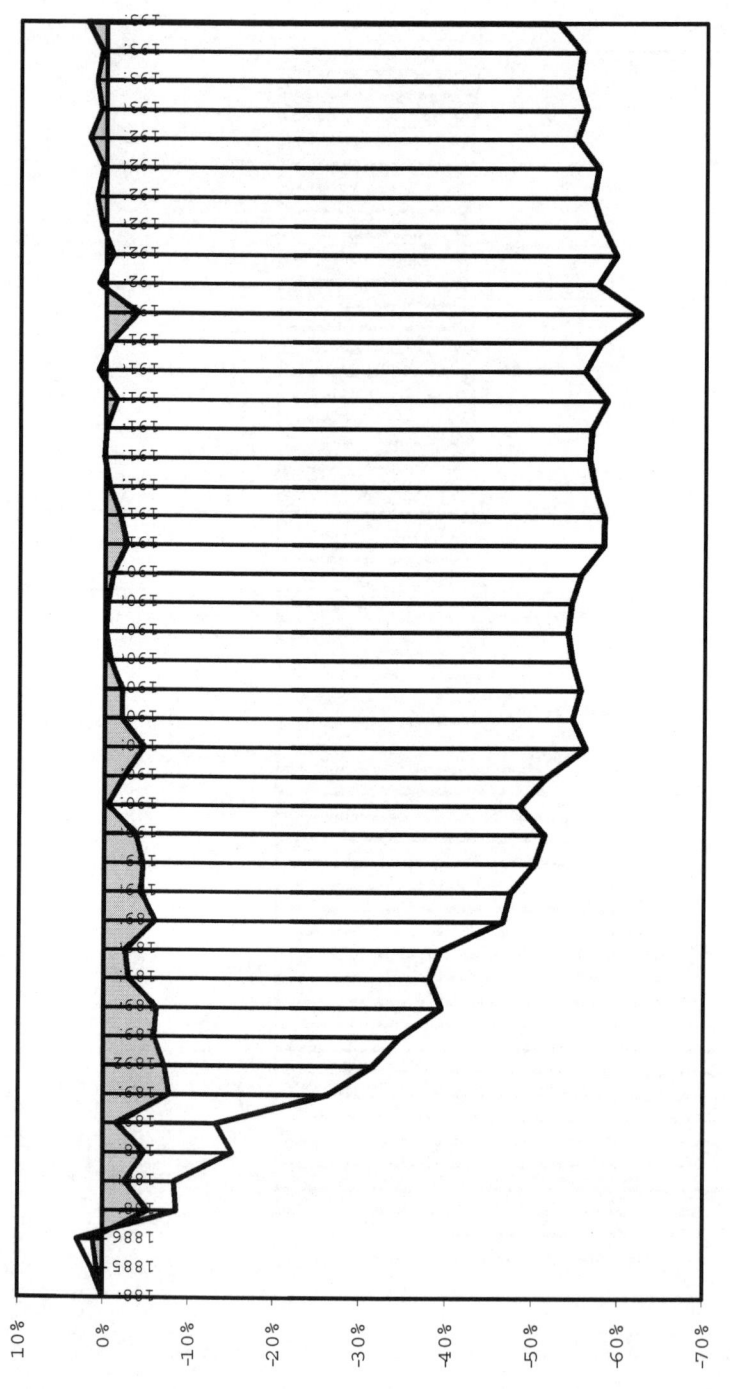

APPENDIX 2

Blackfoot Population Decline in Canada (Yearly and Cumulative), 1877–1933

Prepared by: Blanca Tovías.
Based on *Annual Reports of the Department of Indian Affairs*, Dominion of Canada, 1864–1990; and Hugh A. Dempsey: 1979, *Indian Tribes of Alberta*.

Appendix 3

Blackfoot Population in Canada by First Nation, 1877–1933

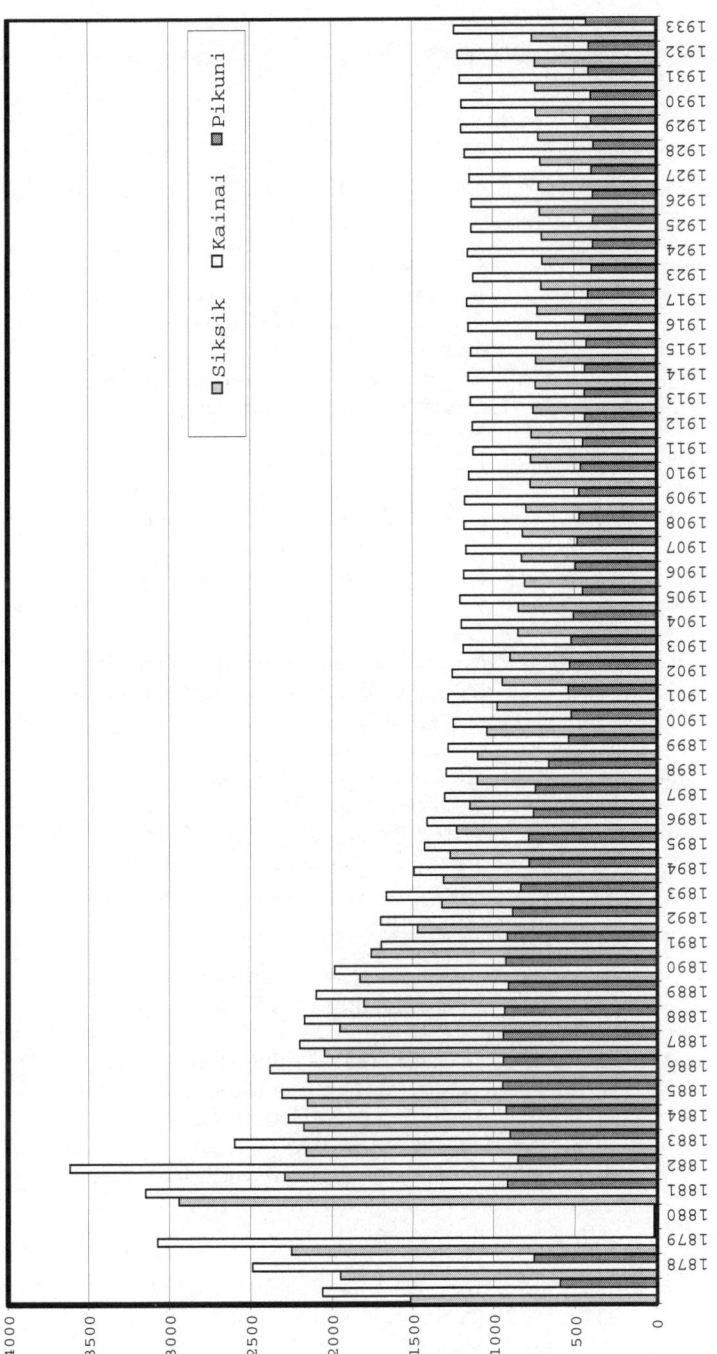

Prepared by: Blanca Tovías.
Based on *Annual Reports of the Department of Indian Affairs*, Dominion of Canada, 1864–1990; and Hugh A. Dempsey: 1979, *Indian Tribes of Alberta*.

Appendices

APPENDIX 4

Blackfoot Population in Canada, 1877–1933

Prepared by Blanca Tovías.
Based on the Annual Reports of the Department of Indian Affairs (AR), Dominion of Canada, 1864–1990; and Hugh A. Dempsey, 1979: *Indian Tribes of Alberta*.

Year	Siksika	Kainai	Pikuni	Total	Observations
1877	1515	2058	589	4162	Dempsey, pp. 20, 27 and 36. Total for Treaty 7 census (includes Sarcee and Stoney) in AR = 4392
1878	1946	2488	750	5184	Dempsey, pp. 20, 27 and 36. Total for Treaty 7 census (includes Sarcee and Stoney) in AR = 4928.
1879	2249	3071	?	6744	Dempsey, pp. 20 and 27. Total for Treaty 7 census (includes Sarcee and Stoney) in AR = 6744 (p. 307); but = 6673 (p. 186). Starvation year. Many died, "principally old people" (AR p. 77).
1880	?	?	?	7549	Total reflects Treaty 7 census (includes Sarcee and Stoney) annuity payments (AR pp. 235 and 315). Large contingent of Siksika and Kainai were in Montana chasing the last of the buffalo.
1881	2940	3146	914	7000	1064 Siksika and all Kainai returned. Total census for Treaty 7 (includes Sarcee and Stony) in AR = 7789.
1882	2292	3615	849	6756	Total was reported to include excess annuity claims paid, corrected numbers shown 1883.
1883	2158	2599	898	5655	Reduction due to annuity claim excess corrected. Treaty 7 census (includes Sarcee and Stoney) = 7701 (AR p. 126 Part II)
1884	2173	2270	922	5365	84 adults and 44 children died at Blood (Kainai) reserve, against 8 births. Total Treaty 7 census (includes Sarcee and Stoney) = 6673 (AR p. 186)
1885	2151	2310	942	5403	Total Treaty 7 census (includes Sarcee and Stoney) = 6415 (AR p. 194).
1886	2147	2382	940	5469	In 1886 Sarcee and Stoney population = 1026
1887	2046	2199	938	5183	Total Blackfoot Treaty 7 = 5222
1888	1952	2169	931	5052	Blackfoot Treaty 7 = 5868 (AR p. 312)
1889	1804	2097	907	4808	Blackfoot Treaty 7 = 5725 (AR p. 257)
1890	1827	1983	924	4734	Blackfoot Treaty 7 = 5648 (AR p. 239)

Appendices

Year	Siksika	Kainai	Pikuni	Total	Observations
1891	1757	1696	914	4367	Blackfoot Treaty 7 = 5717 (AR p. 247)
1892	1472	1701	881	4054	Blackfoot Treaty 7 = 4708 (AR p. 320)
1893	1319	1665	831	3815	Blackfoot Treaty 7 = 4603 (AR p. 311)
1894	1308	1494	780	3579	Blackfoot Treaty 7 = 4428 (AR p. 286)
1895	1267	1427	781	3475	Blackfoot Treaty 7 = 4287 (AR p. 369)
1896	1226	1410	751	3387	Census lists First Nations separately from this point.
1897	1145	1300	739	3184	
1898	1099	1291	658	3048	
1899	1096	1278	536	2910	
1900	1038	1247	519	2804	
1901	975	1279	537	2791	
1902	942	1253	530	2725	
1903	896	1185	519	2600	
1904	845	1196	506	2547	
1905	842	1204	449	2495	
1906	803	1181	493	2477	
1907	824	1168	482	2474	
1908	817	1178	470	2465	
1909	795	1174	471	2440	
1910	768	1149	462	2379	
1911	767	1122	448	2337	
1912	763	1128	435	2326	
1913	752	1140	437	2329	
1914	737	1154	436	2327	
1915	734	1138	424	2296	
1916	731	1154	432	2317	
1917	726	1161	415	2302	From 1917 quinquennial census. Only population per province available in Annual Reports.
1918–1922					Annuity payments reported in lump sum that includes interest on Indian Trust funds, making this figure unreliable to calculate population until 1923, when annuity payments per First Nation are reported.
1923	702	1122	393	2217	Annuities paid, AR Part I, p. 6.
1924	695	1157	385	2237	Annuities paid, AR Part I, p. 5.
1925	698	1134	386	2218	Annuities paid, AR Part I, p, 6.
1926	711	1133	386	2230	Annuities paid, AR Part I, pp. 41–42.
1927	716	1146	394	2256	Annuities paid, AR Part I, pp. 42–43.
1928	707	1176	382	2265	Annuities paid, AR Part I, pp. 44–45.
1929	719	1196	396	2311	Annuities paid, AR Part I, pp. 46–47.
1930	734	1195	397	2326	Annuities paid, AR Part I, pp. 44–45.
1931	737	1206	411	2354	Annuities paid, AR Part I, pp. 48–49.
1932	740	1217	409	2366	Annuities paid, AR Part I, pp. 40–41.
1933	757	1239	424	2420	Annuities paid, AR Part I, pp. 35–36.

Notes

Introduction: The Threads of Continuity

1 George Bird Grinnell, *Blackfoot Lodge Tales: The Story of a Prairie People*, rpt. 2003 edn (Lincoln: University of Nebraska Press [1892] 1962), pp. 208–10. "Lodge" is equivalent to "tepee" or "tipi".
2 Blackfoot Gallery Committee (henceforth BGC), *Nitsitapiisini: The Story of the Blackfoot People* (Buffalo: Firefly Books, 2001), p. 4.
3 Grinnell, *Lodge Tales*, p. 244.
4 Glenbow Archive (GA), M-8458-4, Jane Richardson's Blackfoot (Siksika) Research — Interview with Pitoxpikis (Sleigh), 1938, (henceforth: Richardson's Interview, Pitoxpikis). See other meanings for the term in Duane Mistaken Chief, with Jürgen W. Kremer, "Glossaries", in Betty Bastien, *Blackfoot Ways of Knowing: The Worldview of the Siksikaitsitapi*, Jürgen W. Kremer, ed., and Duane Mistaken Chief, Language Consultant (Calgary: University of Calgary Press, 2004), pp. 194–230, esp. p. 219; Grinnell, *Lodge Tales*, p. 210, translates Ni'-nah as "My father". Donald G. Frantz, Blackfoot Grammar (Toronto: University of Toronto Press, [1991] 2000), p. 9, translates "nínaawa" as "man", and "nínaiksi" as "men". According to Clark Wissler, "The Social Life of the Blackfoot Indians", American Museum of Natural History (henceforth AMNH), *Anthropological Papers* 7, 1 (1911), pp. 1–64; esp. pp. 22–23, there was no "formal right to a title or an office" by the headman who was considered "band chief".
5 Walter McClintock, *The Old North Trail: Life, Legends and Religion of the Blackfeet Indians* ([London: Macmillan and Co., 1910] Lincoln: University of Nebraska Press, 1992), pp. 169 and 517, notes that as a noun "Medicine [. . .] means something endowed with supernatural power; but, when used as an adjective-prefix, it also means sacred, or set apart for use in religious ceremonials". Thus "Medicine Lodge" is the structure where Ookaan takes place; the vower and ceremonialist are referred to as the "Medicine Woman" and "Medicine Man". "Medicine bundles" are sacred objects given to the Blackfoot by creators. Warriors carried into battle their personal "Medicine", which could take many shapes associated with the individual's protector spirits. Blackfoot scholar Nimachia Hernandez, *Mokakssini: A Blackfoot Theory of Knowledge*, Ph.D. Diss., Harvard University, 1999, pp. 7–8, notes that *natoyi*, the Blackfoot equivalent for "Medicine", is the energy or moving force of the universe. However, although she interviewed Blackfoot elders, she relies on Colin Taylor's explanation of the Lakota equivalent for the term (*Skan* or *To*). See Colin F. Taylor, "The Plains", in *idem*, ed., *Native American Myths and Legends* (London: Salamander Books, 1994), pp. 40–53, esp. p. 41. For

the concept of "Sacred Bundles" see Reg Crowshoe and Sybille Manneschmidt, *Akak'stiman: A Blackfoot Framework for Decision-Making and Mediation Processes*, 2nd edn (Calgary: University of Calgary Press, [1997] 2002); pp. 19–26; Audrey Weasel Traveller, *A Shining Trail to the Sun's Lodge: Renewal Through Blackfoot Ways of Knowing*, M.A. Diss., University of Lethbridge, 1990, pp. 27–28; and Gerald T. Conaty, "Economic Models and Blackfoot Ideology", *American Ethnologist* 22, 2 (1995): 403–9.

6   Fraser Taylor, *Standing Alone: A Contemporary Blackfoot Indian* (Halfmoon Bay, BC Canada: Arbutus Bay Publications, 1989), p. 15, where Nii'ta'kaiksa'maikoan (Pete Standing Alone), a "Grandfather of Sacred Horn Society", notes that "The more effective the leadership in any particular band, the more likely other bands would look to them for those decisions affecting the whole tribe."

7   According to missionary John M'Lean (sometimes spelt McLean or MacLean) who, "in the interest of science", attended four Kainai Sun Dances in the late 1880's: "The meaning of Okán is now entirely lost. It is known amongst the white people as the Medicine-Dance or Sun-Dance": *The Blackfoot Sun Dance*, rpt. from Proceedings of the Canadian Institute 151 (Toronto: Copp. Clark, 1889), pp. 1–2. Avail. from Early Canadiana Online @: http://www.canadiana.org/view/30372/0003 [Accessed 3 Sept. 2010]. See Spelling in BGC, *Nitsitapiisini*, p. 20; and Mistaken Chief and Kremer, who use "*Aako'ka'tssin*", in "Glossaries", p. 195.

8   Grinnell, *Lodge Tales*, pp. 219–24; McClintock, *Old North Trail*, pp. 206 and 445–65; Clark Wissler, "Societies and Dance Associations of the Blackfoot Indians", AMNH, *Anthropological Papers* 11, 4 (1913): 359–460, esp. pp. 367 and 430. For a broader look at Plains societies, see Thomas E. Mails, *Dog Soldiers, Bear Men and Buffalo Women: A Study of the Societies and Cults of the Plains Indians* (Englewood Cliffs, NJ: Prentice-Hall, 1973).

9   Alice B. Kehoe. "Blackfoot Persons", in Laura F. Klein and Lillian A. Ackerman, eds, *Women and Power in Native North America* (Norman: University of Oklahoma Press, 1995), pp. 113–25, esp. pp. 119–20.

10 For the fur trade see Oscar Lewis, *The Effects of White Contact upon Blackfoot Culture, with Special Reference to the Role of the Fur Trade* Seattle: University of Washington Press, 1942). See also the extensive writings of Arthur J. Ray: *Indians in the Fur Trade: Their Role as Trappers, Hunters, and Middlemen in the Lands Southwest of Hudson Bay 1660–1870* (Toronto: University of Toronto Press, 1974); *I Have Lived Here Since the World Began: An Illustrated History of Canada's Native People* (Toronto: Lester Publishing Key Porter Books, 1996); "Fur Trade History as an Aspect of Native History", in Ian A. L. Getty and Donald B. Smith, eds., *One Century Later: Western Canadian Reserve Indians Since Treaty 7* (Vancouver: University of British Columbia Press, 1978), pp. 7–19; "The Northern Great Plains: Pantry of the Northwestern Fur Trade, 1774–1885", *Prairie Forum* 9, 2 (1984): pp. 263–79; and "The Hudson's Bay Company and Native People", in Wilcomb E. Washburn, ed., *History of Indian–White Relations*, in William C. Sturtevant, General Editor, *Handbook of North American Indians*, 20 Vols, Vol. 4 (Washington, DC: Smithsonian Institution, 1988) (henceforth *Indian–White Relations*), pp. 335–50. See also E. E. Rich, ed., and A. M. Johnson,

asst ed., *The History of the Hudson's Bay Company*, 2 Vols, Vol. 1, 1670–1763, Vol. 2, 1763–1870, (London: The Hudson's Bay Record Society, 1958–59); Christopher L. Miller and George M. Hamell "A New Perspective to Indian–White Contact: Cultural Symbols and Colonial Trade", *Journal of American History* 73 (1986): 311–28; Irene Spry, *The Palliser Expedition* (Calgary: Fifth House, [1963] 1995); and her "The Great Transformation: The Disappearance of the Commons in Western Canada", in Richard Allen, ed., *Man and Nature on the Prairies* (Regina: Canadian Plains Research Centre, University of Regina, 1976), pp. 21–45. See also Lewis O. Saum, *The Fur Trader and the Indian* (Seattle: University of Washington Press, 1965), and his "The Fur Trader and the Noble Savage", *American Quarterly* 15, 4 (1963): 553–71; and Leslie Wischmann, *Frontier Diplomats: The Life and Times of Alexander Culbertson and Natoyist-Siksina'* (Spokane, WA: Arthur H. Clark Co., 2000).

11 Library and Archives Canada, *Annual Report of The Department of Indian Affairs 1864–1990*, (henceforth LAC, DIA, AR), 1905, pp. 114–16. R. W. Wilson, Indian agent at the Blood Agency, noted that the Blackfoot and their allies "held by force of arms against all comers an extensive territory reaching from the Missouri River north to the Red Deer and from the Rockies east to beyond the Cypress Hills." Avail. @: http://www.collectionscanada.gc.ca/databases/indianaffairs/index-e.html [Accessed 2007–2010].

12 Lewis, *Effects*, pp. 23–25.

13 Stephen E. Ambrose, *Undaunted Courage: Meriwether Lewis, Thomas Jefferson, and the Opening of the American West*, rpt. (New York: Simon and Shuster, 2003), pp. 387–94.

14 Roger L. Nichols, *Indians in the United States and Canada: A Comparative History* (Lincoln: University of Nebraska Press, 1999), p. 203. Eventually, the Pikuni became permanently separated between the Blackfeet Reservation in Montana and the Piegan Reserve in Alberta.

15 Lewis, *Effects*, pp. 28–29.

16 An example of "accommodation", noted by Peter Burke, *Varieties of Cultural History* (Cambridge: Polity Press, 1997), p. 208, is the translation of Christianity by the Jesuit missionaries to China and India "into the local cultural idioms by presenting it as compatible with many of the values of the mandarins and the brahmins."

17 Richard White, *The Middle Ground: Indians, Empires and Republics in the Great Lakes Region, 1650–1815*, rpt. (Cambridge: Cambridge University Press, 1997), pp. x and 50–93.

18 *Ibid.*, p. x.

19 Lewis, *Effects*, pp. 16–17.

20 Alexander Henry The Younger, in Elliott Coues, ed, *New Light on the Early History of the Greater Northwest: The Manuscript Journals of Alexander Henry and David Thompson 1799–1814* (henceforth *Journal*), (Minneapolis: Ross & Haines Inc., [1897] 1965), pp. 525 and 725. Coues's publication is based on 1,642 pages of what is called "the Coventry copy" as the original Journal has not survived: Tyrrell, ed., *David Thompson's Narrative*, 1916.

21 George Catlin, *Letters and Notes on the Manners, Customs, and Conditions of North American Indians*, 2 Vols, rpt. [Minneapolis: Ross and Haines, Inc.,

1844], Avail. from Library of Western Fur Trade Historical Source Documents: *Diaries, Narratives, and Letters of the Mountain Men* @: http://www.xmission.com/~drudy/mtman/html/catlin/index.html [Accessed 21 June 2010]. See also John C. Ewers, *Artists of the Old West* (New York: Doubleday, 1973), pp. 54–63.

22 Brandon K. Ruud, ed., *Karl Bodmer's North American Prints*, annotations by Marsha V. Gallagher, essays by Ron Tyler and Brandon K. Ruud, and foreword by J. Brooks Joyner (Omaha: Joslyn Art Museum and Lincoln: University of Nebraska Press, 2004); and John C. Ewers, Marsha V. Gallagher, David C. Hunt, and Joseph C. Porter, *Views of a Vanishing Frontier* (Omaha: Center for Western Studies/Joslyn Art Museum, 1984). A German naturalist, Duke Paul Wilhelm of Württemberg also travelled in the Upper Missouri, but his papers were lost during the second World War: Sonja Schierle, "Travels in the Interior of North America: The Fascination and Reality of Native American Cultures", in Maximilian Alexander Philipp, Prince of Wied-Neuwied, *Travels in the Interior of North America during the Years 1832–1834*, illustrated by Karl Bodmer rpt. (Köln: Taschen, [1832–34] 2001), p. 18.

23 Among the writings of early missionaries consulted for this study, see especially John Maclean, *Sun Dance; Vanguards of Canada* (Toronto: The Missionary Society of the Methodist Church, 1918); *The Indians of Canada: Their Manners and Customs* (Toronto: William Briggs, 1889); John McDougall, *Opening the Great West: Experiences of a Missionary in 1875–76*, Hugh A. Dempsey, ed., Intro. J. Ernest Nix (Calgary: Glenbow-Alberta Institute, 1970); and Provincial Archives of Alberta, 84.400/1193, *boite* 49, Oblate *fonds*, Emile Legal, esp. "*Cantes pied-noirs, 2 Jan. 1885; suivis de clans et chefs Pied-Noirs et degrés d'initiation Indienne*"; 84.400/1195 "*Notes sur la fête du soleil*; 84.400/1197, "*Legends du Pieds-Noirs, s.d.*".

24 Jacob W. Gruber, "Ethnographic Salvage and the Shaping of Anthropology", *American Anthropologist* 72, 6 (1970): 1289–99, esp. p. 1290.

25 Grinnell, *Lodge Tales;* Clark Wissler and David C. Duvall, *Mythology of the Blackfoot Indians*, Alice Beck Kehoe, Intro. to the Bison Books edn (Lincoln: Bison Books, 1995); McClintock, *Old North Trail;* C. C. Uhlenbeck, ed. and trans., with the help of Joseph Tatsey, *Original Blackfoot Texts: From the Southern Piegans Blackfoot Reservation Teton County Montana* (Amsterdam: Johannes Müller, 1911), and his ed. and trans., with the help of Joseph Tatsey, *A New Series of Blackfoot Texts: From the Southern Piegans Blackfoot Reservation Teton County Montana* (Amsterdam: Johannes Müller, 1912); and Schultz, *Blackfeet and Buffalo*.

26 Uhlenbeck-Melchior, Wilhelmina Maria, "Mrs. Uhlenbeck's Diary", in Mary Eggermont-Molenaar, ed. and trans., *Montana 1911: A Professor and his Wife Among the Blackfeet* (Lincoln: University of Nebraska/University of Calgary Press, 2005), pp. 31–178.

27 Hernandez, *Mokakssini*, 1999; Weasel Traveller, *Shining Trail*, p. 26.

28 For Bull Plume, see GA, M-8188, Arthur Family, "Bull Plume's Winter Count"; and Paul M. Raczka, *Winter Count: A History of the Blackfoot People* (Brocket, AB: Oldman River Culture Centre, 1979). For Bull Plume and Natosi Nepe-e, see McClintock, *Old North Trail* (who spells it Natosin

Notes

Nepe-e). For Duvall, see GA, M-4376-1, David C. Duvall's Blackfoot Research (henceforth Duvall); and Wissler and Duvall, *Mythology*, esp. Kehoe's "Introduction". For Crooked Meat Strings, see Kenneth E. Kidd, *Blackfoot Ethnography*, Archaeological Survey of Alberta Manuscript Series 8, [Masters Diss., University of Toronto, 1937] (Edmonton: Alberta Culture, 1985), who notes that Crooked Meat Strings was "the oldest and one of the most knowledgeable of [his] Blackfoot informants" (p. vii); and GA, 8458-8, Richardson's Interview, Crooked Meat Strings.

29   Mike Mountain Horse, *My People The Bloods*, Hugh A. Dempsey, ed., and intro. (Calgary: Glenbow Museum and Blood Tribal Council, 1989); Bullchild, *Sun Came Down*, and "Foreword" by Woody Kipp; Crowshoe and Manneschmidt, *Akak'stiman*, 2002; Beverly Hungry Wolf, *The Ways of My Grandmothers* (New York: William Morrow and Company, 1980); Hernandez, *Mokakssini*, 1999; Bastien, *Blackfoot Ways of Knowing*; and Weasel Traveller, *Shining Trail*, Taylor, *Standing Alone*.

30   Hugh A. Dempsey, *Red Crow, Warrior Chief* (Lincoln: University of Nebraska Press, 1980); and *Crowfoot: Chief of the Blackfeet*, 3rd rpt. (Norman: University of Oklahoma Press, [1972] 1989).

31   *Saskatchewan Indian*, [Anonymous Obituary] "Senator James Gladstone 1887–1971", September 1971, Avail. @: http://www.sicc.sk.ca/saskindian/a71sep01.htm [Accessed 26 July 2007].

32   This is akin to the method outlined by Clifford Geertz, "Thick Description: Toward an Interpretive Theory of Culture", in Geertz, *The Interpretation of Cultures: Selected Essays* (New York: Basic Books, 1973), pp. 3–30.

Note on Nomenclature

1   BGC, *Nitsitapiisini*, pp. 2–4. The BCG prefers "Pikani", but I use "Pikuni" as this abounds in the documentation. In her *Blackfoot Ways of Knowing*, Bastien refers to Real People, i.e. "Indigenous people", as Niitsitapi, and to the "Blackfoot speaking real people" as "Siksikaitsitapi." See also Weasel Traveller, *A Shining Trail*, p. 41; and in John C. Ewers, *The Blackfeet: Raiders on the Northwestern Plains*, n.d. rpt. (Norman: University of Oklahoma Press, [1958]), pp. 5–6.

2   Ewers, *The Blackfeet*, pp. 27–28.

3   Theodore Binnema, *Common and Contested Ground: A Human and Environmental History of the Northwestern Plains* (Toronto: University of Toronto Press, 2004), p. 75.

4   David Thompson, *David Thompson's Narrative of His Explorations in Western America 1784–1812*, Joseph B. Tyrrell, ed. (Toronto: Champlain Society, 1916).

5   The use of different terms by Blackfoot authors is evident in two volumes: BGC, *Nitsitapiisini: The Story of the Blackfoot People*, follows Canadian use; and Percy Bullchild, *The Sun Came Down: The History of the World as My Blackfeet Elders Told It* (Lincoln: University of Nebraska Press, [1985] 2005), accords with the United States convention.

6   These grammatical rules appear in Frantz, *Blackfoot Grammar*.

7   In 1938, after nearly six decades of reserve life, Lucien M. Hanks and Jane

Notes

Richardson recorded the names of their informants both in the Blackfoot language, as well as in their translation into English. The translations seem to have been used by the informants only for the benefit of outsiders. See, for example, Glenbow Archives (henceforth GA), M-8458-8, Jane Richardson's Blackfoot (Siksika) Research — Interview Crooked Meat Strings, 1938 (henceforth Richardson's Interview, Crooked Meat Strings).

8   Umberto Eco, *Serendipities: Language and Lunacy*, Italian Academy Lectures, William Weaver, trans. (New York: Columbia University Press, 1998), p. viii; Paul Chartrand, "'Terms of Division': Problems of 'Outside Naming' for Aboriginal People in Canada", *Journal of Indigenous Studies* 2, 2 (1991): 1–22, esp. p. 3.

9   Kathryn Shanley, "The Indians America Loves to Love and Read: American Indian Identity and Cultural Appropriation," in Gretchen M. Bataille, ed., *Native American Representations: First Encounters, Distorted Images, and Literary Appropriations* (Lincoln: University of Nebraska Press, 2001, p. 29), apologizes for her "pragmatically narrow use of the term *American*, which for [her] purposes [. . .] includes only the continental United States."

10 For example, Alan Taylor, "The Divided Ground: Upper Canada, New York, and the Iroquois Six Nations, 1783–1815", *Journal of the Early Republic* 22, 1 (2002): 55–75, esp. pp. 74–75, notes the ongoing protests by Six Nations peoples against restrictions of the Canadian–American border. See also Kennerly Clay "On the Medicine Line of the Blackfeet", *Native Peoples* 17, 3 (2004): 34 (one page only).

11 Gerald Vizenor, *Fugitive Poses: Native American Indian Scenes of Absence and Presence*, First Bison Books edn (Lincoln: University of Nebraska Press, 2000), pp. 14–15 and 203, *n*. 22, citing his *The Everlasting Sky: New Voices of the People Named the Chippewa*; and Bullchild, *Sun Came Down*, p. 1.

12 *Ibid.*, pp. 290 and 294; McClintock, *Old North Trail*, pp. 395–405; and Frank Gilbert Roe, *The Indian and the Horse*, 4th rpt. (Norman: University of Oklahoma Press, [1951] 1974), p. 240.

Part I The Blackfoot Sun Dance: Resistance and Persistence, 1877–1920

1 The Sun Dance: Invoking the Sacred

1   Lucien M. Hanks, Jr. and Jane Richardson Hanks, *Tribe Under Trust: A Study of the Blackfoot Reserve of Alberta* (Toronto: University of Toronto Press), p. 6.

2   Clark Wissler, "The Sun Dance of the Blackfoot Indians", AMNH, *Anthropological Papers* 16, 3 (1918): 223–70, esp. p. 229. Wissler and Blackfoot-speaking David Duvall, son of a Peigan woman and a French frontiersman, documented a version of the Sun Dance among the Piegan in Montana "regarded as proper". See also Hanks and Richardson Hanks, *Tribe Under Trust*, p. 25.

3   BGC, *Nitsitapiisini*, p. 13.

4   Should the woman have been unfaithful to her husband, the assembled are obliged to expose any known transgressions. Aptly, one of the early stages of the ceremony is named "the going forward of the tongues": Wissler, "Sun

Dance", p. 233. The punishment from Natosi for making a vow when unchaste was "death to the liar and suffering to the relatives": Hungry Wolf, *Ways of My Grandmothers*, p. 27.

5. Grinnell, *Lodge Tales*, p. 264.
6. Wissler, "Sun Dance", p. 241: the Blackfoot Stories related to this bundle include, "Elk Woman", "The Woman-who-married-a-star", "Scarface", "Cuts-wood", "Otter-woman", and "The Scabby-round-robe". See a version of "Elk Woman" in Wissler and Duvall, *Mythology*, pp. 83–85. McClintock, *Old North Trail*, provides a combined version of "Scarface" (pp. 491–505), and "The Woman Who Married a Star", according to which So-at-sa-ki (Feather Woman), a Blackfoot ancestor who married Morning Star and lived with the Star Beings, was given the Natoas when she returned to her people (pp. 495–96). According to GA, M-8458, Jane Richardson's Blackfoot (Siksika) Research — Interview with Old Bull (henceforth Richardson's Interview, Old Bull), at least four Natoas Bundles were in existence among the Siksika in 1937. It was possible for those with the requisite authority to duplicate them ritually.
7. Leslie Spier, "The Sun Dance of the Plains Indians: Its Development and Diffusion," AMNH, *Anthropological Papers* 16, 7 (1921): 453–527, see the distinct names for the ceremony on p. 463; see also J. A. Jones, "The Sun Dance of the Northern Ute", Smithsonian Institution Bureau of American Ethnology Bulletin 157, *Anthropological Paper* 47 (1955): 207–63; Joseph G. Jorgensen, *The Sun Dance Religion: Power for the Powerless* (Chicago: University of Chicago Press, 1972); Ralph Linton, "The Comanche Sun Dance", *American Anthropologist* 37, 3 (1935): 420–28; Thomas E. Mails, *Sundancing: The Great Sioux Piercing Ritual* (Tulsa: Council Oak Books, [1978] 1998); Darcy Paige, "George W. Hill's Account of the Sioux Sun Dance of 1866", *Plains Anthropologist* 24, 84, (1979): 99–112; William K. Powers, *War Dance: Plains Indian Musical Performance* (Tucson: University of Arizona Press, 1990), p. 120; and Fred W. Voget, *The Shoshoni-Crow Sun Dance* (Norman: University of Oklahoma Press, 1984).
8. Spier, *Sun Dance*, p. 459.
9. Leslie Spier, The Sun Dance of the Plains Indians: Comparison with the Tribal Ceremonial System. In Margaret Mead and Ruth L. Bunzel (eds), *The Golden Age of American Anthropology* (New York: George Braziller, [1960] 1968), pp. 392–97.
10. D. B. Shimkin, "The Wind River Shoshone Sun Dance", Smithsonian Institution Bureau of American Ethnology 151, *Anthropological Papers* 41 (1947): 397–484, esp. pp. 403–5.
11. Ibid., also see Wissler, "Sun Dance", for a full description of Ookaan.
12. Hernandez, *Mokakssini*, pp. 1–2.
13. Conaty, "Economic Models", p. 405.
14. GA, M-8458-5, Jane Richardson's Blackfoot (Siksika) Research — Interview with Many Guns, 1938 (henceforth Richardson's Interview, Many Guns).
15. GA, M-8458-19, Jane Richardson's Blackfoot (Siksika) research — Medicine and Curing Power (henceforth Richardson's Medicine and Curing Power); and Richardson's Interview, Old Bull.

Notes

16 "Old" here has no derisive connotations, being equivalent to "Grandparent", someone worthy of respect.
17 According to Maclean, *Sun Dance*, p. 3, "No child or woman was allowed to supply the fuel, but young men who had performed some valorous deed." See also Grinnell, *Lodge Tales*, pp. 245–50; and Ben Calf Robe, with Adolf and Beverly Hungry Wolf, *Siksiká: a Blackfoot Legacy* (Invermere, BC: Good Medicine Books, 1979), p. 40, who notes that after counting *coup*, Three Suns, a wealthy Siksika warrior, would distribute enough stores to fill two wagons. Conaty, "Economic Models", p. 405, notes that counting *coup* occurs at the beginning and at the end of all Blackfoot ceremonies.
18 Power was bestowed by sacred beings, including Earth Beings, Above Beings, and beings who live in and near the water, such as "water birds, beaver, otter and muskrat" who have taught the Blackfoot "how to use their powers." BGC, *Nitsitapiisinni*, p. 9.
19 Wissler, "Social Life", pp. 22–23.
20 GA, M-8458-8, Richardson's Interview, Crooked Meat Strings.
21 *Ibid.*, Ookaan was the ideal place to display the woman's possessions. Those who were poor would marry prior to the Circle Camp to avoid embarrassment.
22 GA, M-4376, David C. Duvall's Blackfoot Research — Sun Dance (henceforth Duvall, Sun Dance), p. 891.
23 Maclean, *Sun Dance*, pp. 6–7; Grinnell, *Lodge Tales*, p. 264; Wissler, "Sun Dance", pp. 262–63, found no evidence of coercion, although he did not discount the possibility of its having been tolerated. LAC, RG 10, Vol. 3826, f. 60511-3, J. D. McLean, Assistant Deputy and Sec'y, to W. J. Dilworth, Blood Agency, 23 March 1914: to the effect that "any white men attending these dances [. . .] will be liable to be prosecuted".
24 LAC, DIA, AR, 1896, pp. 295–96; See also Wissler, "Sun Dance", p. 263, citing John Maclean's point that "The chief attraction to the pale-face is what has been ignorantly termed 'making braves'"; LAC, RG 10, Vol. 3825, f. 60,511 and 60,511-1, F. C. Cornish to Indian Commissioner, Regina, 13 August 1889, to the effect that the duration of the Sarcee Sun Dance was lengthened "at the special request of the white people, who had given them lots of money to do so." See also Hugh A. Dempsey, *Indians of the Rocky Mountain Parks* (Calgary: Fifth House, 1998), p. 91, who reproduces a photograph taken by Maclean of the Kainai *Ma-toki* (Women's Society) Lodge in the 1890s, which reveals the presence of white visitors.
25 Wissler, "Sun Dance", pp. 265–66. Flesh scarring and the severing of sections of a finger were common when mourning the loss of a relative, and flesh offerings to Natosi took place during times of personal danger, such as during war raids. For an example, see Dempsey, *Crowfoot*, p. 201.
26 Grinnell, *Lodge Tales*, pp. 259 and 269–70.
27 McClintock, *Old North Trail*, p. 491.

2 Colonial Conceits and Indictable Offenses

1 AR, 1864, p. 300.
2 Michael Punke, *Last Stand: George Bird Grinnell, the Battle to Save the*

Buffalo, and the Birth of the New West (New York: HarperCollins, 2007), p. 135.

3   Henry Warner Bowden, *American Indians and Christian Missions: Studies in Cultural Conflict* (Chicago: University of Chicago Press, 1981).

4   John L. Tobias, "Protection, Civilization, Assimilation: An Outline History of Canada's Indian Policy", *Western Canadian Journal of Anthropology* 6, 2 (1976): 13–30, esp. p. 14. Assimilation was the objective of the Indian Act 1876: Andrew Armitage, *Comparing the Policy of Aboriginal Assimilation: Australia, Canada and New Zealand* (Vancouver: UBC Press, 1995), pp. 77–87. The Potlatch of the Pacific First Nations was another ceremony marked for eradication in Canada.

5   Alexander Morris, *The Treaties of Canada with the Indians of Manitoba and The North-West Territories*, rpt. (Toronto: Belfords, Clarke & Co., [1862] 1971).

6   See for example LAC, DIA, AR, 1885, p. 74; 1886, p. 138; and 1895, p. 36. See Ian A. L. Getty, *The Church Missionary Society among the Blackfoot Indians of Southern Alberta, 1880–1895*, M.A. Diss., University of Calgary, 1970, for the role of British missionary organization.

7   Cited in James R. Miller, *Shingwauk's Vision: A History of Native Residential Schools*, rpt. (Toronto: University of Toronto Press, [1997] 2003), p. 151, *n*.1.

8   Paper delivered by Capt. Richard C. Pratt at an 1892 convention. Available from History Matters @: http://historymatters.gmu.edu/d/4929/ [Accessed 31 August 2010].

9   See for example the Annual Report of the U.S. Commissioner of Indian Affairs, 1889, p. 6. Available from Internet Archive @ http://www.archive.org/index.php [Accessed 21 June 2010].

10 LAC, RG 18, North West Mounted Police (henceforth NWMP), vol. 112, f. 665, S. B. Steele, Sup., to Commissioner, 5 October 1895.

11 Hiram Martin Chittenden, and Alfred Talbot Richardson, *Life, Letters and Travels of Father Pierre-Jean De Smet, S.J., 1801–1873*, 4 Vols, Vols 1–2, rpt. (New York: Kraus, [1905] 1969); and Howard L. Harrod, *Mission Among the Blackfeet* (Norman: University of Oklahoma Press, 1971), p. 29. The Jesuit Nicolas Point was the first Christian missionary to spend a winter among the Blackfoot (1846–47): John. C. Ewers, "A Unique Pictorial Interpretation of Blackfoot Indian Religion in 1846–1847", *Ethnohistory* 18, 3 (1971): 231–38.

12 Harrod, *Mission*, p. 68.

13 Ibid., pp. 74–81.

14 James McGregor, *Father Lacombe* (Edmonton: Hurtig, 1975).

15 Bernice Venini, "Father Constantine Scollen, Founder of the Calgary Mission", *CCHA Report* 10 (1942–43): 75–86. Available from the University of Manitoba @: http://www.umanitoba.ca/colleges/st_pauls/ccha/Back%20Issues/CCHA1942-43/Venini.html [Accessed 1 Sept. 2010].

16 See also Ewers, *The Blackfeet*, pp. 193–95, for a summary of attempts to Christianize the Blackfoot.

17 Harrod, *Mission*, p. 102.

18 LAC, DIA, AR, 1896, p. 347, J. Hugonnard's Report; and seven years later, LAC, RG 10, Vol. 3826, f. 60511-3, Hugonnard to Secretary, 20 November

1913, requesting "steps be taken to abolish Indian dances." See also LAC, RG 18, Vol. 205, f. 136-01, Arthur B. Owen, St. Paul's Mission [Blood Reserve], to Major Howe, Commander of the Police Force, Macleod, 24 October 1901.
19 Hugh A. Dempsey, *Firewater: The Impact of the Whiskey Trade on the Blackfoot Nation* (Calgary: Fifth House, 2002), p. 175.
20 Annual Report of Superintendent Deane, Commanding K Division, Appendix E, in *The New West: Being the Official Reports to Parliament of the Activities of the Royal North-West Mounted Police Force From 1888–1889* ([Ottawa: Queen Printer, 1888–89] Toronto: Coles Publishing Co., 1973 facsimile, 1889), pp. 37–53, esp. p. 42; LAC, RG 18, Vol. 205, f. 136-01, Supt. Joseph Howe, Commander of the Police Force, Macleod, to Commissioner, Regina, 30 October 1901; and Rev. Arthur B. Owen to Major Howe, Commander of the Police Force, Macleod, 24 October 1901. In 1900, however, The Commissioner North-West Territories reported that "a missionary who had, unobserved watched some of these dances [. . .] saw nothing of a gross character", in LAC, DIA, AR, 1900, p. 224.
21 LAC, RG 10, Vol. 3826, f. 60,511-3, W. J. Dilworth, Blood Agency, to J. D. McLean, Assistant Deputy and Secretary, 10 March 1914.
22 David Cahill's study "Popular Religion and Appropriation: The Example of Corpus Christi in Eighteenth-Century Cuzco", *Latin American Research Review* 31, 2 (1996): 67–110, is illustrative of how religion, albeit highly syncretic, continued to pose a threat to colonial Spanish rule some 250 years after the initial conquest. See also Cahill, "El Visitador General Areche y su campaña iconoclasta contra la Cultura Andina," in Ramón Mujica, ed., *Visión y Símbolos: del virreinato criollo a la República Peruana* (Lima: Banco de Crédito, 2007), pp. 83–111; and Nicholas A. Robins, *Native Insurgencies and the Genocidal Impulse in the Americas* (Bloomington: Indiana University Press, 2005), for anti-colonial rebellions borne out of religious fervour.
23 James Mooney, *The Ghost Dance Religion and Wounded Knee*, rpt. (New York: Dover Publications, [1896] 1973); Michael Hittman, *Wovoka and the Ghost Dance*, ed. Don Lynch (Lincoln: University of Nebraska Press, Bison Books, 1997); Benjamin R. Kracht, "The Kiowa Ghost Dance, 1894–1916: An Unheralded Revitalization Movement", *Ethnohistory* 39, 4 (1992): 452–57; and Alice Beck Kehoe, *The Ghost Dance: Ethnohistory and Revitalization* (Fort Worth: Holt, Rinehart and Winston, 1989).
24 Morris, *Treaties of Canada*, "Preface".
25 E. Brian Titley, "W. M. Graham: Indian Agent Extraordinaire", *Prairie Forum* 8, 1 (1983): 25–41. See also his *A Narrow Vision: Duncan Campbell Scott and the Administration of Indian Affairs in Canada* (Vancouver: University of British Columbia Press, 1986).
26 Francis Paul Prucha, "Thomas Jefferson Morgan 1889–93", in Robert M. Kvasnicka, and Herman J. Viola, eds, *The Commissioners of Indian Affairs, 1824–1977* (Lincoln: University of Nebraska Press, 1979), pp. 193–203, esp. p. 196.
27 Francis Paul Prucha, *Indian Policy in the United States: Historical Essays* (Lincoln: University of Nebraska Press), 1982, p. 30.
28 Ibid., p. 31.

Notes

29 Corruption was believed to be endemic among Indian Agents in the late nineteenth century, which motivated Washington to create a voluntary Board of Indian Commissioners, and to opt for nominating missionaries as agents, although the measures did not achieve their objective.

30 Wilcomb E. Washburn, *The American Indian and the United States: A Documentary History*, 4 Vols, Vol. 1 (New York: Random House, 1973), p. 425; and Prucha, "Morgan", p. 194.

31 I discuss this massacre in Tovías, "A Blueprint for Massacre".

32 Medicine Springs Library, Special Collections, United States House of Representatives, *Piegan Indians,* 41 Cong., 2 sess. House Executive Document 269, pp. 1–74 (henceforth *Piegan Indians*), p. 13.

33 Robert M. Kvasnicka, "George W. Manypenny (1853–57)", in Kvasnicka and Viola, eds, *Commissioners*, pp. 57–67, esp. p. 58.

34 Patrick Brantlinger, *Dark Vanishings: Discourse on the Extinction of Primitive Races, 1800–1930* (Ithaca, NY: Cornell University Press, 2003), pp. 57; and Prucha, "United States Indian Policies, 1815–1860", pp. 29–39; in *Indian–White Relations*; and Ronald N. Satz, "Elbert Herring 1831–36", in Kvasnicka and Viola, eds, *Commissioners*, pp. 13–6, esp. p. 13.

35 Nichols, *Indians in the United States and Canada*, p. 219; and Frederick E. Hoxie, *A Final Promise: The Campaign to Assimilate the Indians, 1880–1920*, rev. edn (Lincoln: University of Nebraska Press, Bison Books, [1984] 2001); and Steven Conn, *History's Shadow: Native Americans and Historical Consciousness in the Nineteenth Century* (Chicago: The University of Chicago Press, 2004), p. 31.

36 George Bird Grinnell, "Tenure of Land among the Indians," *American Anthropologist* 9, 1 (1907): 1–11, esp. p. 6.

37 Robert F. Berkhofer, Jr., "Commentary", in Jane F. Smith and Robert M. Kvasnicka, eds, *Indian–White Relations: A Persistent Paradox* (Washington, DC: Howard University Press, 1976), p. 81; and George, F. G. Stanley, "As Long As the Sun Shines and Water Flows: An Historical Comment", in Ian A. L. Getty and Antoine S. Lussier, eds, *As Long As the Sun Shines and Water Flows: A Reader in Canadian Native Studies*, Nakoda Institute Occasional Paper 1 (Vancouver: University of British Columbia Press, [1983] 1990), p. 13.

38 Floyd A. O'Neil, "Hiram Price 1881–85", in Kvasnicka and Viola, eds, *Commissioners*, pp. 173–79, esp. p. 174.

39 For population decline in Canada, see Appendices 1–4 of this volume; and Hugh A. Dempsey, *Indian Tribes of Alberta* (Calgary: Glenbow Museum, 1979).

40 Prucha, "Morgan", p. 194.

41 LAC, RG 10, Vol. 3876, f. 91749, Commissioner North-West Territories, to Superintendent General, 21 June 1892, referring to Piapot's Reserve, where a "the agent was compelled to allow the Sun Dance to take place — once all Indians not belonging to the agency were sent away."

42 LAC, DIA, AR, 1885, p. 76; and LAC, RG 10, Vol. 3826, f. 60,511-3, W. J. Dilworth, Blood Agency to J. D. McLean, Assistant Deputy and Secretary, 10 March 1914; and McLean to Dilworth, 23 March 1914.

Notes

43 LAC, DIA, AR, 1893, p. xvii.
44 E. Brian Titley, "Hayter Reed and Indian Administration in the West", in *Swords and Ploughshares: War and Agriculture in Western Canada* (Edmonton: University of Alberta Press, 1993), pp. 108–48, esp. p. 113.
45 *Ibid.*, p. 120.
46 Robert F. Berkhofer, Jr., *The White Man's Indian: Images of the American Indian from Columbus to the Present* (New York: Vintage Books, [1953] 1978), pp. 154–55.
47 Esther Schiff Goldfrank, *Changing Configurations in the Social Organization of a Blackfoot Tribe During the Reserve Period (The Blood of Alberta, Canada)*, Monographs of the American Ethnological Society 8, ed. A. Irving Hallowell (Seattle: University of Washington Press, [1945] 1966), pp. 3 and 70.
48 Quoted in Wilma Mankiller and Michael Wallis, "Asgaya-Dihi", in Susan Lobo and Steve Talbot, eds, *Native American Voices: A Reader* (Upper Saddle River, NJ: Prentice-Hall, 2001), pp. 234–41, esp. p. 236. See also Anthony J. Hall, *American Empire and the Fourth World: The Bowl With One Spoon* (Montreal: McGill–Queen's University Press, 2003), p. 481. For allotment, see Thomas R. Wessel, "Political Assimilation on Blackfoot Indian Reservation, 1887–1934: A Study in Survival", in Douglas H. Ubelaker, and Herman J. Viola, eds, *Plains Indian Studies: A Collection of Essays in Honor of John C. Ewers and Waldo R. Wedel* (City of Washington: Smithsonian Institution Press, 1982), pp. 59–72, esp. p. 65.
49 Tobias, "Protection, Civilization, Assimilation," p. 25.
50 The Blackfoot were excluded from this bill, which envisaged the enfranchisement of "Eastern" First Nations, who had undergone a much longer process of acculturation. Titley, *Narrow Vision*, pp. 50 and 56.
51 Berkhofer, "Commentary", p. 83. Whites complained in 1885 against the presence of Indians (who were in demand as wood cutters) outside their reserves, see LAC, DIA, AR, 1885, p. 76; According to the *Macleod Gazette* in 1887, "the reserve idea was all wrong, not because it segregated Indians [. . .] but because it did not do the job properly", cited in James H. Gray, *Booze: When Whiskey Ruled the West* (Calgary: Fifth House, [1972] 1995), p. 45.
52 In 1889, for example, five Kanai (Young Pine, The Scout, Prairie Chicken Old Man, Wolf Robe, and Crazy Crow) and a South Pikuni stole "lots of horses" from the Crow Reservation in Montana. On their return a large party of Gros Ventres attacked them, and the Kainai killed two of them as well as an Assiniboine. A Scalp Dance was held at the Kainai Reserve: LAC, RG 18, Vol. 35, f. 479, Blood Agent to to Commissioner Regina, 17 May 1889.
53 *Ibid.*, for an example of revenge; and Cecil E. Denny, *The Law Marches West*, ed. W. B. Cameron (Toronto: J. M. Dent and Sons, 1939), pp. 41 and 133.
54 Grinnell, *Lodge Tales*, pp. 289–92. In 1884, a new Agent to the South Pikuni found them starving whilst from 1878 Congress had reduced their appropriations: J. P. Dunn, Jr., *Massacres of the Mountains: A History of the Indian Wars of the Far West 1815–1875* (New York: Archer House, 1958), pp. 537–38.
55 The 1884 Annual Report cited in Bancroft Library, The Indian Rights

Association, "The Action of Congress in Regard to the Piegan Indians of Montana", 12 Dec. 1884, p. 1.

56 Ewers, *The Blackfeet*, p. 294.

57 For population decline of several First Nations, see Dempsey, *Indian Tribes of Alberta*; and Blanca Tovías, "Colonialism and Demographic Catastrophes in the Americas: Blackfoot Tribes of the Northwest," in Patricia Grimshaw and Russell McGregor (eds), *Collision of Cultures and Identities: Settlers and Indigenous Peoples*, Melbourne: Department of History, University of Melbourne, 2006, pp. 72–78.

58 For Treaty Seven see John Leonard Taylor, "Canada's Northwest Indian Policy in the 1870s: Traditional Premises and Necessary Innovations"; and his "Two Views on the Meaning of Treaties Six and Seven," in Richard T. Price, ed., *The Spirit of the Alberta Indian Treaties*, 3rd edn (Edmonton: University of Alberta Press, [1979] 1999), pp. 3–8 and 9–45; Treaty 7 Elders and Tribal Council, with Walter Hildebrandt, Sarah Carter, and Dorothy First Rider, *The True Spirit and Original Intent of Treaty 7* (Montreal: McGill–Queen's University Press, 1996), esp. Wilton Goodstriker, "Introduction: *Otsitsi Pakssaisstoyiih Pi* (the year when the winter was open and cold)", pp. 3–27, pp. 8–9, and for a transcript of Treaty Seven, pp. 230–39. Treaty Seven available online from Treaty Seven Management Corporation @ http://www.treaty7.org/TreatyNo7.aspx [Accessed 31 August 2010]. See also Ian A. Getty and Donald B. Smith, eds, *One Century Later: Western Canadian Reserve Indians Since Treaty 7* (Vancouver: University of British Columbia Press, 1978), esp. the following chapters: Hugh A. Dempsey, "One Hundred Years of Treaty Seven", pp. 20–30; Stan Cuthand, "The Native Peoples of the Prairie Provinces in the 1920s and 1930s", pp. 31–42; and Harold Cardinal, "Treaties Six and Seven: The Next Century", pp. 82–102.

59 Tobias, "Protection, Civilization, Assimilation", pp. 17–18 and 30, citing 47 Vic. cap. 28.

60 LAC, RG 10, Vol. 3825, f. 60,511-1, Reed to C. C. Chipman, HBC, Winnipeg, 9 July 1895; and Robert J. Surtees, "Canadian Indian Policies", in *Indian–White Relations*, pp. 81–95, esp. p. 92.

61 LAC, RG 10, Vol. 3826, f. 60511-3, J. D. McLean to Reverend Ross, 15 March 1917.

62 Alvin M. Josephy, Jr., *Now that the Buffalo's Gone: A Study of Today's American Indians* (Norman: University of Oklahoma Press, 1982), p. 85.

63 Robert H. Lowie, *Indians of the Plains* (Garden City, NY: The Natural History Press, [1954] 1963), p. 197; United States, Bureau of Indian Affairs, *Regulations* [. . .] *Effective April 1, 1904* (Washington 1904), sec. 584, and "Circular Letter 2970" (Washington, 1934), cited in Gordon Macgregor, with the collaboration of Royal B. Hassrick and William E. Henry, *Warriors Without Weapons: A Study of the Society and Personality of the Pine Ridge Sioux* (Chicago: University of Chicago Press, 1946), pp. 91 and 104, *n*.9.

64 See for example, for Canada, LAC, RG 10, Vol. 3826, f. 60511-3, Blood Agency, 2 February 1917; and 60,511-4A James McDonald, Griswold Agent to Assistant Deputy and Secretary, 14 February 1918: "Dances have a demoralizing effect on the Indians and I do not see much use in spending money to

educate them if they are allowed to go back to their old pagan ways." For the United States, see Mails, *Sundancing*, p. 3.
65 For the NWMP, see Sir Cecil E. Denny, *The Law Marches West*, W. B. Cameron, ed. (Toronto: J. M. Dent and Sons (Canada) Ltd, 1939); Dick Harrison, *Best Mounted Police Stories* (Edmonton: University of Alberta Press, [1978] 1996); Commissioners, *New West*; Nichols, *Indians in the United States and Canada*, p. 211. Gray, *Booze*, pp. 24–27, notes that the NWMP began with 318 men and combined "the roles of policeman, judge, and jailer."
66 Washburn, *American Indian and the United States*, pp. 336–37, notes that Congress approved the creation of the Indian Police in 1878 and by 1882 it was in operation in forty agencies.
67 LAC, RG 10, Vol. 3825, f. 60,511-1, Hayter Reed to Deputy Supt. General, 17 August 1889.
68 F. Laurie Barron, "The Indian Pass System in the Canadian West, 1882–1935", *Prairie Forum* 13, 1 (1988): 25–42, esp. pp. 29–34.
69 LAC, RG 18, Vol. 1354, 76, 1896, Part 3, Commissioner to Commissioner, Regina, 9 July 1896; and Supt. Commanding E Division Commissioner, Regina, 22 May 1896, noting a prior circular sent in May 1893 "re sending Indians back, that no order is to be given them to return."
70 Commissioners, *New West*, 1888, p. 68.
71 *Ibid.*, p. 62.
72 LAC, RG 18, Vol. 205, f. 136-01, NWMP, Stand Off Detachment, Corpl. B. H. Robertson's Report, 28 July 1902, including extract from Const. Geoghegan's Report, 12 July 1902.
73 LAC, RG 10, Vol. 3826, F. 60,511-4 Part 1, H. A. Gunn, Indian Agent, Brocket Alberta, to Secretary, Ottawa, 14 June 1917.
74 GA, M-1785-15, Canada, DIA, Blackfoot Indian Agency, General Instructions to Indian Agents in Canada, p. 4, referring to Section 162.
75 LAC, DIA, AR, 1892, p. xix; and Hana Samek, *The Blackfoot Confederacy 1880–1920: A Comparative Study of Canadian and U.S. Indian Policy* (Albuquerque: University of New Mexico Press, 1987), p. 129, n.20: "An Act to Further amend the Indian Act, 1880," S. C. 1884, c. 27 (47 Vict.), clause 3.
76 D. J. Hall, "Clifford Sifton and Canadian Indian Administration 1896–1905", *Prairie Forum* 2, 2 (1977): 127–51, esp. pp. 129–30, and 145.
77 Hall, "Clifford Sifton", pp. 139, and 150, *n*.60.
78 LAC, RG 10, Vol. 3825, f. 60,511-1, F. H. Paget to Indian Agent, Birtle, 9 June 1896: "Can only stop dance if 'give away' feature, mutilation or torture form part of ceremony. Seventeen hundred fourteen amended. If on Reserve may arrest visitors for trespassing: amended sub-section two, section twenty two. If ex pedient [sic] better prevent if possible but proceed cautiously."
79 LAC, DIA, AR, 1889, p. 172.
80 LAC, RG 10, Vol. 3826, f. 60,511-3, Asst. Deputy and Secretary, 17 June 1914.
81 For the United States, see Washburn, *American Indian*, pp. 458–59; and for Canada, LAC, RG 10, Vol. 3826, f. 60511-3, Principal of Indian Industrial School Qu'Appelle, Sask., 6 May 1914, asking to prevent Indians from attending local celebrations.

Notes

82 LAC, RG 10, Vol. 3826, f. 60,511-4-1, J. D. Dilworth, Blood Agent to J. D. McLean, 2 February 1917.
83 Commissioners, *New West*, 1889, pp. 71–72.
84 GA, M-4738-217-6, Articles Written by Gooderham, Lord Burnham and Chief Yellowhorse, Dec. 1955.
85 In 1914 permission was granted to attend the Banff celebrations to the Bearspaw's Band, Stony Agency, after a private company requested it. LAC, RG 10, Vol. 3826, f. 60511-3, General Manager, Brewster Transport Co, Ltd to Mr. J. Waddy, Indian Agent, Morley, 1 July, 1914.
86 LAC, RG 10, Vol. 3826, f. 60511-4A, Asst. Deputy and Secretary, 4 October 1918, Ref. Section 149 of the Indian Act by Sec. 7 of Chap. 26, 8–9 Geo. V.
87 GA, M-4738-259-6 G. H. Gooderham, Articles Written by Gooderham, Weasel Calf and His Favourite Wife, April 1956; and *idem*, M-4738-372-6, Indian Religious Rituals, 16 May 1973.
88 LAC, DIA, AR, 1917, p. 11.
89 The limits of what a community can endure before opting for armed rebellion constitute a "moral economy" according to Kevin Gosner (following E. P. Thompson and James C. Scott). Kevin Gosner, *Soldiers of the Virgin: The Moral Economy of a Colonial Maya Rebellion* (Tucson: University of Arizona Press, 1992); James C. Scott, *The Moral Economy of the Peasant: Rebellion and Subsistence in Southeast Asia* (New Haven: Yale University Press, 1976); and E. P. Thompson, "The Moral Economy of the English Crowd in the Eighteenth Century", *Past and Present* 50 (1971): 76–136.
90 LAC, RG 10, Vol. 3825, f. 60,511-1, Hayter Reed, Telegram 12 June 1893.
91 Titley, "W. M. Graham", pp. 28–29.
92 LAC, RG 10, Vol. 3826, f. 60,511-4A, W. M. Graham to D. C. Scott, Deputy Supt. General, July 1920.
93 O'Neil, "Hiram Price", p. 175.
94 See Prucha, "Thomas Jefferson Morgan 1889–93", pp. 199–200; and Thomas J. Morgan, "Rules for Indian Courts", in Francis Paul Prucha, ed., *Americanizing the American Indians: Writings by the "Friends of the Indian" 1880–1900* (Cambridge, MA: Harvard University Press, 1973), pp. 300–5, esp. pp. 300–2.
95 Josephy, Jr., *Now that the Buffalo's Gone,* pp. 84–85. See also H. Teller, 1883, Courts of Indian Offenses, *Annual Report of the Secretary of the Interior*, Washington, DC: House Executive Document No. 1, 48th. Congress, Serial 2190, pp. x–xiii, cited in Laurence Armand French, "Adaptations of Aboriginal Justice in the United States", *Journal of Human Justice* 6, 2 (1995): 72–78, esp. p. 75.
96 LAC, RG 10, Vol. 3826, f. 60511-3, Blood Agent, Letter 2 February 1917; and f. 60,511-4A, James McDonald, Griswold Agent to Assistant Deputy and Secretary, 14 February 1918.
97 Ewers, *The Blackfeet*, p. 310 (he spells Steel, at variance with the documentation); and Harrod, *Mission*, p. 90.
98 Wessel, "Political Assimilation", p. 62.
99 William E. Farr, *The Reservation Blackfeet 1882–1945: A Photographic History of Cultural Survival*, Foreword by James Welch (Seattle: University of Washington Press, 1984), pp. 78–79.

Notes

100 Samek, *Blackfoot Confederacy*, p. 131.
101 Harrod, *Mission*, pp. 98–99.
102 Farr, *Reservation Blackfeet*, pp. 67–68. Photographs of the 1910 and 1911 Sun Dance on pp. 80–82.

3 Honouring Creator Sun and Praying for Good Crops

1. Jacqueline Gresko, "White 'Rites' and Indian 'Rites': Indian Education and Native Responses in the West, 1870–1910", in Anthony W. Rasporich, ed., *Western Canada Past and Present* (Calgary: McClelland and Stewart West, 1975), pp. 163–81, esp. p. 164; and Alice B. Kehoe, "Maintaining the Road of Life", in William B. Taylor and Franklin Pease G.Y., eds, *Violence, Resistance, and Survival in the Americas: Native Americans and the Legacy of Conquest* (Washington, DC: Smithsonian Institution Press, 1994), pp. 193–207, esp. p. 201.
2. White, *Middle Ground*, p. x.
3. Peter Prando, a Jesuit who built a mission near the Blackfeet reservation in 1881, set as a condition for baptizing chief White Calf, "that he give up three of his four wives." White Calf agreed, but other Blackfeet remained in polygamous marriages into the 1920s. Harrod, *Mission*, pp. 59–65, and 103; and Sarah Carter, *The Importance of Being Monogamous: Marriage and Nation Building in Western Canada to 1915*. Edmonton: University of Alberta Press, 2008, pp. 194–229, esp. pp. 197–200.
4. LAC, DIA, AR, 1889, p. 167.
5. LAC, DIA, AR, 1887, p. 100. The DIA also erected a house for the head chief of the Kainai, Mekasto.
6. GA, M-4738-213-6, George H. Gooderham, "'Black Fever' — Blackfoot Indian", December 1955: "Crowfoot may have embraced Christianity in superficial manner at times, but during his last illness he returned to his native religion [. . .] Black Fever remembered the consternation of the missionaries at the presence of numerous medicine men at the deathbed of the Chief, and the wrangle about his burial when his body was removed from the Christian cemetery."
7. Dempsey, *Crowfoot*, p. 201.
8. *Ibid.*, pp. 207–16; and LAC, DIA, AR, 1888, p. lxvii.
9. GA, M-4376, David C. Duvall, When Men Torture Themselves in the Sun Dance — Interview with Big Bravo, 22 April 1911.
10. Wissler, "Sun Dance," p. 262.
11. LAC, DIA, AR, 1885, p. 76.
12. GA, M-1817, Blackfoot Indian Agency, Notes from Blackfoot Agency Letter Books.
13. GA, M-4738-227-6, G. H. Gooderham, The Making of a Brave, c.1955–56.
14. Mails, *Sundancing*, pp. 4–6; and for a thorough perspective of the survival of the sun dance among the Lakota, see Clyde Holler, *Black Elk's Religion: The Sun Dance and Lakota Catholicism* (Syracuse NY: Syracuse University Press, 1995).
15. GA, M-8458, Richardson's Interview, Old Bull.
16. LAC, RG 18, Vol. 137, S. B. Steele, Supt. to Commissioner NWMP, Regina, 7 May 1897.

Notes

17   LAC, RG 10, Vol. 3826, f. 60511-3, J. A. Markle, Inspector, Crowfoot Boarding School, 14 February 1916.
18   LAC, DIA, AR, 1896, p. 351.
19   LAC, RG 10, Vol. 3826, f. 60,511-3, Bull Plume to DIA, Ottawa, 11 February 1915.
20   LAC, RG 18, Vol. 3290, f. HQ-1034-K-1, RCMP, 'K' Division, Lethbridge, Calgary Sub-District, Gleichen Detachment, Corpl. E. E. Harper's Report, 25 July 1921.
21   LAC, RG 10, Vol. 3825, f. 60511-1, Commissioner, Regina to Blackfoot Agent, 3 June 1897.
22   LAC, DIA, AR, 1899, p. 132.
23   LAC, RG 18, Vol. 3290, f. HQ-1034-K-1, RCMP, K Division, Lethbridge, Calgary Sub-District, Inspector J. W. Spalding's Report 27 July 1921 (henceforth Spalding's Report).
24   GA, M-4738, Gooderham, "Blackfoot Biographies".
25   "Spalding's Report".
26   LAC, RG 18, Vol. 3290, f. HQ-1034-K-1, RCMP, K Division, Lethbridge, Calgary Sub-District, Gleichen Detachment, Corpl. E. E. Harper's Report, 25 July 1921.
27   *Ibid*.
28   GA, M-4738-260-6, Articles Written by Gooderham, The Indian Waltz, April 1956.
29   LAC, RG 18, Series A-1, Vol. 36, File 817-89, Letter from the Department of Justice, Ottawa, 31 October 1889.
30   *Ibid.*, Extract from the report of Supt. Steele, Fort Macleod, 12 August 1889.
31   In 1907 they arrested no less than Day Chief, the head chief of the Kainai in similar circumstances. Dempsey, *Red Crow*, pp. 188–89.
32   LAC, RG 18, Series A-1, Vol. 36, File 817-89, Department of Justice, Ottawa, letter 31 Oct. 1889.
33   Indian Claims Commission, "Report on the Mediation of the Blood Tribe/Kainaiwa Akers Surrender Negotiations," August 2005. Available @ http://www.indianclaims.ca/pdf/bloodmediationenglish.pdf [Accessed June 22, 2010].
34   LAC, RG 10, Vol. 3825, f. 60,511-1, Hayter Reed, Commissioner North-West Territories to Deputy Supt. General, 17 August 1889.
35   LAC, RG 18, Vol. 51, f. 313-1891, Report NWMP Fort Macleod, 9 April 1891.
36   LAC, DIA, AR, 1895, p. 199.
37   Dempsey, *Red Crow*, p. 207.
38   *Ibid.*, 1896, p. 301.
39   *Ibid.*, p. 209, citing Annual Report NWMP, 1898, p. 27.
40   *Ibid.*, p. 214.
41   LAC, RG 18, Vol. 302, f. 658-05, Supt. P. C. H. Primrose, Commanding D Division, to Commissioner, Regina, 5 August 1905.
42   Regulations with reference to rations were tightened again on the Canadian reserves in 1914. LAC, RG 18, Vol. 458, f. 79-14, Correspondence on rationing of Indians on the Blood Reserve.

43 LAC, RG 18, Series A-1, Vol. 36, File 817-89, Department of Justice, Ottawa, 31 October 1889.
44 GA, M-8188, Arthur Family, Bull Plume's Winter Count.
45 LAC, RG 10, Vol. 3826, f. 60511-3, Extract from report Blood Agent, 2 July 1914.
46 LAC, RG 10, Vol. 3826, f. 60,511-3, W. J. Dilworth, Blood Agency, to J. D. McLean, Assistant Deputy and Secretary, 10 March 1914. My emphasis.
47 LAC, DIA, AR, 1914. According to the 1914 census, c.25 per cent Blackfoot listed their religion as Christian.
48 LAC, RG 10, Vol. 3826, f. 60,511-4A, Chief Shot in Both Sides to Commissioner, 24 June 1921.
49 See for example LAC, DIA, AR, 1896, pp. 301–2.
50 LAC, RG 18, Vol. 205, f. 136-01, Correspondence re Blood Sun Dance. Letter 28 February 1902.
51 McClintock, *Old North Trail*, pp. 384–85.
52 Ibid., p. 508.
53 Ibid.
54 Josephy, Jr., *Now that the Buffalo's Gone*, pp. 86–87; and Taylor, *Standing Alone*, p. 159.
55 GA, M-8078 [Old Series] F300/35, Lucien Hanks and Jane Richardson Hanks, Many Guns' Winter Count.
56 Goldfrank, *Changing Configurations*, p. 43.
57 Tobias, "Protection, Civilization, Assimilation," pp. 23 and 30, citing Statutes of Canada, 1951.
58 Ewers, "A Unique Pictorial Interpretation", pp. 236–37.

Part II The Grammar of Blackfoot Leadership Dress, 1830–1920
4 Dress, Sacred Stories, and Worldviews

1 Hildi Hendrickson, "Introduction", in *idem*, ed., *Clothing and Difference: Embodied Identities in Colonial and Post-Colonial Africa* (Durham: Duke University Press, 1996), p. 2.
2 Theodore Binnema, "Allegiances and Interests: Niitsitapi (Blackfoot) Trade, Diplomacy, and Warfare, 1806–1831," *Western Historical Quarterly* 37, 3 (2006): 327–49, esp. p. 331, notes that by 1806 Blackfoot relations with the Cree and Assiniboine had collapsed.
3 Marshall McLuhan, *Understanding Media: The Extensions of Man*, London: Routledge & Kegan Paul, 1964.
4 Stephen Greenblatt, *Renaissance Self-Fashioning: From More to Shakespeare* (Chicago: University of Chicago Press, 1980), p. 1.
5 Ann T. Walton, John C. Ewers, and Royal B. Hassrick, *After the Buffalo were Gone: The Louis Warren Hill, Sr., Collection of Indian Art* (St. Paul, MN: Northwest Area Foundation, 1985), p. 57; and for Blackfoot dress materials, patterns, and distribution, see Clark Wissler, "Material Culture of the Blackfoot Indians", AMNH, *Anthropological Papers* 5, 1 (1910): 1–175; and "Costumes of the Plains Indians," AMNH, *Anthropological Papers* 17, 2 (1915): 39–91.
6 Henry, *Journal*, pp. 525 and 725.

Notes

7   McClintock, *Old North Trail*, p. 352, on achieving supernatural power through vision quest. Big Bear's father, after receiving the design through a dream, made a "red flannel coat trimed (sic) with otter skin around its edges with many brass buttons on it": GA, M-4376, David C. Duvall, pp. 608–9.
8   Ewers, *Vanishing Frontier*, p. 69.
9   For Blackfoot bonnets, see GA, M-4376, David C. Duvall, Dress and Ceremonies; and Clark Wissler, "Ceremonial Bundles of the Blackfoot Indians", AMNH, *Anthropological Papers* 7, 1 (1911): 65–290, esp. pp. 114–16. In contrast, in 1832 Catlin, *Letters*, "Letter 8", described Blackfoot dress as: "chiefly dressed black, or of a dark brown colour; from which circumstance, in all probability, they having black leggings or moccasins, have got the name of Blackfeet".
10 Roland Barthes, *Elements of Semiology*, Annette Lavers and Colin Smith, trans., 2nd rpt. (New York: Hill and Wang, 1977), pp. 10–11.
11 See, for example, Ewers, 'Karl Bodmer's Pictures", pp. 51–93. This is the catalogue for the exhibition of the same title, with essays by Marsha V. Gallagher, David C. Hunt, and Joseph C. Porter. Ewers, once the director of the Museum of the Plains Indian in Browning, had a life-long interest in Blackfoot material culture.
12 See for example Thomas E. Mails, *The Mystic Warriors of the Plains*, rpt. (New York: Marlowe and Co., 1996), an extensive collection of dress traits that combines a wide number of sources. The title, and the first line of the "Introduction": "When I was a little boy", plus the title of the last chapter, "Relocation and Decline", speak volumes about the author's nostalgia for the past.
13 Hernandez, *Mokakssini*, pp. 36–52 and 44–52 for the broader function of the Blackfoot Star Stories; Wissler and Duvall, *Mythology*, pp. 5–18; and for the function of myth, William Bascom, "The Forms of Folklore", *Journal of American Folklore* 78 (1965): 3–20, esp. pp. 4 and 16.
14 For analysis of several versions of this story and their sources see chapter 9 of this volume. There seems to be an unlimited number of ways to spell this name, including Paii, Paiyo, Páieuà, Pàie, Poowaksi, Poiyawa, Ihspowasksski. In English, Scarface is also known as Star Boy. After he died, Scarface became a star, and is known as Paxtsópisòaxs (False Morning Star), Pathsiipissoowasi, and Poks-o-piks-o-aks The-one-you-took-for-Morning-Star, and Mistake Morning Star (Jupiter). See for example, Mistaken Chief and Kremer, "Glossaries", p. 228.
15 The Blackfoot obtained horses from the Shoshone, and "firearms and iron from the Cree and Assiniboine", Lewis, *Effects*, p. 11. Trader Anthony Henday met the Blackfoot in 1754–55, by which time they possessed many horses: Olive Patricia Dickason, "A Historical Reconstruction for the Northwestern Plains", *Prairie Forum* 5, 1 (1980): 19–37, esp. p. 29.
16 Porcupines were found following the western edge of the Great Lakes country, through eastern Montana and Wyoming, and in Alberta, Canada. Mails, *Mystic Warriors*, p. 283.
17 GA, M-4376, David C. Duvall.
18 See GA, M-8458-4, Richardson's Interview with Pitoxpikis, for the path to become akainawa'si; *nina* [which is elsewhere translated as "my father" and

"man"] is also translated as "chief", see Lewis, *Effects*, p. 51, citing Thompson, refers to *Sakatow* or orator, as the term for a civil chief. He also explains changes to the position of war chief after the introduction of the horse.
19 Wissler and Duvall, *Mythology*, p. 14.
20 George Catlin, *Stu-mick-o-súks or Buffalo Bull's Back Fat*, Smithsonian American Art Museum, Gift of Mrs. Joseph Harrison, Accession number 1985.66.149, available @: http://americanart.si.edu/collections/ [Accessed 2 Sept. 2010]; and Catlin, *Letters*, "Letters 4 and 5"; in Letter 5 he notes: "There is no tribe, perhaps, on the Continent, who dress more comfortably, and more gaudily, than the Blackfeet, unless it be the tribe of Crows."
21 Catlin, *Letters*, "Letter 5."
22 Maximilian is cited in Wissler, "Material Culture", pp. 118–19. For the Assiniboine design, see Maximilian, *Travels*, p. 136 and for a Crow disk design, p. 214.
23 Clark Wissler, "Costumes of the Plains Indians", AMNH, *Anthropological Papers* 17, 2 (1915): 39–91, esp. p. 56.
24 Robert J. Moore, *Native Americans A Portrait: The Art and Travels of Charles Bird King, George Catlin and Karl Bodmer* (New York: Stewart, Tabori and Chang, 1997), pp. 130, 142, 178, and 252; Ruud, *Karl Bodmer's North American Prints*; Ewers *et al.*, *Vanishing Frontier*, 1984; and William J. Orr and Joseph C. Porter, eds, "A Journey Through the Nebraska Region in 1833 and 1834: From the Diaries of Prince Maximilian of Wied", trans. William J. Orr, *Nebraska History* 64, 3 (1983): 325–40.
25 GA, M-4421, R. N. Wilson, to the effect that among the Kainai, the leader of the All Brave Dogs Society covered his nose, mouth and chin with red paint, a practice known as "Coyote painting."
26 Wissler and Duvall, *Mythology*, p. 64. For an exemplar of striped leggings, see Ewers *et al.*, *Vanishing Frontier*, p. 23.
27 BGC, *Nitsitapiisini*, p. 28.
28 Contrary to popular belief, "most men did not go to war, only the trying-hard ones did", that is, those seeking to improve their social standing. GA, M-8458-18, Richardson's Research, Horn Society.
29 GA, M-4376, David C. Duvall.
30 According to GA, M-8458-3, Richardson's Interview, Pitoxpikis: A Chief *akainasawa'si* ("full grown in age") can buy a scalp or wear a weasel-fringed suit if he has taken in war: (a) a gun; or (b) one of the following: bow and arrows, spear, shield, Medicine Pipe, and must have killed and/or scalped an enemy; Mails, *Mystic Warriors*, pp. 247 and 324; Henry, *Journal*, p. 726, notes that among the "Fall Indians" (Gros Ventre) who came to trade: "The young men have a more elegant dress which they put on occasionally, the shirt and leggings being trimmed with human hair and ornamented with fringe and quill work; the hair is always obtained from the head of an enemy." Among young Piegan, "The gun which they carry in their arms, and the powder-horn and shot-pouch slung on their backs, are necessary appendages to the full dress [. . .] the bow and quiver of arrows are also slung across the back at all times and seasons". For Blackfoot Sacred Bundles see Wissler, "Ceremonial Bundles", esp. pp. 112–33.

Notes

31 Ewers, *The Blackfeet*, p. 139; and James Axtell and William C. Sturtevant, "The Unkindest Cut, or Who Invented Scalping", *William and Mary Quarterly* 37, 3 (1980): 451–72.
32 Bullchild, *Sun Came Down*, p. 331.
33 Ewers, *The Blackfeet*, p. 9.
34 Wissler, "Social Life", pp. 22–23. For the concept of "Sacred Bundles" see Crowshoe and Manneschmidt, *Akak'stiman*, pp. 19–26; and Conaty, "Economic Models", pp. 403–9.
35 Kehoe, "Blackfoot Persons", p. 119; and Oscar Lewis, "Manly-Hearted Women among the North Piegan", *American Anthropologist* 43, 2 (1941): 173–87, esp. p. 174.
36 Grinnell, *Lodge Tales*, p. 248; and GA, M-8458-4, Richardson's Interview, Pitoxpikis. According to Imiten.a. (Crooked Meat Strings), the Siksika make chiefs by "taking guns, bows, knives and axes — the things that kill us — Crow, Sioux, especially Snakes (Pitsi.ksina) are deprived, especially of their tipi-flags", GA, M-8458-15, Jane Richardson's Blackfoot (Siksika) Research — Agwmaxkayi (Many Swans), 1938, (henceforth Richardson's Research, Agwmaxkayi).
37 McClintock, *Old North Trail*, p. 291.
38 Dempsey provides one example: the Kainai "Braves Warrior Society" had exclusive wear of a shirt with slits on the body and sleeves. It was adorned by several hundred brass tacks, *Indians of the Rocky Mountain Parks*, p. 88; see also Mails, *Dog Soldiers*, for the distinct dress of Plains Indians.
39 GA, M-4421, R. N. Wilson.
40 GA, M-4376-1, David C. Duvall.
41 Bullchild, *Sun Came Down*, p. 350, also notes that, "Creator Sun had the eagle feathers and eagle plume on his head for adornment".
42 Henry, *Journal*, pp. 525–26.
43 GA 8458-8, Richardson's Interview, Crooked Meat Strings: "supernatural ill" would befall those who did not tell "the gospel truth"; and Grinnell, *Lodge Tales*, p. 249.
44 GA, M-4376-1, David C. Duvall, for the economic aspects of Medicine ownership. According to Bear Skin, a man can be considered wealthy if "he has once bought many of the different sacred bundles and lodges [. . .] although he may later on become a poor man".
45 GA 8458-8, Richardson's Interview, Crooked Meat Strings: "All chiefs have power".
46 McClintock, *Old North Trail*, p. 188; and Sidner J. Larson, "Introduction", in *idem*, p. vi. A Blackfoot leader who was "stingy" caused "most of the poor people who had lived [in his camp] to move away". GA, M-8458-3, Richardson's Interview, Pitoxpikis: "A family will up and leave their own bands [. . .] *if the chiefs don't help*" (emphasis in original).
47 Lewis, "Manly-Hearted Women", pp. 173 and 180–81; Hanks and Richardson Hanks, *Tribe Under Trust*, pp. 22 and 36; and Goldfrank, *Changing Configurations*, pp. 7–8.
48 *Minipuka* earned respect for their generosity, but impoverished *Minipuka* continued to receive the respect: Hanks and Richardson Hanks, *Tribe Under Trust*, pp. 34–35.

Notes

49 GA, M-4376, David C. Duvall. The position of *Minipuka* largely disappeared during the reserve era, when government Agents took up their redistributive role: GA, M-8458-3, Richardson's Interview, Pitoxpikis".

50 Kehoe, "Blackfoot Persons", pp. 124–25, based on Wissler and Duvall, and Joe Tatsey's version as given to Uhlenbeck. Moccasins have been made from the skin of the hind leg of the buffalo.

51 Glenbow Museum, *Native North America, Plains*, Exhibit No. AF 3761 a-b.

52 Henry, *Journal*, pp. 525–26.

53 Catlin, *Letters*, "Letter 5".

54 Walter McClintock, *Lanterns of the Prairie: The Blackfoot Photographs of Walter McClintock*, ed. Steven L. Grafe (Norman: University of Oklahoma Press, 2005), p. 166.

55 Bullchild, *Sun Came Down*, p. 331, notes that "Creator Sun" sought honesty and virginity in a girl.

56 GA, M-8458-1, Jane Richardson's Blackfoot (Siksika) Research — Chronological Story of Our Arrival and of the Sundance Events, 28 June–7 July 1938: during the ceremony, the Holy Woman's "face, hands, and clothing are covered with the sacred red paint"; Grinnell, *Lodge Tales*, pp. 265–68; and McClintock, *Old North Trail*, pp. 178–85.

57 Kehoe, "Blackfoot Persons", p. 116.

58 John C. Ewers, "When Red and White Men Met", *Western Historical Quarterly* 2, 2 (1971): 133–50, notes that men intending to go to war sought songs and power from the owners of Medicine Pipes and Beaver Bundles; GA, M-4376, David C. Duvall: wise elders who prayed on their behalf would receive part of their booty.

59 Kehoe, "Blackfoot Persons", p. 116. As mentioned earlier, these stories are: "Elk Woman, the Woman-who-married-a-star, Scar-face, Cuts-wood, Otter-woman, and the Scabby-round-robe".

60 For a version by Natosi Nepe-e (Brings-Down-The-Sun), see McClintock, *Old North Trail*, pp. 491–500; and for one Mrs. Wolf Plume narrated to Duvall in 1911, see GA, M-4376.

61 Wissler and Duvall, *Mythology*, pp. 83–85 provide two versions of the story of Elk Woman. Elk teeth were expensive, and only the incisor teeth were used as dress decoration.

62 Uhlenbeck-Melchior, "Diary", p. 78, notes that in 1911 three women with cut noses lived on the Blackfeet Reservation. Jim Running Wolf's mother had her nose cut off for infidelity in 1894, and in 1895, "All body mutilation and cruel practices were stamped out": GA, M-8458-18, Richardson, Horn Society; McClintock, *Old North Trail*, p. 185; and Grinnell, *Lodge Tales*, pp. 216–20. Grinnell notes that although a husband could justifiably kill a wife, she "was not a chattel that he could trade away [and] he could not sell her to another man" and that "Treachery (that is, when a member of the tribe went over to the enemy and gave them any aid whatever)" was punished by "Death at sight".

63 Lucien M. Hanks, and Jane Richardson, *Observations on Northern Blackfoot Kinship*, Monographs of the American Ethnological Society, ed. A. Irving Hallowell (Seattle: University of Washington Press, [1945] 1966),

p. 26. See also Glenbow Archive, M-8458-18, Richardson, Horn Society.
64 Diamond Jenness, *The Indians of Canada*, rpt. 6th edn (Ottawa: Information Canada, [1932] 1972), p. 320.
65 Kehoe, "Blackfoot Persons", 113–25; and Kiera L. Ladner, "Women and Blackfoot Nationalism", *Journal of Canadian Studies* 35, 2 (2000): 35–60.
66 Michel Foucault, *Power/Knowledge: Selected Interviews & Other Writings 1972–1977*, in Colin Gordon, ed., trans. (New York: Pantheon Books, 1980), p. 98.
67 It is not the intention here to explicate the position of Blackfoot women via Western feminist theory, which addresses radically different kinds of oppression and does not engage with structures of female power within the indigenous cultures of North America.
68 According to Grinnell, *Lodge Tales*, p. 216: "Many of the doctors of the highest reputation in the tribe were women." Quilling was deemed to be a sacred occupation that required ceremonial initiation. Failure to undergo this initiation "led the quiller to go blind": Conaty, "Economic Models", p. 407. For moccasins, see Dempsey, *Red Crow*, p. 42.
69 Ray, *I Have Lived Here*, p. 95.
70 Kehoe, "Blackfoot Persons", p. 115, citing Clark Wissler, *Indian Cavalcade*, p. 290.
71 GA, M-8078 [Old Series] F300/35, Lucien Hanks and Jane Richardson Hanks, Many Guns' Winter Count.
72 GA, M-8188, Arthur Family, Bull Plume's Winter Count; and M-1100-127, Claude E. Schaeffer, Big Brave's Winter Count.
73 Grinnell, *Lodge Tales*, p. 216.
74 Catlin, *Letters*, "Letter 8".
75 McClintock, *Old North Trail*, p. 189; Grinnell, *Lodge Tales*, p. 216. A woman could be killed by her father if she refused to marry the man of his choice: "A girl ordered to marry a man whom she did not like would often [. . .] hang herself"; Henry, *Journal*, pp. 525–26, 724, and 730.
76 Grinnell, *Lodge Tales*, p. 217; McClintock, *Old North Trail*, p. 188; Wissler, "Social Life", p. 11 uses the term "she who sits beside him".
77 Grinnell, *Lodge Tales*, p. 218.
78 *Ibid.* Seen From Afar, a Kainai, reportedly had ten wives *c*.1850: Wischmann, *Frontier Diplomats*, p. 163. Grinnell heard of a man who had sixteen wives: *Lodge Tales*, p. 218.
79 GA, M-8458-3, Richardson's Interview, Pitoxpikis; and Hugh A. Dempsey, *The Amazing Death of Calf Shirt and Other Blackfoot Stories* (Saskatoon, SK: Fifth House, 1994), p. 73, in respect of Many Buffalo Stones Woman.
80 Cited in Lewis, "Manly-Hearted Women", p. 181, note 7.
81 For an example of such a woman, who was also a Sits-beside-him wife, see GA, M-8458-3, Richardson's Interview, Pitoxpikis. See also Beverly Hungry Wolf, *Daughters of the Buffalo Women* (Canadian Caboose Press), 1996, p. 100, to the effect that "Ninnaki, which means Chief Woman" is "the Blackfoot word for Queen" (also nínàke, according to Uhlenbeck).
82 GA, 8458-15, Richardson, Agwmaxkayi. Narrated by Imiten.a (Crooked Meat Strings), and Little Back Bone. See also Dempsey, *Amazing Death*, pp. 67–79.

Notes

83 Georgia Green Fooks, "The First Women: Southern Alberta Native Women Before 1900 (1)", *Alberta History* 51, 4 (2003): 23–28.

84 GA, 8458-15, Richardson, Agwmaxkayi.

85 See GA, M-4376-1, David C. Duvall, pp. 622–24, for a recount of how four women being abducted by a Cree killed and scalped him. John C. Ewers, *Plains Indian History and Culture: Essays on Continuity and Change* (Norman: University of Oklahoma Press, 1997), p. 203, was told by Kainai Weasel Tail that his wife had been in five fights with him: "She carried a revolver — a six shooter. Once she took a horse with a saddle, a bag of ammunition and a war club on it"; Ewers photographed Annie Bear Shield in 1943, "who, as a young woman, accompanied her husband on war parties". Uhlenbeck-Melchior, "Diary", p. 38, recorded meeting Elk Yells in the Water, Bear Chief's wife, who went on horse raids with her husband.

86 GA, M-8458 [Old Series], Lucien Hanks and Jane Richardson Hanks, Interview with Imiten.a (Crooked Meat Strings).

87 Joseph Bruchac, *Our Stories Remember: American Indian History, Culture, and Values through Storytelling* (Golden, CO: Fulcrum Publishing, 2003), p. 165.

88 James Willard Schultz, *Blackfeet Tales of Glacier National Park* (Helena: Montana Historical Society / Riverbend Pub., [1916] 2002), pp. 10–18. Beverly Hungry Wolf recounts a slightly different story to that of Schultz in *Ways of My Grandmothers*, pp. 59–68.

89 Schultz, *Blackfeet Tales*, p. 14.

90 Ewers, *Plains Indian History*, citing Weasel Tail's account, Ewers notes that it differs from that of James Willard Schultz, *Running Eagle* (Boston and New York: Houghton Mifflin Co., 1919); see also Schultz, *Blackfeet and Buffalo*, pp. 347–68, for a story of Lance Woman, a Pikuni who went on the warpath wearing men's clothing so as to be inconspicuous.

91 Schultz, *Blackfeet Tales of Glacier*, pp. 14–15, and 18.

92 GA, M-4376, David C. Duvall, pp. 622–24, regarding four women being abducted by a Cree, who killed and scalped him.

93 Sarah Carter with Dorothy First Rider, *Capturing Women: The Manipulation of Cultural Imagery in Canada's Prairie West* (Montreal: McGill–Queen's UP, 1997), p. 27.

94 Kehoe, "Blackfoot Persons," pp. 122–24.

95 Lewis, "Manly-Hearted Women"; and Goldfrank, *Changing Configurations*, pp. 48–49.

96 Lewis, "Manly-Hearted Women", pp. 178, 185–87.

97 Cited in Kehoe, "Blackfoot Persons," p. 116.

98 Hugh A. Dempsey, *The Vengeful Wife and Other Blackfoot Stories* (Norman: University of Oklahoma Press, 2003), p. 62, notes: "women who took a male role commanded much more respect" than males who took on a female role.

99 Lewis, "Manly-Hearted Women", p. 175. Males chose a *tak.a* or *takai* (friend) from early childhood. This relationship was formalized through joint participation in societies, warfare, and at times even through the sharing of a woman.

100 Grinnell, *Lodge Tales*, p. 194.

Notes

5 Fur Trade, Success, and Dress

1. Lewis, *Effects*, 1942; Ray, *Indians in the Fur Trade*, 1974; and Miller and Hamell, "Indian White Contact", 1986.
2. This term was coined by Fernando Ortiz Fernández, in his *Contrapunto Cubano del Tabaco y el Azúcar*, in María Fernanda Ortiz Herrera, ed. (Madrid: EditoCubaEspaña, [1940] 1999).
3. Burke, *Varieties*, p. 208.
4. *Ibid*. Burke does not define *bricolage*, which in the original French means "do-it-yourself". *The Oxford English Dictionary* notes the term was used in 1960 by R. G. Cohn to refer to "fiddling and tinkering with [literary] devices", and by C. Lévi-Strauss in his 1962 *La Pensée Sauvage*.
5. Burke, *Varieties*, p. 188.
6. Ewers, *The Blackfeet*, 198–99; and Thomas F. Schilz, "Robes, Rum, and Rifles", *Montana: The Magazine of Western History* 40, 1 (1990): 2–13, esp. p. 4, for prehistoric trade at Mandan and Arikara villages.
7. Ambrose, *Undaunted Courage*, p. 182; and Ewers, "Karl Bodmer's Pictures," pp. 54–55.
8. Nancy Bonvillain, *Native Nations: Cultures and Histories of Native North America* (Upper Saddle River, NJ: Prentice Hall, 2001), p. 180, cites one Arapaho individual whose lexicon included 3,500 signs. McClintock, *Old North Trail*, p. 403, attended a meeting where representatives of sixteen First Nations "talked freely and rapidly in gesture speech". For intertribal rivalry see Dempsey, *Indians of the Rocky Mountain Parks*, pp. 81–84: the Blackfoot defended their territory from Cree and Métis from the north, Kootenay and Stoney from the west, Crow and Shoshoni from the south, and Assiniboine and Sioux from the east.
9. According to Nii'ta'kaiksa'maikoan (Pete Standing Alone), the Kainai used weasel pelts for their clothing, and, for this reason "were referred to as the weasel people" or Aapaitsitapi by other groups, a name which was mistakenly translated as Blood. Cited in Bastien, *Blackfoot Ways of Knowing*, p. 10.
10. For intertribal kinship see David Smyth, *The Niitsitapi Trade: Euroamericans and the Blackfoot-Speaking Peoples, to the mid-1830s*, PhD Diss. Carleton University, 2001, pp. 38–42.
11. James Willard Schultz, and Jessie Louise Donaldson, *The Sun God's Children* (Boston: Houghton Mifflin Co., 1930), p. 229.
12. Wischmann, *Frontier Diplomats*, pp. 42–43. Hugh Welch, a Blackfoot, confirmed the story in correspondence with Wischmann.
13. Marshall Joseph Becker, "Matchcoats: Cultural Conservatism and Change in One Aspect of Native American Clothing", *Ethnohistory* 52, 4 (2005): 727–87, esp. p. 767. Manufactured in Stroud, England, this cloth was made from recycled woollen rags; Catlin noted some changes in Blackfoot dress patterns and decoration "since the days of Alexander Henry twenty years earlier", with trade beads providing decorations on Blackfoot women's dresses. Ewers, *The Blackfeet*, p. 59.
14. McClintock, *Old North Trail*, p. 291, described horse adornment during a Sun Dance parade as follows: "The saddle had deer-antler pommels with beaded pendants and a beaded buck-skin crupper. Brightly coloured feathers

were fastened to [the] horse's tail and a large cluster of eagle feathers hung from his neck"; for martingales and cruppers, see John C. Ewers, "The Horse in Blackfoot Indian Culture; with Comparative Material from Other Western Tribes", *Bureau of American Ethnology Bulletin* 159, rpt. (Washington, DC: Smithsonian Institution Press, [1955] 1980): 95–7. The *Oxford English Dictionary* lists a crupper as a "strap buckled to the back of a saddle and looped under the horse's tail, to prevent the saddle from slipping forward," and a martingale as a "strap or arrangement of straps fastened at one end to the noseband, bit or reins of a horse, and at the other to its girth". See more descriptions of horse adornment in Mails, *Mystic Warriors*, p. 242.

15 GA, 8458-15, Richardson, Agwmaxkayi. See horse painting in Mails, *Mystic Warriors*, pp. 219–23 and 234. Horses were also given names, and some became widely known: M-8078 [Old Series] F300/35, Lucien Hanks and and Jane Richardson Hanks, Many Guns' Winter Count. A parade preceding the erection of the Sun Dance Pole is described by McClintock, *Old North Trail*, p. 290, at which women wore their husbands' eagle feathers during a Scalp Dance.

16 The HBC built Fort Edmonton in 1795 on the North Saskatchewan River, and Rocky Mountain House in 1799 on the mouth of the Saskatchewan.

17 In 1845 the Kainai "separated in two parties for trading, the one going to [Fort] Benton and the other to Rocky Mountain House." GA, M-4421, Bad Head's Winter Count [Blood], 1810–1883, published by Hugh A. Dempsey, *A Blackfoot Winter Count*, Occasional Paper 1, rpt. (Calgary: Glenbow Museum, [1965] 1988); and Lewis, *Effects*, p. 28.

18 Dempsey, *Indians of the Rocky Mountain Parks*, pp. 82–83.

19 Sylvia Van Kirk, *Many Tender Ties: Women in Fur Trade Society, 1670–1870* (Norman: University of Oklahoma Press, [1980] 1983).

20 White, *Middle Ground*, esp. pp. 50–93; and Ray, *Indians in the Fur Trade*, p. xi.

21 Ray, "Northern Great Plains", pp. 263–79. In August 1794, Gros Ventres attacked an HBC post, killing three traders and five or six women and children.

22 Ray, *Indians in the Fur Trade*, pp. 67–68, and 137.

23 After 1796 trade was regulated in the United States through a "factory system", where "factor" was the name given to the chief of a trading post: Reginald Horsman, "United States Indian Policies, 1776–1815", in *Indian–White Relations*, pp. 29–39, esp. p. 34.

24 Henry, *Journal*, p. 507; Ray, *Indians in the Fur Trade*, pp. 137–9, and 162 n.5, citing Morton, ed., *The Journal of Duncan M'Gillivray* (Toronto: 1929), p. 74: "if a band failed to obtain a sufficient quantity of furs or provisions to pay off its debts, the band leader was denied these symbols of office."

25 Wischmann, *Frontier Diplomats*, p. 44, citing Reuben Gold Thwaites, ed., *Early Western Travels: 1748–1846*, 32 Vols, Vol. 23, p. 88.

26 Ewers, "Karl Bodmer's Pictures", p. 56.

27 Smyth, *Niitsitapi Trade*, p. 60.

28 Nicholas Biddle, ed., *The Journals of the Expedition under the Command of Capts. Lewis and Clark to the sources of the Missouri, thence across the Rocky Mountains and down the river Columbia to the Pacific Ocean, per-*

formed during the years 1804-5-6 by Order of the Government of the United States, 2 Vols (Norwalk, Conn.: Heritage Press, 1993), Volume 1, p. 75.

29 Ray, *Indians in the Fur Trade*, pp. 139 and 162, n.4, citing Glyndwr Williams, *Andrew Graham's Observations on Hudson's Bay 1767–1791*, p. 317. See GA, 8458-15, Richardson, Agwmaxkayi, to the effect that the only presents women received were "buttons".

30 Herman J. Viola, *After Columbus: The Smithsonian Chronicle of the North American Indians* (Washington DC: Smithsonian Books, 1990), pp. 94 and 118.

31 During the first encounter with the Delawares, the Dutch gave them "a round of liquor [. . .] iron and cloth gifts". James Axtell, *After Columbus: Essays in the Ethnohistory of Colonial North America* (Oxford: Oxford University Press, 1988), p. 131; and Becker, "Matchcoats", pp. 771–73.

32 J. R. Miller, "Compact, Contract, Covenant: The Evolution of Indian Treaty Making", in Ted Binnema and Susan Neylan, eds, *New Histories for Old: Changing Perspectives on Canada's Native Pasts* (Vancouver: University of British Columbia Press, 2007), p. 71.

33 Henry, *Journal*, p. 728.

34 Flags were highly prized, coveted trophies of war. A Pikuni year count records the most salient event of 1801 as follows: "When we took the Stars and Stripes from the River Indians": GA, M-8188, Bull Plume's Winter Count. Flying a flag was a sign of peaceful intentions, although this was not always observed in practice as noted by Ewers, *The Blackfeet*, p. 60, citing an attack on white traders by a Gros Ventre band flying the American flag.

35 Lewis, *Effects*, pp. 42–43; and Henry, *Journal*, p. 654: "Black Bear having given me 10 large beavers, I gave him a chief's coat and hat."

36 Biddle, *Journals*, Vol. 1, p. 76.

37 *Ibid.*, citing Thwaites, Vol. 23, p. 127; Schultz, *Signposts of Adventure: Glacier National Park as the Indians Knew It* (Boston: Houghton Mifflin Co., 1926), pp. 39–41; Smyth, *Niitsitapi Trade*, p. 490, cites fur trader Harriot's report to the effect that a battle between the Kainai and Pikuni took Place at Burnt River, "in which three Peagan Camps were totally routed."

38 Dempsey, *Crowfoot*, p. 57.

39 Treaty 7 Elders, *Original Intent*, pp. 241–42.

40 Dempsey, *Amazing Death*, p. 73; and GA, 8458-15, Richardson, Agwmaxkayi.

41 GA, 8458-15, Richardson, Agwmaxkayi.

42 See for example the photographic collection at the Glenbow Archives, with early images of the Blackfoot, available online at: http://ww2.glenbow.org; and Farr, *Reservation Blackfeet*, 1984.

43 Writing of the Piegan in 1787, trader Thompson reported "all those who have it in their power buy woolen (*sic*) clothing". Women, he noted "took to cotton and woolen (*sic*) clothing much later than the men"; Grinnell, *Lodge Tales*, p. 293; and Lewis, *Effects*, p. 37.

44 Henry, *Journal*, pp. 541–43.

45 *Ibid.*, pp. 525–27; and Bullchild, *Sun Came Down*, p. 350, who explains Creator Sun's use of red paint on his own clothes.

Notes

46 See for example, Dee Garceau, "Mediations of Women on *The Big Sky*", in William E. Farr, and William W. Bevis, *Fifty Years After* The Big Sky: *New Perspectives on the Fiction and Films of A. B. Guthrie, Jr.* (Missoula: University of Missoula), pp. 119–56, esp. p. 132.
47 Wissler, "Social Life", p. 11.
48 Catlin, *Letters*, "Letter 5" and "Letter 8".
49 *Ibid.*, "Letter 5".
50 Lewis, "Manly-Hearted Women", p. 174, claims that *ninauake* or favourite wife was an ideal wife: "kind, loyal, and deeply attached to her husband". *Ninauake* departed from conventional sex behaviour, allowing a great deal of sex play, to the point of satisfying their husbands sexually.
51 Ray, *I Have Lived Here*, p. 169.
52 According to a trader, cited in Ewers, "Karl Bodmer's Pictures", p. 60, a Blackfoot man with five or six wives, and twenty of thirty children, would occupy two or three lodges, own between 50 and 100 horses, and trade *c*.$2,000 per year.
53 Lewis, *Effects*, p. 40.
54 Wischmann, *Frontier Diplomats*, pp. 95, 162 and 210–11.
55 It appears that the character had some influence in the United States, where a trout of the St. Mary's Lakes and River was also named "Dolly Varden." Schultz, *Blackfeet and Buffalo*, p. 90.
56 Wischmann, *Frontier Diplomats*, pp. 93 and 219, citing Schultz, *Signposts*, p. 113. Culbertson had to divorce his then Pikuni wife to marry Natuyitsixina, who could not be a secondary wife.
57 *Ibid.*, p. 224.

6 The Longevity of Buckskins

1 Wealthy leaders could fulfil their reciprocal obligations to their followers independently and therefore did not require white approval to maintain their authority. In contrast, chiefs sanctioned by white officials relied on white supplied rations to fulfil their obligation to provide for their followers.
2 Hanks and Richardson Hanks, *Tribe Under Trust*, p. 15.
3 LAC, DIA, AR 1879, pp. 76–103.
4 Hanks and Richardson Hanks, *Tribe Under Trust*, p. 17.
5 Farr, *Reservation Blackfeet*, p. 13; and Lewis, *Effects*, pp. 28–29 and 69. Among dress materials provided to Blackfoot at their agency in Montana, Ewers cites 48 yards of duck, blue and red flannel, and 196 yards of print materials. GA, M-9141-8c, John Ewers' Blood field notes, pp. 224–25.
6 Grinnell, *Lodge Tales*, p. 293.
7 Medals were extensively used in diplomacy. During an encounter with eight Pikuni in 1806, Meriwether Lewis presented three individuals, who claimed to be chiefs, with a flag, a handkerchief, and a medal with Thomas Jefferson's likeness on the obverse side and a handshake between an Indian and a white hand, with a peace pipe crossed with a tomahawk, and the engraved words "peace and friendship" on the reverse side: Ambrose, *Undaunted Courage*, pp. 158, and 387–88; Viola, *Diplomats*, p. 104: "With the exception of John Adams, each president from George Washington to Benjamin Harrison issued

an Indian peace medal"; medals were also used by the Dominion: Dempsey, "One Hundred Years", pp. 20–30, esp. p. 21.
8   Viola, *Diplomats*, pp. 94 and 118.
9   Grinnell, *Lodge Tales*, p. 293; and Ewers, *Story of the Blackfeet*, p. 51.
10 LAC, DIA, AR, 1906, p. 165.
11 During the Laramy Treaty negotiations at Horse Creek in 1851, First Nations were asked to nominate a "Chief of the whole nation" to be recognized by the Great Father, when the Sioux (a white misnomer for the combined Dakota and Lakota nations) failed to do so, a chief was chosen by the American negotiator and ratified by the chiefs who took treaty. Chiefs received military uniforms and gilt swords. Wischmann, *Frontier Diplomats*, pp. 201–7, *note* 20.
12 LAC, DIA, AR, 1891, p. 83.
13 After Crowfoot's death in 1890, Pitoxpikis was offered the chief's medal, which he refused saying: "I don't want a dead man's medal nor to be made chief in the white way. I am an Indian chief and I'm chief enough." GA, M-8458-14, Richardson's Blackfoot (Siksika) Research — History of the Skunk Band.
14 Hanks and Richardson Hanks, *Tribe Under Trust*, p. 14: "Eagle Ribs, even though he signed the treaty, refused to obligate himself to the Whites, by accepting a medal. Little Person, Eagle Robe, Chief Calf, all respected men and chiefs, were excluded or refused to be honoured in this manner. They knew they were chiefs even without a medal and a gold-braided uniform".
15 The signatories to Treaty Seven agreed to live in peace with Indians, Métis and whites, but horse raiding continued: GA, M-8458-17, Jane Richardson's Blackfoot (Siksika) Research — Life in Crowfoot's Camp. ca. 1870–1877 (henceforth Richardson, Crowfoot's Camp); and Commissioners, *New West*, 1888, p. 48; and 1889, p. 84.
16 Tobias, "Protection, Civilization, Assimilation", p. 20.
17 *Ibid.*, noting that in 1902 several chiefs were removed during efforts "to suppress illegal dancing"; and LAC, RG 10, Vol. 3826, f. 60511-4-1, J. D. McLean, Assistant Deputy and Secretary, 2 June 1917.
18 GA, M-4738-255-6, Articles Written by Gooderham, Biography, Joe Calfchild, Blackfoot [Siksika] 1875–1942.
19 LAC, RG 18, Vol. 302, f. 658-05, Supt. P. C. H. Primrose, Commanding D Division, to Commissioner, Regina, 5 August 1905. As noted in chapter 3, Day Chief asked Primrose to notify his superiors about the Indian agent's threat to demote the chief.
20 Lucien Hanks collated these figures in 1938. GA, M-8458-31, Lucien Hanks' Blackfoot (Siksika) research — Typed notes and interviews.
21 In 1921, when Agent George Gooderham and NWMP Inspector J. W. Spalding attempted to stop Ookaan, some women tried to join the negotiations, but were unceremoniously dismissed by Chief Weasel Calf. Spalding noted: "these old fellows do not sympathize with women's suffrage." LAC, RG 18, Vol. 3290, f. HQ-1034-K-1, RCMP, K Division, Lethbridge, Calgary Sub-District, Inspector J. W. Spalding's Report 27 July 1921. As for whites, including Gooderham, they were still using the term "squaw" well into the twentieth century: GA, M-4738, George H. Gooderham.

Notes

22 Dempsey, *Crowfoot*; and *Red Crow*. Red Crow proudly noted "I was never struck by an enemy in my life, with bullet, arrow, axe, spear or knife!", a significant achievement given that he had participated in more than thirty battles: GA, M-4421, R. N. Wilson, Part IV, esp. p. 227. For the importance of Crowfoot's chieftainship see LAC, DIA, AR, 1883, p. xi.
23 Hanks, and Richardson Hanks, *Tribe Under Trust*, p. 10.
24 LAC, DIA, AR, 1883, p. 103: "Already the news of negotiations with the Blackfeet had reached the Stonies, and these Indians informed me (as subsequently did the Sarcees, Peigans and Bloods), that they all were of the same mind as Crowfoot, and 'what he said, they all said." See also Hanks, and Richardson Hanks, *Tribe Under Trust*, p. 22.
25 GA, M-8458-17, Richardson, Crowfoot's Camp.
26 For attitudes to Crowfoot, see GA, M-8078, Lucien Hanks and Jane Richardson Hanks, Many Guns' Winter Count; and Hanks and Richardson Hanks, *Tribe Under Trust*, pp. 10, 21 and 31.
27 Homi K. Bhabha, ed., *The Location of Culture*, rpt. (London: Routledge, 1997), pp. 86–88. Italics in original.
28 Viola, *Diplomats*, p. 118.
29 Both the Latin *mimicus* and the Greek *mimikos* relate to imitation.
30 Hanks, and Richardson Hanks, *Tribe Under Trust*, p. 19.
31 GA, M-4394-19, Joe Little Chief, "Joe Little Chief's Stories: From 1880 the Year the Blackfoot Moved South."
32 GA, M-8458 [Old Series], Lucien Hanks and Jane Richardson Hanks, Interview with Imiten.a. (Crooked Meat Strings). According to Jane Richardson Hanks, the Blackfoot "think that we are dirty and do not eat with us." However, one of her informants claimed that the "Main complaint against white people is they refuse to eat Indian food." For the treatment of Blackfoot children, see Grinnell, *Lodge Tales*, pp. 188–91.
33 LAC, DIA, AR, 1887, p. 125.
34 McClintock, *Old North Trail*, p. 389.
35 Hanks and Richardson Hanks, *Tribe Under Trust*, p. 26.
36 McClintock, *Old North Trail*, p. 23, was told by Spotted Eagle "that he had never been able to understand how people could live on the food eaten by white men". See also Schultz, *Blackfeet and Buffalo*, p. 30.
37 Hanks and Richardson Hanks, *Tribe Under Trust*, p. 22.
38 The Siksika bands were divided into two main groups, one settled on the north side of the reserve and the other on the south, and each group had its own leaders.
39 The hat was a present from the HBC in 1912, later replaced with a present from Lord Burnham, British newspaper magnate in 1920. GA, M-4738-217-6, Gooderham, Lord Burnham and Chief Yellowhorse. John C. Ewers, "Artifacts and Pictures as Documents", in Smith and Kvasnicka, eds, *Indian–White Relations*, pp. 101–11, esp. 102, notes that in the Kainai Reserve in Alberta, as late as 1968 "one hundred or more Indians still [wore] moccasins daily, except in winter."
40 *Ibid*.
41 Hanks and Richardson Hanks, *Tribe Under Trust*, pp. 24–25: horse ownership played a part on these transfers.

42 GA, M-4376, Duvall, pp. 317–18.
43 Walton et al., *After the Buffalo*, p. 51.
44 See Goldfrank, *Changing Configurations*, pp. 21–31 for a view of give-aways at the Blood Reserve during the early twentieth century, including buckskin suits.
45 Bill Ashcroft, "Resistance and Transformation", in Bruce Bennet, Susan Cowan, Jacqueline Lo, Satendra Nandan and Jennifer Webb, eds, *Resistance and Reconciliation: Writing in the Commonwealth* (Canberra: Association for Commonwealth Literature and Language Studies (ACLALS), 2003), pp. 384–85 and 389.
46 Farr, *Reservation Blackfeet*, p. 90.
47 According to Ben Calf Robe, *Siksiká*, pp. 85–91, who was a participant in the first Calgary Stampede in 1912, the organizers invited the Blackfoot to camp on the grounds and parade in their regalia, for which they were given rations and money. In 1891 the then Commissioner of Indian Affairs at Regina, Hayter Reed, complained that whites were encouraging sun dances "not only by their presence but in other ways". GA, M-1234-7, Archdeacon J. W. Tims Family, Archdeacon Tims General Correspondence 1885–1953, John W. House to the Archdeacon, 19 June 1939.
48 Blackfoot headdresses were distinct in that eagle feathers were arranged in an upright position similar to that of a crown. These headdresses are practically absent from early twentieth-century photographs of the Blackfoot. See Walton et al., *After the Buffalo*, pp. 100–3.
49 DIA, 1895, pp. 196–97; and Viola, *Diplomats*, p. 111. The Canadian Blackfoot travelled to Regina in 1895 to meet with the Governor General and Lady Aberdeen. At this meeting they wore their buckskin regalia. Pikuni Chief Little Plume attended Theodore Roosevelt's Inaugural Parade in 1905. In 1923 a group of Pikuni attending a "Shrine convention" in Washington, DC were photographed wearing Sioux-style headdress. A photograph titled "Dedication of oil well, ca. 1928" shows a contingent of Pikuni dressed in buckskin suits, both photos in Farr, *Reservation Blackfeet*, pages 122 and 125.
50 During the 1920s and 1930s, Blackfoot from the reservation "would dance for the tourists or sell trinkets and pose for pictures" at East Glacier Lodge, and were employed as tourist bus drivers: Farr, *Reservation Blackfeet*, pp. 191 and 197–98.
51 Angelika Bammer, "Introduction", in Bammer, ed., *Displacements: Cultural Identities in Question* (Bloomington and Indianapolis: Indiana University Press, 1994), pp. xi–xx.
52 Interpretive frames are formulated by "popular intellectuals" and "framing specialists", who act as intermediaries to shape collective views in social interaction: Michiel Baud, and Rosanne Rutten, "Framing Protest: Popular Intellectuals and Social Movements in Asia, Africa, and Latin America (Nineteenth–Twentieth centuries)", Position Paper, *International Review of Social History*, pp. 1–4, available @: http://www.iisg.nl/irsh/protest.pdf [Accessed 31 August 2010].
53 GA, Photograph NA-350-1, where Chief Yellow Horse is photographed with his "wife", whose name is not stated.

Notes

54 See for example List of Crops Sown and Harvested for 1890, where the crops belonging to two deceased men appear against the names of their widows, respectively. LAC, DIA, AR, 1890, pp. 242 and 308.
55 John C. Ewers, "The Persistent Tradition: The Hill Collection from the Viewpoint of a Student of Blackfeet Indian Arts and Crafts", in Walton *et al.*, *After the Buffalo*, 1984, pp. 37–46, esp. p. 40.
56 Hanks and Richardson Hanks, *Tribe Under Trust*, pp. 112–15.
57 Numerous photographs of Blackfoot at the Calgary Stampede are available online from the Glenbow Archive and Museum.
58 Hanks and Richardson Hanks, *Tribe Under Trust*, p. 25.
59 Wissler, "Social Life", p. 23.
60 In 1920, Chief Yellowhorse presented newspaper magnate Lord Burnham with a beaded buckskin suit. GA, M-4738, George H. Gooderham. In 1977 Prince Charles was inducted into the "Kainai Chieftainship", a symbolic office reserved for distinguished non-Blackfoot, during the Centennial Commemoration of the Signing of Treaty Seven. He received a beaded buckskin suit, and several presents including a horse and saddle: Taylor, *Standing Alone*, pp. 223–24.

Part III Ethnographic Encounters: Cultural Transactions and Translations

7 Between Orality and Text: The Encounter with "Salvage" Ethnography

1 Blackfoot authors who acknowledge these volumes as sources are: Hernandez, *Mokakssini*, pp. 41 and 53 (Grinnell, McClintock, and Wissler and Duvall); Hungry Wolf, *Ways of My Grandmothers*, p. 9 (Schultz, Grinnell, and Wissler and Duvall); Bastien, *Blackfoot Ways of Knowing*, pp. 9 and 16 (McClintock and Grinnell); and Darrel Robes Kipp, "Completing the Circle", in *Lanterns of the Prairie: The Blackfoot Photographs of Walter McClintock*, Steven L. Grafe, ed. (Norman: University of Oklahoma Press, 2005), pp. 99–103 (McClintock).
2 Thedis B. Crowe, "Introduction", in Grinnell, *Lodge Tales*, pp. v–xvii, esp. p. xi.
3 Malcolm McFee, *Modern Blackfeet: Montanans on a Reservation* (New York: Holt, Rinehart and Winston, Inc., 1972), p. 50, notes that in the Montana Reservation, those who could speak or read English were a tiny minority.
4 Hungry Wolf, *Ways of My Grandmothers*, p. 9.
5 Helen Carr, *Inventing the American Primitive: Politics, Gender, and the Representation of Native American Literary Traditions, 1789–1936* (New York: New York University Press, 1996), p. 147; and Jerry D. Moore, *Visions of Culture: An Introduction to Anthropological Theories and Theorists* (Walnut Creek, CA: AltaMira Press, 1997), pp. 15–16.
6 For Frantz Boas's approach to his discipline, see Alan Barnard, *History and Theory in Anthropology* (Cambridge: Cambridge University Press, 2000).
7 Sherry L. Smith, *Reimagining Indians: Native Americans through Anglo Eyes, 1880–1940* (Oxford University Press, 2000), p. 47, citing Margot Liberty.

8   Bruce G. Trigger, "Ethnohistory: The Unfinished Edifice", *Ethnohistory* 33, 3 (1986): 253–67, esp. pp. 255–56.
9   Francis Jennings, "A Growing Partnership: Historians, Anthropologists and American Indian History", *Ethnohistory* 29, 1 (1982): 21–34, p. 26, cites Edward Burnett Taylor, the first Professor of Anthropology at Oxford University, to elucidate the distinctions between anthropology, ethnology and ethnohistory. These distinctions were based on the 1910 *Encyclopedia Britannica*: anthropology was "the science which, in its strictest sense, has as its object the study of man in the animal kingdom. It is distinguished from ethnology, which is devoted to the study of man as a *racial* unit, and from ethnography, which deals with the *distribution* of the races formed by the aggregation of such units."
10 James Clifford, "On Ethnographic Authority", *Representations* 1, 2 (1983): 118–46, esp. pp. 120–21.
11 Crowe, "Introduction", p. xi.
12 Grinnell, *Lodge Tales*, p. xxvi.
13 George Peter Murdock, "Clark Wissler, 1870–1947", *American Anthropologist* 50 (1948): 292–304.
14 Frederick E. Hoxie, ed. and intro., *Talking Back to Civilization: Indian Voices from the Progressive Era* (Boston: Bedford/St Martin's, 2001), pp. 16–20; Clara Sue Kidwell, and Alan Velie, *Native American Studies* (Lincoln: University of Nebraska Press, 2005), p. 2; and Robert Bringhurst, "That Also Is You: Some Classics of Native Canadian Literature", in William H. New, ed., *Native Writers and Canadian Writing*, rpt. (Vancouver: UBC Press, 1992), pp. 32–47.
15 Throughout The Americas, categories of race and caste imposed by colonial powers were 'slippery', such that individuals might find themselves listed under more than one category depending on context. See for example Jennifer Brown and Theresa Schenck, "Métis, Mestizo, and Mixed-Blood", in Phillip J. Deloria and Neal Salisbury, eds, *A Companion to American Indian History* (Malden, MA: Blackwell Publishers, 2004), pp. 321–38; Tony A. Culjak, "Searching for a Place in Between: The Autobiographies of Three Canadian Metis Women", *American Review of Canadian Studies* 31, 1–2 (2001): 137–57, discussing the problematic use of terms such as "mixed-blood", "halfbreed", and Métis, in Canada and the United States.
16 Malcolm McFee, "The 150% Man, a Product of Blackfeet Acculturation," *American Anthropologist* 70, 6 (1968): 1096–1107, esp. pp. 1098–1101.
17 See for example, the contributors to Bernd C. Peyer, ed., *The Singing Spirit: Early Short Stories by North American Indians* (Tucson: University of Arizona Press, 1989), including of Mohawk-English descent Pauline Johnson (Tekahionwake or Double Wampum Woman), "A Red Girl's Reasoning". See also Alanna Kathleen Brown, "Mourning Dove's Canadian Recovery Years, 1917–1919," in W. H. New, ed., *Native Writers and Canadian Writing*, rpt. (Vancouver: UBC Press, 1992), pp. 113–22, esp. p. 113.
18 Ewers, *The Blackfeet*, pp. 326–27.
19 Between 1870 and 1885 Grinnell undertook nine trips to the West. Shawn Patrick Bailey, *Colonization of the Crown: Hunting, Class, and the Creation of Glacier National Park, 1885–1915*, MA Diss., University of Montana, 2009, pp. 56–57.

Notes

20 Harris, *Preserving a Vision*, pp. 380–81 and 408.
21 This New York-based publication became influential in shaping public opinion on matters of environmental conservation. As a component of the "outdoors", the lifeways of First Nations also interested readers. Bailey, *Colonization of the Crown*, p. 57.
22 *Ibid.*, p. 48.
23 Smith, *Reimagining Indians*, pp. 46 and 53.
24 Grinnell, *Lodge Tales*, pp. xxxi and 289.
25 Sidner J. Larson, "Introduction", McClintock, *Old North Trail*, pp. v–x, esp. p. vi; and Smith, *Reimagining Indians*, p. 67.
26 Smith, *Reimagining Indians*, p. 68.
27 Uhlenbeck spent three months among the Blackfoot in 1910. He returned in 1911 and collected more material. See his *Original Blackfoot Texts*, pp. iv and 4–5; and Uhlenbeck-Melchior, "Diary".
28 Klaas van Berkel, and Mary Eggermont-Molenaar, "The Uhlenbecks and the Burdens of Life: A Biographical Introduction", in Mary Eggermont-Molenaar, ed., *Montana 1911: A Professor and his Wife Among the Blackfeet* (Lincoln: University of Nebraska, and University of Calgary Press, 2005), pp. 7–1, esp. p. 12.
29 C. C. Uhlenbeck, *A Concise Blackfoot Grammar: Based on Materials from the Southern Peigans* (Amsterdam: Noord-Hollandsche Uitgevers-maatschappij, 1938), "Preface".
30 Mary Eggermont-Molenaar, "Collage of Blackfoot Texts Recorded by C. C. Uhlenbeck", in Eggermont-Molenaar, ed., *Montana 1911: A Professor and his Wife Among the Blackfeet*, trans. from Dutch by Mary Eggermont-Molenaar (Lincoln: University of Nebraska, and University of Calgary Press, 2005), pp. 203–346, esp. pp. 207 and 211.
31 Seele, Keith C., "Introduction", in Seele, ed., James Willard Schultz, *Blackfeet and Buffalo: Memories of Life Among the Indians* (Norman: University of Oklahoma Press, [c. 1878–1915] 1962), pp. vii–xii, esp. p. viii.
32 Grinnell, *Lodge Tales*, p. xxx.
33 Seele, "Introduction", pp. ix and xi (italics in the original).
34 Smith, *Reimagining Indians*, p. 55.
35 Grinnell, *Lodge Tales*, p. xxx.
36 Larson, "Introduction", *Old North Trail*, p. x; and Wissler and Duvall, *Mythology*, p. 6.
37 Carr, *Inventing the American Primitive*, p. 155, citing Curtis Hinsley.
38 Grinnell, *Lodge Tales*, p. 180.
39 Grinnell, "Tenure of Land", p. 6.
40 Carr, *Inventing the American Primitive*, p. 156.
41 Mary Eggermont-Molenaar, "Mrs. Uhlenbeck: An Informed Diarist?", in Eggermont-Molenaar, ed. and trans., *Montana 1911*, pp. 17–27, esp. p. 21.
42 Grinnell, *Lodge Tales*, p. xxiii.
43 *Ibid.*, p. 5.
44 McClintock, *Old North Trail*, p. xi.
45 Smith argues that McClintock must have been aware of Grinnell's work: *Reimagining Indians*, p. 68. For the citation of Wissler, see McClintock, *Old North Trail*, p. xii.

46 Smith, *Reimagining Indians*, p. 81.
47 James Welch, *Fools Crow* (New York: Viking, 1986).
48 James Clifford and George E. Marcus, eds, *Writing Culture: The Poetics and Politics of Ethnography* (Berkeley, California: University of California Press, 1986).
49 Grinnell, *Lodge Tales*, p. xxvii.
50 Gayatri Chakravorty Spivak, "Can the Subaltern Speak? Speculations on Widow Sacrifice", *Wedge* 7, 8 (1985): 120–30.
51 Edward W. Said, *Orientalism*, rpt. (London: Penguin Books, [1978] 1995), p. 335.
52 For definitions of *testimonio*, see John Beverley, *Against Literature* (Minneapolis: University of Minnesota Press, 1993), pp. 70–71; and his *Subalternity and Representation: Arguments in Cultural Theory* (Durham: Duke University Press, 1999), p. 65; see also George Yúdice, "Testimonio *and* Postmodernism", in Georg M. Gugelberger, ed., *The Real Thing: Testimonial Discourse and Latin America* (Durham: Duke University Press, 1996), pp. 42–57, esp. p. 44.
53 Seele, "Introduction", p. xii.
54 Schultz, *Blackfeet and Buffalo*, p. 282.
55 *Ibid.*, p. 95.
56 Seele, "Introduction", p. vii.
57 Jonathan E. Reyman, "Note on Clark Wissler's Contribution to American Archeology, *American Anthropologist* 87 (1985): 389–90.
58 Alice B. Kehoe, "Introduction", Wissler and Duvall, *Mythology*, pp. v-xxxiii, esp. p. vi; and Murdock, "Clark Wissler," pp. 292–304.
59 David Murray, *Forked Tongues: Speech, Writing, and Representation in North American Indian Texts* (Bloomington: Indiana UP, 1991), p. 102.
60 Wissler cited from the publications of Grinnell and McClintock, among others. See for example his introductory remarks to "Social Life".
61 Wissler, "In Memoriam".
62 In 1850, George Copway's *The Traditional History and Characteristic Sketches of the Ojibway Nation* became one of the earliest writings of "Indian history written by an Indian": Penny Petrone, *Native literature in Canada from the Oral Tradition to the Present* (Toronto: Oxford University Press, 1990); and her *First People, First Voices* (Toronto: University of Toronto Press, 1991), p. 77.
63 Kehoe, "Introduction", pp. xii and xxvi–xxvii.
64 Harris, *Preserving a Vision*, p. 428, citing Grinnell's letter to S. M. Brosius in 1901.
65 Kehoe, "Introduction", pp. vi–vii.
66 Uhlenbeck-Melchior, "Diary", pp. 95–96.
67 Kehoe, "Introduction", p. xi.
68 Alice Kehoe, "Legendary Histories" in Eggermont-Molenaar, ed., *Montana 1911*, pp. 195–202, esp. p. 201, notes that contemporary Blackfoot attribute his death to the fact that he "'fooled around' with Medicine Bundles, sending some to New York and getting Tom Kyaio (Kiyo) to perform the great Beaver bundle ritual just for the museum man's publication."
69 Uhlenbeck-Melchior, "Diary", pp. 95–96, and 405 *n*.39, to the effect that the

Notes

Grinnells launched their first 'Glacier' experience on 4 July 1911. The Uhlenbecks stayed with Grinnell and his wife in New York after their visit to Montana: Eggermont-Molenaar, "Collage", p. 258.

70 James L. Dempsey, *Blackfoot War Art: Pictographs of the Reservation Period, 1880–2000* (Norman: University of Oklahoma Press, 2007), p. 60.
71 Uhlenbeck-Melchior, "Diary", pp. 71 and 109.
72 *Ibid.*, p. 406, *n*.45.
73 *Ibid.*, pp. 126–29. Italics by editor to indicate words untranslated from the Dutch manuscript.
74 Uhlenbeck, *Original Blackfoot Texts*, p. v.
75 Kehoe, "Legendary Histories," p. 197.

8 Blackfoot Genres into Written History and Literature

1 Peter Nabokov, *A Forest of Time: American Indian Ways of History* (Cambridge: Cambridge University Press, 2002), pp. vii–viii.
2 Harris, *Preserving a Vision*, p. 400, citing Grinnell, "Teachers for the Indians," *Forest and Stream*, 15 October 1885. See also Grinnell, *Lodge Tales*, pp. xxvii–xxviii.
3 Gordon Brotherston, *Book of the Fourth World: Reading the Native Americas Through Their Literature* (Cambridge: Cambridge University Press, 1992).
4 See Burke, *Varieties*, pp. 195–96, on the ideas of cultural "reproduction" by Althusser, and Bourdieu and Passeron; and "reception theory" by Michel De Certeau.
5 Cited in Gerald Vizenor, *Wordarrows: Native American States of Literary Sovereignty* (Lincoln: University of Nebraska Press, 2003), p. xii.
6 BGC, *Nitsitapiisini*, p. 8. See also Lawrence W. Gross, "The Comic Vision of the Anishinaabe Culture and Religion", *American Indian Quarterly* 26, 3 (2002): 436–59, esp. p. 449, noting that among the Anishinaabe (or Saulteaux) "it is commonly thought that religion and life way are one in [*sic*] the same".
7 For Blackfoot perspectives, see BGC, *Nitsitapiisini*, p. 10; and Hernandez, *Mokakssini*, p. 259.
8 This is the attitude of an anonymous informant in Hernandez, *Mokakssini*, p. 68, and of Crowe, "Introduction", pp. x–xiii.
9 Jacques Derrida, "What is a "Relevant" Translation?", Trans. by Lawrence Venuti, *Critical Inquiry* 27, 2 (2001): 174–200, esp. p. 179; and Lawrence Venuti, "Introduction" in *idem*, pp. 169–73.
10 Crowe, "Introduction", p. xiii.
11 Nabokov, *A Forest*, 2002, p. 57.
12 Hernandez, *Mokakssini*, pp. v and 53, from her own interviews.
13 Paul Radin, *The Trickster: A Study in American Indian Mythology*, with commentaries by Karl Kerényi and C. G. Jung (New York: Bell Publishing, 1956), p. 118, notes that the Winnebago termed these two sets *waikan* ("a past irretrievably gone") and *worak* ("present workaday world").
14 Mircea Eliade, *Myth and Reality*, rpt. (New York: Harper Colophon Books, [1963] 1975), p. 1.

Notes

15 Hernandez, *Mokakssini*, pp. 36–52, and 44–52 for the function of the Star Stories, although Blackfoot scholar Woody Kipp uses myth without qualification for the same in "Foreword", in Bullchild, *Sun Came Down*, p. vi; see also Wissler and Duvall, *Mythology*, pp. 5–18. For a general perspective on definitions of myth, legend and folktale, including a discussion of Crow narratives that bear similarity to the Blackfoot Stories, see Bascom, "The Forms of Folklore", pp. 4, 9 and 16.
16 Nabokov, *A Forest*, p. 66.
17 BGC, *Nitsitapiisini*, p. 10; and Hernandez, *Mokakssini*, p. 259.
18 Nabokov, *A Forest*, p. 65.
19 M. I. Finley, *The Use and Abuse of History*, rpt. (London: Pimlico, [1975] 2000), pp. 15 and 215, *n.9*, citing I. Meyerson.
20 Walter J. Ong, *Orality and Literacy: The Technologizing of the Word*, rpt. (London: Routledge, [1982] 1991), p. 11.
21 Dell Hymes, *Now I Know Only So Far: Essays in Ethnopoetics* (Lincoln: University of Nebraska Press, 2003), pp. 15–16.
22 Robert H. Lowie, "The Oral Literature of the Crow Indians", *Journal of American Folklore* 72, 284 (1959): 97–104. See also Petrone, *Native Literature in Canada*, pp. 3–8, for a discussion on the changing perspectives regarding Canadian oral literatures. See also William M. Clements, "The Jesuit Foundations of Native North American Literary Studies", *American Indian Quarterly* 18, 1 (1994): 43–59; Rodney Frey, ed., *Stories That Make the World: Oral Literatures of the Indian Peoples of the Inland West, As Told by Lawrence Aripa, Tom Yellowtail, and Other Elders* (Norman: University of Oklahoma Press, 1995); and Andrew Wiget, *Native American Literature* (Boston: G. K. Hall & Co., 1985).
23 Uhlenbeck, *Original Blackfoot Texts*, pp. 50–51.
24 Wissler and Duvall, *Mythology*, p. 61. In GA, M-4376, Duvall, the version of Scarface is narrated by Three Bears. Here the chum, not the sister, asks the chief's daughter to marry Scarface.
25 Oliver La Farge in his foreword to an anthology of California Indian Legends, claims that "The literary value of a great deal of primitive literature, whether myths or tales, is *nil*." See Theodora Kroeber, *The Inland Whale: Nine Stories Retold from California Indian Legends*, rpt. (Berkeley: University of California Press, [1959] 1984), p. 7. For a claim of the devaluation of oral stories, see Brotherston, *Book of the Fourth World*, p. 4.
26 Grinnell, *Lodge Tales*, pp. xix–xx.
27 Wissler and Duvall, *Mythology*, pp. 53–58, use the title "Blood-Clot, or Smoking Star".
28 Nabokov, *A Forest*, p. 65.
29 Bascom, "The Forms of Folklore", p. 4.
30 *Ibid.*, and Nabokov, *A Forest*, p. 66.
31 R. David Edmunds, "Native Americans, New Voices: American Indian History, 1895–1995", *American Historical Review* 100, 3 (1995): 717–40, esp. p. 721.
32 Bascom, "The Forms of Folklore", p. 4.
33 Michael Foucault, *The Order of Things*, rpt. (London: Routledge, 2003), pp. xxi–xxii.

Notes

34 Dell H. Hymes, *"In Vain I Tried to Tell You": Essays in Native American Ethnopoetics* (Lincoln: University of Nebraska Press, 2004), p. 80, notes that "In contemporary transformational generative grammar the term performance treats overt realization, quite likely imperfect, of an underlying knowledge on the part of a speaker"; pp. 79–141 provide perspectives on performance; see also Adam Kendon, *Gesture: Visible Action as Utterance* (Cambridge: Cambridge University Press, 2004).
35 Geertz, *Interpretation of Cultures*, p. 15, claims that by definition "only a 'native' makes first order ones: it's his[/her] culture.) They are, thus, fictions; fictions, in the sense that they are 'something made,' 'something fashioned' — the original meaning of *fictio* — not that they are false, unfactual, or merely 'as if' thought experiments'.
36 Vizenor, *Fugitive Poses*, pp. 63–64.
37 Ibid., pp. 64 and 67.
38 *The Oxford English Dictionary* defines "survivance" as: "The succession to an estate, office, etc. of a survivor nominated before the death of the existing occupier or holder; the right of such succession in case of survival".
39 Vizenor, *Fugitive Poses*, pp. 15 and 23.
40 The writings of Foucault and Barthes provide a good point of departure to view the differences between both types. They both point to a prior time when the author did not occupy a central role. Foucault emphasizes a key moment in the history of ideas, when recounting the lives of heroes was replaced by the recounting of the lives of authors. He locates the Greek epic in the earlier period, when a desire for immortality makes the hero accept death willingly while still young: Michel Foucault, "What is an Author?", trans. by Joseph V. Harari, in David Lodge, ed., *Modern Criticism and Theory: A Reader*, rpt. (London: Longman, [1988] 1994), pp. 197–210, esp. p. 198; and Roland Barthes, "The Death of the Author," in Lodge, ed., *Modern Criticism and Theory*, pp. 166–72, esp. p. 168. Barthes' prior time points to ethnographic societies, where "responsibility for a narrative did not reside on a person, but on a mediator or shaman, who 'performed' rather than 'created' the text".
41 Wissler and Duvall, *Mythology*, p. 5.
42 When White Horse, a Kootenay chief, was killed by a Blood leader called Many Spotted Horses in 1862, the Bloods marked the spot where he fell with an effigy made of stones. Dempsey, *Indians of the Rocky Mountain Parks*, p. 64.
43 Grinnell, *Lodge Tales*, pp. 137–44 ("The Blackfoot Genesis"); and Ewers, *The Blackfeet*, p. 4.
44 Hernandez, *Mokakssini*, p. 8.
45 Grinnell, *Lodge Tales*, p. 249.
46 Raczka, *Winter Count*, p. 13.
47 Nabokov, *A Forest*, p. 160.
48 Raymond D. Fogelson coined the term "epitomizing event": see "On the Varieties of Indian History: Sequoyah and Traveller Bird," *Journal of Ethnic Studies* 2, 1 (1974): 106–7.
49 Linea Sundstrom, "Smallpox Used Them up: References to Epidemic Disease in Northern Plains Winter Counts, 1714–1920", *Ethnohistory* 44, 2 (1997): 305–43, esp. pp. 305–8. Also see ten Lakota winter counts (1701–1902) in

Notes

Smithsonian National Museum of Natural History, "Lakota Winter Counts", available @: http://wintercounts.si.edu/index.html [Accessed 6 Sept. 2010].

50 The Bad Head's Winter Count is in GA, M-4421, R. N. Wilson, Bad Head's Winter Count, 1810–1883. See also Hugh A. Dempsey, *A Blackfoot Winter Count*, Occasional Paper 1, rpt. (Calgary: Glenbow Museum, [1965] 1988).

51 GA, M-8188, Arthur Family, Bull Plume's Winter Count; and Raczka, *Winter Count*.

52 Raczka, *Winter Count*, pp. 13–16; McClintock, *Old North Trail*, pp. 418–22; Moore, *Native Americans*, pp. 218–19, and 251. Mehkskéhme-Sukáhs greeted the 60-foot keelboat *Flora* on its arrival at Fort McKenzie, the westernmost outpost of the Missouri Fur Trade, nearly 3,000 river miles from St. Louis, carrying Prince Maximilian and Karl Bodmer.

53 McClintock, *Old North Trail*, p. 57. Grinnell, *Lodge Tales*, p. 225 cites a Pikani band called "Fat Roasters", which may be another translation for the same band. See Uhlenbeck, *Original Blackfoot Texts*, p. 1, for an explanation of the name.

54 McClintock, *Old North Trail*, p. 387, photographed Bull Plume while he was leading a Medicine Pipe ceremony. Raczka, *Winter Count*, pp. 13–16. Bull Plume is referred to as a minor chief.

55 *Ibid.*, pp. 384–85 and 414–16.

56 *Ibid.*, p. 417.

57 Raczka, *Winter Count*, pp. 4–5.

58 Grinnell, *Lodge Tales*, p. 249.

59 Alvin M. Josephy, Jr., *500 Nations: An Illustrated History of North American Indians*, rpt. (New York: Gramercy Books, 2002), p. 363.

60 Hugh A. Dempsey, "Introduction", in H. Dempsey, ed., Mike Mountain Horse, *My People The Bloods*, pp. v–xi. It has already been mentioned in an earlier chapter that the Blackfoot considered the obtaining of guns as a great deed: GA, M-8458-15, Richardson's Research, Agwmaxkayi.

61 Larson, "Introduction", p. ix.

62 Mountain Horse, *My People The Bloods*, pp. 59–65.

63 Larson, "Introduction", p. ix.

64 Mountain Horse, *My People The Bloods*, p. 106.

65 GA 8458-8, Richardson's Interview, Crooked Meat Strings: "supernatural ill" would befall those who do not tell "the gospel truth"; and Grinnell, *Lodge Tales*, p. 249.

66 Taylor, *Standing Alone*, p. 168.

67 James Dempsey, *Blackfoot War Art*, pp. 25 and 39.

68 Referring to the Mandans, with whom the Blackfoot maintained trade before the arrival of whites, Moore, *Native Americans*, p. 223, observes that "the production of Indian art was divided among gender lines; women produced geometric patterns in porcupine quills and beadwork to decorate clothing [. . .] while men represented their exploits in pictographs made in paints derived from clay, minerals and charcoal, as well as pigments obtained through trade with Euro-Americans."

69 Nabokov, *A Forest*, p. 160.

70 Schultz, *Blackfeet and Buffalo*, pp. 264–70.

71 Grinnell, *Lodge Tales*, p. 249.

Notes

72 Moore, *Native Americans*, p. 249.
73 See for example McClintock, *Old North Trail*, p. 418.
74 Nabokov, *A Forest*, pp. 5–6.
75 According to Foucault, *Power/Knowledge*, p. 131, "truth isn't outside power, or lacking in power [. . .] truth is a thing of this world: it is produced only by virtue of multiple forms of constraint. And it induces regular effects of power. Each society has its régime of truth, its 'general politics' of truth: that is, the types of discourse which it accepts and makes function as true; the mechanisms and instances which enable one to distinguish true and false statements, the means by which each is sanctioned; the techniques accorded value in the acquisition of truth; the status of those who are charged with saying what counts as true."
76 Bullchild, *Sun Came Down*, p. 337. A young man would climb a mountain and fast and pray for four days and night in the hope of receiving a vision from a protective spirit through which power can be received.
77 GA, M-4376-1, David C. Duvall, pp. 619, 644, and 649.
78 Grinnell, *Lodge Tales*, pp. xxx–xxxi.
79 *Ibid.*, p. 256. European names are hardly used by Blackfoot of this era, unless they are of mixed ancestry.
80 Schultz, *Blackfeet and Buffalo*, pp. 70, 91 and 290; and his *Blackfeet Tales*, pp. 1–6. Monroe was sent by the Hudson's Bay Company to winter with the Pikani in 1815 and 1816, in order to learn their language; he served the pioneer Jesuit, Father Lacombe, as a guide.
81 Grinnell, *Lodge Tales*, p. xxviii.
82 Smith, *Reimagining Indians*, p. 68.
83 Grinnell, *Lodge Tales*, p. xxvii.
84 See Clifford and Marcus, eds., *Writing Culture*.
85 Luke Eric Lassiter, "Authoritative Texts, Collaborative Ethnography and Native American Studies," *American Indian Quarterly* 24, 4 (2000): 601–14.
86 GA, M-8458-5, Richardson's Interview, Many Guns, for the motivations of the keepers of the Many Guns Winter Count, discussed later in this chapter.
87 Ong, *Orality and Literacy*, p. 6.
88 On early ethnological endeavours in The Americas, see Anthony Pagden, *The Fall of Natural Man: The American Indian and the Origins of Comparative Ethnology* (Cambridge: Cambridge University Press, 1982).
89 According to Bullchild, *Sun Came Down*, p. 335, Sweet Grass Hills — a small mountain range that runs West to East in north-central Montana — is a mistranslation for the Pikuni name for "Sweet Pine Mountains," which Independent Scholar Mary Scriver notes is "katoyísix" (plural for sweet pines) or "balsam fir." Scriver points out that the sweetness is from coumadin, known to be a blood thinner. She notes that McClintock's translation was "katoya" or "abies lasiocarpa." Available @: http://prairiemary.blogspot.com/2005/06/sam-worm-man-in-sweet-grass-hills.html [Accessed 6 Sept. 2010].
90 Ong, *Orality and Literacy*, p. 9.
91 María Lucía G. Pallares-Burke, *The New History* (Cambridge: Polity Press, 2002), interview with Jack Goody, p. 23.
92 Wissler and Duvall, *Mythology*, p. 6.

Notes

93 GA, M-4738, George H. Gooderham, excerpt.
94 Hanks and Richardson Hanks, *Tribe Under Trust*, p. xv.
95 Morris, *Treaties of Canada*, p. 269. Despite this provision, many Blackfoot resisted sending their children to school because they feared they would become like white people.
96 Ewers, *The Blackfeet*, pp. 290–96.
97 Schultz, *Blackfeet and Buffalo*, pp. 84–85; Grinnell, *Lodge Tales*, p. 292; and Smith, *Reimagining Indians*, p. 59.
98 Harris, *Preserving a Vision*, pp. 420–22, citing Grinnell, "He Ought to be Removed", *New York Times*, 4 March 1889, 2, col. 3; and 426–27 about being made an honorary chief.
99 McClintock, *Old North Trail*, pp. 51, and 70–71.
100 Ibid., pp. 26–27.
101 Smith, *Reimagining Indians*, p. 72.
102 Taylor, *Standing Alone*, pp. 223–24.
103 This winter count is reproduced in Colin G. Calloway, ed., *Our Hearts Fell to the Ground: Plains Indian Views of How the West was Lost* (Boston: Bedford Books, 1996), pp. 105–10.
104 GA, M-8078 [Old Series] F300/35, Lucien Hanks and Jane Richardson Hanks, Many Guns' Winter Count.
105 James Westfall Thompson and Bernard J. Holm, *A History of Historical Writing: From the Earliest Times to the End of the Seventeenth Century*, rpt. (Gloucester, MA: Peter Smith, [1942] 1967), p. 158.
106 Rachel Ermineskin and Darin Howe, "On Blackfoot Syllabics and the Law o Finals", Paper presented at the 37th Algonquian Conference, Ottawa, 22 October 2005. Available @: http://www.ucalgary.ca/dflynn/files/dflynn/ErmineskinHowe2005.pdf [Accessed 6 Sept. 2010]. Ermineskin and Howe note that the Blackfoot Syllabary was designed "ca. 1890 by Anglican missionaries John William Tims and Harry W. Gibbon Stocken, and unknown Blackfoot [. . .] Tim's main interpreter/teacher was a certain Paul Bird".
107 GA, M8458-5, Richardson's Interview, Many Guns".
108 E. P. Thompson, *The Making of the English Working Class* (London: Penguin Books, 1965), pp. 12–13.
109 See Carr, *What is History?*, esp. Richard J. Evans, "Introduction", pp. ix–xlvi.
110 Petrone, *Native Literature in Canada*, p. 109, notes that although completed by 1936, this volume was not published until 1979.

Part IV The Oral Tradition in Contemporary Native Literature
9 Hero Quests, Sun Dancing, and the Story of "Scarface"

1 Scarface is also Star Boy or Jupiter. There are many variations of the name, including Paii, Poïa, Poakskii, Aksskii and Payoa, Boh-yi-yi or Welt on Face. See McClintock, *The Old North Trail*, p. 491; Hernandez, *Mokakssini*, p. 8; and Bullchild, *Sun Came Down*, p. 344.
2 Weasel Traveller, *Shining Trail*, 1990, pp. 31–33 and 35–37.
3 Hernandez, *Mokakssini*, p. v, uses Spumatapiiwa or "Sky People".
4 BGC, *Nitsitapiisini*, p. 9; and Bastien, *Blackfoot Ways of Knowing*, p. 11.

Notes

5   Bastien, *Blackfoot Ways of Knowing*, p. 11.
6   Thomas King, ed., *All My Relations: An Anthology of Contemporary Canadian Native Fiction*, Toronto: McClelland & Stewart, 1990, p. ix. See also storyteller and author of Abenaki, English and Slovak ancestry, Joseph Bruchac, "All Are My Relations: Native People and Animals," in *Native American Animal Stories Told by Joseph Bruchac*, rpt. (Golden, Colorado: Fulcrum Publishing, 1992), pp. xiii–xvi.
7   King, *All My Relations*, p. ix.
8   Woody Kipp, "Foreword", p. ix.
9   Hernandez, *Mokakssini*, pp. 94–115.
10 Conaty, "Economic Models", p. 403.
11 Kipp, "Foreword," p. viii. Compassion in *The Oxford English Dictionary* is "The feeling or emotion, when a person is moved by the suffering or distress of another, and by the desire to relieve it; pity that inclines one to spare or to succour. Thus 'to have' or 'to take' pity is 'to feel or show pity; to be merciful or compassionate.'" Lakota ceremonialist Black Elk, through Joseph Epes Brown, "Hanblecheyapi: Crying for a Vision," in Dennis Tedlock and Barbara Tedlock, eds, *Teachings from the American Earth: Indian Religion and Philosophy* (New York: Liveright, 1975), pp. 20–41, esp. pp. 20–21, utilizes "lamenter" to describe a vision seeker. He notes that "lamenting" is a very important way of praying and is "at the center of [Lakota] religion, for from it [the Lakota] have received many good things".
12 Bastien, *Blackfoot Ways of Knowing*, pp. 1–2.
13 Hernandez, *Mokakssini*, p. 2; and BGC, *Nitsitapiisini*, p. 8.
14 *The Oxford English Dictionary* defines ætiological as "assigning or tending to assign a cause or reason.
15 McClintock, *The Old North Trail*, pp. 491–505 and 523–24. McClintock notes that Morning Star is Venus and Star Boy, who became Scarface, is Jupiter. After he died, Scarface became known among the Blackfoot as Pokso-piks-o-aks or Paxtsópisòaxs (Mistake Morning Star).
16 Schultz, *Blackfeet and Buffalo*, including "The Story of Scarface" (pp. 338–44), and "The Tobacco Food Planters" (pp. 344–47). Sikochkeka (Chewing Black Bone) was a venerable Pikuni "Grandfather", and an excellent storyteller. He was a grandson of Lame Bull, the Pikuni leader who signed the first treaty between the Blackfoot and the United States in 1855.
17 Grinnell, *Lodge Tales*, pp. 93–103. In his introduction, Grinnell thanks Miss Ross, p. xxx.
18 Wissler and Duvall, *Mythology*, pp. 58–65.
19 Uhlenbeck, *Original Blackfoot Texts*, pp. 50–57.
20 Hernandez, *Mokakssini*, pp. 86–89; Bullchild, *Sun Came Down*, pp. 328–86; GA, M-4422, R. N. Wilson, "The Blackfoot Legend of Scarface" (Wilson translates Scarface as *Uk-ske*, "a scar on the face"); and GA, M-4376, David C. Duvall, "Scarface".
21 McClintock, *The Old North Trail*, pp. 491–92. The "dog days" came to an end when horses replaced dogs as beasts of burden during "the very first years" of the eighteenth century: Grinnell, *Lodge Tales*, pp. 177 and 186.
22 In Schultz, *Blackfeet and Buffalo*, p. 339, he has parents. According to Bullchild, *Sun Came Down*, p. 331, "an old lady," who was his grandmother, raised Scarface.

Notes

23 Grinnell, *Lodge Tales*, pp. 93–95; Bullchild, *Sun Came Down*, pp. 329–31.

24 Grinnell, *Lodge Tales*, p. 93.

25 Kehoe, "Blackfoot Persons", p. 124.

26 Elk Woman, a role model for Blackfoot women, proved her strength to be superior to that of her husband, who had accused her of not being chaste.

27 Grinnell, *Lodge Tales*, pp. 95–96. In McClintock, *The Old North Trail*, p. 497, "an old medicine woman" helps Scarface.

28 Hernandez, *Mokakssini*, pp. 86–89. Mike Swims Under explains that the "Old Lady" asked Scarface to wait for her husband, who gives him directions. Her husband is Napi, Old Man, who is the same as the Sun. In other stories, Napi and the Sun are represented as different beings. For example, in "The Theft From The Sun", Old Man (the Blackfoot creator and trickster also known as Na'pi) tries to steal Sun's leggings. During the night he steals away from Sun's lodge, but each morning he finds himself back inside Sun's lodge. According to Grinnell, *Lodge Tales*, pp. 167–68, Old Man didn't know that "the whole world is the Sun's lodge."

29 Grinnell, *Lodge Tales*, pp. 96–97. This cycle relates to the sacredness with which the Blackfoot view the four directions, North, South, East, and West. The two versions in Wissler and Duvall, *Mythology*, pp. 61–66, differ greatly in this section, but the Piegan Man's version contains more fourfold cycles. In Schultz's *Blackfeet and Buffalo*, p. 341, Wolverine, "Chief Lynx, Chief Elk, Chief Buffalo, and other four-footed chiefs" cannot help, but Chief Badger tells Scarface where to find the Sun. "Chief" in this case, is probably a literal translation pointing to the power of these sacred helpers.

30 According to Hymes, *Now I Know Only So Far*, pp. 17–19, in the late nineteenth century Boas argued that rhythmic repetition was a formal aspect fundamental to the stories of many First Nations.

31 Among the Blackfoot there are myriad references to four being a sacred number. For example, in a Blackfoot story, when Napi first created "a woman and a child [. . .] her son," out of clay, he kept them covered, and each morning during four consecutive days he would uncover and inspect them. On the fourth morning "he told them to rise and walk; and they did so": Moreover, up until the early reserve era, the Blackfoot camp moved four times before Ookaan could begin: Grinnell, *Lodge Tales*, pp. 138 and 263–6.

32 Wissler and Duvall, *Mythology*, pp. 61–66.

33 See Grinnell, *Lodge Tales*, p. 141.

34 In Natosi Nepe-e's version in McClintock, *The Old North Trail*, p. 497, Morning Star, or a "bright trail leading across the water", possibly related to the former, guides Scarface. In Uhlenbeck, *Original Blackfoot Texts*, p. 52, Scarface hides from the heat of the Sun, when morning comes, Morning Star assists him.

35 The attackers are variously described as "angry birds" (Schultz, *Blackfeet and Buffalo*, p. 340); "seven enormous birds" (McClintock, *The Old North Trail*, p. 498); "seven geese" (the Piegan Man's version in Wissler and Duvall, *Mythology*, p. 63); and four cranes (Uhlenbeck, *Original Blackfoot Texts*, p. 53).

36 Grinnell, *Lodge Tales*, pp. 189–90.

37 *Tak.a*, or *itakkaa*, is usually translated as "partner", it refers to a special rela-

tionship between two males of the same age, who go to war and undertake other activities together, including joining age societies.
38 Scarface is also known as Poks-o-piks-o-aks or Mistake Morning Star: McClintock, *The Old North Trail*, p. 499.
39 Grinnell, *Lodge Tales*, p. 101; and Uhlenbeck, *Original Blackfoot Texts*, p. 55.
40 According to the story of "The Woman Who Married a Star," the digging stick was used by So-at-sa-ki, the Morning Star's wife and Scarface's mother, to dig a sacred turnip. She had been forbidden to do so. When she saw the camps of her people through the hole left by the turnip, she became homesick and returned to join them: McClintock, *The Old North Trail*, pp. 494–96.
41 Schultz, *Blackfeet and Buffalo*, p. 343; Wissler and Duval, *Mythology*, p. 64; Grinnell, *Lodge Tales*, p. 102.
42 Wissler and Duvall, *Mythology*, p. 65.
43 Uhlenbeck, *Original Blackfoot Texts*, p. 57.
44 Hernandez, *Mokakssini*, p. 6; and BGC, *Nitsitapiisini*, p. 9.
45 Hernandez, *Mokakssini*, pp. 77 and 83.

10 The Blackfoot Hero in James Welch's *Fools Crow*

1 Welch, *Fools Crow*. Welsh was born on the Blackfeet Reservation in Montana. One grandmother was Pikani and the other was Gros Ventre (also At-séna, Atsina, or Entrails People). The Gros Ventre were allies of the Blackfoot, but became their enemies c.1862: Grinnell, *Lodge Tales*, p. 244.
2 Dempsey, *Crowfoot*, pp. 59–60.
3 Mary Jane Lupton, *James Welch: A Critical Companion*, in Kathleen Gregory Klein, ed., Critical Companion to Popular Contemporary Writers Series (Westport, CT: Greenwood Press, 2004), p. 84.
4 Schultz, *Blackfeet and Buffalo*, pp. 282–305. One of Welch's Pikuni great-grandmothers was a survivor of the massacre, while Malcolm Clarke, the settler whose murder by a Pikuni precipitated the massacre, was also his relative. His mother was a Gros Ventre, and his father was a Blackfeet (Pikuni). However, he had two Irish grandfathers who had married Native women. He considered himself an Indian. Lupton, *James Welch*, pp. 2–4.
5 Louis Owens, *Other Destinies: Understanding the American Indian Novel* (Norman and London: University of Oklahoma Press, 1992), p. 157.
6 Grinnell, *Lodge Tales*, pp. 208–10.
7 Lupton, *James Welch*, p. 88.
8 McClintock, *Old North Trail*, p. 322. According to Grinnell, *Lodge Tales*, pp. 190–91, a father would encourage his daughter to live a worthy life by pointing to the Medicine Woman during Ookaan as an example of virtue.
9 Owens, *Other Destinies*, p. 157.
10 See for example Nora Barry, "'A Myth to Be Alive': James Welch's Fools Crow", *MELUS* 17, 1 (1991–2): 3–20; and Lupton, *James Welch*, wherein Lupton paraphrases the previous essay by Barry.
11 Bette S. Weidman, "Closure in James Welch's *Fools Crow*," *Studies in American Indian Literatures* 18, 3 (2006): 90–97, esp. p. 93. Weidman's

appraisal of other critics on *Fools Crow* provides a useful context to view the novel from different perspectives.

12 Owens, *Other Destinies*, p. 166. Welch cited on p. 157.
13 The name Mika'pi — Red Old Man, is the title of a Blackfoot Story in George Bird Grinnell, *Blackfeet Indian Stories*, rpt (New York: Riverbend Publishing, [1913] 2005), pp. 78–87.
14 See Thomas E. Mails, *Fools Crow: Wisdom & Power* (Tulsa, OK: Council Oaks Books, 1991); Mails, *Sundancing*, p. 8.
15 Owens, *Other Destinies,* p. 165.
16 The Lone Eaters is one of twenty-four Pikani bands listed in Grinnell, *Lodge Tales*, pp. 208–10.
17 Displays of courage have, among other purposes, to show the superiority of Pikuni warriors in order to demoralize their enemies.
18 King, *All My Relations*, p. xi.
19 Lupton, *James Welch*, p. 4, only mentions Grinnell, McClintock and Wissler and Duvall. However, the testimony of the massacre appears in Schultz, *Blackfeet and Buffalo*, pp. 282–305.
20 Grinnell, *Lodge Tales*, p. 101.
21 Lupton, *James Welch*, p. 86.
22 Grinnell, *Lodge Tales*, p. 289.
23 *Ibid.*, p. xxiii.
24 Owens, *Other Destinies*, p. 164.
25 McClintock, *Old North Trail*, p. 408.
26 The opening of this Bundle usually took place in spring, during April or May. Ewers, *The Blackfeet*, p. 89.

11 Ethics in Emma Lee Warrior's *Compatriots*

1 Renate Eigenbrod, "'Stranger and Stranger': The (German) Other in Canadian Indigenous Texts", in Colin G. Calloway *et al.*, *Germans and Indians: Fantasies, Encounters, Projections* (Lincoln: University of Nebraska Press, 2002), pp. 259–86, esp. p. 275.
2 In urban legend the name has been humorously bestowed to ridicule, for example, President George W. Bush See http://urbanlegends.about.com/library/bl_walking_eagle.htm [Accessed 20 May 2010].
3 Ann McKinnon, "Morality Destabilised: Reading Emma Lee Warrior's 'Compatriots'", *Studies in American Literatures* 10, 4 (1998): 53-66, esp. p. 65, *n*.1.
4 Eigenbrod, "'Stranger and Stranger'", p. 276, who cites from Hartmut Lutz.
5 For a short biography of Beverly Hungry Wolf, see the University of Minnesota, "Voices from the Gaps", available @: http://voices.cla.umn.edu/artistpages/hungrywolfbeverly.php [Accessed 7 Sept. 2010]. Among the many books by Beverly Hungry Wolf are the already cited *Ways of My Grandmothers*, and *Daughters of the Buffalo Women*. Adolf Hungry Wolf's publications include: *Traditional Dress: Knowledge and Methods of Old-Time Clothing* (Skookumchuck, BC: Good Medicine Books, 1990); *The Blood People: A Division of the Blackfoot Confederacy: An Illustrated Interpretation of the Old Ways* (New York: Harper & Row, 1977); books co-

Notes

authored with Beverly Hungry Wolf include: *Children of the Sun: Stories by and about Indian Kids* (New York: Quill William Morrow, 1987); and their jointly edited *Indian Tribes of the Northern Rockies* (Summertown, TN: Native Voices, 1989).
6   Hungry Wolf, *Ways of My Grandmothers*, p. 8.
7   See, for example Thedis Crowe, "Introduction", *Lodge Tales*.
8   Eigenbrod, "Stranger and Stranger", p. 276.
9   See Eigenbrod and Fachinger cited earlier.
10 Hungry Wolf, *Ways of My Grandmothers*, p. 32.

Conclusion

1   Jack Goody, *The Theft of History* (Cambridge: Cambridge University Press, 2006), p. 1. Goody, an Asianist and Africanist anthropologist, who writes widely on comparative world history, refers to "the take-over of history by the west. That is, the past is conceptualized and presented according to what happened on the provincial scale of Europe, often western Europe, and then imposed upon the rest of the world."

Select Biblography

UNPUBLISHED PRIMARY SOURCES

Bancroft Library
Indian Rights Association, Actions of Congress, 12 Dec. 1884.

Glenbow Archives
Arthur Family
M-8188, Bull Plume's Winter Count.

Blackfoot Indian Agency
M-1817, Notes from Blackfoot Agency Letter Books.

Canada, Department of Indian Affairs
M-1785-15, Blackfoot Indian Agency, General Instructions to Indian Agents in Canada.

David C. Duvall's Blackfoot Research
M-4376, Blackfoot Research, pp. 1–1256:
When Men Torture Themselves in the Sun Dance — Interview with Big Bravo, 22 April 1911.
Sun Dance.
Scarface.
Dress and Ceremonies.

John C. Ewers
M-9141-8c, John Ewers' Blood field notes.

George H. Gooderham
M-4738-31-2, Indian Agent correspondence and reports 1920–1928, Royal Canadian Mounted Police, K Division, Lethbridge, Calgary Sub-District, Gleichen Detachment, Corpl. E. E. Harper's Report, 25 July 1921.
Series 6, Articles Written by Gooderham:
M-4738-213-6, 'Black Fever' — Blackfoot Indian, December 1955.
M-4738-217-6, Lord Burnham and Chief Yellowhorse, December 1955.
M-4738-227-6, The Making of a Brave, c.1955–56.
M-4738-255-6, Biography, Joe Calfchild, Blackfoot, 1875–1942.
M-4738-259-6, Weasel Calf and His Favourite Wife, April 1956.
M-4738-260-6, Articles Written by Gooderham, The Indian Waltz [1921], April 1956.

Select Bibliography

M-4738-372-6, Articles Written by Gooderham, Indian Religious Rituals, 16 May 1973.

Lucien Hanks and Jane Richardson Hanks
M-8078 [Old Series], F300/35, Many Guns' Winter Count.
M-8458 [Old Series], Interview with Old Bull, 26 July 1937.
M-8458 [Old Series], Crooked Meat Strings via Mary White Elk.
M-8458 [Old Series], Interview with Imiten.a (Crooked Meat Strings)

Jane Richardson's Blackfoot (Siksika) Research
M-8458-1, Chronological Story of Our Arrival and of the Sundance Events, 28 June–7 July 1938.
M-8458-3, Interview with Pitoxpikis (Sleigh), 24 August 1938.
M-8458-4, Interview with Pitoxpikis (Sleigh), 25 and 30 August 1938.
M-8458-5, Interview with Many Guns, August 1938.
M-8458-8, Interview with Crooked Meat Strings, 1938.
M-8458-14, History of the Skunk Band, 1938.
M-8458-15, Agwmaxkayi (Many Swans), 1938.
M-8458-17, Life in Crowfoot's Camp, c.1870–1877.
M-8458-18, Husband and Wife Relations and Horn Society, 1938.
M-8458-19, Medicine and Curing Power, 1938.

Lucien Hanks' Blackfoot (Siksika) Research
M-8458-31, Typed notes and interviews.

Joe Little Chief
M-4394, Joe Little Chief's Winter Count, 1830–1913.
M-4394-18, Joe Little Chief's Stories: From 1830 the Year Crowfoot was Born.
M-4394-19, Joe Little Chief's Stories: From 1880 the Year the Blackfoot Moved South.

Houghton Running Rabbit
M-4233 and M-2787, Houghton Running Rabbit's Winter Count, 1830–1937.

Claude E. Schaeffer
M-1100-127, Big Brave's Winter Count.

Archdeacon J. W. Tims Family
M-1234-7, Archdeacon Tims General Correspondence 1885–1953, John W. House to the Archdeacon, 19 June 1939.

R. N. Wilson
M-4421, Bad Head's Winter Count, 1810–1883.
M-4422, The Blackfoot Legend of Scarface.

Teddy Yellow Fly
M-4423, Teddy Yellow Fly's Winter Count, 1831–1877.

Select Bibliography

Library and Archives Canada, Dominion of Canada
Annual Reports of The Department of Indian Affairs 1864–1990.
Available online at: http://www.collectionscanada.ca/indianaffairs/

Public Archives Canada, Public Records Division, RG 10 Indian Affairs
Vol. 3825, f. 60511, F. C. Cornish to Indian Commissioner, Regina, 13 August 1889.
Vol. 3825, f. 60,511-1:
Hayter Reed, Telegram 12 June 1893.
Hayter Reed to Deputy Supt. General, 17 August 1889.
Reed to C. C. Chipman, Hudson's Bay Company, Winnipeg, 9 July 1895.
F. H. Paget to Indian Agent, Birtle, 9 June 1896.
Hayter Reed, Commissioner North-West Territories to Deputy Supt. General, 17 August 1889.
Commissioner, Regina to Blackfoot Agent, 3 June 1897.
Vol. 3826, f. 60511-4-1, Asst. Deputy and Secretary, J. D. McLean to Chief Inspector, Winnipeg 8 August 1913.
Vol. 3826, f. 60511-3:
Hugonnard to Secretary, 20 November 1913.
W. J. Dilworth, Blood Agency to J. D. McLean, Assistant Deputy and Secretary, 10 March 1914.
J. D. McLean, Assistant Deputy and Secretary to W. J. Dilworth, Blood Agency, 23 March 1914.
Principal of Indian Industrial School Qu'Appelle, Sask., 6 May 1914.
Asst. Deputy and Secretary, 17 June 1914.
General Manager, Brewster Transport Co, Ltd to Mr. J. Waddy, Indian Agent, Morley, 1 July 1914.
Extract from report from Blood Agent, 2 July 1914.
Bull Plume to Department of Indian Affairs, Ottawa, 11 February 1915.
J. A. Markle, Inspector, Crowfoot Boarding School, 14 February 1916.
J. D. McLean to Reverend Ross, 15 March 1917.
Blood Agent, 2 February 1917.
Vol. 3826, f. 60511-4-1:
J. D. Dilworth, Blood Agent to J. D. McLean, 2 February 1917.
J. D. McLean, Assistant Deputy and Secretary, 2 June 1917.
H. A. Gunn, Indian Agent, Brocket Alberta to Secretary, Ottawa, 14 June 1917.
Vol. 3826, f. 60,511-4A:
James McDonald, Griswold Agent to Assistant Deputy and Secretary, 14 February 1918.
Asst. Deputy and Secretary, 4 October 1918.
W. M. Graham to D. C. Scott, Deputy Supt. General, July 1920.
Vol. 3826, f. 60,511-4A, Chief Shot in Both Sides to Commissioner, 24 June 1921.
Vol. 3876, f. 91749, Commissioner North-West Territories to Superintendent General, 21 June 1892.

Select Bibliography

Public Archives Canada, Public Records Division, RG 18, North-West Mounted Police (NWMP)
Vol. 35, f. 479, Blood Agent to Commissioner Regina, 17 May 1889.
Series A-1, Vol. 36, f. 817-89, Department of Justice, Ottawa, 31 October 1889.
Vol. 51, f. 313-1891, Report NWMP Fort Macleod, 9 April 1891.
Vol. 1354, 75-1895-3, Correspondence re Blood Sun Dance, 1893.
Vol. 1354, 76-1896-3, Correspondence re Blood Sun Dance, 1895.
Supt. Commanding E Division, Calgary to Commissioner, Regina, 22 May 1896.
Vol. 112, f. 665, S. B. Steele, Supt. to Commissioner, 5 October 1895.
Commissioner to Commissioner, Regina, 9 July 1896.
Vol. 137, S. B. Steele, Supt. to Commissioner NWMP, Regina, 7 May 1897.
Vol. 205, f. 136-01:
Arthur B. Owen, St. Paul's Mission [Blood Reserve], to Major Howe, Commander of the Police Force, Macleod, 24 October 1901.
Supt. Joseph Howe, Commander of the Police Force, Macleod to Commissioner, Regina, 30 October 1901.
Correspondence re Blood Sun Dance, 28 February 1902.
Corpl. B. H. Robertson's Report 28 July 1902.
Vol. 302, f. 658-05, Supt. P. C. H. Primrose, Commanding D Division to Commissioner, Regina, 5 August 1905.
Vol. 458, f. 79-14, Correspondence on rationing of Indians on the Blood Reserve, 1914.
Vol. 3290, f. HQ-1034-K-1:
RCMP, K Division, Lethbridge, Corpl. E. E. Harper's Report, 25 July 1921.
RCMP, K Division, Lethbridge, Inspector J. W. Spalding's Report 27 July 1921.

Medicine Springs Library
U.S. House of Representatives, *Piegan Indians*, 41 Cong., 2 sess. House Executive Document 269, 1–74.

Montana Historical Society
Bradley Manuscript

Montana State University, Bozeman
Merrill G. Burlingame Special Collections

Historical Report Regarding Lands Ceded to the United States Government by the Blackfeet and Gros Ventre Tribes of Indians, Residing upon the Blackfeet and Fort Belknap Reservations in the State of Montana, in the Agreement of May 1, 1888.

Provincial Archives of Alberta
Oblate fonds
84.400/1193, Emile Legal, *Cantes pied-noirs, 2 janvier* 1885; *suivis de clans et chefs Pied-Noirs et degrés d'initiation Indienne.*
84.400/1195, Emile Legal, *Notes sur la fête du soleil.*

Select Bibliography

84.400/1197, Emile Legal, *Legendes du Pieds-Noirs*, s.d.
71.220/6852, Jean Lessard, *La Religion naturelle chez les Indiennes du Canada*.
71.220/6739, *Jules Lechevallier, Un Conte ou Legende Pied Noir*. Dec. 1922.
71.220/6400, Leon Doucet, *Notes diverses sur les missions et les Amerindiens du Sud d l'Alberta*.

R.N. Wilson
84.28/15, Our Betrayed Wards: A story of 'Chicanery, Infidelity and the Prostitution of Trust'. Indians of the Prairie Provinces (Indian Affairs Branch) (32 pages).

Prelinger Library, San Francisco, CA
United States, Office of Indian Affairs, *Annual Reports of the U.S. Commissioner of Indian Affairs*. Available from Internet Archive online @ http://www.archive.org/index.php

PUBLISHED PRIMARY SOURCES

Bradley, James H. 1917 and 1923: *The Bradley Manuscript*. Montana Historical Society Contributions, Vols 8–9. Helena: Montana Historical Society.
Burpee, Lawrence J. (ed.) 1907: *York Factory to the Blackfoot Country: The Journals of Anthony Hendry [Henday], 1754–1755*. Proceedings and Transactions of the Royal Society of Canada, 3rd Series, Vol. 1.
Catlin, George 1841: *Letters and Notes on the Manners, Customs, and Conditions of North American Indians*. Minneapolis: Ross and Haines, Inc.
Chambers, James H. 1940: *Original Journal of James H. Chambers*. In Anne McDonnell (ed.), Contributions to the Historical Society of Montana 10, pp. 106–7.
Chateaubriand, 1847: *Viages de Chateaubriand, en América, Italia y Suiza*. Madrid: Establecimiento Tipográfico de D. F. de P. Mellado.
Chittenden, Hiram Martin and Richardson, Alfred Talbot [1905] 1969: *Life, Letters and Travels of Father Pierre-Jean De Smet, S. J., 1801–1873*, 4 Vols, Vols 1 & 2, New York: Kraus.
Commissioners of the Royal North-West Mounted Police, The, 1973 facsimile of Ottawa: Queen Printer, 1888–1889: *The New West: Being the Official Reports to Parliament of the Activities of the Royal North-West Mounted Police Force From 1888–1889*. Toronto: Coles Publishing Co.
Coues, Elliott [1897] 1965: *New Light on the Early History of the Greater Northwest: The Manuscript Journals of Alexander Henry and David Thompson 1799–1814*. Minneapolis: Ross & Haines Inc.
Denny, Sir Cecil E. 1939: *The Law Marches West*, W. B. Cameron (ed.), Toronto: J. M. Dent and Sons (Canada) Ltd.
Duvall, David C. and Wissler, Clark [1908] 1995: *Mythology of the Blackfoot Indians*. Lincoln: Bison Books.
Ege, Robert J. 1970: *Tell Baker to Strike Them Hard: Incident on the Marias, 23 Jan. 1870*. Fort Collins: The Old Army Press.
Eggermont-Molenaar, Mary 2005: Preface and Acknowledgments; Mrs.

Select Bibliography

Uhlenbeck: An Informed Diarist?; Collage of Blackfoot Texts Recorded by C. C. Uhlenbeck. In Eggermont-Molenaar (ed. and trans.), *Montana 1911: A Professor and his Wife Among the Blackfeet*, Lincoln and Calgary: University of Nebraska/University of Calgary Press, pp. ix–xii, 17–27 and 203–346.

French, Laurence Armand 1995: Adaptations of Aboriginal Justice in the United States. *Journal of Human Justice* 6 (2): 72–78.

Grinnell, George Bird [1892] 2003: *Blackfoot Lodge Tales: The Story of a Prairie People*. Lincoln: University of Nebraska Press.

Hanks, Lucien M. and Richardson, Jane [1945] 1966: *Observations on Northern Blackfoot Kinship*. Monographs of the American Ethnological Society, Irving Hallowell (ed.), Seattle: University of Washington Press.

Henday, Anthony A. [1748–1755] 2000: *A Year Inland: The Journal of a Hudson's Bay Company Winterer*, Barbara Belyea (ed.), Waterloo, ON: Wilfrid Laurier University Press.

Henry The Younger, Alexander, see Elliot Coues.

Kelsey, Henry 1929: *The Kelsey Papers*, A. G. Doughty and C. Martin (eds), Ottawa: Public Archives of Canada and Public Records Office in Northern Ireland.

Lewis, Oscar 1942: *The Effects of White Contact upon Blackfoot Culture, with Special Reference to the Role of the Fur Trade*. In Monographs of the American Ethnological Society 6, Seattle: University of Washington Press.

——. 1941: Manly-Hearted Women among the North Piegan. *American Anthropologist* 43 (2): 173–87.

Lamb, W. Kaye (ed.) 1970: *The Journals and Letters of Sir Alexander Mackenzie*, Cambridge: Hakluyt Society at the University Press.

McClintock, Walter 2005: *Lanterns of the Prairie: The Blackfoot Photographs of Walter McClintock*, ed. S. L. Grafe, Norman: University of Oklahoma Press.

——. [1910] 1992: *The Old North Trail or Life, Legends and Religion of the Blackfeet Indians*. Lincoln: Bison Books.

Mackenzie, Sir Alexander, see W. Kaye Lamb

Maclean, John 1918: *Vanguards of Canada*. Toronto: The Missionary Society of the Methodist Church.

M'Lean [Maclean], John 1889: *The Blackfoot Sun Dance*, Proceedings of the Canadian Institute 151, Toronto: Copp, Clark Co.

——. 1889: *The Indians of Canada: Their Manners and Customs*. Toronto: W. Briggs, 1889.

Maximilian, Prince of Wied, [1832–34] 2001: *Travels in the Interior of North America during the years 1832–1834*, illustrated by Karl Bodmer, Malcolm Green, trans. [from *Reise in das innere Nord-Amerika in den Jahren 1832–1834*, Coblens, 1839], Köln and London: Taschen.

Middleton, Samuel Henry [1953] 1954: *Kainai Chieftainship: History, Evolution and Culture of the Blood Indians: Origin of the Sun Dance*. Lethbridge, AB: The Lethbridge Herald (James Muir Edition).

Orr, William J. and Porter, Joseph C. (eds) 1983: *A Journey Through the Nebraska Region in 1833 and 1834: From the Diaries of Prince Maximilian of Wied*, trans. by William J. Orr, *Nebraska History* 64 (3): 325–40.

Raczka, Paul M. 1979: *Winter Count: A History of the Blackfoot People*. Brocket, AB: Oldman River Culture Centre.

Select Bibliography

Schultz, James Willard 2002: *Blackfeet Tales from Apikuni's World*, David C. Andrews (ed.), Norman: University of Oklahoma Press.

——. 1974: *Why Gone Those Times?: Blackfoot Tales*, Eugene Lee Silliman (ed.), Norman: University of Oklahoma Press.

——. 1926: *Signposts of Adventure: Glacier National Park as the Indians Knew It*. Boston: Houghton Mifflin.

——. 1919: *Running Eagle*. Boston and New York: Houghton Mifflin.

——. [1916] 2002: *Blackfeet Tales of Glacier National Park*. Helena: Montana Historical Society/ Riverbend Publishing.

——. [c.1878–1915] 1962: *Blackfeet and Buffalo: Memories of Life among the Indians*. Keith C. Seele, (ed. and intro.), Norman: University of Oklahoma Press.

——. [1907] 1973: *My Life as an Indian: The Story of a Red Woman and a White Man in the Lodges of the Blackfeet*. New York: Doubleday, Page & Company.

——. [1902] 2003: *Floating on the Missouri: 100 Years after Lewis and Clark*. Helena: [*Forest and Stream*] Riverbend Publishing.

——. and Donaldson, Jessie Louise 1930: *The Sun God's Children*. Boston: Houghton Mifflin.

——. 1957: Return to the Beloved Mountains, *Montana: The Magazine of Western History* 7 (3): 26–33.

——. 1884: Life Among the Blackfeet, *Forest and Stream* 21 (26): 512.

——. 1882: The 'Pis-Kan' of the Blackfeet, *Forest and Stream* 18 (18): 344.

Thompson, David 1916: *David Thompson's Narrative of His Explorations in Western America 1784–1812*, Joseph Burr Tyrrell (ed.), Toronto: Champlain Society.

Tims, John William, 1967: Anglican Beginnings in Southern Alberta, *Alberta Historical Review* 15 (2): 1–11.

Uhlenbeck, C. C. [Christianus Cornelius] 1938: *A Concise Blackfoot Grammar: Based on Materials from the Southern Peigans*. Amsterdam: Noord-Hollandsche Uitgevers-maatschappij.

——. (ed. and trans., with the help of Joseph Tatsey) 1912: *A New Series of Blackfoot Texts from the Southern Piegans Blackfoot Reservation Teton County Montana*. Amsterdam: Johannes Müller.

——. (ed. and trans., with the help of Joseph. Tatsey) 1911: *Original Blackfoot Texts from the Southern Piegans Blackfoot Reservation Teton County Montana*. Amsterdam: Johannes Müller.

Uhlenbeck-Melchior, Wilhelmina Maria [1911] 2005: Mrs. Uhlenbeck's Diary. In Mary Eggermont-Molenaar (ed.), *Montana 1911: A Professor and his Wife Among the Blackfeet*, Mary Eggermont-Molenaar, trans., Lincoln and Calgary: University of Nebraska/University of Calgary Press, pp. 31–178.

Wissler, Clark 1927: Distribution of Moccasin Decorations among the Plains Tribes, American Museum of Natural History, *Anthropological Papers* 29 (1).

——. 1918: The Sun Dance of the Blackfoot Indians, American Museum of Natural History, *Anthropological Papers* 16 (3): 223–70.

——. 1915: Costumes of the Plains Indians, American Museum of Natural History, *Anthropological Papers* 17 (2): 39–91.

——. 1913: Societies and Dance Associations of the Blackfoot Indians, American Museum of Natural History, *Anthropological Papers* 11 (4): 359–460.

Select Bibliography

——. 1911: The Social Life of the Blackfoot Indians, American Museum of Natural History, *Anthropological Papers* 7 (1): 1–64.
——. 1911: Ceremonial Bundles of the Blackfoot Indians, American Museum of Natural History, *Anthropological Papers* 7 (1): 65–290.
——. 1911: *In Memoriam* [of David C. Duvall], American Museum of Natural History, *Anthropological Papers* 7 (1).
——. 1910: Material Culture of the Blackfoot Indians, American Museum of Natural History, *Anthropological Papers* 5 (1): 1–175.
——. 1914: The Influence of the Horse in the Development of Plains Culture, *American Anthropologist* 16 (1): 1–25.
——. and Duvall, David C. 1995: *Mythology of the Blackfoot Indians*. Lincoln: Bison Books.

SECONDARY SOURCES

Aberle, David F. 1962: A Note on Relative Deprivation Theory as Applied to Millenarian and Other Cult Movements. In Sylvia L. Thrupp (ed.), *Millenial Dreams in Action: Studies in Revolutionary Religious Movements*, The Hague: Mouton and Co., pp. 209–14.
——. 1959: The Prophet Dance and Reactions to White Contact. *Southwestern Journal of Anthropology* 15 (1): 74–83.
Adam, Ian and Tiffin, Helen (eds) 1991: *Past the Last Post: Theorizing Post-colonialism and Post-modernism*. New York: Harvester Wheatsheaf.
Adas, Michael [1979] 1987: *Prophets of Rebellion: Millenarian Protest Movements against the European Colonial Order*. Cambridge: Cambridge University Press.
Alcoff, Linda (1991–1992): The Problem of Speaking for Others. *Cultural Critique*, 5–32.
Allen, Paula Gunn 1986: *The Sacred Hoop: Recovering the Feminine in American Indian Traditions*. Boston: Beacon Press.
——. 1991: *Grandmothers of the Light: A Medicine Woman's Source Book*. Boston: Beacon Press.
Allen, Richard (ed.) 1976: *Man and Nature on the Prairies*. Canadian Plains Studies 6, Regina: Canadian Plains Research Centre, University of Regina.
Ambrose, Stephen E. 2003: *Undaunted Courage: Meriwether Lewis, Thomas Jefferson, and the Opening of the American West*. New York: Simon and Shuster.
Anner, John 2001: To the U.S. Census Bureau, Native Americans are Practically Invisible. In Susan Lobo and Steve Talbot (eds) *Native American Voices: A Reader*. Upper Saddle River, NJ: Prentice-Hall, pp. 48–55.
Anderson, Benedict [1983] 1993: *Imagined Communities: Reflections on the Origins and Spread of Nationalism*. London: Verso.
Armitage, Andrew 1995: *Comparing the Policy of Aboriginal Assimilation: Australia, Canada and New Zealand*. Vancouver: UBC Press.
Arnold, A. James 1996: *Monsters, Tricksters and Sacred Cows: Animal Tales and American Identities*. Charlottesville: University Press of Virginia.
Arthur, George 1984: The North American Plains Bison: A Brief History. *Prairie Forum* 9 (2): 281–89.

Select Bibliography

Ashcroft, Bill 2001: *Post-Colonial Transformation*. London: Routledge.
——. 2003: Resistance and Transformation. In Bruce Bennet, Susan Cowan, Jacqueline Lo, Satendra Nandan and Jennifer Webb (eds), *Resistance and Reconciliation: Writing in the Commonwealth*, Canberra: ACLALS, pp. 382–90.
Austin, Alvyn and Scott, Jamie S. (eds) 2005: *Canadian Missionaries, Indigenous Peoples: Representing Religion at Home and Abroad*. Toronto: University of Toronto Press.
Axtell, James 1992: *Beyond 1492: Encounters in Colonial North America*. Oxford: Oxford University Press.
——. 1988: *After Columbus: Essays in the Ethnohistory of Colonial North America*. Oxford: Oxford University Press.
——. 1979: Ethnohistory: An Historian's Viewpoint. *Ethnohistory* 26 (1): 1–13.
——. and Sturtevant, William C. 1980: The Unkindest Cut, or Who Invented Scalping. *William and Mary Quarterly* 37 (3): 451–72.
Bailey, Shawn Patrick 2009: *Colonization of the Crown: Hunting, Class, and the Creation of Glacier National Park*, 1885–1915. MA Diss., University of Montana.
Bakhtin, Mikhail M. 1981: *The Dialogic Imagination: Four Essays*. Michael Holquist (ed.), Caryl Emerson and Michael Holquist, trans., Austin: University of Texas Press.
Bammer, Angelika 1994: Introduction. In Angelika Bammer (ed.), *Displacements: Cultural Identities in Question*, Bloomington and Indianapolis: Indiana University Press, pp. xi–xx.
Barber, Russell J. and Berdan, Frances F. 1998: *The Emperor's Mirror: Understanding Cultures through Primary Sources*. Tucson: University of Arizona Press.
Barnard, Alan 2000: *History and Theory in Anthropology*. Cambridge: Cambridge University Press.
Barron, F. Laurie 1988: The Indian Pass System in the Canadian West, 1882–1935. *Prairie Forum* 13 (1): 25–42.
——. and Waldram, James B. (eds) 1986: *1885 And After: Native Society in Transition*. Regina: Canadian Plains Research Center, University of Regina.
Barry, Nora 1991–2: 'A Myth to Be Alive': James Welch's *Fools Crow*. *MELUS* 17 (1): 3–20.
Barthes, Roland 1977: *Elements of Semiology*. Annette Lavers and Colin Smith, trans., New York: Hill and Wang.
——. [1988] 1994: The Death of the Author. In David Lodge (ed.), *Modern Criticism and Theory: A Reader*, London: Longman, pp. 167–72.
Bascom, William 1965: The Forms of Folklore. *Journal of American Folklore* 78: 3–20.
Bastien, Betty 2004: *Blackfoot Ways of Knowing: The Worldview of the Siksikaitsitapi*. Jürgen W. Kremer (ed.), Duane Mistaken Chief, Language Consultant. Calgary: University of Calgary Press.
——. 1999: *Blackfoot Ways of Knowing: Indigenous Science*. Ph.d. Diss., California Institute of Integral Studies.
Bataille, Gretchen M. (ed.) 2001: *Native American Representations: First*

Select Bibliography

Encounters, Distorted Images, and Literary Appropriations. Lincoln: University of Nebraska Press.

Battiste, Marie (ed.) 2000: *Reclaiming Indigenous Voice and Vision.* Vancouver: UBC Press.

Baylie, Sharon M. 1999: The Arbitrary Nature of the Story: Poking Fun at Oral and Written Authority in Thomas King's *Green Grass, Running Water. World Literature Today* 73 (1): 43–52.

Becker, Marshall Joseph 2005: Matchcoats: Cultural Conservatism and Change in One Aspect of Native American Clothing. *Ethnohistory* 52 (4): 727–87.

Belanger, Yale 2005: 'An All Round Indian Affair': The Native Gatherings at Macleod, 1924 & 1925. *Alberta History*: 13–23.

Benham, Mary Lile 1980: *La Vérendrye, Pierre Gaultier de Varennes, sieur de, 1685–1749.* Don Mills, ON: Fitzhenry & Whiteside Ltd.

Bennett, Ben 1982: *Death, Too, For the Heavy Runner.* Missoula: Mountain Press.

Berkhofer Jr, Robert F. [1953] 1978: *The White Man's Indian: Images of the American Indian from Columbus to the Present.* New York: Vintage Books.

——. 1976: Commentary. In Jane F. Smith and Robert M. Kvasnicka (eds), *Indian–White Relations: A Persistent Paradox*, Washington, DC: Howard University Press, pp. 79–86.

Berry, Gerald L. 1995: *The Whoop-Up Trail: Early Days in Alberta ... Montana*, Occasional Paper 29, Lethbridge, AB: Lethbridge Historical Society.

Beverley, John 1999: *Subalternity and Representation: Arguments in Cultural Theory.* Durham: Duke University Press.

——. 1993: *Against Literature.* Minneapolis: University of Minnesota Press.

——. 1996: The Margin at the Centre: On Testimonio. In Georg M. Gugelberger (ed.), *The Real Thing: Testimonial Discourse and Latin America*, Durham: Duke University Press, pp. 23–41.

Bhabha, Homi K. (ed.) 1997: *The Location of Culture.* London: Routledge.

Biddle, Nicholas (ed.) 1993: *The Journals of the Expedition under the Command of Capts. Lewis and Clark to the sources of the Missouri, thence across the Rocky Mountains and down the river Columbia to the Pacific Ocean, performed during the years 1804–5–6 by Order of the Government of the United States*, 2 Vols. Norwalk, CT: Heritage Press.

Binnema, Theodore 2004: *Common and Contested Ground: A Human and Environmental History of the Northwestern Plains.* Toronto: University of Toronto Press.

——. 2006: Allegiances and Interests: Niitsitapi (Blackfoot) Trade, Diplomacy, and Warfare, 1806–1831. *Western Historical Quarterly* 37 (3): 327–49.

——. and Melanie Niemi 2006: 'Let the Line Be Drawn Now': Wilderness, Conservation, and the Exclusion of Aboriginal People from Banff National Park in Canada. *Environmental History* 11: 724–50.

Black Elk, through John G. Neihardt [1972] 1988: *Black Elk Speaks: Being the Life Story of a Holy Man of the Oglala Sioux.* Lincoln: Bison Books.

Black Elk, through Joseph Epes Brown 1975: Hanblecheyapi: Crying for a Vision. In Dennis Tedlock and Barbara Tedlock (eds), *Teachings from the American Earth: Indian Religion and Philosophy*, New York: Liveright, pp. 20–41.

Blackfoot Gallery Committee, The 2001: *Nitsitapiisini: The Story of the Blackfoot People.* Buffalo: Firefly Books.

Select Bibliography

Blaeser, Kimberly M. 1999: Writing Voices Speaking: Native Authors and an Oral Aesthetic. In Laura J. Murray and Keren Rice (eds), *Talking on the Page: Editing Aboriginal Oral Texts*. Toronto: University of Toronto Press, pp. 53–68.

Boas, Franz 1914: Mythology and Folk Tales of the North American Indians. *Journal of American Folklore* 27 (106): 374–410.

Bonvillain, Nancy 2001: *Native Nations: Cultures and Histories of Native North America*. Upper Saddle River, NJ: Prentice-Hall.

Bouma, Janis and Keyser James D. 2004: Dating the Deadmont Bison Robe: a Seriation of Blackfeet Biographic Art. *Plains Anthropologist* 49 (189): 9–24.

Bowden, Henry Warner 1981: *American Indians and Christian Missions: Studies in Cultural Conflict*. Chicago: University of Chicago Press.

Bracken, Christopher 1997: *The Potlatch Papers: A Colonial Case History*. Chicago: University of Chicago Press.

Brantlinger, Patrick 2003: *Dark Vanishings: Discourse on the Extinction of Primitive Races, 1800–1930*. Ithaca, NY: Cornell University Press.

Braroe, Niels Winther [1975] 1993: *Indian & White: Self-Image and Interaction in a Canadian Plains Community*. Stanford: Stanford University Press.

Brettell, Caroline B. 1986: Introduction: Travel Literature, Ethnography, and Ethnohistory. *Ethnohistory* 33 (2): 127–38.

Brightman, Robert 1989: Tricksters and Ethnopoetics. *International Journal of American Linguistics* 55 (2): 179–203.

Bringhurst, Robert 1992: That Also Is You: Some Classics of Native Canadian Literature. In W. H. New (ed.), *Native Writers and Canadian Writing*, Vancouver: UBC Press, pp. 32–48.

Brinton, Daniel G. [1876] 1968: *The Myths of the New World: A Treatise on the Symbolism and Mythology of the Red Race of America*. New York: Haskell House.

Brotherston, Gordon 1992: *Book of the Fourth World: Reading the Native Americas Through Their Literature*. Cambridge: Cambridge University Press.

Brown, Alanna Kathleen 1992: Mourning Dove's Canadian Recovery Years, 1917–1919. In W. H. New (ed.), *Native Writers and Canadian Writing*, Vancouver: UBC Press, pp. 113–22.

Brown, Dee 1971: *Bury My Heart at Wounded Knee: A History of the Sioux Uprising of 1870*. London: Barrie and Jenkins.

——. (ed.) 1993: *Dee Brown's Folktales of the Native American: Retold for our Times*. New York: Henry Holt and Company.

Brown, Jennifer S. H., and Vibert, Elizabeth (eds) 1998: *Reading Beyond Words: Contexts for Native History*. Orchard Park, NY: Broadview Press.

Brown, Jennifer and Schenck, Theresa 2004: Métis, Mestizo, and Mixed-Blood. In P. J. Deloria and N. Salisbury (eds), *A Companion to American Indian History*, Malden, MA: Blackwell Publishers, pp. 321–38.

Brown, Joseph Epes 1990: *The Spiritual Legacy of the American Indian*. New York: Crossroad.

——. (comp.) 1975: Black Elk, Hanblecheyapi: Crying for a Vision. In Dennis Tedlock and Barbara Tedlock (eds) *Teachings from the American Earth: Indian Religion and Philosophy*, New York: Liveright, pp. 20–41.

Bruchac, Joseph 2003: *Our Stories Remember: American Indian History, Culture, and Values through Storytelling*. Golden, CO: Fulcrum Publishing.

Select Bibliography

———. 1992: All Are My Relations: Native People and Animals. In J. Bruchac (ed.), *Native American Animal Stories Told by Joseph Bruchac*, from Michael J. Caduto and Joseph Bruchac [*Keepers of the Animals*], Golden, CO: Fulcrum Publishing, pp. xiii–xvi.

Bullchild, Percy [1985] 2005: *The Sun Came Down: The History of the World as My Blackfeet Elders Told It*. Lincoln: University of Nebraska Press.

Burke, Peter 1997: *Varieties of Cultural History*. Cambridge: Polity Press.

Burns, Robert I. 1988: Roman Catholic Missions in the Northwest. In Wilcomb E. Washburn (ed.), *History of Indian–White Relations*. In William C. Sturtevant, General Editor, *Handbook of North American Indians*, 20 Vols, Vol. 4. Washington, DC: Smithsonian Institution, pp. 494–500.

Cahill, David 1994: Colour by Numbers: Racial and Ethnic Categories in the Viceroyalty of Peru, 1532–1824. *Journal of Latin American Studies* 26 (2): 325–34.

———. 1996: Popular Religion and Appropriation: The Example of Corpus Christi in Eighteenth-Century Cuzco. *Latin American Research Review* 31 (2): 67–110.

———. 2007: El Visitador General Areche y su campaña iconoclasta contra la Cultura Andina. In Ramón Mujica (ed.), *Visión y Símbolos: del virreinato criollo a la República Peruana*, Lima: Banco de Crédito, pp. 83–111.

Calder, Alison and Wardhaugh, Robert (eds) 2005: *History, Literature, and the Writing of the Canadian Prairies*. Winnipeg: University of Manitoba Press.

Calf Robe, Ben with Adolf and Beverly Hungry Wolf, 1979: *Siksiká: a Blackfoot Legacy*. Invermere, BC: Good Medicine Books.

Calloway, Colin G. 2004: *First Peoples: A Documentary Survey of American Indian History*. Boston: Bedford/St. Martin's.

———. 2003: *One Vast Winter Count: The Native American West before Lewis and Clark*. Lincoln: University of Nebraska Press.

———. 1994: *The World Turned Upside Down: Indian Voices from Early America*. Boston: Bedford Books.

———. (ed.) 1996: *Our Hearts Fell to the Ground: Plains Indian Views of How the West was Lost*. Boston: Bedford Books.

Cardinal, Harold 1977: *The Rebirth of Canada's Indians*. Edmonton: Hurtig Publishers.

———. 1978: Treaties Six and Seven: The Next Century. In Ian A. L. Getty and Donald B. Smith (eds), *One Century Later: Western Canadian Reserve Indians Since Treaty 7*, Vancouver: UBC Press, pp. 82–102.

Careless, J. M. S. 1971: *Colonists & Canadiens 1760–1867*. Toronto: Macmillan.

Carr, Helen 1996: *Inventing the American Primitive: Politics, Gender, and the Representation of Native American Literary Traditions, 1789–1936*. New York: New York University Press.

Carrière, Gaston (O.M.I.) 1979: The Early Efforts of the Oblate Missionaries in Western Canada. *Prairie Forum* 4 (1): 1–25.

Carroll, Michael P. 1984: The Trickster as Selfish-Buffoon and Culture Hero, *Ethos* 12 (2): 105–31.

———. 1981: Levi-Strauss, Freud, and the Trickster: A New Perspective upon an Old Problem. *American Ethnologist* 8 (2): 301–13.

Carter, Sarah 2008: *The Importance of Being Monogamous: Marriage and Nation Building in Western Canada to 1915*. Edmonton: University of Alberta Press.

Select Bibliography

———. 1999: *Aboriginal People and Colonizers of Western Canada to 1900*. Toronto: University of Toronto Press.

———. 1993: *Lost Harvests: Prairie Indian Reserve Farmers and Government Policy*. Montreal: McGill–Queen's University Press.

———. with Dorothy First Rider, 1997: *Capturing Women: The Manipulation of Cultural Imagery in Canada's Prairie West*. Montreal: McGill–Queen's University Press.

———. Erickson, Lesley, Roome, Patricia, and Smith, Char (eds) 2005: *Unsettled Pasts: Reconceiving the West through Women's History*. Calgary: University of Calgary Press.

———. 1984: The Missionaries' Indian: The Publications of John McDougall, John Maclean and Egerton Ryerson Young. *Prairie Forum* 9 (1): 27–44.

Cave, Alfred A. 2006: *Prophets of the Great Spirit: Native American Revitalization Movements in Eastern North America*. Lincoln: University of Nebraska Press.

Champagne, Duane (ed.) 1994: *Native America: Portrait of the Peoples*. Detroit: Visible Ink.

Chartrand, Paul 1991: 'Terms of Division': Problems of 'Outside Naming' for Aboriginal People in Canada. *Journal of Indigenous Studies* 2 (2): 1–22.

Chester, Blanca 1999: *Green Grass, Running Water*: Theorizing the World of the Novel. *Canadian Literature/Littérature canadienne* 161–62: 44–61.

Cheyfitz, Eric 2006: The (Post)Colonial Construction of Indian Country: U.S. American Indian Literatures and Federal Indian Law. In Eric Cheyfitz (ed.), *The Columbia Guide to American Indian Literatures of the United States Since 1945*, New York: Columbia University Press, pp. 1–124.

Churchill, Ward 1997: *A Little Matter of Genocide: Holocaust and Denial in the Americas 1492 to the Present*. San Francisco: City Lights Books.

———. 2004: Genocide by Any Other Name: North American Residential Schools in Context. In Adam Jones (ed.), *Genocide, War Crimes and the West: History and Complicity*, London: Zed Books, pp. 78–115.

Clark, Ella Elizabeth [1960] 1992: *Indian Legends of Canada*. Toronto: McClelland and Stewart Inc.

———. 1966: *Indian Legends from the Northern Rockies*. Norman: University of Oklahoma Press.

———. 1953: *Indian Legends of The Pacific Northwest*. Berkeley: University of California Press.

Clay, Kennerly 2004: On the Medicine Line of the Blackfeet, *Native Peoples* 17 (3): 34.

Clements, Forrest 1931: Plains Indian Tribal Correlations with Sun Dance Data. *American Anthropologist* 33 (2): 216–27.

Clements, William M. 1994: The Jesuit Foundations of Native North American Literary Studies. *American Indian Quarterly* 18 (1): 43–59.

Clifford, James 1988: *The Predicament of Culture*. Cambridge, MA: Harvard University Press.

———. and George E. Marcus (eds) 1986: *Writing Culture: The Poetics and Politics of Ethnography*. Berkeley: University of California Press, 1986.

———. 1986: On Ethnographic Allegory. In James Clifford and George E. Marcus

Select Bibliography

(eds), *Writing Culture: The Poetics and Politics of Ethnography*, Berkeley: University of California Press, pp. 98–121.

——. 1983: On Ethnographic Authority. *Representations* 1 (2): 118–46.

Clifton, James A. (ed.) 1990: *The Invented Indian*. New Brunswick: Transaction Publishers.

—— (ed.) 1989: *Being and Becoming Indian: Biographical Studies of North American Frontiers*. Chicago: Dorsey Press.

Coleman, William S. E. 2002: *Voices of Wounded Knee*. Lincoln: University of Nebraska Press.

Conaty, Gerald T. 1995: Economic Models and Blackfoot Ideology. *American Ethnologist* 22 (2): 403–9.

Conn, Steven 2004: *History's Shadow: Native Americans and Historical Consciousness in the Nineteenth Century*. Chicago: University of Chicago Press.

Cook, Barbara 2000: A Tapestry of History and Reimagination: Women's Place in James Welch's '*Fools Crow*'. *American Indian Quarterly* 24 (3): 441–53.

Cook-Lynn, Elizabeth 1998: American Indian Intellectualism and the New Indian Story. In Devon A. Miheshua (ed.), *Natives and Academics: Researching and Writing about American Indians*, Lincoln: University of Nebraska Press, pp. 111–38.

Crosby, Alfred W. 1972: *The Columbian Exchange: Biological and Cultural Consequences of 1492*. Westport, CT: Greenwood Press.

——. 1976: Virgin Soil Epidemics as a Factor in the Aboriginal Depopulation of America. *William and Mary Quarterly* 33 (2): 289–99.

Crowe, Thedis Berthelson 2003: Introduction. In George Bird Grinnell, *Blackfoot Lodge Tales: The Story of a Prairie People*, Lincoln: Bison Books, pp. v–xvii.

Crowshoe, Reg and Manneschmidt, Sybille [1997] 2002: *Akak'stiman: A Blackfoot Framework for Decision-Making and Mediation Processes*. Calgary: University of Calgary Press.

Crozier-Hogle, Lois, and Wilson, Darryl Babe 1997: *Surviving in Two Worlds: Contemporary Native American Voices*, Jay Leibold (ed.), Austin: University of Texas Press.

Culjak, Tony A. 2001: Searching for a Place in Between: The Autobiographies of Three Canadian Metis Women. *American Review of Canadian Studies* 31 (1–2): 137–57.

Curtis, Edward S. [1907–1930] 2003: *The North American Indian: The Complete Portfolios*. London: Taschen.

Cuthand, Stan 1978: The Native Peoples of the Prairie Provinces in the 1920s and 1930s. In Ian A. L. Getty and Donald B. Smith (eds), *One Century Later: Western Canadian Reserve Indians since Treaty 7*, Vancouver: UBC Press, pp. 31–42.

Cutright, Paul Russell 1968: Lewis on the Marias 1806. *Montana: The Magazine of Western History* 18 (3): 30–43.

Daniells, Roy 1969: *Alexander Mackenzie and the North West*. London: Faber and Faber.

Davis R. and Zannis, M. 1973: *The Genocide Machine in Canada: The Pacification of the North*. Montreal: Black Rose Books.

Debo, Angie [1970] 1995: *A History of the Indians of the United States*. London: Pimlico.

Select Bibliography

Decker, Jody F. 1998: Country Distempers: Deciphering Disease and Illness in Rupert's Land before 1870. In Jennifer S. H. Brown and Elizabeth Vibert (eds), *Reading Beyond Words: Contexts for Native History*, Orchard Park, NY: Broadview Press, pp. 156–81.

Deloria, Phillip Joseph 2004: *Indians in Unexpected Places*. Lawrence, KS: University Press of Kansas.

——. and N. Salisbury (eds) 2004: *A Companion to American Indian History*. Malden, MA: Blackwell Publishers.

Deloria Jr, Vine 1999: *For this Land: Writings on Religion in America*, James Treat (ed.), New York: Routledge.

——. 1995: *Red Earth, White Lies: Native Americans and the Myth of Scientific Fact*. New York: Scribner.

——. 1973: *God is Red*. New York: Grosset and Dunlap.

——. 1969: *Custer Died for your Sins: An Indian Manifesto*. New York: Macmillan.

—— (ed.) 1992: *American Indian Policy in the Twentieth Century*. Norman: University of Oklahoma Press.

——. 1998: Comfortable Fictions and the Struggle for Turf: An Essay Review of The Invented Indian: Cultural Fictions and Government Policies. In Devon A. Miheshua (ed.), *Natives and Academics: Researching and Writing about American Indians*, Lincoln: University of Nebraska Press, pp. 65–83.

——. 1996: Vision and Community: A Native American Voice. In James Treat (ed.), *Native and Christian Indigenous Voices on Religious Identity in the United States and Canada*, New York: Routledge, pp. 105–14.

——. 1987: Revision and Reversion. In Calvin Martin (ed.), *The American Indian and the Problem of History*, New York: Oxford University Press, pp. 84–90.

DeMallie, Raymond J. 1993: 'These Have No Ears': Narrative and the Ethnohistorical Method. *Ethnohistory* 40 (4): 515–38.

——. and Douglas R. Parks (eds) 1988: *Sioux Indian Religion: Tradition and Innovation*. Norman: University of Oklahoma Press.

Dempsey, Hugh A. 2003: *The Vengeful Wife and Other Blackfoot Stories*. Norman: University of Oklahoma Press.

——. 2002: *Firewater: The Impact of the Whiskey Trade on the Blackfoot Nation*. Calgary: Fifth House.

——. 1998: *Indians of the Rocky Mountain Parks*. Calgary: Fifth House.

——. 1994: *The Amazing Death of Calf Shirt and Other Blackfoot Stories*. Saskatoon, SK: Fifth House.

——. 1980: *Red Crow, Warrior Chief*. Lincoln: University of Nebraska Press.

——. 1979: *Indian Tribes of Alberta*. Calgary: Glenbow Museum.

——. [1978] 1998: *Charcoal's World: The True Story of a Canadian Indian's Last Stand*. Calgary: Fifth House.

——. [1972] 1989: *Crowfoot: Chief of the Blackfeet*. Norman: University of Oklahoma Press.

——. (ed. and intro.) 1989: Mike Mountain Horse, *My People The Bloods*. Calgary: Glenbow Museum and Blood Tribal Council, pp. v–xi.

—— (ed.) 1989: *Heaven is Near the Rocky Mountains: The Journals and Letters of Thomas Woolsey 1855–1869*. Calgary: Glenbow Museum.

Select Bibliography

———. 1994: Native Peoples and Calgary. In *Centennial City: Calgary 1894–1994*, Calgary: University of Calgary.

———. 1978: One Hundred Years of Treaty Seven. In Ian A. L. Getty and Donald B. Smith (eds), *One Century Later: Western Canadian Reserve Indians since Treaty 7*, Vancouver: UBC Press, pp. 20–30.

———. [1968] 1982: *A Blackfoot Ghost Dance*, Occasional Paper 3, Calgary: Glenbow Museum.

———. [1966] 1989: *Jerry Pots: Plainsman*, Occasional Paper 2, Calgary: Glenbow Museum.

———. [1965] 1988: *A Blackfoot Winter Count*, Occasional Paper 1, Calgary: Glenbow Museum.

———. and Lindsay Moir 1989: *Bibliography of the Blackfoot*. Metuchen, NJ: The Scarecrow Press Inc.

Dempsey, L. James 2007: *Blackfoot War Art: Pictographs of the Reservation Period, 1880–2000*. Norman: University of Oklahoma Press.

———. 2003: 'A Warrior's Robe': Mike Mountain Horse, a Blood Indian Veteran of World War I. *Alberta History* 51 (4): 18–22.

Denevan, William M. (ed.) 1992: *The Native Population of the Americas in 1492*. Madison: University of Wisconsin Press.

Denig, Edwin Thompson 1953: *Of the Crow Nation: Crow Relationship to the Hidatsa*, edited with biographical sketch and footnotes by J. C. Ewers, Smithsonian Institution Bureau of American Ethnology 151, *Anthropological Papers* 33. Washington, DC: United States Government Printing Office, pp. 19–74.

———. rpt. of 1961: *Five Indian Tribes of the Upper Missouri: Sioux, Arikaras, Assiniboines, Crees, Crows*, edited with introduction by J. C. Ewers, The Civilization of the American Indian Series 59, Norman and London: University of Oklahoma Press.

Denman, Clayton Charlton 1968: *Cultural Change Among the Blackfeet Indians of Montana*. Ph.D. Diss., University of California, Berkeley.

Derrida, Jacques 2001: What is a Relevant" Translation? Lawrence Venuti, trans., *Critical Inquiry* 27 (2): 174–200.

Dickason, Olive Patricia 1993: *The Myth of the Savage: And the Beginnings of French Colonialism in the Americas*. Toronto: McClelland & Stewart.

———. [1984] 1997: *Canada's First Nations: A History of Founding Peoples from Earliest Times*. Edmonton: University of Alberta Press.

———. 1980: A Historical Reconstruction for the Northwestern Plains. *Prairie Forum* 5 (1): 19–37.

Dickson, Lovat [1974] 1976: *Wilderness Man: The Strange Story of Grey Owl*. London: ABACUS.

Dilworth, Leah 1996: *Imagining Indians in the Southwest: Persistent Visions of a Primitive Past*. Washington, DC: Smithsonian Institution Press.

Dippie, Brian W. 1982: *The Vanishing American: White Attitudes and U.S. Indian Policy*. Lawrence, KS: University Press of Kansas.

Dundes, A. (ed.) [1965] 1984: *Sacred Narrative: Readings in the Theory of Myth*. Berkeley: University of California Press.

Dunn Jr, J. P. 1958: *Massacres of the Mountains: A History of the Indian Wars of the Far West 1815–1875*. New York: Archer House.

Select Bibliography

Eastman, Charles A. – see Ohiyesa

Eco, Umberto 1998: *Serendipities: Language and Lunacy*, Italian Academy Lectures, William Weaver, trans. New York: Columbia University Press.

Edmunds, R. David 1995: Native Americans, New Voices: American Indian History, 1895–1995. *American Historical Review* 100 (3): 717–40.

——. Hoxie, Frederick E. and Salisbury, Neal 2005: *The People: A History of Native America*. Boston: Houghton Mifflin.

Eigenbrod, Renate 2005: *Travelling Knowledges: Positioning the Im/Migrant Reader of Aboriginal Literatures in Canada*. Winnipeg: University of Manitoba Press.

——. 2002: 'Stranger and Stranger': The (German) Other in Canadian Indigenous Texts. In Colin G. Calloway *et al. Germans and Indians: Fantasies, Encounters, Projections*, Lincoln: University of Nebraska Press, pp. 259–86.

——. 1995: The Oral in the Written: A Literature Between Two Cultures. *Canadian Journal of Native Studies* 15 (1): 89–102.

Eliade, Mircea [1963] 1975: *Myth and Reality*. New York: Harper Colophon Books.

Erdoes, Richard 1972: *The Sun Dance People: The Plains Indians, Their Past and Present*. New York: Vintage Sundial.

——. and Alfonso Ortiz, 1984: *American Indian Myths and Legends*. New York: Pantheon Books.

Evans, Richard J. [1961] 2001: Introduction. In E. H. Carr, *What is History?* London: Palgrave, pp. ix–xlvi.

Ewers, John Canfield 1997: *Plains Indian History and Culture: Essays on Continuity and Change*. Norman: University of Oklahoma Press.

——. 1973: *Artists of the Old West*. New York: Doubleday.

——. 1958: *The Blackfeet: Raiders on the Northwestern Plains*. Norman: University of Oklahoma Press.

——. 1955: *The Horse in Blackfoot Indian Culture; with Comparative Material from Other Western Tribes*. Smithsonian Institution, Bureau of American Ethnology Bulletin 159, Washington, DC: Government Printing Office.

——. Marsha V. Gallagher, David C. Hunt, and Joseph C. Porter 1984: *Views of a Vanishing Frontier*. Omaha: Center for Western Studies/Joslyn Art Museum.

——. 1984: The Persistent Tradition: The Hill Collection from the Viewpoint of a Student of Blackfeet Indian Arts and Crafts. In Anne T. Walton, John C. Ewers and Royal B. Hassrick, *After the Buffalo Were Gone: The Louis Warren Hill, Sr., Collection of Indian Art*, St. Paul, MN: Northwest Area Foundation, pp. 37–46.

——. 1984: An Appreciation of Karl Bodmer's Pictures of Indians. In John C. Ewers *et al.* (eds), *Views of a Vanishing Frontier*, Omaha: Center for Western Studies/Joslyn Art Museum, pp. 51–93.

——. 1976: Artifacts and Pictures as Documents. In Jane F. Smith and Robert M. Kvasnicka (eds), *Indian–White Relations: A Persistent Paradox*, Washington, DC: Howard University Press, pp. 101–11.

——. 1971: A Unique Pictorial Interpretation of Blackfoot Indian Religion in 1846–1847. *Ethnohistory* 18 (3): 231–38.

——. 1971: When Red and White Men Met. *Western Historical Quarterly* 2 (2): 133–50.

Select Bibliography

———. 1945: The Case for Blackfoot Pottery. *American Anthropologist* 47 (2): 289–99.

———. 1944: The Blackfoot War Lodge: Its Construction and Use. *American Anthropologist* 46 (2): 182–92.

———. 1943: Were the Blackfoot Rich in Horses? *American Anthropologist* 45 (4): 601–10.

———. n.d. [after 1937]: *The Story of the Blackfeet: Indian Life and Customs*, Education Division Pamphlet 6, United States Indian Service.

Fachinger, Petra 1996: Cross-Dressing as Appropriation in the Short Stories of Emma Lee Warrior. *Studies in American Indian Literatures* 8 (3): 36–48.

Farb, Peter 1968: *Man's Rise to Civilization as Shown by the Indians of North America from Primeval Times to the Coming of the Industrial State*. New York: E. P. Dutton.

Farr, William E., 1984: *The Reservation Blackfeet 1882–1945: A Photographic History of Cultural Survival*. Seattle: University of Washington Press.

———. 2003–2004: Going to Buffalo: Indian Hunting Migrations across the Rocky Mountains. Part 1: Making Meat and Taking Robes, *Montana: The Magazine of Western History* 53 (4): 2–21; Part 2: Civilian Permits, Army Escorts, *Montana: The Magazine of Western History* 54 (1): 26–43.

Fee, Margery 2004: What Use is Ethnicity to Aboriginal Peoples in Canada? In Cynthia Ingars (ed.), *Unhomely States: Theorizing English Canadian Postcolonialism*, Peterborough: Broadview Press, pp. 267–76.

———. 1999: Introduction, *Canadian Literature/Littérature canadienne* 161–62: 9–11.

———. 1997: Writing Orality: Interpreting Literature in English by Aboriginal Writers in North America, Australia and New Zealand. *Journal of Intercultural Studies* 18 (1): 23–39.

———. and Jane Flick, 1999: Coyote Pedagogy: Knowing Where the Borders Are in Thomas King's Green Grass, Running Water. *Canadian Literature/Littérature canadienne* 161–62: 131–39.

Felman, Soshana and Laub, Dori, M.D. 1992: *Testimony: Crises of Witnessing in Literature, Psychoanalysis, and History*. New York: Routledge.

Ferguson, Laurie L. 2002: *Trickster Shows the Way: Humour, Resiliency, and Growth in Modern Native American Literature*. Ph.D. Diss., Wright Institute Graduate School of Psychology.

Fiedler, Leslie Aaron 1988: The Indian in Literature in English. In Wilcomb E. Washburn (ed.), *History of Indian–White Relations*. In William C. Sturtevant, General Editor, *Handbook of North American Indians*, 20 Vols, Vol. 4, Washington, DC: Smithsonian Institution, pp. 573–81.

Finley, M. I. [1975] 2000: *The Use and Abuse of History*. London: Pimlico.

Fitzgerald, Michael Oren 1991: *Yellowtail, Crow Medicine Man and Sun Dance Chief: An Autobiography*. Norman: University of Oklahoma Press.

Fixico, Donald L. (ed.) 1997: *Rethinking American Indian History*. Albuquerque: University of New Mexico Press.

———. 1998: Ethics and Responsibilities in Writing American Indian History. In Devon A. Miheshua (ed.), *Natives and Academics: Researching and Writing about American Indians*, Lincoln: University of Nebraska Press, pp. 84–99.

Select Bibliography

Flanagan, Thomas E. 1996: *Louis David Riel: Prophet of the New World*. Toronto: Toronto University Press.

Flick, Jane 1999: Reading Notes for Thomas King's *Green Grass, Running Water*. *Canadian Literature/Littérature canadienne* 161–62: 140–72.

Fludernik, Monika (ed.) 1998: *Hybridity and Postcolonialism: Twentieth-Century Indian Literature*, Stauffenburg: Verlag.

Fogelson, Raymond D. 1989: The Ethnohistory of Events and Nonevents. *Ethnohistory* 36 (2): 133–47.

——. 1974: On the Varieties of Indian History: Sequoyah and Traveller Bird. *Journal of Ethnic Studies* 2 (1): 106–7.

Fooks, Georgia Green 2003: The First Women: Southern Alberta Native Women Before 1900, *Alberta History* 51 (4): 23–28.

Foucault, Michel, 2003: *The Order of Things*, London: Routledge.

——. 1980: *Power/Knowledge: Selected Interviews & Other Writings 1972–1977*. Colin Gordon (ed.), trans. Colin Gordon, Leo Marshall, John Mepham and Kate Soper, New York: Pantheon.

——. 1971: Orders of Discourse, Lecture delivered in French at the Collège de France on 2 December 1970 [*L'ordre du discourse*, Paris: Gallimard, 1971], trans. Rupert Swyer. *Social Science Information* 10 (2): 7–30.

——. [1988] 1994: What is an Author? Joseph V. Harari, trans. In David Lodge (ed.), *Modern Criticism and Theory: A Reader*, London: Longman, pp. 197–210.

Francis, Daniel 1992: *The Imaginary Indian: The Image of the Indian in Canadian Culture*. Vancouver: Arsenal Pulp Press.

Francis, Mark 1998: The 'Civilizing' of Indigenous People in Nineteenth-Century Canada. *Journal of World History* 9 (1): 51–87.

Frantz, Donald G. [1991] 2000: *Blackfoot Grammar*. Toronto: University of Toronto Press.

Freed, Stanley A. and Freed, Ruth. S. 1983: Clark Wissler and the Development of Anthropology in the United States. *American Anthropologist* 85 (4): 800–25.

Frey, Rodney (ed.) 1995: *Stories That Make the World: Oral Literatures of the Indian Peoples of the Inland West, as Told by Lawrence Aripa, Tom Yellowtail, and Other Elders*. Norman: University of Oklahoma Press.

Frideres, James S., 1974: *Canada's Indians: Contemporary Conflicts*. Scarborough, ON: Prentice-Hall of Canada.

——. 1996: The Royal Commission on Aboriginal Peoples: The Route to Self-Government? *Canadian Journal of Native Studies* 16 (2): 247–66.

Galbraith, John S. 1957: *The Hudson's Bay Company as an Imperial Factor 1821–1869*. Berkeley: University of California Press.

Garceau, Dee 2001: Mediations of Women on *The Big Sky*. In William E. Farr, and William W. Bevis, *Fifty Years After* The Big Sky: *New Perspectives on the Fiction and Films of A. B. Guthrie, Jr.*, Missoula: University of Missoula, pp. 119–56.

Gasco, Janine L., 2005: Spanish Colonialism and Processes of Social Change in Mesoamerica. In Gil J. Stein (ed.), *The Archaeology of Colonial Encounters:*

Select Bibliography

Comparative Perspectives, Santa Fe and Oxford: School of American Research Press/James Currey, pp. 69–108.

Geertz, Clifford [1973] 1975: *The Interpretation of Cultures*. London: Hutchinson & Co.

Getty, Ian A. L. 1970: *The Church Missionary Society among the Blackfoot Indians of Southern Alberta, 1880–1895*. MA Diss., University of Calgary.

———. 1974: The Failure of the Native Church Policy of the CMS in the North-West. In Richard Allen (ed.), *Religion and Society in the Prairie West*, Canadian Plains Studies 3, Regina: Canadian Plains Research Center, University of Regina.

———. and Lussier, Antoine S. (eds) [1983] 1990: *As Long as the Sun Shines and the Water Flows: A Reader in Canadian Native Studies*. Vancouver: UBC Press.

———. and Smith, Donald B. (eds) 1978: *One Century Later: Western Canadian Reserve Indians since Treaty 7*. Vancouver: UBC Press.

Gibbins, Roger and Ponting, J. Rick 1978: 'Prairie Canadians' Orientations towards Indians. In Ian A. L. Getty and Donald B. Smith (eds), *One Century Later: Western Canadian Reserve Indians Since Treaty 7*, Vancouver: UBC Press, pp. 82–102.

Gibbon, Guy 2003: *The Sioux: The Dakota and Lakota Nations*. Malden, MA: Blackwell Publishing.

Gibson, Arrell M., 1988: Indian Land Transfers. In Wilcomb E. Washburn (ed.), *History of Indian–White Relations*. In William C. Sturtevant, General Editor, *Handbook of North American Indians*, 20 Vols, Vol. 4, Washington, DC: Smithsonian Institution, pp. 211–29.

Gilman, Carolyn 1982: *Where Two Worlds Meet: The Great Lakes Fur Trade*. Minnesota: Minnesota Historical Society.

Gilham Sr, Dan 1979: *Handbook of Blackfeet Tribal Law*. R. De Marce (comp. and ed.), Browning MT: Blackfoot Heritage Program.

Giraud, Marcel [1945] 1986: *The Métis of the Canadian West*. Trans., G. Woodcock, [from Paris: *Le Métis Canadien*, Institut d'Ethnologie, Museum National d'Histoire Naturelle], Edmonton: University of Alberta Press.

Glancy, Diane 1998: Sun Dance. In J. Weaver (ed.), *Native American Religious Identity: Unforgotten Gods*, Maryknoll, NY: Orbis, pp. 117–23.

Goldfrank, Esther Schiff [1945] 1966: *Changing Configurations in the Social Organization of a Blackfoot Tribe During the Reserve Period (The Blood of Alberta, Canada)*. In A. Irving Hallowell (ed.), *Monographs of the American Ethnological Society* 8, Seattle: University of Washington Press.

Goldie, Terry 1989: *Fear and Temptation: The Image of the Indigene in Canadian, Australian and New Zealand Literatures*. Kingston: McGill–Queen's University Press.

Gone, Joseph P. 2006: As If Reviewing His Life: Bull Lodge's Narrative and the Mediation of Self-Representation. *American Indian Culture and Research Journal* 30 (1): 67–86.

Goody, Jack 2006: *The Theft of History*. Cambridge: Cambridge University Press.

Goodstriker, Wilton 1996: Introduction: *Otsitsi Pakssaisstoyiih Pi* (the year when the winter was open and cold). In Treaty 7 Elders and Tribal Council, with Walter Hildebrandt, Sarah Carter, and Dorothy First Rider, *The True Spirit and Original Intent of Treaty 7*, Montreal: McGill–Queen's University Press, pp. 3–27.

Select Bibliography

Gosner, Kevin 1992: *Soldiers of the Virgin: The Moral Economy of a Colonial Maya Rebellion*. Tucson: University of Arizona Press.

Grant, Agnes 1996: *No End to Grief: Indian Residential Schools in Canada*. Winnipeg: Pemmican Publications Inc.

Gray, James H. [1972] 1995: *Booze: When Whiskey Ruled the West*. Calgary: Fifth House.

Green, Michael D. 1982: *The Politics of Indian Removal: Creek Government and Society in Crisis*. Lincoln: University of Nebraska Press.

Green, Rayna 1988: The Indian in Popular American Culture. In Wilcomb E. Washburn (ed.), *History of Indian–White Relations*. In William C. Sturtevant, General Editor, *Handbook of North American Indians*, 20 Vols, Vol. 4, Washington, DC: Smithsonian Institution, pp. 587–606.

Greenblatt, Stephen 1980: *Renaissance Self-Fashioning: From More to Shakespeare*. Chicago: University of Chicago Press.

Greene, Jerome A. (ed.) 1993: *Battles and Skirmishes of the Great Sioux War, 1876–1877: The Military View*. Norman: University of Oklahoma Press.

Gresko, Jacqueline 1975: White 'Rites' and Indian 'Rites': Indian Education and Native Responses in the West, 1870–1910. In Anthony W. Rasporich (ed.), *Western Canada Past and Present*, Calgary: McClelland and Stewart West Limited, pp. 163–81.

——. 1992: Everyday Life at Qu'Appelle Industrial School. In Raymond Huel (ed.), *Western Oblate Studies* 2, Lewiston NY: Edwin Mellen Press, pp. 71–94.

Grinnell, George Bird [1913] 2005: *Blackfeet Indian Stories*. New York: Riverbend Publishing.

——. 1972: *The Passing of the Great West: Selected Papers of George Bird Grinnell*, John F. Reiger (ed.), New York: Winchester Press.

——. 1895: *The Story of the Indian*. New York: D. Appleton & Co.

——. 1922: The Medicine Wheel. *American Anthropologist* 24 (3): 299–310.

——. 1907: Tenure of Land among the Indians. *American Anthropologist* 9 (1): 1–11.

——. 1901: The Lodges of the Blackfeet. *American Anthropologist* 4 (1): 650–68.

——. 1888: Notes and News. *American Anthropologist* 3 (1): 194–96.

——. 1893: A Blackfoot Sun and Moon Myth. *Journal of American Folklore* 6 (20): 44–7.

——. 1892: Early Blackfoot History. *American Anthropologist* 5 (2): 153–64.

Grobsmith, Elizabeth S. 2002: The Changing Role of the Giveaway Ceremony in Contemporary Lakota Life. *Plains Anthropologist* 47 (183): 75–79.

Gross, Lawrence W. 2002: The Comic Vision of the Anishinaabe Culture and Religion. *American Indian Quarterly* 26 (3): 436–59.

Ground, Mary 1978: *Grass Woman Stories*. Browning, MT: Blackfeet Heritage Program.

Grounds, Richard A., Tinker, George E., and Wilkins, David E. (eds) 2003: *Native Voices: American Indian Identity and Resistance*. Lawrence, KS: University Press of Kansas.

Gruber, Jacob W. 1970: Ethnographic Salvage and the Shaping of Anthropology. *American Anthropologist* 72 (6): 1289–99.

Gunther, Erna 1950: The Westward Movement of Some Plains Traits. *American Anthropologist* 52 (2): 174–80.

Select Bibliography

Hackett, Paul 2004: Averting Disaster: The Hudson's Bay Company and Smallpox in Western Canada during the Late Eighteenth and Early Nineteenth Centuries. *Bulletin of Historical Medicine* 78: 575–609.

Hagan, William T. 2003: *Taking Indian Lands: The Cherokee (Jerome) Commission, 1889–1893*. Norman: University of Oklahoma Press.

——. 1988: United States Indian Policies, 1860–1900. In Wilcomb E. Washburn (ed.), *History of Indian–White Relations*. In William C. Sturtevant, General Editor, *Handbook of North American Indians*, 20 Vols, Vol. 4, Washington, DC: Smithsonian Institution, pp. 51–65.

Haines, Francis 1938: The Northward Spread of Horses among the Plains Indians. *American Anthropologist* 40 (3): 429–37.

Hall, Anthony J. 2003: *American Empire and the Fourth World: The Bowl With One Spoon*. Montreal: McGill–Queen's University Press.

Hall, D. J. 1977: Clifford Sifton and Canadian Indian Administration 1896–1905. *Prairie Forum* 2 (2): 127–51.

Hall, Robert L. 1885: Medicine Wheels, Sun Circles and the Magic of the World Center Shrines. *Plains Anthropologist* 30 (109): 181–94.

Hall, Stuart 1996: When was 'The Post-Colonial'? Thinking at the Limit. In Iain Chambers and Lidia Curti (eds), *The Post-Colonial Question: Common Skies, Divided Horizons*, London: Routledge, pp. 242–60.

Hanke, Lewis [1959] 1975: *Aristotle and the American Indians: A Study in Race Prejudice in the Modern World*. Bloomington: Indiana University Press.

Hanks, Lucien M., Jr., and Richardson Hanks, Jane 1950: *Tribe under Trust: A Study of the Blackfoot Reserve of Alberta*. Toronto: University of Toronto Press.

Hanna, Warren L. 1986: *The Life and Times of James Willard Schultz (Apikuni)*. Norman: University of Oklahoma Press.

Harkin, Michael E. (ed.) 2004: *Reassessing Revitalization Movements: Perspectives from North America and the Pacific Islands*. Lincoln: University of Nebraska Press.

Harmon, Alexandra 1990: When is an Indian not an Indian? The 'Friends of the Indian' and the Problems of Indian Identity. *Journal of Ethnic Studies* 18: 95–123.

Harootunian, Harry 2000: *History's Disquiet: Modernity, Cultural Practice and the Question of Everyday Life*. New York: Columbia University Press.

Harris, Edward Day 1995: *Preserving a Vision of the American West: The Life of George Bird Grinnell*. Ph.D. Diss., University of Texas at Austin.

Harrison, Dick [1978] 1996: *Best Mounted Police Stories*. Edmonton: University of Alberta Press.

Harrod, Howard L. 1971: *Mission Among the Blackfeet*. Norman: University of Oklahoma Press.

Hefflin, Ruth J. 2001: *"I Remain Alive": The Sioux Literary Renaissance*. Syracuse, NY: Syracuse University Press.

Hendrickson, Hildi 1996: *Clothing and Difference: Embodied Identities in Colonial and Post-Colonial Africa*. Durham: Duke University Press.

Hernandez, Nimachia 1999: *Mokakssini: A Blackfoot Theory of Knowledge*, Ph.D. Diss., Harvard University.

Hester, James J. 1968: Pioneer Methods in Salvage Anthropology. *Anthropological Quarterly* 41 (3): 132–46.

Select Bibliography

Hines, Jack 1998: The Buffalo Runners: Hoofbeats Across the Centuries. *Montana: The Magazine of Western History* 152: 24–29.

Hirschfelder, Arlene and Molin, Paulette 2000: *Encyclopedia of Native American Religions: An Introduction*. New York: Facts on File.

Hittman, Michael 1997: *Wovoka and the Ghost Dance*. Don Lynch (ed.). Lincoln: University of Nebraska Press.

Holler, Clyde 1995: *Black Elk's Religion: The Sun Dance and Lakota Catholicism*. Syracuse, NY: Syracuse University Press.

Honko, Lauri and Vopigt, Vilmos (eds) 1980: *Genre, Structure and Reproduction in Oral Literature*. Budapest: Akadémiai Kiadó.

Horsman, Reginald 1988: United States Indian Policies, 1776–1815. In Wilcomb E. Washburn (ed.), *History of Indian–White Relations*. In William C. Sturtevant, General Editor, *Handbook of North American Indians*, 20 Vols, Vol. 4, Washington, DC: Smithsonian Institution, pp. 29–39.

Howard, Robert E., 1965: *A Historical Survey of the Formation and Growth of Education on the Blackfoot Indian Reservation 1872–1964*. MA Diss., Western Montana College of Education.

Horton, Andrew 1978: The Bitter Humour of '*Winter in the Blood*'. *American Indian Quarterly* 4 (2): 131–39.

Hoxie, Frederick E. [1984] 2001: *A Final Promise: The Campaign to Assimilate the Indians, 1880–1920*. Lincoln: Bison Books.

——. (ed. and Intro.) 2001: *Talking Back to Civilization: Indian Voices from the Progressive Era*. Boston: Bedford/St Martin's.

——, Mancall, Peter C., and Merrell, James H. (eds) 2001: *American Nations: Encounters in Indian Country, 1850 to the Present*. New York: Routledge.

Huel, Raymond J. A. 1974: French Speaking Bishops and the Cultural Mosaic in Western Canada. In Richard Allen (ed.), *Religion and Society in the Prairie West*. Canadian Plains Studies 3, Regina: Canadian Plains Research Center, University of Regina.

Hulme, Peter 1999: Voice from the Margins? Walter Mignolo's The Darker Side of the Renaissance. *Journal of Latin American Cultural Studies* 8 (2): 9–33.

Hultkrantz, Åke 1976: The Contribution of the Study of North American Indian Religions to the History of Religions. In W. H. Capps (ed.), *Seeing with a Native Eye*, New York: Harper and Row, pp. 86–106.

Hungry Wolf, Adolf 1990: *Traditional Dress: Knowledge and Methods of Old-Time Clothing*. Skookumchuck, BC: Good Medicine Books.

——. 1977: *The Blood People: A Division of the Blackfoot Confederacy: An Illustrated Interpretation of the Old Ways*. New York: Harper & Row.

——. and Hungry Wolf, Beverly 1989: *Children of the Sun: Stories by and about Indian Kids*. New York: Quill William Morrow.

——. and Hungry Wolf, Beverly (comps) 1989: *Indian Tribes of the Northern Rockies*. Summertown, TN: Native Voices.

Hungry Wolf, Beverly 1980: *Daughters of the Buffalo Women*. Skookumchuck, BC: Canadian Caboose Press.

——. 1980: *The Ways of My Grandmothers*. New York: William Morrow and Company.

Hurtado, Albert L. and Iverson Peter (eds) 2001: *Major Problems in American Indian History*. Boston: Houghton Mifflin.

Select Bibliography

Hutchison, Gerald M. 1991: Robert Terrill Rundle: He went to Them. *Alberta History* 39 (1): 9–14.

Hymes, Dell H. 2004: *In Vain I Tried to Tell You": Essays in Native American Ethnopoetics*. Lincoln: University of Nebraska Press.

———. 2003: *Now I Know Only So Far: Essays in Ethnopoetics*. Lincoln: University of Nebraska Press.

———. 1996: Coyote, The Thinking (Wo)man's Trickster. In A. James Arnold (ed.), *Monsters, Tricksters and Sacred Cows: Animal Tales and American Identities*, Charlottesville: University Press of Virginia, pp. 108–37.

———. 1965: Some North Pacific Coast Poems: A Problem in Anthropological Philology. *American Anthropologist* 67: 316–41.

———. and Simpson, Louis 1984: Bungling Host, Benevolent Host: Louis Simpson's 'Deer and Coyote'. *American Indian Quarterly* 8 (3): 171–98.

Inderwick, Mary E. 1967: A Lady and Her Ranch. *Alberta Historical Review* 15 (2): 1–9.

Irving, Washington [1865] revised ed. 1967: *A Tour of the Prairies*. New York: Pantheon Books.

Irwin, Lee 2004: Native American Spirituality: History, Theory, and Reformulation. In Phillip J. Deloria and Neal Salisbury (eds), *A Companion to American Indian History*, Malden, MA: Blackwell Publishers, pp. 103–20.

Isenberg, Andrew C. 2000: *The Destruction of the Bison: An Environmental History, 1750–1920*. Cambridge: Cambridge University Press.

Jackson, John C. 2000: *The Piikani Blackfeet: A Culture Under Siege*. Missoula: Mountain Press Publishing Co.

Jenish, D'arcy. 1999: *Indian Fall: The Last Great Days of the Plains Cree and the Blackfoot Confederacy*. Harmondsworth, Middlesex: Viking.

Jenness, Diamond [1932] 1972: *The Indians of Canada*. Ottawa: Information Canada.

Jennings, Francis 1982: A Growing Partnership: Historians, Anthropologists and American Indian History. *Ethnohistory* 29 (1): 21–34.

Johnson, Lester R. 2005: *Perceptions of Leadership Expectations on the Blackfeet Reservation*. MA Diss., University of Montana.

Johnson, Pauline 1989: A Red Girl's Reasoning; and The Tenas Klootchman. In Bernd C. Peyer (ed.), *The Singing Spirit: Early Short Stories by North American Indians*, Tucson: University of Arizona Press, pp. 15–33 and 34–42.

Jones, J. A. 1955: *The Sun Dance of the Northern Ute*. Smithsonian Institution, Bureau of American Ethnology Bulletin 157, Anthropological Papers 47, pp. 207–63.

Jorgensen, Joseph G. 1972: *The Sun Dance Religion: Power for the Powerless*. Chicago: University of Chicago Press.

Josephy, Alvin M., Jr., 2002: *500 Nations: An Illustrated History of North American Indians*. New York: Gramercy Books.

———. 1982: *Now that the Buffalo's Gone: A Study of Today's American Indians*, Norman: University of Oklahoma Press.

Judy, Mark A. 1987: Powder Keg on the Upper Missouri: Sources of Blackfoot Hostility 1730–1810. *American Indian Quarterly* 11 (2): 127–44.

Justice, Daniel Heath 2001: We're Not There Yet, Kemo Sabe: Positing a Future for American Indian Literary Studies. *American Indian Quarterly* 25 (2): 256–69.

Select Bibliography

Katanski, Amelia V. 2005: *Learning to Write "Indian": The Boarding-School Experience and American Indian Literature*. Norman: University of Oklahoma Press.

Kehoe, Alice Beck 2000: *Shamans and Religion*. Prospect Heights, IL: Waveland Press.

——. 1989: *The Ghost Dance: Ethnohistory and Revitalization*. Fort Worth: Holt, Rinehart and Winston.

——. 2005: Legendary Histories. In Mary Eggermont-Molenaar (ed.), *Montana 1911: A Professor and his Wife Among the Blackfeet*, Lincoln and Calgary: University of Nebraska Press/University of Calgary Press, pp. 195–202.

——. 1998: Transcribing Insima, A Blackfoot 'Old Lady'. In Jennifer S. H. Brown and Elizabeth Vibert (eds), *Reading Beyond Words: Contexts for Native History*, Orchard Park, NY: Broadview Press, pp. 381–402.

——. 1995: Blackfoot Persons. In Laura F. Klein and Lillian A. Ackerman (eds), *Women and Power in Native North America*. Norman: University of Oklahoma Press, pp. 113–25.

——. 1995: Introduction. In Clark Wissler and David C. Duvall, *Mythology of the Blackfoot Indians*, Lincoln: Bison Books, pp. v–xxxiii.

——. 1994: Maintaining the Road of Life. In William B. Taylor and Franklin Pease G. Y. (eds), *Violence, Resistance, and Survival in the Americas: Native Americans and the Legacy of Conquest*, Washington, DC: Smithsonian Institution Press, pp. 193–207.

——. 1980: The Giveaway Ceremony of Blackfoot and Plains Cree. *Plains Anthropologist* 25 (87): 17–26.

——. and Thomas F. Kehoe, 1977: Stones, Solstices and Sun Dance Structures. *Plains Anthropologist* 22 (76-1): 85–95.

Kehoe, Thomas F. 1959: Boulder Effigy Monuments in the Northern Plains. *Journal of American Folklore* 72 (284): 115–27.

——. 1958: Tipi Rings: The 'Direct Ethnological' Approach Applied to an Archeological Problem. *American Anthropologist* 60 (5): 861–73.

Keller, Betty 1999: *Pauline Johnson: First Aboriginal Voice of Canada*. Montreal: XYZ Publishing.

Kellog, Susan 1991: Histories for Anthropology: Ten Years of Historical Research and Writing by Anthropologists, 1980–1990. *Social Science History* 15 (4): 417–55.

Kelly, Lawrence C. 1988: United States Indian Policies, 1900–1980. In Wilcomb E. Washburn (ed.), *History of Indian–White Relations*. In William C. Sturtevant, General Editor, *Handbook of North American Indians*, 20 Vols, Vol. 4, Washington, DC: Smithsonian Institution, pp. 66–80.

Kelm, Mary Ellen 2005: Diagnosing the Discursive Indian: Medicine, Gender, and the 'Dying Race'. *Ethnohistory* 52 (2): 371–406.

Kendon, Adam 2004: *Gesture: Visible Action as Utterance*. Cambridge: Cambridge University Press.

Kerstetter, Todd 1997: Spin Doctors at Santee: Missionaries and the Dakota-Language Reporting of the Ghost Dance and Wounded Knee. *Western Historical Quarterly* 28 (1): 45–67.

Keyser, James D. and Mitchell, Mark 2001: Decorated Bridles: Horse Tack in Plains Biographic Rock Art. *Plains Anthropologist* 46 (176): 195–210.

Select Bibliography

Kicza, John. E. 2003: *Resilient Cultures: America's Native Peoples Confront European Colonization, 1500–1800*. Upper Saddle River, NJ: Prentice Hall.

Kidd, Kenneth E. [1937] 1985: *Blackfoot Ethnography*. Archaeological Survey of Alberta Manuscript Series 8, Edmonton: Alberta Culture.

Kidwell, Clara Sue 2004: Native American Systems of Knowledge. In Phillip J. Deloria and Neal Salisbury (eds) *A Companion to American Indian History*, Malden, MA: Blackwell, pp. 85–102.

——. and Velie, Alan 2005: *Native American Studies*. Lincoln: University of Nebraska Press.

King, Thomas 2003: *The Truth About Stories: A Native Narrative*. Toronto: Anansi Press.

——. 2002: *A Coyote Columbus Story*. Toronto: A Groundwood Book Douglas & McIntyre.

——. writing as Hartley GoodWeather 2002: *DreadfulWater Shows Up*. Toronto: HarperCollins.

——. 2000: *Truth and Bright Water*. New York: Grove Press.

——. [1990] 1995: *Medicine River*. Ontario: Penguin Canada.

——. 1993: *One Good Story. That One*. Toronto: Harper Perennial.

—— (ed.) 1990: *All My Relations: An Anthology of Contemporary Canadian Native Fiction*. Toronto: McClelland & Stewart.

——, Calver, Cheryl, and Hoy, Helen (eds) 1987: *The Native in Literature*. Winnipeg: ECW Press.

——. Introduction. In Thomas King, Cheryl Calver, and Helen Hoy (eds) 1987: *The Native in Literature*. Winnipeg: ECW Press, pp. 7–14.

——. 1999: A Short History of Indians in Canada. *Canadian Literature/Littérature canadienne* 161–62: 62–64.

Kipp, Darrel Robes 2005: Completing the Circle. In Steven L. Grafe (ed.), *Lanterns of the Prairie: The Blackfoot Photographs of Walter McClintock*, Norman: University of Oklahoma Press, pp. 99–103.

Kipp, Woody 1985: Foreword. In Percy Bullchild, *The Sun Came Down: The History of the World as My Blackfeet Elders Told It*, San Francisco: Harper and Row, pp. v–ix.

Klein, Alan, The Political Economy of Gender. In Patricia Albers and Bea Medicine (eds), *The Hidden Half: Studies of Plains Indian Women*, Washington, DC: Catholic University Press, pp. 151–52.

Koch, Ronald P. 1977: *Dress Clothing of the Plains Indians*. Norman: University of Oklahoma Press.

Kracht, Benjamin R. 1992: The Kiowa Ghost Dance, 1894–1916: An Unheralded Revitalization Movement. *Ethnohistory* 39 (4): 452–77.

Krech, Shepard 1991: The State of Ethnohistory. *Annual Review of Anthropology* 20: 345–75.

Kroeber, Karl [1988] 2004: *Native American Storytelling: A Reader of Myths and Legends*. Malden, MA: Blackwell.

Kroeber, Theodora [1959] 1984: *The Inland Whale: Nine Stories Retold from California Indian Legends*. Berkeley: University of California Press.

Krupat, Arnold 1992: *Ethnocriticism: Ethnography, History, Literature*. Berkeley: University of California Press.

———. 1989: *The Voice in the Margin: Native American Literature and the Canon*. Berkeley: University of California Press.

———. (ed.) 1994: *Native American Autobiography: An Anthology*, Madison: University of Wisconsin Press.

Kvasnicka, Robert M. 1979: George W. Manypenny (1853–57). In Robert Kvasnicka and Herman J. Viola (eds), *The Commissioners of Indian Affairs, 1824–1977*, Lincoln: University of Nebraska Press, pp. 57–67.

Ladner, Kiera L. 2001: *When Buffalo Speaks: Creating an Alternative Understanding of Traditional Blackfoot Governance*. Ph.D. Diss., Carlton University.

———. 2000: Women and Blackfoot Nationalism. *Journal of Canadian Studies* 35 (2): 35–60.

Laga, Barry E. 1994: Gerald Vizenor and his 'Heirs of Columbus': A Postmodern Quest for More Discourse. *American Indian Quarterly* 18 (1): 71–86.

Lansing, Michael 2000: Plains Indian Women and Interracial Marriage in the Upper Missouri Trade, 1804–1868. *Western Historical Quarterly* 31 (4): 413–33.

Laronde, Sandra (ed.) 2005: *Sky Woman: Indigenous Women Who Have Shaped, Moved or Inspired Us*. Penticton, BC: Theytus Books.

Larson, Sidner J. 2005: Colonization as Subtext in James Welch's *Winter in the Blood*. *American Indian Quarterly* 29 (1–2): 274–80.

———. 1992: Introduction. In Walter McClintock, *The Old North Trail or Life, Legends and Religion of the Blackfeet Indians*, Lincoln: University of Nebraska Press, Bison Books, pp. v–x.

Lassiter, Luke Eric. 2000: Authoritative Texts, Collaborative Ethnography and Native American Studies. *American Indian Quarterly* 24 (4): 601–14.

Laubin, Reginald and Laubin, Gladys 1989: *Indian Dances of North America: Their Importance to Indian Life*. Norman: University of Oklahoma Press.

Leacock, Eleanor Burke and Lurie, Nancy Oestreich 1971: *North American Indians in Historical Perspective*. New York: Random House.

Lenz, Mary Jane 2004: *Small Spirits: Native American Dolls from the National Museum of the American Indian*. Washington, DC: Smithsonian National Museum of the American Indian/University of Washington Press.

Lewis, Thomas H. 1982: The Evolution of the Social Role of the Oglala Heyoka. *Plains Anthropologist* 27 (97): 249–53.

———. 1972: The Oglala (Teton Dakota) Sun Dance: Vicissitudes of its Structures and Functions. *Plains Anthropologist* 17 (55): 44–49.

Liebersohn, Harry 2001: *Aristocratic Encounters: European Travelers and North American Indians*. Cambridge: Cambridge University Press.

Lincoln, Kenneth 1983: *Native American Renaissance*. Berkeley: University of California Press.

Linderman, Frank B. [1931] 1996: *Old Man Coyote (Crow)*. Lincoln: Bison Books.

———. 2004: *Indian Why Stories: Sparks from War Eagle's Lodge-Fire*. Lincoln: University of Nebraska Press.

Linklater, Andro 2003: *Measuring America: How the United States was Shaped by the Greatest Land Sale in History*. London: HarperCollins.

Linton, Patricia 1999: Ethical Reading and Resistant Texts. In Deborah L.

Select Bibliography

Madsden (ed.), *Post-colonial Literatures: Expanding the Canon*, London: Pluto Press, pp. 29–44.

———. 1999: 'And Here's How it Happened': Trickster Discourse in Thomas King's *Green Grass, Running Water*. *Modern Fiction Studies* 45 (1): 212–34.

Linton, Ralph 1943: Nativistic Movements. *American Anthropologist* 45 (2): 230–40.

———. 1935: The Comanche Sun Dance. *American Anthropologist* 37 (3): 420–28.

Lobo, Susan and Talbot, Steve (eds) 2001: *Native American Voices: A Reader*. Upper Saddle River, NJ: Prentice Hall.

Logan, Brad 1980: The Ghost Dance among the Paiute: An Ethnohistorical View of the Documentary Evidence 1889–1893. *Ethnohistory* 27 (3): 267–88.

Lone-Knapp, Faye 2000: Rez Talk. *American Indian Quarterly* 24 (4): 635–40.

Loomba, Ania 2005: *Colonialism/Postcolonialism*. London: Routledge.

Lowie, Robert H. 1963: *Indians of the Plains*. Garden City, NY: The Natural History Press.

———. 1916: *Plains Indian Age-Societies: Historical and Comparative Summary*. American Museum of Natural History. *Anthropological Papers* 11: 877–1031.

———. 1959: The Oral Literature of the Crow Indians. *Journal of American Folklore* 72 (284): 97–104.

———. 1955: Reflections on the Plains Indians. *Anthropological Quarterly* 28: 63–86.

———. 1909: The Hero-Trickster Discussion. *Journal of American Folklore* 22 (86): 431–33.

———. 1908: The Test Theme in North American Mythology. *Journal of American Folklore* 21 (81): 97–148.

Lundquist, Suzanne Evertsen 1991: *The Trickster: A Transformation Archetype*. San Francisco: Mellen Research University Press.

Lupton, Mary Jane 2004: *James Welch: A Critical Companion*. Westport CT: Greenwood Press.

———. 2005: Interview with James Welch (1940–2003), 17 November 2001. *American Indian Quarterly* 29 (1–2): 198–211.

Lurie, Nancy Oestreich 1965: An American Indian Renascence? *Midcontinent American Studies Journal* 6 (2): 25–50.

McAllester, David 1941: Water as a Disciplinary Agent among the Crow and Blackfoot. *American Anthropologist* 43 (4): 593–604.

McClintock, Anne 1995: *Imperial Leather: Race, Gender and Sexuality in the Colonial Contest*. New York, Routledge.

———. 1992: The Angel of Progress: Pitfalls of the Term 'Post-colonialism'. *Social Text*: 1–15.

McDougall, John 1970: *Opening the Great West: Experiences of a Missionary in 1875–76*. Occasional Paper 6, Hugh A. Dempsey (ed.), Calgary: Glenbow-Alberta Institute.

McFarland, Ron (ed.) 1986: *James Welch*. Lewiston, ID: Confluence Press.

McFee, Malcolm 1972: *Modern Blackfeet: Montanans on a Reservation*. New York: Holt, Rinehart and Winston, Inc.

———. 1968: The 150% Man, a Product of Blackfeet Acculturation. *American Anthropologist* 70 (6): 1096–1107.

McGowan, Mark G. 2003: *Michael Power: The Struggle to Build the Catholic*

Church on the Canadian Frontier. Montreal: McGill–Queen's University Press.

Macgregor, Gordon, with the collaboration of Hassrick, Royal B., and Henry, William E. (Indian Education Research Staff) 1946: *Warriors Without Weapons: A Study of the Society and Personality of the Pine Ridge Sioux*. Chicago: University of Chicago Press.

McGregor, James 1975: *Father Lacombe*. Edmonton: Hurtig.

McIntyre John W. R., MB BS and Houston, C. Stuart, MD 1999: Smallpox and its control in Canada. *Canadian Medical Association Journal*: 161–72.

McKinnon, Ann 1998: Morality Destabilised: Reading Emma Lee Warrior's 'Compatriots'. *Studies in American Literatures* 10 (4): 53–66.

McLuhan, Marshall 1964: *Understanding Media: The Extensions of Man*, London: Routledge & Kegan Paul.

McNickle, D'Arcy 1973: *Native American Tribalism: Indian Survivals and Renewals*. London: Oxford University Press.

McPherson, Dennis 1998: A Definition of Culture: Canada and First Nations. In Jace Weaver (ed.), *Native American Religious Identity: Unforgotten Gods*, Maryknoll, NY: Orbis Books, pp. 77–98.

Mails, Thomas E. [1978] 1998: *Sundancing: The Great Sioux Piercing Ritual*. Tulsa: Council Oak Books.

——. 1996: *The Mystic Warriors of the Plains*. London: Aurum Press.

——. 1995: *Deadly Medicine: Indians and Alcohol in early America*. Ithaca: Cornell University Press.

——. 1991: *Fools Crow: Wisdom & Power*, Tulsa: Council Oaks Books.

——. 1978: *Sundancing at Rosebud and Pine Ridge*. Sioux Falls, SD: Center for Western Studies, Augustana College.

——. 1973: *Dog Soldiers, Bear Men and Buffalo Women: A Study of the Societies and Cults of the Plains Indians*. Englewood Cliffs, NJ: Prentice-Hall.

——. and Merrell, James H. (eds) 2000: *American Encounters: Natives and Newcomers from European Contact to Indian Removal, 1500–1850*. New York: Routledge.

Mankiller, Wilma, and Wallis, Michael 2001: Asgaya-Dihi. In Susan Lobo and Steve Talbot (eds), *Native American Voices: A Reader*. Upper Saddle River, NJ: Prentice-Hall, pp. 234–41.

Many Guns, Tom 1979: *Pinto Horse Rider*. Browning, MT: Blackfeet Heritage Program.

Manypenny, George W. 1880: *Our Indian Wards*, Cincinnati: Robert Clarke & Co.

Markley, Janet Katherine 2002: *Walking in the Footsteps of Our Ancestors: Present-day Representation of Peigan/Blackfoot Cultural Identity*. MA Diss., University of Calgary.

Marks, Paula Mitchell, 2002: *In a Barren Land: The American Indian Quest for Cultural Survival, 1607 to the Present*. New York: HarperCollins.

Marsden, Michael T., and Nachbar, Jack 1988: The Indian in the Movies. In Wilcomb E. Washburn (ed.), *History of Indian–White Relations*. In William C. Sturtevant, General Editor, *Handbook of North American Indians*, 20 Vols, Vol. 4, Washington, DC: Smithsonian Institution, pp. 607–16.

Martin, Calvin 1987: The Metaphysics of Writing Indian–White History. In

Select Bibliography

Martin Calvin (ed.), *The American Indian and the Problem of History*, New York: Oxford University Press, pp. 27–34.

Marule, Marie Smallface 1978: The Canadian Government's Termination Policy: From 1969 to the Present Day. In Ian A. L. Getty and Donald B. Smith (eds), *One Century Later: Western Canadian Reserve Indians Since Treaty 7*, Vancouver: UBC Press, pp. 82–102.

Maud, Ralph 1982: *A guide to B.C. Indian Myth and Legend: A Short History of Myth-Collecting and a Survey of Published Texts*. Vancouver: Talonbooks.

Mauss, Marcel [1950] 2002: *The Gift*. London: Routledge Classics.

Mayfield, Barbara J. 1979: *The North-West Mounted Police and the Blackfoot Peoples, 1874–1884*. MA Diss., University of Victoria (Canada).

Maynard, Jill (ed.) 1996: *Through Indian Eyes: The Untold Story of Native American Peoples*. Pleasantville, NY: Reader's Digest Association.

Means, Angelia K. 2002: Narrative Argumentation: Arguing with Natives. *Constellations* 9 (2): 221–45.

Medicine, Bea 1981: Native American Resistance to Integration: Contemporary Confrontations and Religious Revitalization, *Plains Anthropologist* 26 (94-1): 277–86.

Michaelsen, Scott 1997: Resketching Anglo-Amerindian Identity Politics. In Scott Michaelsen and David E. Johnson (eds), *Border Theory: The Limits of Cultural Politics*, Minneapolis: University of Minnesota Press, pp. 221–51.

Middleton, Rev. S. H. 1945: The Story of the Blood Indians. *Alberta Folklor and Local History Collection* 1 (3): 100–5.

Mielke, Laura L. 2002: 'Native to the Question' Wiliam Apess, Black Hawk, and the Sentimental Context of Early Native American Autobiography. *American Indian Quarterly* 26 (2): 246–70.

Miheshua, Devon A. (ed.) 1998: *Natives and Academics: Researching and Writing about American Indians*. Lincoln: University of Nebraska Press.

——. 1996: Commonalty of Difference: American Indian Women and History. *American Indian Quarterly* 20 (1): 15–27.

——. and Wilson, Angela Cavender 2002: Indigenous Scholars versus the Status Quo. *American Indian Quarterly* 26 (1): 145–48.

Miles, John 1997: *Infectious Diseases: Colonising the Pacific?* Dunedin, NZ: University of Otago Press.

Miller, Chistopher L., and Hamell, George M. 1986: A New Perspective to Indian–White Contact: Cultural Symbols and Colonial Trade. *Journal of American History* 73: 311–28.

Miller, David Reed 1998: Licensed Trafficking and Ethnogenetic Engineering. In Devon A. Miheshua (ed.), *Natives and Academics: Researching and Writing about American Indians*, Lincoln: University of Nebraska Press, pp. 100–10.

——. 1994: Definitional Violence and Plains Indian Reservation Life: Ongoing Challenges to Survival. In William B. Taylor and Franklin Pease G. Y. (eds), *Violence, Resistance, and Survival in the Americas: Native Americans and the Legacy of Conquest*, Washington, DC: Smithsonian Institution Press, pp. 226–48.

Miller, James R. [1997] 2003: *Shingwauk's Vision: A History of Native Residential Schools*. Toronto: University of Toronto Press.

——. 2007: Compact, Contract, Covenant: The Evolution of Indian Treaty

Select Bibliography

Making. In T. Binnema and S. Neylan (eds), *New Histories for Old: Changing Perspectives on Canada's Native Pasts*, Vancouver: UBC Press, pp. 66–91.

———. 1992: Denominational Rivalry in Indian Residential Education. In Raymond Huel (ed.), *Western Oblate Studies 2*, Lewiston, NY: Edwin Mellen Press, pp. 139–55.

———. 1990: Owen Glendower, Hotspur, and Canadian Indian Policy. *Ethnohistory* 37 (4): 386–415.

Miller, Jay 1992: *Oral Literature*. Occasional Papers in Curriculum Series 13, Chicago: D'Arcy McNickle Center for History of the American Indian, Newberry Library.

Miller, John C. 1967: *The First Frontier: Life in Colonial America*. New York: Dell Publishing.

Milloy, John 1983: The Early Indian Acts: Development Strategy and Constitutional Change. In Ian A. L. Getty and A. S. Lussier (eds), *As Long as the Sun Shines and the Water Flows: A Reader in Canadian Native Studies*, Vancouver: UBC Press, pp. 56–64.

Mistaken Chief, Duane with Kremer, Jürgen W. 2004: Glossaries. In Betty Bastien, *Blackfoot Ways of Knowing: The Worldview of the Siksikaitsitapi*. Jürgen W. Kremer (ed.), and Duane Mistaken Chief, Language Consultant, Calgary: University of Calgary Press, pp. 194–230.

Mitchell, Ken 1974: The Universality of W. O. Mitchell's Who Has Seen the Wind. In Richard Allen (ed.), *Religion and Society in the Prairie West*, Canadian Plains Studies 3, Regina: Canadian Plains Research Center, University of Regina.

Momaday, N. Scott 1978: *House Made of Dawn*. New York: Harper & Row.

———. Personal Reflections. In Calvin Martin (ed.), *The American Indian and the Problem of History*, New York: Oxford University Press, 1987, pp. 156–61.

Moodie, D. W. 1976: Early British Images of Rupert's Land. In Richard Allen (ed.), *Man and Nature on the Prairies*, Canadian Plains Studies 6, Regina: Canadian Plains Research Centre, University of Regina.

Mooney, James [1896] 1973: *The Ghost Dance Religion and Wounded Knee*. New York: Dover Publications.

Moore, Irene 1927: *Valiant La Vérendrye*. Quebec: L.S.A. Proulx.

Moore, Jerry D. 1997: *Visions of Culture: An Introduction to Anthropological Theories and Theorists*. Walnut Creek, CA: AltaMira Press.

Moore, Robert J., Jr. 1997: *Native Americans A Portrait: The Art and Travels of Charles Bird King, George Catlin and Karl Bodmer*. New York: Stewart, Tabori and Chang.

Moreau, William E. (ed.) [1850] 2009: *The Writings of David Thompson, Vol. 1, The Travels*, Montreal, Seattle and Toronto: McGill–Queen's University Press, University of Washington Press, and Champlain Society.

Morgan, Thomas J. 1973: "Rules for Indian Courts", in Francis Paul Prucha, ed., *Americanizing the American Indians: Writings by the "Friends of the Indian" 1880–1900*, Cambridge, MA: Harvard University Press, pp. 300–5.

Morris, Alexander [1862] 1971: *The Treaties of Canada with the Indians of Manitoba and The North-West Territories*. Toronto: Belfords, Clarke & Co.

Mossmann, Manfred 1985: The Charismatic Pattern: Canada's Riel Rebellion of 1885 as a Millenarian Protest Movement. *Prairie Forum* 10 (2): 307–25.

Select Bibliography

Mountain Horse, Mike 1989: *My People The Bloods*. Hugh A. Dempsey (ed. and intro.) Calgary: Glenbow Museum and Blood Tribal Council.

Murdock, George Peter 1948: Clark Wissler, 1870–1947. *American Anthropologist* 50: 292–304.

Murray, David 1991: *Forked Tongues: Speech, Writing, and Representation in North American Indian Texts*. Bloomington: Indiana University Press.

Murray, Laura J. and Rice, Keren (eds) 1999: *Talking on the Page: Editing Aboriginal Oral Texts*. Toronto: University of Toronto Press.

Nabokov, Peter 2002: *A Forest of Time: American Indian Ways of History*. Cambridge: Cambridge University Press.

—— (ed.) 1992: *Native American Testimony: A Chronicle of Indian–White Relations From Prophecy to Present, 1492–1992*. New York: Penguin Books.

Nagel, Joane 1996: *American Indian Ethnic Renewal: Red Power and the Resurgence of Identity and Culture*. New York: Oxford University Press.

Nazareth, Peter 1994: *In the Trickster Tradition*. London: Bogle-L'Overture Press.

Neihardt, Hilda, and Utecht, Lori (eds) 2003: *Black Elk Lives: Conversations with the Black Elk Family*, by Esther Black Elk DeSersa, Olivia Black Elk Pourier, Aaron DeSersa Jr, and Clifton DeSersa. Lincoln: University of Nebraska Press.

Neihardt, John G. (ed.) [1972] 1988: *Black Elk Speaks: Being the Life Story of a Holy Man of the Oglala Sioux*. Lincoln: Bison Books.

Nettl, Bruno 1968: Biography of a Blackfoot Indian Singer. *Musical Quarterly* 54 (2): 199–207.

New, W. H. (ed.), 1992: *Native Writers and Canadian Writing*. Vancouver: UBC Press.

Nichols, R. L. 1999: *Indians in the United States and Canada: A Comparative History*. Lincoln: University of Nebraska Press.

Nii'ta'kaiksa'maikoan (Pete Standing Alone) 2004: Foreword. In Betty Bastien, *Blackfoot Ways of Knowing: The Worldview of the Siksikaitsitapi*, Jürgen W. Kremer (ed.), and Duane Mistaken Chief, Language Consultant, Calgary: University of Calgary Press, pp. vii–ix.

Nock, David A. 1982: A Chapter in the Amateur Period of Canadian Anthropology: A Missionary Case Study. *Canadian Journal of Native Studies* 2 (2): 249–67.

Nugent, David 1993: Property Relations, Production Relations, and Inequality: Anthropology, Political Economy, and the Blackfeet. *American Ethnologist* 20 (2): 336–62.

Ohiyesa (Charles A. Eastman) 1989: The Gray Chieftain. In Bernd C. Peyer (ed.), *The Singing Spirit: Early Short Stories by North American Indians*, Tucson: University of Arizona Press, pp. 99–106.

——. 1989: The Singing Spirit. In B. C. Peyer (ed.), *The Singing Spirit: Early Short Stories by North American Indians*, Tucson: University of Arizona Press, pp. 107–18.

Omura, Rob K. 1995: *Blackfoot Legal Culture: Wrongful Injuries Law on the Canadian Blackfoot Reserves, 1880–1920*. MA Diss., University of Calgary.

O'Neil, Floyd A. 1979: Hiram Price 1881–85. In Robert M. Kvasnicka and Herman J. Viola (eds), *The Commissioners of Indian Affairs, 1824–1977*, Lincoln: University of Nebraska Press, pp. 173–79.

Select Bibliography

Ong, Walter J. [1982] 1991: *Orality and Literacy: The Technologizing of the Word*. London: Routledge.

Orr, William J., and Porter, Joseph C. (eds) 1983: A Journey Through the Nebraska Region in 1833 and 1834: From the Diaries of prince Maximilian of Wied. William J. Orr (trans.) *Nebraska History* 64 (3): 325–40.

Ortiz Fernández, Fernando [1940] 1999: *Contrapunto Cubano del Tabaco y el Azúcar*. María Fernanda Ortiz Herrera (ed.), Madrid: EditoCubaEspaña.

Ostler, Jeffrey 1999: 'They Regard Their Passing as Wakan', Interpreting Western Sioux Explanations for the Bison's Decline. *Western Historical Quarterly* 30 (4): 475–97.

Outram, Dorinda 1995: *The Enlightenment*. Cambridge: Cambridge University Press.

Owens, Louis 1992: *Other Destinies: Understanding the American Indian Novel*. Norman: University of Oklahoma Press.

——. 2001: As If an Indian Were Really an Indian: Native American Voices and Postcolonial Theory. In Gretchen M. Bataille (ed.), *Native American Representations*, Lincoln: University of Nebraska Press, pp. 11–24.

Pagden, Anthony 1982: *The Fall of Natural Man: The American Indian and the Origins of Comparative Ethnology*. Cambridge: Cambridge University Press.

Paget, Amelia M. [1909] 2004: *People of the Plains*. Regina, Saskatchewan: Canadian Plains Reprint Series.

Paige, Darcy 1979: George W. Hill's Account of the Sioux Sun Dance of 1866. *Plains Anthropologist* 24 (84): 99–112.

Pallares-Burke, María Lucía G. 2002: *The New History*. Cambridge: Polity Press.

Pannekoek, Fritz 1974: The Rev. James Evans and the Social Antagonisms of the Fur Trade Society, 1840–1846. In Richard Allen (ed.), *Religion and Society in the Prairie West*. Canadian Plains Studies 3, Regina: Canadian Plains Research Center, University of Regina.

Patterson, Michelle Wick 2002: 'Real' Indian Songs: The Society of American Indians and the Use of Native American Culture as a Means of Reform. *American Indian Quarterly* 26 (1): 44–66.

Peeterse, Natalie 2002: Can the Subaltern Speak . . . Especially without a Tape Recorder?: A Postcolonial Reading of Ian Frazier's On the Rez. *American Indian Quarterly* 26 (2): 271–85.

Penman, Sarah (ed.) 2000: *Honor the Grandmothers*. St. Paul, MN: Minnesota Historical Society Press.

Perdue, Theda (ed.) 2001: *Sifters: Native American Women's Lives*. New York: Oxford University Press.

Peterson, Nancy J. 1999: Introduction: Native American Literature——From the Margins to the Mainstream. *Modern Fiction Studies* 45 (1): 1–9.

Petrone, Penny 1991: *First People, First Voices*. Toronto: University of Toronto Press.

——. 1990: *Native Literature in Canada from the Oral Tradition to the Present*. Toronto: Oxford University Press.

Pettipas, Katherine. 1994: *Severing the Ties that Bind: Government Repression of Indigenous Religious Ceremonies on the Prairies*. Winnipeg, MB: University of Manitoba Press.

Select Bibliography

Peyer, Bernd C. (ed.) 1989: *The Singing Spirit: Early Short Stories by North American Indians*. Tucson: University of Arizona Press.

Podruchny, Carolyn 2006: *Making the Voyageur World: Travelers and Traders in the North American Fur Trade*. Lincoln and London: University of Nebraska Press.

Ponting, J. Rick (ed.) 1986: *Arduous Journey: Canadian Indians and Decolonisation*. Toronto: McClelland & Stewart.

Porter, Harry Culverwell 1979: *The Inconstant Savage: England and the North American Indian 1500–1660*. London: Duckworth & Co.

Potvin, Annette 1966: *The Sun Dance Liturgy of the Blackfoot Indians*. MA Diss., University of Ottawa.

Powers, William K. 1990: *War Dance: Plains Indian Musical Performance*. Tucson: University of Arizona Press.

Pratt, Mary Louise 1997: *Imperial Eyes: Travel Writing and Transculturation*. London: Routledge.

Price, Richard T. (ed.) [1979] 1999: *The Spirit of the Alberta Indian Treaties*. Edmonton: University of Alberta Press.

Prince, Joseph M. and Steckel, Richard H. 2003: Nutritional Success on the Great Plains: Nineteenth-Century Equestrian Nomads. *Journal of Interdisciplinary History* 33 (3): 353–84.

Propp, Vladimir 1968: *Morphology of the Folktale*, L. Scott (trans.). Austin: University of Texas Press.

Prucha, Francis Paul 1984: *The Great Father: The United States Government and the American Indians*. 2 Vols, Lincoln: University of Nebraska.

——. 1982: *Indian Policy in the United States: Historical Essays*. Lincoln: University of Nebraska Press.

——. 1976: *American Indian Policy in Crisis: Christian Reformers and the Indian, 1865–1900*. Norman: University of Oklahoma Press.

——. 1970: *American Indian Policy in the Formative Years: The Indian Trade and Intercourse Acts, 1790–1834*. Lincoln: Bison Books.

——. 1988: United States Indian Policies, 1815–1860. In Wilcomb E. Washburn (ed.), *History of Indian–White Relations*. In William C. Sturtevant, General Editor, *Handbook of North American Indians*, 20 Vols, Vol. 4, Washington, DC: Smithsonian Institution, pp. 40–50.

——. 1979: Thomas Jefferson Morgan 1889–93. In Robert M. Kvasnicka, and Herman J. Viola (eds), *The Commissioners of Indian Affairs, 1824–1977*. Lincoln: University of Nebraska Press, pp. 193–203.

——. 1973: Thomas Jefferson Morgan 1889–93. In Francis Paul Prucha, ed., *Americanizing the American Indians: Writings by the "Friends of the Indian" 1880–1900*, Cambridge, MA: Harvard University Press, 1973, pp. 199–200.

Pulitano, Elvira 2003: *Toward a Native American Critical Theory*. Lincoln: University of Nebraska Press.

Punke, Michael 2007: *Last Stand: George Bird Grinnell, the Battle to Save the Buffalo, and the Birth of the New West*. New York: HarperCollins.

Purdy, John L., and Ruppert, James (eds) 2001: *Nothing but the Truth: An Anthology of Native American Literature*. Upper Saddle River, NJ: Prentice Hall.

——, and Hausman, Blake 2005: The Future of Print Narratives and Comic

Select Bibliography

Holotropes: A Conversation with Gerald Vizenor. *American Indian Quarterly* 29 (1–2): 212–25.

Purple, Edwin Ruthven 1995: *Perilous Passage: A Narrative of the Montana Gold Rush, 1862–1863*. Kenneth N. Owens (ed.). Helena: Montana Historical Society.

Pyne, Garry H. 1970: *The Pre-Reserve Blackfoot: Cultural Persistence and Change*. MA Diss., Simon Fraser University.

Quennet, Fabienne C. 2000: *Where Indians" Fear to Tread?: A Postmodern Reading of Louise Erdrich's North Dakota Quarter*. London: LIT Verlag Münster.

Rabinow, Paul (ed.), 1997: *The Essential Works of Foucault*. New York: The New Press.

Radin, Paul 1956: *The Trickster: A Study in American Indian Mythology*. New York: Bell Publishing.

Raheja, Michelle and Fitzgerald, Stephanie 2006: Literary Sovereignties: New Directions in American Indian Autobiography. *American Indian Cultural and Research Journal* 30 (1): 1–3.

Raibmon, Paige 2005: *Authentic Indians: Episodes of Encounter from the Late-Nineteenth-Century Northwest Coast*. Durham: Duke University Press.

Rama, Ángel 1985: *La Crítica de la cultura en América Latina*. Caracas: Biblioteca Ayacucho.

Rapport, Nigel, and Overing, Joanna 2000: *Social and Cultural Anthropology: The Key Concepts*. London: Routledge.

Rasporich, Anthony W. (ed.) 1975: *Western Canada Past and Present*. Calgary: McClelland and Stewart West.

——. 1987: Utopia, Sect and Millennium in Western Canada, 1870–1940. *Prairie Forum* 12 (2): 217–43.

Ray, Arthur J. 1996: *I Have Lived Here Since the World Began: An Illustrated History of Canada's Native People*. Toronto: Lester Publishing, Key Porter Books.

——. 1974: *Indians in the Fur Trade: Their Role as Trappers, Hunters, and Middlemen in the Lands Southwest of Hudson Bay 1660–1870*. Toronto: University of Toronto Press.

——, and Freeman, Donald B. 1978: *'Give Us Good Measure': An Economic Analysis of Relations Between the Indians and the Hudson's Bay Company Before 1763*. Toronto: University of Toronto Press.

——. 1988: The Hudson's Bay Company and Native People. In Wilcomb E. Washburn (ed.), *History of Indian–White Relations*. In William C. Sturtevant, General Editor, *Handbook of North American Indians*, 20 Vols, Vol. 4, Washington, DC: Smithsonian Institution, pp. 335–50.

——. 1978: Fur Trade History as an Aspect of Native History. In Ian A. L. Getty and Donald B. Smith (eds), *One Century Later: Western Canadian Reserve Indians Since Treaty 7*, Vancouver: UBC Press, pp. 7–19.

——. 1984: The Northern Great Plains: Pantry of the Northwestern Fur Trade, 1774–1885. *Prairie Forum* 9 (2): 263–79.

Reiss, Winold 1997: *Native Faces*. P. Riess (ed.), Bozeman, MT: Nygard & Elliott Pub.

Select Bibliography

Remington, Frederic 1981: *Selected Writings.* F. Oppel (comp.). Secaucus, NJ: Castle.

Reyman, Jonathan E. 1985: Note on Clark Wissler's Contribution to American Archeology. *American Anthropologist* 87: 389–90.

Rich, E. E. (ed.), and Johnson A. M. (asst. ed.) 1958–59: *The History of the Hudson's Bay Company,* 2 Vols, Vol. 1, 1670–1763, Vol. 2, 1763–1870. London: The Hudson's Bay Record Society.

Riley, Patricia (ed.) 1993: *Growing Up Native American: An Anthology.* New York: William Morrow.

Robins, Nicholas A. 2005: *Native Insurgencies and the Genocidal Impulse in the Americas.* Bloomington: Indiana University Press.

Robinson, Charles M. 2003: *The Plains Wars, 1757–1900.* New York: Routledge.

Roe, Frank Gilbert [1951] 1974: *The Indian and the Horse.* Norman: University of Oklahoma Press.

Roosevelt, Theodore [1899] 1966: *Ranch Life and the Hunting Trail.* Washington, DC: Library of Congress, Readex Microprint.

——. 1963: *The Winning of the West, A Modern Abridgment With Introduction.* Christopher Lasch (ed.), New York: Hastings House.

Rosenblatt, Daniel 2004: An Anthropology Made Safe for Culture: Patterns of Practice and the Politics of Difference in Ruth Benedict. *American Anthropologist,* 106 (3): 459–72.

Rosier, Paul C. 2001: *Rebirth of the Blackfeet Nation 1912–1954,* Lincoln: University of Nebraska Press.

Ross, Eric B. 1985: The 'Deceptively Simple' Racism of Clark. *American Anthropologist* 87, 390–92.

Rowand, John 1963: A Letter from Fort Edmonton. *Alberta Historical Review* 11 (1): 1–6.

Rowley, Kelley E. 2002: Re-inscribing Mythopoetic Vision in Native American Studies. *American Indian Quarterly* 26 (3): 491–500.

Ruby, Robert H., and Brown, John A. [1989] 2002: *Dreamer Prophets of the Columbia Plateau: Smohalla and Skolaskin.* Norman: University of Oklahoma Press.

Ruud, Brandon K. (ed.) 2004: *Karl Bodmer's North American Prints,* Omaha and Lincoln: Joslyn Art Museum/University of Nebraska Press.

Ruoff, A. LaVonne Brown 1990: *American Indian Literatures: An Introduction, Bibliographic Review and Selected Bibliography.* New York: Modern Language Association of America.

——. 1981: American Indian Oral Literatures. *American Quarterly* 33 (3): 327–38.

Rutherford, Jonathan 1990: A Place Called Home: Identity and the Cultural Politics of Difference. In Jonathan Rutherford (ed.), *Identity, Community, Culture, Difference,* London: Lawrence & Wishart, pp. 9–27.

Sahlins, Marshall 1993: Goodbye to *Tristes Tropes*: Ethnology in the Context of Modern World History. *Journal of Modern History* 65, 1–25.

Said, Edward W. [1978] 1995: *Orientalism.* London: Penguin Books.

Samek, Hana 1987: *The Blackfoot Confederacy 1880–1920: A Comparative Study of Canadian and U.S. Indian Policy.* Albuquerque: University of New Mexico Press.

Select Bibliography

Sanders, Douglas 1988: Government Indian Agencies in Canada. In Wilcomb E. Washburn (ed.), *History of Indian–White Relations*. In William C. Sturtevant, General Editor, *Handbook of North American Indians*, 20 Vols, Vol. 4, Washington, DC: Smithsonian Institution, pp. 276–83.

Sarkowsky, Katja 2003: Writing (and) Art – Native American/First Nations' Art and Literature Beyond Resistance and Reconciliation. In Bruce Bennet, Susan Cowan, Jacqueline Lo, Satendra Nandan and Jennifer Webb (eds), *Resistance and Reconciliation: Writing in the Commonwealth*, Canberra: ACLALS, pp. 90–101.

Satz, Ronald N. 1979: Elbert Herring 1831–36. In Robert M. Kvasnicka and Herman J. Viola (eds), *The Commissioners of Indian Affairs, 1824–1977*, Lincoln: University of Nebraska Press, pp. 13–16.

Saum, Lewis O. 1965: *The Fur Trader and the Indian*. Seattle: University of Washington Press.

——. 1963: The Fur Trader and the Noble Savage. *American Quarterly* 15 (4): 553–71.

Schaeffer, Claude E. 1951: Was the California Condor Known to the Blackfoot Indians? *Journal of the Washington Academy of Sciences* 41 (6): 181–91.

——. 1950: Bird Nomenclature and Principles of Avian Taxonomy of the Blackfeet Indians. *Journal of the Washington Academy of Sciences* 40 (2): 37–46.

Schierle, Sonja 2001: Travels in the Interior of North America: The Fascination and Reality of Native American Cultures. In Maximilian Alexander Philipp, Prince of Wied-Neuwied, *Travels in the Interior of North America during the Years 1832–1834*, Köln: Taschen, pp. 16–35.

Schilz, Thomas F. 1990: Robes, Rum, and Rifles. *Montana: The Magazine of Western History* 40 (1): 2–13.

Schlesier, Karl H. 1990: Rethinking The Midewiwin and The Plains Ceremonial Called The Sun Dance. *Plains Anthropologist* 35 (127): 1–27.

Schoenberg, Wilfred P., SJ 1961: Historic St. Peter's Mission: Landmark of the Jesuits and the Ursulines Among the Blackfeet. *Montana* 11 (1): 68–85.

Scott, James C. 1990: *Domination and the Arts of Resistance: Hidden Transcripts*. New Haven: Yale University Press.

——. 1985: *Weapons of the Weak: Everyday Forms of Peasant Resistance*. New Haven: Yale University Press.

——. 1976: *The Moral Economy of the Peasant: Rebellion and Subsistence in Southeast Asia*. New Haven: Yale University Press.

Scriver, Bob 1990: *The Blackfeet: Artists of the Northern Plains: The Scriver Collection of Blackfeet Indian Artifacts and Related Objects, 1894–1990*. Kansas City: The Lowell Press.

Seele, Keith C. (ed. and intro.) 1962: James Willard Schultz, *Blackfeet and Buffalo: Memories of Life among the Indians*. Norman: University of Oklahoma Press, pp. vii–xii.

Shanley, Kathryn 2001: The Indians America Loves to Love and Read: American Indian Identity and Cultural Appropriation. In Gretchen M. Bataille (ed.), *Native American Representations: First Encounters, Distorted Images, and Literary Appropriations*, Lincoln: University of Nebraska Press, pp. 26–51.

Shannon, Timothy J. 1996: Dressing for Success on the Mohawk Frontier:

Select Bibliography

Hendrick, William Johnson, and the Indian Fashion. *William and Mary Quarterly* 53 (1): 13–42.
Sharp, Paul F. 1855: *Whoop-up Country: the Canadian-American West, 1865–1885*. Minneapolis: University of Minnesota Press.
Shieffelin, Edward L. 2005: Moving Performance to Text: Can Performance be Transcribed? *Oral Tradition* 20 (1): 80–92.
Shimkin, D. B. 1947: *The Wind River Shoshone Sun Dance*, Smithsonian Institution, Bureau of American Ethnology Bulletin 151, *Anthropological Papers* 41, 399–484.
Shoemaker, Nancy 2004: *A Strange Likeness: Becoming Red and White in Eighteenth-Century North America*. New York: Oxford University Press.
——. 1999: *American Indian Population Recovery in the Twentieth Century*. Albuquerque: University of New Mexico Press.
—— (ed.) 2002: *Clearing a Path: Theorizing the Past in Native American Studies*. New York: Routledge.
—— (ed.) 2001: *American Indians*. Malden, MA: Blackwell.
Silversides, Brock V. 1994: *The Face Pullers: Photographing Native Canadians 1871–1939*. Calgary: Fifth House.
Simpson, Louis, and Hymes, Dell 1984: Bungling Host, Benevolent Host: Louis Simpson's 'Deer and Coyote'. *American Indian Quarterly* 8 (3): 171–98.
Simpson, Thomas 1843: *Narrative of the Discoveries on the North Coast of America Effected by the Officers of the Hudson's Bay Company during the Years 1836–39*. London: R. Bentley [microform].
Sissons, Jeffrey 2005: *First Peoples: Indigenous Cultures and their Futures*. London: Reaktion Books.
Smith, Donald B. 2000: *Chief Buffalo Child Long Lance: The Glorious Impostor*. Red Deer, AB: Red Deer Press.
Smith, Dwight L. and Ewers, John C. (eds) 1974: *Indians of the United States and Canada: A Bibliography*. Santa Barbara CA: ABC-CLIO.
Smith, Linda Tuhiwai 2003: *Decolonizing Methodologies: Research and Indigenous Peoples*. Dunedin: University of Otago Press.
Smith, Sherry L. 2000: *Reimagining Indians: Native Americans through Anglo Eyes, 1880–1940*. Oxford: Oxford University Press.
——. 2001: Francis LaFlesche and the World of Letters. *American Indian Quarterly* 25 (4): 579–603.
——. 2000: George Bird Grinnell and the 'Vanishing' Plains Indians. *Montana The Magazine of Western History* 50 (13): 18–31.
Smoak, Gregory E. 2006: *Ghost Dances and Identity: Prophetic Religion and American Indian Ethnogenesis in the Nineteenth Century*. Berkeley: University of California Press.
Smyth, David 2001: *The Niitsitapi Trade: Euroamericans and the Blackfoot-Speaking Peoples, to the mid-1830s*. Ph.D. Diss., Carleton University.
Snow, (Chief) John 1978: Treaty Seven Centennial: Celebration or Commemoration? In Ian A. L. Getty and Donald B. Smith (eds), *One Century Later: Western Canadian Reserve Indians Since Treaty 7*, Vancouver: UBC Press, pp. 1–6.
Sokolow, Jayme A. 2003: *The Great Encounter: Native Peoples and European Settlers in the Americas, 1492–1800*. New York: M. E. Sharpe.

Select Bibliography

Spivak, Gayatri Chakravorty 1985: Can the Subaltern Speak? Speculations on Widow Sacrifice. *Wedge* 7 (8): 120–30.

Spier, Leslie 1935: *The Prophet Dance of the Northwest and its Derivatives: The Source of the Ghost Dance*. Menasha: University of Wisconsin Press.

——. 1927: *The Ghost Dance of 1870 Among the Klamath of Oregon*. University of Washington Publications in Anthropology, Vol. 2, Seattle: University of Washington.

——. 1921: *Notes on the Kiowa Sun Dance*. American Museum of Natural History. New York: The Trustees.

——. 1921: *The Sun Dance of the Plains Indians: Its Development and Diffusion*. American Museum of Natural History, *Anthropological Papers* 16 (7): 453–527.

——. [1960] 1968: The Sun Dance of the Plains Indians: Comparison with the Tribal Ceremonial System. In Margaret Mead and Ruth L. Bunzel (eds), *The Golden Age of American Anthropology*, New York: George Braziller, pp. 392–97.

Spores, Ronald 1980: New World Ethnohistory and Archaeology, 1970–1980. *Annual Review of Anthropology* 9, 575–603.

Spry, Irene [1963] 1995: *The Palliser Expedition*. Calgary: Fifth House.

——. 1976: *The Great Transformation: The Disappearance of the Commons in Western Canada*. In Richard Allen (ed.), *Man and Nature on the Prairies*, Canadian Plains Studies 6, Regina: Canadian Plains Research Centre, University of Regina, pp. 21–45.

Standing Alone, see Nii'ta'kaiksa'maikoan

Stanley, George F. G. [1983] 1990: As Long As the Sun Shines and Water Flows: An Historical Comment. In Ian A. L. Getty and Antoine S. Lussier (eds), *As Long As the Sun Shines and Water Flows: A Reader in Canadian Native Studies*. Nakoda Institute Occasional Paper 1, Vancouver: UBC Press.

Stannard, David E. 1992: *American Holocaust: The Conquest of the New World*. New York: Oxford University Press.

Starna, William A. 1992: The Biological Encounter: Disease and the Ideological Domain. *American Indian Quarterly* 16 (4): 511–19.

St. Germain, Jill 2001: *Indian Treaty-Making Policy in the United States and Canada 1867–1877*. Lincoln: University of Nebraska Press.

Sturtevant, William C. 1966: Anthropology, History, and Ethnohistory, *Ethnohistory* 13 (1–2): 1–51.

Sullivan, Lawrence E. (ed.) 2003: *Native Religions and Cultures of North America: Anthropology of the Sacred*. London: Continuum International Publishing Group.

Sundstrom, Linea 1997: Smallpox Used Them up: References to Epidemic Disease in Northern Plains Winter Counts, 1714–1920. *Ethnohistory* 44 (2): 305–43.

Surtees, Robert J. 1988: Canadian Indian Policies; Canadian Indian Treaties. In Wilcomb E. Washburn (ed.), *History of Indian–White Relations*. In William C. Sturtevant, General Editor, *Handbook of North American Indians*, 20 Vols, Vol. 4, Washington, DC: Smithsonian Institution, pp. 81–95 and 202–10.

Swagerty, William R. 1988: Indian Trade in the Trans-Mississippi West to 1870. In Wilcomb E. Washburn (ed.), *History of Indian–White Relations*. In William

Select Bibliography

C. Sturtevant, General Editor, *Handbook of North American Indians*, 20 Vols, Vol. 4, Washington, DC: Smithsonian Institution, pp. 351–74.

Swann, Brian (ed.) 1983: *Smoothing the Ground: Essays on Native American Oral Literature*. Berkeley: University of California Press.

——, and Krupat, Arnold (eds) 1987: *Recovering the Word: Essays on Native American Literature*. Berkeley: University of California Press.

Swanton, John R. 1952: *The Indian Tribes of North America*. Smithsonian Institution Bureau of American Ethnology Bulletin 145. Washington, DC: Government Printing Office.

Szasz, Margaret Connell 1977: *Between Indian and White Worlds: The Cultural Broker*. Norman: University of Oklahoma Press.

Taiaiake, Alfred 2005: *Wasáse: Indigenous Pathways of Action and Freedom*. Peterborough, ON: Broadview Press.

Tanner, Adrian 1983: Introduction: Canadian Indians and the Politics of Dependency. In Adrian Tanner (ed.), *The Politics of Indianness: Case Studies of Ethnopolitics in Canada*, St. John, Newfoundland: Institute of Social and Economic Research, Memorial University of Newfoundland, pp. 1–36.

Tarrow, Sidney 1996: The People's Two Rhythms: Charles Tilly and the Study of Contentious Politics, A Review Article. *Comparative Studies in Society and History* 38 (3): 586–600.

Tatonetti, Lisa 2004: Behind the Shadows of Wounded Knee: The Slippage of Imagination in Wynema: A Child of the Forest. *Sail* 16 (1): 1–31.

Tatz, Colin (ed.), Tatz, Sandra and Tatz, Paul (assoc. eds) 1997: *Genocide Perspectives I: Essays in Comparative Genocide*. Centre for Comparative Genocide Studies, Sydney: Macquarie University.

Taylor, Alan 1998: *Buckskin & Buffalo: The Artistry of the Plains Indians*. New York: Rizzoli.

——. 2002: The Divided Ground: Upper Canada, New York, and the Iroquois Six Nations, 1783–1815. *Journal of the Early Republic* 22 (1): 55–75.

Taylor, Colin F. 2002: *The American Indian*. Philadelphia: Courage Books.

——. 1994: The Plains. In Colin Taylor (ed.), *Native American Myths and Legends*, London: Salamander Books, pp. 40–53.

——, and Dempsey, Hugh A. (eds) 2003: *The People of the Buffalo*, Vol. 1, *The Plains Indians of North America, Military Art, Warfare, and Changes: Essays in Honor of John C. Ewers*. Wyk auf Foehr, Germany: Tatanka Press.

Taylor, Fraser 1989: *Standing Alone: A Contemporary Blackfoot Indian*. Halfmoon Bay, BC: Arbutus Bay.

Taylor, John Leonard [1979] 1999: Canada's Northwest Indian Policy in the 1870s: Traditional Premises and Necessary Innovations; and Two Views on the Meaning of Treaties Six and Seven. In Richard T. Price (ed.), *The Spirit of the Alberta Indian Treaties*, Edmonton: University of Alberta Press, pp. 3–8 and 9–45.

Taylor, William, and Pease G. Y., Franklin (eds) 1994: *Violence, Resistance, and Survival in the Americas: Native Americans and the Legacy of Conquest*. Washington, DC: Smithsonian Institution Press.

Teuton, Sean Timothy 2002: *Homelands: Politics, Identity, and Place in American Indian Novel*. Ph.D. Diss., Cornell University.

——. 2001: Postmodernism, 'Realism,' and American Indian Identity in James

Welch's *Winter in the Blood*. *American Indian Quarterly* 25 (4): 626–50.
Thomas, David Hurst (ed.) 1986: *The North American Indian*. New York: Garland Publishing Inc.
Thomas, Rodney G., 2000: Thomas Online: Daughters of the Lance: Native American Women Warriors. *Journal of the Indian Wars* 1 (3): 147–54.
Thomasma, Kenneth 1986: *Om-kas-toe of the Blackfeet*. Jackson WY: Grandview Publishing Company.
Thompson, E. P. 1971: The Moral Economy of the English Crowd in the Eighteenth Century. *Past and Present* 50, 76–136.
——. 1965: *The Making of the English Working Class*. London: Penguin Books.
Thompson, James Westfall, and Holm, Bernard J. [1942] 1967: *A History of Historical Writing: From the Earliest Times to the End of the Seventeenth Century*. Gloucester, MA: Peter Smith.
Thompson, Paul 1984: *The Voice of the Past: Oral History*. Oxford: Oxford University Press.
Thornton, Martin 2001: Aspects of the History of Aboriginal People in their Relationships with Colonial, National and Provincial Governments in Canada. In Martin Thornton and Roy Todd (eds), *Aboriginal People and Other Canadians: Shaping New Relationships*. Ottawa: University of Ottawa Press, pp. 7–24.
Thornton, Russell 1990: *American Indian Holocaust and Survival: A Population History Since 1492*. Norman: University of Oklahoma Press.
—— (ed.) 1998: *Studying Native America: Problems and Prospects*. Madison: University of Wisconsin Press.
——. 2002: A Rosebud Reservation Winter Count. *Ethnohistory* 49 (4): 723–41.
Tilly, Charles 2003: *The Politics of Collective Violence*. Cambridge: Cambridge University Press.
Titley, E. Brian 1986: *A Narrow Vision: Duncan Campbell Scott and the Administration of Indian Affairs in Canada*. Vancouver: UBC Press.
——. 1993: Hayter Reed and Indian Administration in the West. In R. C. Macleod, (ed.), *Swords and Ploughshares: War and Agriculture in Western Canada*, Edmonton: University of Alberta Press, pp. 108–48.
——. 1992: Dunbow Indian Industrial School: An Oblate Experiment in Education. In Raymond Huel (ed.), *Western Oblate Studies* 2, Lewiston, NY: Edwin Mellen Press, pp. 95–107.
——. 1983: W. M. Graham: Indian Agent Extraordinaire. *Prairie Forum* 8 (1): 25–41.
Tobias, John L. 1976: Protection, Civilization, Assimilation: An Outline History of Canada's Indian Policy. *Western Canadian Journal of Anthropology* 6 (2): 13–30.
Tovías, Blanca and Cahill, David (eds) 2006: *New World, First Nations: Native Peoples of Mesoamerica and the Andes under Colonial Rule*, Brighton, UK: Sussex Academic Press.
——. Forthcoming 2010: A Blueprint for Massacre: The United States Army and the 1870 Massacre of Blackfeet on the Marias River, Montana. In Philip Dwyer and Lyndall Ryan (eds), *Theatres of Violence: The Massacre, Mass Killing and Atrocity in History*. New York: Berghahn.
——. 2008: Navigating the Cultural Encounter: Blackfoot Religious Resistance in

Select Bibliography

Canada (c.1870–1930). In Dirk Moses (ed.), *Empire, Colony, Genocide: Conquest, Occupation and Subaltern Resistance in World History*, New York: Berghahn Books, pp. 271–95.

——. 2007: Power Dressing on the Prairies: The Grammar of Blackfoot Leadership Dress. In Louise Edwards and Mina Roces (eds), *Gender, Nation and the Politics of Dress in Asia and the Americas*, Brighton, UK: Sussex Academic Press, pp. 139–62.

——. 2006: Colonialism and Demographic Catastrophes in the Americas: Blackfoot Tribes of the Northwest. In Patricia Grimshaw and Russell McGregor (eds), *Collision of Cultures and Identities: Settlers and Indigenous Peoples*, Melbourne: Department of History, University of Melbourne, pp. 72–78.

——. 2010: A Hero for all Seasons: A Late Nineteenth-Century Scarface in James Welch's *Fools Crow*. *Australasian Canadian Studies* 27 (1–2): 129–47.

——. 2006: Infected by the Hybrid? Framing Blackfoot Stories across Genres. *New Literatures Review* 43: 83–97.

——. 2006: Fur and Skin Trades in the Americas. In Thomas Benjamin (ed.), *Encyclopedia of Western Colonialism since 1450*, 3 Vols, Detroit: Macmillan Reference USA.

Trachtenberg, Alan 2004: *Shades of Hiawatha: Staging Indians, Making Americans, 1880–1930*. New York: Hill and Wang.

Trafzer, Clifford E. 2000: *As Long as the Grass Shall Grow and the Rivers Flow: A History of Native Americans*. Fort Worth: Harcourt Brace.

Treat, James (ed.) 1996: *Native and Christian Indigenous Voices on Religious Identity in the United States and Canada*. New York: Routledge.

Treaty 7 Elders and Tribal Council, with Hildebrandt, Walter, Carter, Sarah and First Rider, Dorothy 1996: *The True Spirit and Original Intent of Treaty 7*. Montreal: McGill–Queen's University Press.

Trigger, Bruce G. 2001: Early Native North American Responses to European Contact. In Albert L. Hurtado and Peter Iverson (eds), *Major Problems in American Indian History: Documents and Essays*, Boston: Houghton Mifflin, pp. 63–77.

——. 1986: Ethnohistory: The Unfinished Edifice. *Ethnohistory* 33 (3): 253–67.

Trigger, David, and Griffiths, Gareth (eds) 2003: *Disputed Territories: Land, Culture and Identity in Settler Societies*. Hong Kong: Hong Kong University Press.

Turner, John Peter 1950: *The North-West Mounted Police 1873–1893*. Vol. 2. Ottawa: Edmond Cloutier, King's Printer and Controller of Stationery.

Tuttle, Edmund B. [1871] 2002: *Three Years on the Plains: Observations of Indians 1867–1870*. Norman: University of Oklahoma Press.

Twofeathers, Manny 1996: *The Road to the Sundance: My Journey into Native Spirituality*. Hyperion: New York.

Ubelaker, Douglas H. 1992: The Sources and Methodology for Mooney's Estimates of North American Indian Populations. In William M. Denevan (ed.), *The Native Population of the Americas in 1492*, Madison: University of Wisconsin Press, pp. 243–88.

Utley, Robert M. 1993: *The Lance and the Shield: The Life and Times of Sitting Bull*. New York: Ballantine Books.

Van Berkel, Klaas, and Eggermont-Molenaar, Mary 2005: The Uhlenbecks and the Burdens of Life: A Biographical Introduction. In Mary Eggermont-Molenaar (ed.), *Montana 1911: A Professor and his Wife Among the Blackfeet*, Lincoln: University of Nebraska, and University of Calgary Press, pp. 7–1.

———. 1984: *The Indian Frontier of the American West 1846–1890*. Albuquerque: University of New Mexico Press.

Van Kirk, Sylvia [1980] 1983: *Many Tender Ties: Women in Fur Trade Society, 1670–1870*. Norman: University of Oklahoma Press.

Vaughan, Alden T. 1982: From White Man to Redskin: Changing Anglo-American Perceptions of the American Indian. *American Historical Review* 87 (4): 917–53.

Venne, Sharon 2004: She Must be Civilized: She Paints Her Toe Nails. In Stephen Greymorning (ed.), *A Will to Survive: Indigenous Essays on the Politics of Culture, Language, and Identity*, Boston: McGraw–Hill, pp. 126–39.

Venuti, Lawrence (intro. and trans.) 2001: Jacques Derrida, What is a Relevant" Translation? *Critical Inquiry* 27 (2): 174–200.

Vernon, Irene, S. 2005: A Happiness That Sleeps with Sadness: An Examination of 'White Scabs' in Fools Crow. *American Indian Quarterly* 29 (1–2): 178–97.

Vest, Jay Hansford C. 1988: Traditional Blackfeet Religion and the Sacred Badger–Two Medicine Wildlands. *Journal of Law and Religion* 6: 455–89.

Vibert, Elizabeth 1995: 'The Natives Were Strong to Live': Reinterpreting Early-Nineteenth-Century Prophetic Movements in the Columbia Plateau. *Ethnohistory* 42 (2): 197–229.

Viola, Herman J. 1990: *After Columbus: The Smithsonian Chronicle of the North American Indians*. Washington, DC: Smithsonian Books.

———. 1981: *Diplomats in Buckskin: A History of Indian Delegations in Washington City*. Washington, DC: Smithsonian Institution Press.

Vizenor, Gerald 2003: *Wordarrows: Native American States of Literary Sovereignty*. Lincoln: University of Nebraska Press.

———. 2000: *Fugitive Poses: Native American Indian Scenes of Absence and Presence*. Lincoln: University of Nebraska Press, Bison Books.

———. 1994: *Manifest Manners: Postindian Warriors of Survivance*. Hanover: Wesleyan University Press.

———, and A. Robert Lee 1999: *Postindian Conversations*. Lincoln: University of Nebraska Press.

——— (ed.) [1989] 1993: *Narrative Chance: Postmodern Discourse on Native American Literatures*. Norman: University of Oklahoma Press.

———. 1993: Trickster Discourse: Comic Holotropes and Language Games. In Gerald Vizenor (ed.), *Narrative Chance: Postmodern Discourse on Native American Indian Literatures*. Norman: University of Oklahoma Press.

———. 1990: Trickster Discourse. *American Indian Quarterly* 14 (3): 277–87.

Voget, Fred W. 1984: *The Shoshoni–Crow Sun Dance*. Norman: University of Oklahoma Press.

Waldram, James B., and Barron, F. Laurie (eds) 1986: *1885 And After: Native Society in Transition*. Regina: Canadian Plains Research Center, University of Regina.

Walker, James R. 1991: *Lakota Belief and Ritual*. Raymond J. DeMallie and Elaine A. Jahner (eds). Lincoln: University of Nebraska Press/Colorado Historical Society.

Select Bibliography

——. 1982: *Lakota Society*. Raymond J. DeMallie (ed.). Lincoln: University of Nebraska Press/Colorado Historical Society.

Wallace, Anthony F. C. 2003: *Revitalizations and Mazeways: Essays on Culture Change*. Robert S. Grumet (ed.). Lincoln: University of Nebraska Press.

——. 1956: Revitalization Movements: Some Theoretical Considerations for Their Comparative Study. *American Anthropologist* 58 (2): 264–81.

Wallace, Jim 1998: *A Trying Time: The North West Mounted Police in The 1885 Rebellion*. Winnipeg: Bunker to Bunker.

——. 1997: *A Double Duty: The Decisive First Decade of the North West Mounted Police*. Winnipeg: Bunker to Bunker.

Walton, Ann T., Ewers, John C., Hassrick Royal B. 1985: *After the Buffalo were Gone: The Louis Warren Hill, Sr., Collection of Indian Art*. St. Paul, MN: Northwest Area Foundation.

Warrior, Emma Lee 1990: Compatriots. In Thomas King (ed.), *All My Relations: An Anthology of Contemporary Canadian Native Fiction*, Toronto: McClelland & Stewart, pp. 48–59.

Washburn, Wilcomb E. 1973: *The American Indian and the United States: A Documentary History*, 4 Vols, Vol. 1. New York: Random House.

Waterman, T. T. 1914: The Explanatory Element in the Folk-Tales of the North-American Indians, *Journal of American Folklore* 27 (103): 1–54.

Weasel Traveller, Audrey 1990: *A Shining Trail to the Sun's Lodge: Renewal Through Blackfoot Ways of Knowing*. MA Diss., University of Lethbridge.

Weaver, Jace 2001: *Other Words: American Indian Literature, Law, and Culture*. Norman: University of Oklahoma Press.

—— (ed.) 2002: *Native American Religious Identity: Unforgotten Gods*. New York: Orbis Books.

——, Womack, Craig S., and Warrior, Robert 2006: *American Indian Literary Nationalism*. Albuquerque: University of New Mexico Press.

Weber, David J. 2005: *Bárbaros: Spaniards and Their Savages in the Age of Enlightenment*. New Haven: Yale University Press.

Weidman, Bette S. 2006: Closure in James Welch's *Fools Crow*. *Studies in American Indian Literatures* 18 (3): 90–97.

Welch, James 2001: *The Heartsong of Charging Elk*. New York: Anchor Books.

——. 1986: *Fools Crow*. New York: Viking.

——. 1974: *Winter in the Blood*. New York, Harper and Row.

——, with Paul Steckler 1994: *Killing Custer: The Battle of the Little Bighorn and the Fate of the Plains Indians*. New York: W. W. Norton & Co.

Wessel, Thomas R., Political Assimilation on the Blackfoot Indian Reservation, 1887–1934: A Study in Survival. In Douglas H. Ubelaker, and Herman J. Viola (eds), *Plains Indian Studies: A Collection of Essays in Honor of John C. Ewers and Waldo R. Wedel*, Washington, DC: Smithsonian Institution Press, 1982, pp. 59–72.

West, Helen B. 1970: *Flood: The Story of the 1964 Blackfeet Disaster*. Browning, MT: Blackfeet Tribal Council.

Whillans, James W. 1955: *First in the West: The Story of Henry Kelsey Discoverer of Canadian Prairies*. Edmonton: Applied Art Products.

White, Jon Manchip [1979] 2003: *Everyday Life of the North-American Indian*, Mineola. NY: Dover Publications.

Select Bibliography

White, Richard 1997: *The Middle Ground: Indians, Empires and Republics in the Great Lakes Region, 1650–1815*. Cambridge: Cambridge University Press.

——. 2001: Indian Peoples and the Natural World: Asking the Right Question. In Albert L. Hurtado and Peter Iverson (eds), *Major Problems in American Indian History: Documents and Essays*, Boston: Houghton Mifflin, pp. 8–16.

Whitehead, Neil L. (ed. and intro.) 2003: *Historicities in Amazonia*. Lincoln: University of Nebraska Press.

Wiebe, Rudy 1975: On the Trail of Big Bear. In Anthony W. Rasporich (ed.), *Western Canada Past and Present*, Calgary: McClelland and Stewart West, pp. 183–92.

Wiget, Andrew O. 1985: *Native American Literature*. Boston: G. K. Hall & Co.

Wild, Peter 1983: *James Welch*. Boise, ID: Boise State University Printing and Graphic Services.

Wilson, Angela Cavender 1998: American Indian History or Non-Indian Perceptions of American Indian History. In Devon A. Miheshua (ed.), *Natives and Academics: Researching and Writing about American Indians*, Lincoln: University of Nebraska Press, pp. 23–26.

Wilson, James 1998: *The Earth Shall Weep: A History of Native America*. New York: Grove Press.

Wilson, Wesley C. 1965: The U.S. Army and the Piegans——The Baker Massacre of 1870. *North Dakota History* 32 (1): 40–58.

Wischmann, Leslie 2000: *Frontier Diplomats: The Life and Times of Alexander Culbertson and Natoyist-Siksina'*. Spokane, WA: Arthur H. Clark.

Wissler, Clark [1940] 1966: *Indians of the United States*. Revised ed. by Lucy Wales Kluckhohn. Garden City, NY: Doubleday.

Wolf, Eric R. 1982: *Europe and the People Without History*. Berkeley: University of California Press.

Wong, Hertha D. 1987: Pre-literate Native American Autobiography. *MELUS* 14 (1): 17–32.

Yellowhorn, Caroline 2004: *Niipáitapiiyssin Life* by Naatóyiohsokaakiiwa (Medicine Trails Woman), Brocket, AB: Medicine Trails Publishing.

Yellowtail, Thomas 1991: *Yellowtail Crow Medicine Man and Sun Dance Chief: An Autobiography*. Norman: University of Oklahoma Press.

Young, Egerton Ryerson 1903: *Stories from Indian Wigwams and Northern Camp Fires*. London: Charles H. Kelly.

Yúdice, George 1996: Testimonio *and Postmodernism*. In Georg M. Gugelberger (ed.), *The Real Thing: Testimonial Discourse and Latin America*, Durham: Duke University Press, pp. 42–57.

Zentner, Henry 1970: The Impending Identity Crisis Among Native Peoples. In David P. Gagan (ed.), *Prairie Perspectives: Papers of the Western Canadian Studies Conference*, Toronto: Holt Rinehart and Winston, pp. 78–89.

Zimmerman, Larry J. 2003: *American Indians The First Nations: Native North American Life, Myth and Art*. London: Duncan Baird Publishers.

Weblinks

Anonymous, 1971: Senator James Gladstone 1887–1971. *Saskatchewan Indian* 2

Select Bibliography

(7): 1 (Obituary). Available @: http://www.sicc.sk.ca/saskindian/a71sep01.htm [Accessed 1 Sept. 2010].

Burke, Barry. Antonio Gramsci and Informal Education. *The Encyclopedia of Informal Education*. Available online at: http://www.infed.org/thinkers/et-gram.htm. [Accessed 16 Sept. 2010].

Baud, M. and Rutten R. n.d.: Framing Protest: Popular Intellectuals and Social Movements in Asia, Africa, and Latin America (Nineteenth-Twentieth centuries), Position Paper, *International Review of Social History*, 1–4, available @: http://www.iisg.nl/irsh/protest.pdf [Accessed 31 August 2010].

Chewing Black Bones, *Blackfeet Creation Tale*. Ella E. Clark (ed.). Available from Blackfeet Community College @: http://www.montana.edu/%7Ewwwbcc/legend.html [Accessed 16 Sept. 2010].

Curtis, Edward S. 1907–30: *The North American Indian*. F. W. Hodge (ed.) 20 Vols, Norwood, Mass.: Plimpton Press, Vol. 6, *The Piegan. The Cheyenne. The Arapaho*, Available from Northwestern University @: http://curtis.library.northwestern.edu/ocrtext.cgi?vol=6 [Accessed 16 Sept. 2010].

Dempsey, Hugh A. 1987: Treaty Research Report — Treaty Seven (1877). Treaties and Historical Research Centre, Comprehensive Claims Branch, Self-Government, Indian and Northern Affairs Canada, available http://www.ainc-inac.gc.ca/al/hts/tgu/pubs/t7/tre7-eng.asp [Accessed 16 Sept. 2010]

Encyclopaedia Britannica, Available @: http://www.britannica.com/ [Accessed 16 Sept. 2010].

Ermineskin, Rachel and Howe, Darin 2005: On Blackfoot Syllabics and the Law o Finals. Paper presented at the 37th. Algonquian Conference, Ottawa, 22 October. Available @: http://www.ucalgary.ca/dflynn/files/dflynn/ErmineskinHowe2005.pdf [Accessed 16 Sept. 2010].

Glenbow Archives, M-8188 Bull Plume's Winter Count. Available @: http://asalive.archivesalberta.org:8080/access/asa/documents/display/GLEN-22 [Accessed 1 Sept. 2010].

Government of the United States, Annual Report of the U.S. Commissioner of Indian Affairs, 1889, Available from Internet Archive @ http://www.archive.org/index.php [Accessed 21 June 2010].

Hungry Wolf, Beverly, University of Minnesota, Voices from the Gaps. Available @: http://voices.cla.umn.edu/artistpages/hungrywolfbeverly.php [Accessed 7 Sept. 2010].

Indian Claims Commission, Report on the Mediation of the Blood Tribe / Kainaiwa Akers Surrender Negotiations, August 2005. Available @: http://www.indianclaims.ca/pdf/bloodmediationenglish.pdf [Accessed 22 June 2010].

Library and Archives Canada, *Annual Report of The Department of Indian Affairs 1864–1990*. Avail. @: http://www.collectionscanada.gc.ca/databases/indianaffairs/index-e.html [Accessed 2007–2010]

Library and Archives Canada, *Dictionary of Canadian Biography Online*, Natawista Iksana or Natoyist-Siksina' (Medicine Snake Woman). Available @: http://www.biographi.ca/009004-119.01-e.php?BioId=40450 [Accessed 16 Sept 2010].

Select Bibliography

M'Lean [Maclean], John, *The Blackfoot Sun Dance*, rpt. from Proceedings of the Canadian Institute 151 (Toronto: Copp, Clark Co., 1889). Available from Early Canadiana Online @: http://www.canadiana.org/view/30372/0003 [Accessed 3 Sept. 2010].

Oxford English Dictionary, Available @: http://dictionary.oed.com [Accessed 2005–2010].

Pratt, Capt. Richard C., 'Kill the Indian, and Save the Man', Capt. Richard C. Pratt on the Education of Native Americans, Paper delivered at an 1892 convention. Available from *History Matters* @: http://historymatters.gmu.edu/d/4929/ [Accessed 31 August 2010].

Scriver, Mary, Prairie Mary Blogspot: Available at http://prairiemary.blogspot.com/2005/06/sam-worm-man-in-sweet-grass-hills.html [Accessed 6 Sept. 2010].

Smithsonian National Museum of Natural History, Lakota Winter Counts, available @: http://wintercounts.si.edu/index.html [Accessed 6 September 2010].

Treaty Seven available online from Treaty Seven Management Corporation at: http://www.treaty7.org/Article.asp?ArticleID=1 [Accessed 31 August 2010].

Urban Legends, Walking Eagle — President George W. Bush, Available @ http://urbanlegends.about.com/library/bl_walking_eagle.htm [Accessed 20 May 2010].

Venini, Bernice, *CCHA Report* 10 (1942–1943): 75–86; Father Constantine Scollen, Founder of the Calgary Mission, Available from the University of Manitoba at: http://www.umanitoba.ca/colleges/st_pauls/ccha/Back% 20Issues /CCHA1942-43/Venini.html [Accessed 1 Sept. 2010].

Other Media

Glenbow Museum, *Native North America, Plains*, Siksika quilled suit, 1900s, Exhibit AF 3761 a-b.

Index

A-pe-ech-eken (White Weasel Moccasin) see McClintock, Walter
A-pe-so-muckka (Running Wolf), 90, 140, 141, 238n
  see also Iron Shirt (Mehkskéme-Sukáhs)
Above Beings, 207n
  Ookaan, 17, 159
  Scarface Story, 160, 164–6
  Warrior's "Compatriots", 180
  Welch's *Fools Crow*, 176, 177, 178
  see also Ipiso-Waahsa (the Morning Star); Kokomi-kisomm (the Moon); Natosi (the Sun)
acculturation, 85
  flow in two directions, 90, 125
acculturation policies, 16, 19, 25–6, 28, 30–2, 188
  adoption of European dress, 85, 90, 93, 98
  Blackfoot resistance, 7, 37, 46, 47, 49, 51, 57, 59, 65, 106, 189
  "Eastern" First Nations, 211n
  Grinnell's views, 122
  McFee's views, 119
  Warrior's "Compatriots", 181, 184
  see also assimilationist policies; civilization policies
age-graded societies see I-kun-uh'-kah-tsi
Agwmaxkayi (Many Swans), 79, 92–3
Ah-kay-ee-pix-en (The Woman Who Strikes Many), 95
Ahkiiwa Iyoumako Mistewaw, Sokapiiwa (Good Crooked Stick Woman) see Crowe, Thedis
Ahko Pitsu see Chewing Black Bone (Sikochkeka)
akáinauasiu, 66, 171, 219n
Akai'niskimyaki (Many Buffalo Stones Woman), 79
Akay-Namuka (Many Guns) see Gladstone, James
Ako-katssinn see Circle Camp gathering
Alberta Blackfoot reserves see Kainai (Blood Reserve Alberta); Pikuni (Piegan Reserve Alberta); Siksika (Blackfoot Reserve Alberta)

All-are-his-Children, 148
all-comrades societies see I-kun-uh'-kah-tsi
Almost-a-Dog, 34, 147
American Fur Company, 3, 4, 89, 90
Anderson, Benedict, 84
anthropology, 116–17, 125, 232n
Apikuni (Far-Off White Robe) see Schultz, James Willard
Apináko'tamiso (Tomorrow Coming Over The Hill), 153
Ashcroft, Bill, 109
assimilationist policies, 24, 25, 30–2, 99, 111
  Blackfoot resistance, 46, 193
  Chiefs' co-operation, 102, 107
  missionaries, 35
  Ookaan, 16, 23, 27, 37–42, 45, 59–60
  see also acculturation policies; civilization policies
Assiniboine First Nation
  Assiniboine dress, 67, 68, 69, 84
  Blackfoot name for, 11
  relations with Blackfoot, 89, 217n
  trade, 63–4, 85, 87, 88, 218n
At-séna (Gros Ventre) First Nation, 1, 8, 219n, 243n
Audubon, John James, 96

Bad Guns band (Siksika), 79
Bad Head, 140
Bahktin, Mikhail, 143
Baker, Eugene M., 30, 124
Baldwin, Major, 43–4, 152
Bammer, Angelika, 109–10
Banks, Constable, 50
Barthes, Roland, 237n
Bascom, William, 136–7
Bastien, Betty, 6, 160, 161, 183, 193
beads, introduction of, 67, 73, 93, 110, 224n
Bear Chief, 92, 120, 223n
Bear Head (Kai Otokan), 124, 155, 169, 177–8
Bear Shield, Annie, 223n
Bear Skin, 220n
Beaver Bundles, 20, 71, 74, 160

Index

Begg, Magnus, 31, 47–8
Belaney, Archie (Grey Owl), 180
Benedict, Ruth, 81
Bent, George, 121
Berkhofer, Jr., Robert, 30, 32–3, 34, 118
Bhabha, Homi, 105
bicultural individuals
  Blackfoot knowledge, 118–19, 121, 126–8, 147, 148, 154
  Blackfoot women, 96, 97, 98
Big Brave, 124, 125
Big Brave's Winter Count, 77
Big Bravo, 47, 215n
Big Nose (Three Suns), 124, 144–5, 147, 207n
Big Plume, Louise, 118
Big Swan, 92
Big Wolf, 52
Bird Chief, 124
bison, 25, 99
  see also buffalo herds
Black Bear, 125
Black Fever, 215n
Blackfeet Reservation (Montana) *see* Pikuni (Blackfeet Reservation Montana)
Blackfoot First Nations
  acquire the horse, 2, 66, 76, 87–8, 218n
  adoption of European dress, 85, 90, 93, 98, 101
  adoption of Western technologies, 2–3, 106, 152, 188
  adoption of whites, 121, 148, 152–3
  American lack of knowledge, 118
  band leadership, 1–2, 69–73, 189–90
  children, 106
  counting coup (*Naamaahkaani*), 18, 21–2, 71, 80, 86, 142–3, 144, 207n
  dependency on government food rations, 25, 30, 32, 100
  honour code, 34, 75
  horse adornments, 88, 224–5n
  nomenclature, 8–9
  population in Canada, 195, 196, 197, 198–9
  resistance to acculturation 7, 37, 46–7, 49, 51, 57, 59, 65, 106, 189
  revenge parties, 34
  smallpox outbreaks, 34, 140, 169
  stereotypes, 33, 106, 118, 143, 148, 151, 155, 178
  tourist entertainment, 109, 110, 111
  treaty with Crees, 79
  treaty with Canada (1877), 7, 9, 27, 29, 32, 33, 35, 38, 52, 56, 64, 92, 101–2, 104–5, 106, 110, 145, 152, 153, 198–9, 228n, 265n
  treaty with United States (1855), 9, 26, 33, 64, 101, 168, 228n, 241n
  warring and horse raiding, 34, 80, 102, 171
  see also Kainai First Nation; Pikuni First Nation; Siksika First Nation; Treaty Seven (1877)
Blackfoot Gallery Committee, 8
Blackfoot Reserve Alberta *see* Siksika (Blackfoot Reserve Alberta)
Blackfoot Stories, 129–38, 190–2
  "Cuts-wood", 206n, 221n
  "Elk Woman", 17, 73–5, 166, 206n, 221n, 242n
  "Everyday Stories", 131, 132, 137, 139
  "The First Marriage" story, 73
  "How the Blackfeet got the Pinto Ponies", 87
  as literature, 133, 192
  "Old People Stories", 131, 132, 138
  "Otter-woman", 206n, 221n
  rejection of myth, 132
  "The Scabby-round-robe", 206n, 221n
  "Story of Kutóyis", 135
  "Story of the Lost Children", 148
  "Story of the Medicine Lodge (Ookaan)", 148
  "The Theft from the Sun", 136
  toponomies, 139
  truth claims, 146–9, 154, 191
  "The Woman-who-married-a-star", 74, 206n, 221n, 243n
  see also Scarface Story
Blackfoot-Man, 120
Blood Reserve *see* Kainai (Blood Reserve Alberta)
Boas, Frantz, 117, 125, 132, 137, 139, 242n
Bodmer, Karl, 5, 65, *col. plate 1*, *col. plate 3*, *col. plate 5*
  Blackfoot in a Navajo blanket, 84
  native dress, 90
  painted robes, 145
  portrait of Mehkskéhme-Sukáhs, 140
  portrait of Stu-mick-o-súks (1833), 67, 93
  shirt decorations, 68
Bow River, 27
Braves Warrior Society, 71, 220n
bricolage, 85, 224n
Brings-down-the-Sun *see* Natosi Nepe-e (Brings-down-the-Sun)
Brotherston, Gordon, 130
Bruchac, Joseph, 80
buckskin suits
  circulation of, 71
  continuity of, 84
  as exchange gift, 91

✦ 294 ✦

Index

manly-hearted women, 81
Scarface Story, 66, 67, 68–9, 70, 71, 84, 86
  symbolism to Blackfoot, 100, 106, 108–11, 190
Buffalo Bull's Back Fat *see* Stu-mick-o-súks (Buffalo Bull's Back Fat)
buffalo herds
  destruction of, 15, 19, 23, 24, 25, 99, 169, 188
  Ookaan, 15
  robes trade, 4, 24, 25, 88, 169–70
Buffalo Women's Society *see* Ma'toki Society
Bull Bear, David, 50
Bull Child, George, 153
Bull Plume, 6
  gifts and "giveaways", 48–9
  technology of writing, 141–2, 151
  winter count, 55, 77, 140–2, 153
Bull Shield, 172
Bullchild, 6, 10, 69, 71
Bulls Head, 53
Bundles, transfer of
  Beaver Bundles, 20, 71, 74, 160
  Natoas Bundle, 17–18, 74, 166, 206*n*
  see also Medicine Pipe Bundles; Sacred Bundles
Burke, Peter, 85
Burnham, Lord, 229*n*, 231*n*

Calfchild, Joe, 102
Calf Old Woman, 80
Calf Robe, 51
Calf Robe, Ben, 207*n*, 230*n*
Calgary Stampede, 40, 41, 109, 110, 111, 230*n*
Canada
  Blackfoot leadership positions, 102
  Blackfoot population, 195, 196, 197, 198–9
  Blackfoot warring and horse raiding, 34
  Indian Act (1876), 33–4, 35–7, 40, 41, 48, 52
  Indian Act (1884), 102
  residential schools, 26
  Vagrant Act, 38
  see also Treaty Seven (1877)
Canadian Department of Indian Affairs (DIA)
  Blackfoot gifts and "giveaways", 48–9
  Blackfoot polygamous marriages, 46
  First Nations advance to civilization, 42
  First Nations confined to reserves, 32
  local Fairs, 40, 41
  Pass System, 38
  promotion of agriculture and pastoral pursuits, 26

sun dances, 42, 45, 51, 56, 57
Canadian officials
  attempts to eliminate sun dances, 16–17, 19–20, 23, 25, 28, 31–2, 37–42, 46–59, 107, 189
  "civilization" policies, 25, 28–35
  see also acculturation policies; assimilationist policies; North-West Mounted Police (NWMP)
Carlisle Indian School, 26
Carnegie, Andrew, 120
Carpenter, James, 118
Carroll, John B., 27, 44–5
Carter, Sarah, 80
Catlin, George, 5, 65
  Assiniboine dress, 67
  Blackfoot women, 73, 78, 94–5
  portrait of Eeh-nís-kim, 73, col. plate 4
  portrait of Stu-mick-o-súks, 66–7, col. plate 2
  shirt decorations, 68
Charles, Prince of Wales, 153, 231*n*
Chartrand, Paul, 9
Chewing Black Bone (Sikochkeka), 124, 162, 241*n*
Chief Calf, 228*n*
Christianity
  Blackfoot attitudes, 46, 56, 106–7, 108
  Blackfoot expected to adopt, 26, 32
  as first step to civilization, 27, 28
  Pikuni in Montana, 59
  self-mortification, 23
  sun dances as obstacle, 16, 25, 27, 32, 44
  Warrior's "Compatriots", 180, 182, 184
  see also missionaries
Circle Camp gathering, 2, 15–23
  Beaver Bundles, 20, 71, 74, 160
  buffalo tongues sacramental meal, 19, 23, 49–50, 54–5
  counting coup (*Naamaahkaani*), 18, 21–2, 80, 86, 142–3, 144, 207*n*
  Crowfoot's attendance, 47
  dress, 71
  generosity, 19–20, 21–2, 23, 33, 36, 71, 167, 170–1
  gifts and "giveaways", 19, 20, 21–2, 48–9, 161
  I-kun-uh'-kah-tsi, 20, 21
  initiation rites, 71
  Kainai Circle Camp (1893), 53
  Kainai Circle Camp (1902), 38
  marriages, 22, 134, 207*n*
  missionaries and officials fear of, 28
  Natoas Bundle, 17–18, 74, 166, 206*n*
  reciprocity, 17–18, 19–21, 23, 33, 36, 170–1
  renewing acquaintance role, 15, 37
  sacrifice, 19–20, 22, 23, 36, 160

✦ 295 ✦

Index

Circle Camp gathering *(continued)*
 Scarface Story, 134
 Siksika, 15, 21, 38, 48, 50
 see also Medicine Pipe Bundles; Ookaan; Sacred Bundles
civilization policies, 24, 28–35, 190–1
 Blackfoot leaders' obligations, 102
 DIA reports, 42
 effects on Blackfoot, 188
 Medicine Men as obstacle, 42–3
 sun dances as obstacle, 16, 25, 27, 32, 44, 109
 white superiority claims, 27, 30, 37, 58, 117, 128, 130, 173
 see also acculturation policies; assimilationist policies
Clark, William, 85, 86, 90, 92, 101, 144
Clarke, Malcolm, 173, 243*n*
Clifford, James, 117, 123
Cocking, Matthew, 3, 5, 8
Cody, Buffalo Bill, 40
Cold Band, 93
Cold Maker, Welch's *Fools Crow*, 174, 175, 177
Collier, John, 58
colonization
 asymmetrical power relations, 116
 Blackfoot leadership positions, 100
 dominance of First Nations, 24, 100
 extinction discourse, 30–1
 fur traders' role, 169
 influence on Native literatures, 186
 Warrior's "Compatriots", 182, 186
 see also acculturation policies; assimilationist policies; civilization policies; Indian agents; missionaries; reserves and reservations era; settlers
Columbus, Christopher, 9–10, 28, 149
compassion, 161, 241*n*
Conaty, Gerald, 5, 20, 161
Cook, Lorenzo, 44
Cooke, L.W., 145
Cornish, F.C., 52, 53
Corps of Discovery, 85
Coues, Elliott, 5
coups, 68, 70
 counting of, 21, 22, 71, 80, 86, 142–3, 144, 207*n*
"Coyote painting", 71, 219*n*
Crazy Dogs Society, 2
Cree First Nation
 Blackfoot name for, 11
 interference in their ceremonies, 55
 relations with Blackfoot, 79, 92, 217*n*
 trade with Blackfoot, 63–4, 87, 88, 218*n*
 Treaty Six, 27
Crooked Meat Strings (Imiten.a), 6, 79, 204*n*, 220*n*

Crop-eared Wolf, 52
Crow First Nation, 73
Crowe, Thedis, 116, 117, 131, 155
Crowfoot (Isapo-Muxica), *104*
 death of, 47, 215*n*
 Dempsey's biography, 7, 47, 104, 190
 as leading negotiator, 7, 104–5, 189
 name changes, 9
 self-mortification rituals, 47
 trading visits, 92
 Treaty Seven, 7, 9, 35, 92, 104–5
 white habits, 106
Crowshoe, Reg, 6
The Crystal Stone (Eeh-nís-kim), 73, 94–5, col. plate 4
Culbertson, Alexander, 96, 98, 227*n*
cultural relativism, 150
Curtis, Edward, 151
Custer, George Armstrong, 119
"Cuts-wood", 206*n*, 221*n*

Dakota First Nation, 18
Dawes Act (1887), 33
Dawson, Thomas, 148
Day Chief, 52, 55, 102–3, 216*n*, 228*n*
De Smet, Pierre-Jean, 26
Deane, Superintendent, 38, 54, 55
Dempsey, Hugh
 Bad Head's Winter Count, 140
 biography of Crowfoot, 7, 47, 104, 190
 biography of Red Crow, 7, 53, 76, 104, 190, 229*n*
 Mountain Horse's autobiography, 142
Dempsey, James, 127, 144, 145
Department of Indian Affairs (DIA) *see* Canadian Department of Indian Affairs (DIA)
Derrida, Jacques, 131, 137
Dewdney, Edgar, 47, 100–1
DIA *see* Canadian Department of Indian Affairs (DIA)
Dickens, Charles, 97
Dilworth, W.J., 31, 56
dog days, 66, 67, 68, 159, 162, 241–2*n*
Donaldson, Jessie Louise, 86, 121
Double Runner, 122, 124, 148, 152, 155, 177
Dream Helper (Nitsokan), Welch's *Fools Crow*, 145
dreams
 dress designs, 65, 69
 sacred power, 147
dress, Blackfoot, 63–5, 189–90
 age-graded societies, 70
 band leadership, 69–73
 bonnet styles, 65, 109
 ceremonial, 70–1
 decorations, 65

✦ 296 ✦

Index

diplomatic transactions, 64, 65
elites, 63, 68, 69, 82, 98, 99, 105
European style adoption, 85, 90, 93, 96, 97, 98–9, 100, 105, 108, 190
fur trade impact, 63–4, 84–5, 88–93, 94, 95, 96–9, 189
as gifts, 65, 71
hair locks, 66, 67, 68–9, 86, 102, Piegan, 219–20n
headdress, 86, 109, 230n
hybridity, 65, 95, 98, 99
intertribal exchange, 84–8
Kainai First Nation, 71, 220n
as a marker of status, 64
materials, 65, 66, 93, 99, 100
military-style uniforms, 90, 91, 92–3, 94, 98, 101–2, 105, 106, 190
prohibitions and taboos, 69, 83
quilling, 73, 93, 222n
received in dreams, 65, 69
reserves and reservations, 100–2, 105–11
restrictions, 72
sacred dimension of, 66–9, 82–3
sacred and secular worldview, 65–6, 68–9, 72, 82
"story" robes, 67
variety of designs, 64, 65
and war success, 69, 70, 84, 86, 87–8
women, 73–5, 78, 79, 80, 82, 93, 94, 95, 96–8, 190
see also beads; buckskin suits
Durkheim, Emile, 117
Duvall, Charles, 118
Duvall, David, 142
background, 126
death of, 126–7, 234–5n
mixed ancestry, 6, 118, 126, 146, 205n
Mythology of the Blackfoot Indians, 5, 115, 116, 118, 125–6, 134, 136, 150
Scarface Story, 66, 134, 162, 164
translation skills, 118, 125, 126

Eagle Ribs, 228n
Eagle Robe, 228n
Earth Beings, 160, 207n
Eco, Umberto, 9
Edmunds, R. David, 136
Edward, Prince of Wales, 153
Eeh-nís-kim (The Crystal Stone), 73, 94–5, col. plate 4
Elbow River, 27
Eliade, Mircea, 132
elites, Blackfoot
as cultural brokers, 110
dress, 63, 68, 69, 82, 98, 99, 105
as organic intellectuals, 146
privileges, 110–11
traders' gifts, 91

women, 75, 78–9, 89, 96, 110
elk teeth, 73, 74–5, 93, 221n
Elk Woman, 17, 73–5, 166, 206n, 221n, 242n
epistemology, Blackfoot
Blackfoot Stories, 138, 190
knowledge and power, 147, 151
oral tradition, 116
preservation of knowledge, 130
transmission of knowledge, 6, 138
truth of discourses, 138, 143, 145, 146, 191
ethnography, 115–28, 146–55, 232n
ethnology, 232n
see also salvage ethnology
Ewers, John, 7
Blackfoot trade, 85
Bodmer's portraits, 90
famine (1883–84), 152
in Browning (1941–44), 59
Running Eagle's life, 80
sun dances, 59

Far-Off White Robe, 125
Feather Woman *see* So-at-sa-ki (Feather Woman)
Fine Shield Woman (Mutsi-Awotan-Ahki), 121
Finley, M.I., 132
First Nations peoples
absence of writing, 129
"All my Relations" concept, 160, 173–5, 192
causes of poverty according to missionaries, 22
"civilization" policies, 28–32, 42, 188, 190–1
colonial dominance, 24, 100
communitarian lifeways, 33
conflict with Americans, 30
dependency on government food rations, 16
early chroniclers, 149
eradication of cultural practices, 25
extinction discourse, 30–1, 121–3, 128
Fort Laramie Treaty, 26, 228n
hospitality to white travellers, 94
"Indian problem", 31, 33
individualism, 32–3
intermarriage, 87
intertribal exchange, 84–8
missionary enterprise, 27–8
negative stereotyping of enemies, 11
sign language, 86, 224n
stereotypes, 179, 186–7
storytelling, 130
virgin soil diseases, 27
westward movement of, 4

Index

First Nations peoples *(continued)*
  see also acculturation policies;
    assimilationist policies; Blackfoot First
    Nations; colonization; reserves and
    reservations era; sun dances
flags, 91, 226*n*
folktales, definition, 136
Fools Crow (a.k.a. White Man's Dog),
  Welch's *Fools Crow*, 123, 168–78
Fools Crow, Frank (Lakota ceremonialist),
  58, 172
Forest and Stream, 30, 119, 121, 135, 152,
  233*n*
Forget, A.E., 50, 53, 54
Fort Benton, 24, 96, 126, 169
Fort Edmonton, 27, 92, 93, 96, 225*n*
Fort Laramie Treaty, 26, 228*n*
Fort York, 5, 87, 90
Foucault, Michel, 137
  power concept, 75–6
  role of authors, 237*n*
  "rules of exclusion", 143
  truth and power, 146, 154, 239*n*
  universities' constraint on knowledge,
    117
Four Bears, 147
Fuller, Thomas, 44
fur trade, 3–4
  Blackfoot cultural transformation, 25,
    169, 189
  Blackfoot women, 89, 93–9
  diplomatic ties, 64
  impact on Blackfoot dress, 63–4, 84–5,
    88–93, 94, 95, 96–9, 189
  reciprocity practices, 89–92
  see also American Fur Company;
    Hudson's Bay Company; Northwest
    Company; trading posts

Gaultier de Varennes et de la Vérendrye,
  Pierre, 85
Geertz, Clifford, 137
generosity practices
  Blackfoot leaders, 2, 69, 70, 71, 72,
    161
  Circle Camp gathering, 19–20, 21–2, 23,
    33, 36, 71, 167, 170–1
  dress gifts, 71
  minipuka, 72
  Scarface Story, 86, 161, 165
  as social imperative, 161
  universe in balance, 160
  Warrior's "Compatriots", 179, 181, 184,
    186
Gerring, Elbert, US Superintendent Indian
  Affairs, 30
Ghost Dance religion, 28
Glacier National Park, 109, 111, 127, 149

Gladstone, James (a.k.a. Akay-Namuka
  (Many Guns), 7
Goldfrank, Esther S., 33, 59, 81
Good Crooked Stick Woman *see* Crowe,
  Thedis
Good Young Man, 53
Gooderham, George, 41, 48, 50, 51, *51*,
  102
Gooderham, John, 48, 151
Goody, Jack, 150, 191, 245*n*
Graham, William Morris, 42
Grandparents (respected elders), 43, 118,
  128, 131, 147, 151, 191
Grant, Ulysses S., 26
Grease Melters (*Ich-poch-semo*) Band, 140
Greenblatt, Stephen, 65
Gretchen (Duvall's wife), 126
Grinnell, George Bird
  attitude to First Nations peoples, 130,
    148
  attitude to mixed ancestry, 126
  background, 119
  Blackfoot bands, 1
  Blackfoot by adoption, 121, 152
  Blackfoot dress, 101
  Blackfoot extinction threat, 30, 121–2
  Blackfoot Lodge Tales, 5, 115, 116, 117,
    118, 121, 122–3, 124, 135–6, 147–9,
    155
  Blackfoot name, 152
  Blackfoot Stories as literature, 133, 192
  Duvall's death, 127
  expeditions, 119
  famine (1883-84), 119, 152
  Forest and Stream journal, 30, 119, 121,
    152
  lobbying for Blackfoot, 119
  painted robes, 145
  recognition to Schultz, 121
  sale of Pikuni land (1895), 149
  Scarface Story, 162, 165
  self-mortification rituals, 23
  superiority of civilization, 173
  women's position, 78, 221*n*
Gros Blanc, 93
Gros Ventre *see* At-séna (Gros Ventre) First
  Nation
guns
  First Nations dependence on, 89
  obtained through war, 87

Hall, D.J., 39
Hamilton, Robert J., 44, 45
Hanks, Lucien, 75, 110, 111, 151, 154
Harper, Corporal, 48, 50
Harris III, Edward Day, 119, 152
Harrod, Howard, 44
Haynes, William, 141, 151

Index

Hearne, Samuel, 77
Heavy Gun, 125, 126
Heavy Runner, 30, 34, 147, 153, 169, 176, 177
Heavy Shield Woman, 175
Henday, Anthony, 3, 5
Henry, Alexander, 73
Henry the Younger, Alexander, 5, 71, 91, 93–4
Hernandez, Nimachia, 6, 193
  Blackfoot ideals, 161
  Blackfoot Stories, 132, 135, 137, 139
  natoyi ("Medicine"), 200*n*
Hewitt, John N.B., 118
Hidatsa people, 84
history, Western conceptions of, 132–3
history, Blackfoot, 138–55
  see also Blackfoot Stories; oral tradition; pictographs; war art; winter counts
Holy Milk, 77
Holy Snake Woman (Natuyitsixina), 96–8, 97, 227*n*
Holy Woman, Ookaan, 17, 19, 74–5, 77, 154, 163, 166, 175
Homer, 133
Horn Society, 2, 21, 54, 70, 83, 111, 142
horse
  Blackfoot acquisition, 2, 66, 76, 87–8, 218*n*
  raiding for horses, 34, 80, 102, 171
  adornments, 88, 224–5*n*
  "How the Blackfeet got the Pinto Ponies", 87
Hudson's Bay Company
  Blackfoot trade, 3, 88, 92, 94, 96
  expeditions, 77
  Fort Edmonton, 27, 92, 93, 96, 225*n*
  Fort York, 5, 87, 90
  Mandan trade, 85
  military-style uniform gifts, 79, 90, 92
Huggonard, J., 27
Hungry Wolf, Adolf, 180, 181
Hungry Wolf, Beverly, 6, 116, 185
Hunt, George, 118, 125
Hürlimann, Johann, *col. plate 3*
Hyde, George, 121
Hymes, Dell, 133, 164, 192

I-kun-uh'-kah-tsi, 2, 20, 21, 70, 71, 75, 83
Ich-poch-semo (Grease Melters) Band, 140
Imiten.a (Crooked Meat Strings), 6, 79, 204*n*, 220*n*
Indian agents
  colonialism, 37
  corruption, 29, 210*n*
  as *ex officio* Justice of the Peace, 39
  measures of success, 31
  Pass System, 38–9
  provision for future needs, 22
  reserves and reservations, 101, 102–3, 108
  self-mortification rituals, 22
  sun dances, 31, 37, 38–40, 41, 42, 50–7, 109
  tutelage role, 26
Indian Trade and Intercourse Act (1790), 25
Ipiso-Waahsa (the Morning Star)
  Ookaan, 17, 206*n*
  Scarface story, 66, 68, 134, 159, 160, 162, 164, 165, 166, 168
  "Story of a Woman Who Married a Star", 74
  Welch's *Fools Crow*, 168, 176
Iron Shirt (Mehkskéme-Sukáhs), 90, 140, 141, 238*n*
Isapo-muxica *see* Crowfoot (Isapo-Muxica)
istuisanaps, 72

Jackson, William (a.k.a. Siksikakoan or Blackfoot-Man), 120, 148
Jenness, Diamond, 75
Jesuits, 26, 202*n*
Josephy, Alvin, 142
Josselin de Jong, J.P.B. de, 120
Joyce, James, 179

Kai Otokan (Bear Head), 124, 155, 169, 177–8
Kainai (Blood Reserve Alberta)
  Circle Camp gathering, 31, 38, 53
  Governor-General visit (1889), 41
  individualism, 33
  Ookaan, 16, 17, 51, 53, 56
  settlement due to starvation, 25
Kainai First Nation
  adoption of whites, 153
  attack on Fort Piegan (1833), 3
  bands, 1–2
  Braves Warrior Society, 71, 220*n*
  dress, 71, 220*n*
  Hungry Wolfs, 180
  individualism, 33
  manly-hearted women, 81
  nomenclature, 8–9
  Ookaan, 16, 17, 51–2, 53–6, 59
  population in Canada, 197, 198–9
  trading visits, 92
  war trophies, 142
  weasel pelts, 224*n*
  see also Red Crow (Mekasto)
Katoyisiks (the Sweetgrass Hills), 139
Kehoe, Alice
  Blackfoot autonomy, 80–1
  Blackfoot women, 163

Index

Kehoe, Alice *(continued)*
  Holy Woman, 74
  Mythology of the Blackfoot Indians
    introduction, 125–6
  Ookaan, 74
  power in Blackfoot culture, 74, 75, 76, 79, 82, 163
  Uhlenbeck's texts, 128, 135
  Wissler's work on Blackfoot, 126, 127
Kelsey, Henry, 90
King, Thomas, 160, 173, 192
Kipp, Darrell Robes, 123
Kipp, (Joe) Joseph (Raven Quiver), 124, 127
Kipp, Woody, 6, 160, 161, 236*n*
knowledge, Blackfoot
  bicultural individuals, 118–19, 121, 126–8, 147, 148, 154
  "Everyday Stories", 131, 132, 137, 139
  Grandparents, 43, 118, 128, 131, 147, 151, 191
  mnemonic tools, 139, 143, 145
  "Old People Stories", 131, 132, 138
  sacred and secular worldview, 135
  salvage ethnology, 5–6, 115–28, 146–55, 191
  "ways of knowing", 138–46
  see also Blackfoot Stories; *natoyi* ("Medicine"); oral tradition; pictographs; Sacred Bundles; war art; winter counts
Kokomi-kisomm (the Moon)
  Ookaan, 17
  Scarface story, 66, 159, 160, 164, 166
Ksahkomi-tapiksi (Earth Beings), 160, 207*n*
Ksisstsi'ko'm (Thunder), 160

Lacombe, Albert, 27, 239*n*
LaFlesche, Francis, 118
Laird, David, 57
Lakota First Nation
  lamenting, 241*n*
  ritual piercing, 48, 58
  Sun Dance, 48, 58, 172
Laramy Treaty negotiations (1851), 26, 228*n*
Larson, Sidner, 123, 142, 143
legends, 116, 136–7
Lethbridge Herald, 140
Lewis, Meriwether
  conflict with Pikuni (1806), 3
  gifts to leaders, 90, 92, 101
  guns and ammunition trade, 3, 86
  painted buffalo robes, 144
  peace treaty with the Mandans, 90
  presentation of medals, 227*n*
  winter with the Mandan (1804-5), 85, 86

Lewis, Oscar
  elite Blackfoot women, 110
  manly-hearted women, 81–2, 83
  slave wives, 95
liquor, effects of, 27
Lisa, Manuel, 3
Little Bear, Beverly, 180
Little Dog, 152
Little Light, 50
Little Person, 228*n*
Little Pine, 52
Little Plume, 152, 230*n*
Lone Eaters band, 170, 172, 173, 177, 178
Lone Fighters Band, 140
Lone Medicine Person, 148
Louise Big Plume, 118
Lupton, Mary Jane, 169, 175

Ma-kwi'-i-po-wak-sin (Rising Wolf) *see* Monroe, Hugh
McClintock, Walter (A-pe-ech-eken (White Weasel Moccasin))
  background, 119–20
  Blackfoot by adoption, 121, 152
  Blackfoot children, 106
  Blackfoot extinction threat, 123
  Blackfoot leaders, 72
  Blackfoot travels, 85
  dress with elk teeth, 73
  first contact with Blackfoot, 119–20
  The Old North Trail, 5, 23, 115, 116, 118, 122–3, 136, 148, 170
  Ookaan, 23, 58
  photographs of the Blackfoot, 123
  relations with Bull Plume, 140–1, 142, 151
  relations with Natosi Nepe-e, 58, 140–1, 142, 148, 151, 162
  Scarface Story, 162, 166, 206*n*
  superiority of civilization, 173
  winter counts, 140–1, 142
  women's position, 78
McDonald, James, 213*n*
McDougall, John, 27
McFee, Malcolm, 118–19
McKenzie, Kenneth, 89
McKinnon, Ann, 180
Maclean, John, 27, 201*n*
Macleod, Justice, 51, 52, 53
McLuhan, Marshall, 64
Mad Dog Society, 2
Mad Wolf (Siyeh), 152, 170
Makúya.to'si (Wolf Sun), 153
Mandan people, 85, 90, 92, 144
Many Buffalo Stones Woman (Akai'niskimyaki), 79
Many Guns (Akay-Namuka) *see* Gladstone, James

Index

Many Guns, 154
Many Guns Winter Count, 59, 77, 153–4, 247
Many Spotted Horses, 237n
Many Swans, 79, 92–3
Many-Tail-Feathers, 124
Marcus, George, 123
Marias River, 30
Markle, J.A., 107
Marsh, Otheniel, 119
Ma'toki Society, 21, 54
  bundle, 54
Matonabbee, 76–7, 94
Maximilian of Wied-Neuwied, Alexander Philipp, 5, 65, 67, 68, 84, 90, 145
medals, 101, 102–3, 227–8n
Medicine Lodge, built to Natosi, 17, 18, 154, 166, 200n
  see also Ookaan
Medicine Men, 42–3, 200n, 215n
"Medicine" (natoyi), 2, 69, 71, 72, 147, 200n
Medicine Pipe Bundles
  changed Blackfoot views on, 108
  dress, 71, 108
  received from sacred beings, 20, 74, 160, 200n
  Singing Before's vow, 54
  transfer of, 20–1, 48, 50, 71
Mehkskéhme-Sukáhs (Iron Shirt), 90, 140, 141, 238n
Mekasto see Red Crow (Mekasto)
M'Gillivray, Duncan, 78
Miller, James, 91
mimicry, 105–6
minipuka, 72–3, 78, 81, 83, 108, 221n
Minto, Lord, 39
missionaries
  assimilation efforts, 35
  attempts to eliminate sun dances, 16, 25, 27–8, 31, 189
  baptism of Blackfoot, 35, 46, 106
  conversion efforts, 25–8, 46
  education of First Nation children, 26
  friendships with Blackfoot, 46
  Indian children donations, 48
  poverty among First Nations, 22
  provision for future needs, 22
  self-mortification rituals, 22, 23
  as vanguard of colonialism, 37
Mitchell, David, 90
Moccasin Band, 47, 105
Momaday, N. Scott, 130
Monroe, Hugh, (Ma-kwi'-i-po-wak-sin (Rising Wolf)), 124, 148, 239n
Monroe, John, 148
Montana
  arrival of railways, 24, 25

Blackfoot and settler violence, 34
  discovery of gold, 24–5
Montana Blackfeet Reservation see Pikuni (Blackfeet Reservation Montana)
the Moon see Kokomi-kisomm (the Moon)
Morgan, Lewis Henry, 117, 122
Morgan, Thomas Jefferson, 29, 30, 43
the Morning Star see Ipiso-Waahsa (the Morning Star)
Morris, Alexander, 28, 33
Motokix see Ma'toki Society
Mountain Chief (South Pikuni head chief), 125
Mountain Chief, Walter (South Pikuni), 128
Mountain Chief, Welch's Fools Crow, 170, 173, 176
Mountain Horse, Mike, 6, 142, 143, 155, 169
mourning practices, Blackfoot, 23, 47, 82, 176, 207n
Mutsi-Awotan-Ahki (Fine Shield Woman), 121
myth
  meaning of, 132, 136, 137
  older stories, 132
  pre-colonial histories, 191
  see also white mythologies

Naa-to-yi-ta-piiksi (Spirit Beings), 17
Naamaahkaani (counting coup), 21, 22, 71, 80, 86, 142–3, 144, 207n
Nabokov, Peter, 129, 132, 136, 139, 144, 146
Napi (Napiwa or Old Man), 136, 139, 164, 242n
  stories, 127, 136, 161
Natawista (Natuyitsixina), 96–8, 97, 227n
Natoas Bundle, 17–18, 74, 166, 206n
Natosi Nepe-e (Brings-down-the-Sun), 6
  McClintock's studies, 58, 140–1, 142, 148, 151, 162
  Ookaan, 57–8
  Scarface Story, 162, 168, 176
  "Story of a Woman Who Married a Star", 74
  views on whites, 57–8
  winter count, 140–2
Natosi (the Sun)
  Ookaan, 17, 18, 19, 20, 22, 74, 159, 161, 167, 171
  Scarface story, 66, 68, 69, 70, 71, 84, 159, 160, 161, 163–4, 165–6, 175, 242n
  Welch's Fools Crow, 170, 172, 175
natoyi ("Medicine"), 2, 69, 71, 72, 147
Natuyitsixina (Natawista), 96–8, 97, 227n
Naywatame poets, 90

◆ 301 ◆

Index

Nicholas (first baptized Blackfoot), 26
Night-Light *see* Kokomi-kisomm (the Moon)
Nii't'kaiksa'maikoan (Pete Standing Alone), 6, 143, 201*n*, 224*n*
Niitsitapiksi (Real People), 8
Nin-ais-tukku, 139
ninauake wives, 78–9, 82, 95, 227*n*
ninauposkitzipxpe (manly-hearted women), 81–2, 83
Ninnaa, 1
Ninonista, 96
Nitsi-poi-yiksi (speakers of the Real Language), 8
Nitsitapiisinni ("Our Way of Life"), 131
Nitsokan (Dream Helper), Welch's *Fools Crow*, 145
North-West Mounted Police (NWMP)
  Blackfoot warring and raiding for horses, 34
  functions of, 37, 213*n*
  Pass System, 38
  relations with Blackfoot, 34, 103
  residential schools' practices, 26
  Riel Rebellion (1885), 38
  Sarcee Sun Dance, 37
  sun dances, 41, 45, 50–2, 54–5
Northwest Company
  Blackfoot trade, 3, 88, 94
  gifts to Blackfoot, 91–2
  Mandan trade, 85

Old Bull, 20
Old Man (Napiwa, Napi), 136, 139, 164, 242*n*
  stories, 127, 136, 161
Old Sun, 80, 105
Old Women's Society *see* Ma'toki Society
Ong, Walter, 133, 149–50
Ookaan, 15–23
  attempts to eliminate, 16–17, 19–20, 23, 43–4, 46–59, 107, 189
  colonial legislation, 35–7
  cultural centrality of, 2, 17–19, 37, 167
  dress, 71
  fourfold repetition, 164
  generosity practices, 19–20, 21–2, 23, 33, 36, 71, 167, 170–1
  Holy Woman, 17, 19, 74–5, 77, 154, 163, 166, 175
  Ipiso-Waahsa (the Morning Star), 17, 206*n*
  Many Guns Winter Count, 154
  Medicine Lodge, 17, 18, 154, 166, 200*n*
  Natosi (the Sun), 17, 18, 19, 20, 22, 74, 159, 161, 167, 171
  prayers for "good crops", 50
  reciprocity practices, 17–18, 19–21, 23, 33, 36, 170–1
  Scarface Story, 15, 19, 66
  self-mortification rituals, 19, 20, 22–3, 36, 47–8, 207*n*
  significance of, 7, 15–23, 35
  sombrero offering, 87
  sponsorship of, 109
  survival of, 109
  transformations of, 109
  Warrior's "Compatriots", 179–80, 184–5
  see also Circle Camp gathering
oral tradition
  behaviour guidelines, 159–60
  genres, 138–46
  literary value, 133, 192
  mnemonic tools, 139, 143, 145
  transformed into text, 115–28, 130, 131–5, 137, 146–55, 188–9, 190–1
  Western devaluation of, 135, 136
  see also Blackfoot Stories
"organic intellectuals", 126, 128, 146, 191
o'totamin.ai (Sits-beside-him wife), 78
"Otter-woman", 206*n*, 221*n*
Owens, Louis, 169, 170, 171, 172, 177
Owl Child, Welch's *Fools Crow*, 173–4, 176
Owl Top Feathers, 126

Pacific First Nations, 16, 208*n*
Paii *see* Scarface Story
Painted Feather, 93, 94
Parkapotokan (Bad Head), 140
Parker, Arthur, 118
Pass System, 38–9, 48
Percy Bullchild, 6, 10, 69, 71
Pi-nut-ú-ye is-tsím-okan, 152
Piapot's Reserve, 210–11*n*
pictographs, 129, 139, 238*n*
  painted robes, 67, 70, 144–5, 153
  see also war art; winter counts
Piegan First Nation *see* Pikuni First Nation
Piegan Reserve Alberta *see* Pikuni (Piegan Reserve Alberta)
Pikuni (Blackfeet Reservation Montana)
  allotment effects, 33
  bicultural individuals, 119
  buckskin suits, 110
  famine, 34, 119, 152, 176
  Grinnell's lobbying, 119
  Jesuits banned, 26
  official neglect, 119
  Ookaan, 16, 17, 45
  Pikuni separation, 3, 202*n*
  self-mortification rituals, 48
  settlement due to starvation, 25
Pikuni First Nation, *col. plate 1*
  adoption of whites, 148, 152–3

Index

at Kainai Circle Camp (1902), 38
bands, 1–2
Bull Plume's winter count, 55, 77, 140–2, 153
clash with Lewis (1806), 3
dress, 219–20n
encampment, 29
manly-hearted women, 81–2
massacre of Heavy Runner's band, 30, 34, 153, 169, 177
nomenclature, 8–9
Ookaan, 44, 54, 59
permanent separation of, 3, 202n
population in Canada, 197, 198–9
sale of land (1895), 149
smallpox outbreaks, 34, 169
Sun Dance camp, 16
tourist entertainment, 110
trading visits, 91, 92
use of white goods, 169–70
Welch's *Fools Crow*, 168–78
women's war exploits, 79–80
Pikuni (Piegan Reserve Alberta)
Blackfoot women, 110
Circle Camp (1902), 38
Ookaan, 17, 44, 54, 59
Pikuni separation, 3, 202n
settlement due to starvation, 25
Pikuni Yellow Bird, 118
Pinchot, Gifford, 119–20
Pi'tamakan (Running Eagle), 70, 79–80, 83
Pitoxpikis, 228n
pity, 161, 241n
Pocklington, William, 52, 53
Poïa *see* Scarface Story
Point, Nicolas, 208n
Porcupine Hills, 139
porcupine quills, 65, 66–7, 81, 218–19n, 238n
Potlatch, 16, 208n
power
  and truth, 146, 154, 239n
  see also natoyi ("Medicine")
Prairie Chicken Old Man, 51
Prando, Peter, 26, 215n
Pratt, Richard, 26
Pressick, Henry, 5
Price, Hiram, 31, 42, 43
Primrose, Superintendent, 55, 228n
prostitution, 27
Prucha, Francis, 29
Punke, Michael, 25

quillwork
  as a sacred occupation, 73, 222n
  see also porcupine quills

Rabid Wolf, 147

Raczka, Paul, 140, 141
railways, advent of, 24, 25
Raven Quiver (Joseph (Joe) Kipp), 124, 127
Raven, Welch's *Fools Crow*, 172, 174, 175
Raw Eater, 151
reciprocity practices
  achievement of balance, 161
  Circle Camp gathering, 17–18, 19–21, 23, 33, 36, 170–1
  dress gifts, 71
  minipuka, 72
  as social imperative, 161
  trading rituals, 89–92
  universe in balance, 160
  war trophies, 70
  Warrior's "Compatriots", 179, 181, 184, 186
Red Crane, 145
Red Crow (Mekasto), 103
  Dempsey's biography, 7, 53, 76, 104, 190, 229n
  as leading negotiator, 7
  Medicine Bundle, 54
  Ookaan, 53, 54, 55
  Pass System, 48
  sale of Kainai lands, 52
  Treaty Seven (1877), 7, 153
Red Crow, Mrs. *see* Singing Before
Red Deer Industrial School, 27
Red Eagle, 147
red paint, 67, 71, 219n, 221n, 227n
Red Plume, 125
Reed, Hayter
  eradication of indigenous cultures, 32
  Kainai lands, 52
  Pass System, 38
  replaced (1896), 39
  sun dances, 31, 37, 39, 53, 230n
reserves and reservations era, 100–11
  allotment effects, 33
  Blackfoot divisions, 106
  Blackfoot dress, 100, 101–2, 105, 106, 108–11
  ceremonial life, 108
  cultural change, 23
  dependence on government rations, 16, 25, 30
  forced settlement, 116, 188
  generosity practices prohibited, 161
  military-style uniforms, 101–2, 105, 106
  mimicry, 105–6
  missionary enterprise, 26–8
  population decline, 29, 34
  transitional time, 115–16
  war art, 144–6
  white concerns and white actions, 105–6

Index

reserves and reservations era *(continued)*
 see also acculturation policies; assimilationist policies; Kainai (Blood Reserve Alberta); Pikuni (Blackfeet Reservation Montana); Pikuni (Piegan Reserve Alberta); Siksika (Blackfoot Reserve Alberta)
residential schools, 26
Richardson Hanks, Jane, 75, 110, 111, 151, 154
Riel Rebellion (1885), 38, 190
Rising Wolf, *see* Monroe, Hugh
rituals *see* Bundles, transfer of; Ookaan; sun dances
Rivois, Charles, 124
Roessel, Ruth, 129
Roosevelt, Franklin D., 58
Roosevelt, Theodore, 33, 120, 135
Ross, Cora M., 148, 162
Rundle, Robert, 27
Runner, George, Sarcee artist, 145
Running Eagle (Pi'tamakan), 70, 79–80, 83
Running Rabbit, 147
Running Wolf (A-pe-so-muckka), 90, 140, 141, 238*n*
 see also Iron Shirt (Mehkskéme-Sukáhs)
Running Wolf (A-pe-so-muckka), son of Iron Shirt, *see* Natosi Nepe-e (Brings-down-the-Sun)
Running Wolf, Jim, (South Pikuni) 221*n*
Running Wolf (minor Kainai chief), 53–4
Running Wolf, Mrs., 53–54

Sacred Beings, 20, 74, 207*n*
Sacred Bundles
 Blackfoot leaders, 2, 69
 knowledge and songs, 138–9
 received from beings, 74, 160
 transfer of, 15, 20, 22, 37, 49, 138–9, 147
 see also Beaver Bundles; Medicine Pipe Bundles
sacred power *see natoyi* ("Medicine")
sacred and secular worldview
 Blackfoot dress, 65, 66, 68, 72, 82
 Blackfoot knowledge, 135
 Blackfoot Stories, 131, 136
 female power, 70, 190
 interrelatedness of, 7, 35, 171
 reciprocity, 17
sacred stories
 and dress, 66–9, 73, 82–3
 origins of Sun Dance, 18–19
sacrifice principle, 19–20, 22, 23, 36, 160
Said, Edward, 123–4, 149, 180
Salteaux, 55
salvage ethnology, 5–6, 115–28, 146–55, 191

 see also Duvall, David; Grinnell, George Bird; McClintock, Walter; Schultz, James Willard; Uhlenbeck, C.C.; Wissler, Clark
Sarcee *see* Tsúùt'ínà (Many People, or Every One [in the tribe]) First Nation
scalping, 69
Scarface Story, 159–67, 186, 187, 191–2
 Blackfoot ideologies, 155
 bravery and courage, 161, 165
 dress, 66, 67, 68–9, 70, 71, 84, 86
 Duvall's version, 66, 134, 162, 164
 ethical behaviour, 162–4, 192
 generosity, 86, 161, 165
 Grinnell's version, 162, 165
 Ipiso-Waahsa (the Morning Star), 66, 68, 134, 159, 160, 162, 164, 165, 166, 168
 Kokomi-kisomm (the Moon), 66, 159, 160, 164, 166
 McClintock's version, 162, 166, 206*n*
 Natosi (the Sun), 66, 68, 69, 70, 71, 84, 159, 160, 161, 163–4, 165–6, 175, 242*n*
 Ookaan, 15, 19, 66
 repetition, 164
 Scarface as Blackfoot model, 75
 Schultz's version, 162, 164
 Uhlenbeck's translation, 133–5, 162
 Welch's *Fools Crow*, 168, 176
 Wissler's version, 134, 162, 164
Schultz, James Willard
 background, 120–1
 Blackfeet and Buffalo, 5, 115, 116, 118, 124–5, 136, 169
 Blackfoot by adoption, 121, 152
 famine (1883-84), 152
 Grinnell's recognition, 121
 influence on Grinnell, 119
 Running Eagle, 80
 sale of Pikuni land (1895), 149
 Scarface Story, 162, 164
 Sun God's Children, 86
 superiority of civilization, 173
 Three Suns' Robe, 144–5
 see also Apikuni (Far-Off White Robe)
Scollen, Constantine, 27
Scott, Duncan Campbell, 33, 55, 56
Scriver, Mary, 239*n*
Seele, Keith, 121, 125, 136
settlers
 conflict with Blackfoot, 25, 34
 demise of the buffalo, 30
 land secured by treaties, 28, 31, 33
 Pass System, 38
 westward expansion, 4, 24, 25, 99, 169
sham fights, 41, 143
Sheridan, Philip Henry, 30

✦ 304 ✦

Index

Sherman, William Tecumesh, 30
Shimkin, D.B., 18
Shoshone First Nation, 88, 218*n*
Shot in Both Sides, 56
Sifton, Clifford, 39
Sikochkeka (Chewing Black Bone), 124, 162, 241*n*
Siksika (Blackfoot Reserve Alberta)
    Ookaan, 16, 17, 47–8, 49–51, 54
    self-mortification rituals, 47–8
    settlement due to starvation, 25
Siksika First Nation
    bands, 1–2
    Circle Camp gatherings, 15, 21, 38, 48, 50
    dress, 110
    making of chiefs, 220*n*
    Natoas Bundle, 206*n*
    nomenclature, 8–9
    Pass System, 48
    peace treaty with Cree, 79
    population in Canada, 197, 198–9
    trading visits, 92
    white concerns and white actions, 105
    women's reputation as cowards, 79
    see also Crowfoot (Isapo-Muxica)
Siksikakoan (Blackfoot-Man), *see* Jackson, William
Singing Before (Mrs. Red Crow), 54
Sioux Wars, 4
Sits-beside-him wife (*o'totamin.ai*), 78
Sitting Bull, 190
Siyeh (Mad Wolf), 152, 170
Sleeping on Top, 52
smallpox outbreaks, 34, 140, 169
Smart, James A., 39
Smith, Sherry, 123, 148, 153
Smithsonian Institution, 117, 128
So-at-sa-ki (Feather Woman),
    Scarface Story, 162, 166, 168, 206*n*
    Story of a Woman Who Married a Star, 74, 206*n*, 243*n*
    Welch's *Fools Crow*, 168, 176, 177
Social Darwinism, 122
Sonny, Warrior's "Compatriots", 182, 183–4
Soyii-tapiksi (Water Beings), 160, 177, 178, 207*n*
Spalding, Jim, 50, 51
Spier, Leslie, 18
Spirit Beings (Naa-to-yi-ta-piiksi), 17
Spivak, Gayatri Chakravorty, 123
Spomi-tapi-ksi *see* Above Beings
Standing Alone, Pete (Nii't'kaiksa'maikoan), 6, 143, 201*n*, 224*n*
Star Boy *see* Scarface Story

Star People, 159, 160, 161, 164–6, 167, 168
    see also Ipiso-Waahsa (the Morning Star); Kokomi-kisomm (the Moon); Natosi (the Sun)
Star Stories cycle, 66
Steele, Superintendent, 44, 53, 55
Stock-stchi, 58
Stoney (Nakoda) First Nation, 27
Stu-mick-o-súks, 66–7, 68, 73, 93, 94–5, col. plate 2
the Sun *see* Natosi (the Sun)
"Sun Dance Pole", Ookaan, 18, 23, 74
sun dances
    attempts to eliminate, 16–17, 19–20, 23, 25, 28, 31–2, 37–45, 46–59, 107, 189
    common characteristics of, 18
    dress, 71
    First Nation differences, 18
    obstacles to Christianity and civilization, 16, 25, 27, 32, 44, 109
    see also Ookaan
Sundstrom, Linea, 140
survivance, 137–8, 142, 151, 237*n*
Sweetgrass, (Cree chief), 79
Sweetgrass Hills, 139, 239*n*
Swims Under, Mike, 162, 164, 242*n*

takai (friend), 165, 166, 223*n*, 243*n*
Tatsey, Joseph, 115, 120, 127, 142
Tatsey, Mrs, 127
Taylor, Fraser, 6
Teller, Henry M., 43
testimonios, 124
Thompson, David, 5, 8
Thompson, James Westfall, 153
Three Bears, 66, 67, 68
Three Persons, Tom, 41
Three Suns (Big Nose), 124, 144–5, 147, 207*n*
Thunder (Ksisstsi'ko'm), 160
Tims, John William, 47
Titley, E. Brian, 32
Tocqueville, Alexis de, 33
Tom Kiyo, 126
Tomorrow Coming Over The Hill, 153
tourist entertainment, 109, 110, 111
trading posts, 3–4
    Blackfoot attacks, 3
    Blackfoot reaction, 3, 88
    competition, 88
    conflicts, 89
    earliest representations of First Nations, 64
    reciprocity practices, 89–92
    see also American Fur Company; fur trade; Hudson's Bay Company; Northwest Company

Index

transculturation, 85, 92, 129, 193
Treaty Seven (1877), 35
  Blackfoot education, 152
  Blackfoot negotiators, 7, 9, 35, 92, 104–5, 153
  Blackfoot signatories, 9
  commemoration of, 153
  diplomatic ties, 64
  missionary presence, 27
  Sarcee signatories, 52
Treaty Six, 27
trickster, 136
  see also Old Man (Napiwa, Napi)
Trivett, Samuel, 53
Trombley, Cecile, 126
Tsúùt'ínà (Many People, or Every One [in the tribe]), or Sarcee First Nation, 8
  at Kainai Circle Camp (1902), 38
  Blackfoot allies, 1
  Sun Dance, 22, 37, 52–3, 207n
  Treaty Seven, 27
Tylor, Edward, 117

Uhlenbeck, C.C.
  A New Series of Blackfoot Texts, 5–6, 115, 117, 127–8, 136
  background, 120
  Blackfoot extinction threat, 122
  A Concise Blackfoot Grammar, 118, 120
  Duvall's death, 127
  reliance on Tatsey, 120
  Scarface Story, 133–5, 162
Uhlenbeck-Melchior, Wilhelmina Maria, 6, 120, 127
United States
  Board of Indian Commissioners, 210n
  Bureau of Indian Affairs (BIA), 26, 28–9, 33, 34
  Court of Indian Offenses, 36–7, 42, 43
  Fort Laramie Treaty, 26, 228n
  General Allotment Act (1887), 33
  Indian Police, 37, 43–4, 103, 213n
  Indian Reorganization Act (Wheeler–Howard Act), 58
  Removal Act (1830), 30
  residential schools, 26
  treaty with Blackfoot (1855), 9, 64, 168, 241n
  see also Montana
United States Army
  assistance to Indian Agents, 37
  massacre of Heavy Runner's band, 30, 34, 153, 169, 177
  repression of the Ghost Dance religion, 28
  Sioux Wars, 4
United States officials
  attempts to eliminate sun dances, 16–17, 19–20, 23, 25, 28, 31–2, 42–5, 46–59, 107, 189
  Blackfoot leadership positions, 101–2
  "civilization" policies, 25, 28–35
  see also acculturation policies; assimilationist policies
Upson, Gad E., 24

Van Kirk, Sylvia, 89, 96
Venus *see* Ipiso-Waahsa (the Morning Star)
Victoria, Queen, 82
Viola, Herman J., 91, 101, 105
vision quests, 80, 147, 239n
Vizenor, Gerald, 10, 137–8, 151

war
  Blackfoot dress, 69, 70, 84, 86, 87–8
  Blackfoot leaders' achievements, 69, 70
  Blackfoot women, 79–80, 223n
war art, 139, 144–6
war trophies, 70, 87, 88, 98, 142
Warrior, Emma Lee, 159, 179–87, 188, 191, 192
Water Beings, 160, 177, 178, 207n
Weasel Calf, 50, 51, 56
Weasel Tail, 80, 223n
Weasel Traveller, Audrey, 6, 159–60
Weasel Woman, 80
Weidman, Bette, 171
Welch, James
  background, 243n
  Fools Crow, 123, 159, 168–78, 179, 186, 187, 188, 191, 192
Wheatley, G.H., 49, 50
Wheeler–Howard Act, 58
White Calf, 53, 147, 215n
"white chief" label, 102, 105, 108
White, Fred, 39, 57
White Horse, 237n
white mythologies
  "civilization", 25, 28–35
  salvation, 28
White Quiver, 124
White, Richard, 4, 89
White Weasel Moccasin (A-pe-ech-eken), 152
  see McClintock, Walter
whites
  Blackfoot adoption of, 121, 148, 152–3
  Blackfoot views on, 57–8, 106
  Blackfoot war narratives, 143
  curiosity towards First Nations, 40, 41
  deleterious effects on First Nations, 27
  First Nations hospitality, 94
  "Middle Ground" relations, 4, 89, 100, 169, 189

nomenclature, 10–11
opening of the West, 24, 188
self-mortification rituals, 22, 207n
settlement on Pikuni lands, 169
sun dances, 22, 44–5, 50, 51, 52–3, 109
see also Canadian officials; fur trade; Indian agents; missionaries; settlers; trading posts; United States officials
"Wild West Shows", 40
Wilson, James, 53–5, 59
Wilson, Robert N., 55, 102–3, 140, 162, 202n
Wilson, R.W. (sic), 202n
winter counts, 59, 77–8, 129, 139–42, 153–4
  Bad Head's Winter Count, 140
Wischmann, Leslie, 96
Wissler, Clark
  Assiniboine dress, 67
  background, 125
  Blackfoot artifacts, 127
  Blackfoot women, 77, 94
  cited by McClintock, 122–3
  I-kun-uh'-kah-tsi, 2
  Mythology of the Blackfoot Indians, 5, 115, 116, 118, 125, 134, 136, 150
  "Old People Stories", 138
  Ookaan, 15
  published papers, 126
  reputation, 118
  reserves and reservations era, 111
  Scarface Story, 134, 162, 164
  self-mortification rituals, 47
  Sun Dance, 205n
  "Tales of Old Man", 136
"*wiwanyag wacipi*", 18
Wolf Calf, 147
Wolf Child, 141
Wolf Collar, Paul, 145
Wolf Collar's Story Robe, 145, *col. plate 6*
Wolf Sun, 153
Wolf Tail, 147
Wolverine, Welch's *Fools Crow*, 172, 175, 176

Woman Who Strikes Many (Ah-kay-ee-pix-en), 95
women, Blackfoot
  bicultural individuals, 96, 97, 98
  chastity, 74, 75, 163
  diplomatic role, 79
  dress, 73–5, 78, 79, 80, 82, 93, 94, 95, 96–8, 190
  elites, 75, 78–9, 89, 96, 110
  fur trade, 89, 93–9
  ideal qualities of, 74
  intermediary role, 74, 96
  manly-hearted women, 81–2, 83
  marriage to fur traders, 96–8
  "Medicine women", 81, 83
  mobility, 95–6
  neglected representations of, 179
  ninauake wives, 78–9, 82, 95, 227n
  position *vis-à-vis* their husbands, 78, 94
  power and leadership, 70, 74, 75–83, 96, 103–4, 110, 190
  principal wives, *see* Sits-beside-him wife (*o'totamin.ai*)
  quillwork, 73, 93, 222n
  silenced voices, 50
  social stratification, 78–9, 83
  stereotypes, 79, 80, 179, 190
  tepee ownership, 76
  traditional occupations, 76
  use of red earth, 71
  valued role of, 76–7, 94
  violence against, 75, 78, 221n
  war exploits, 79–80, 223n
  Warrior's "Compatriots", 179, 183, 184, 186
  "The Woman-who-married-a-star", 74, 206n, 221n, 243n
women, mixed ancestry, 96, 97, 98
women, white, 76

year counts *see* winter counts
Yellow Bird, 126
Yellow Horse, 107–8, 107, 231n
Young Bear Chief, 147
Young, John, 26, 43, 152